# European and Chinese Histories of Economic Thought

The Western literature on the history of Chinese economic thought is sparse, and comparisons with the history of Western economic thought even more so. This pioneering book brings together Western and Chinese scholars to reflect on the historical evolution of economic thought in Europe and China.

The international panel of contributors covers key topics such as currency, usury, land tenure, the granary system, welfare and government, with special attention given to monetary institutions and policies. The problem of "good government" emerges as the unifying thread of a complex analysis that includes both theoretical issues and applied economics. Chinese lines of evolution include the problem of the agency of the state, its ideological justification, the financing of public expenditure, the role played by the public administration and the provision of credit. The early radical condemnation of usury in the Near East and in the West gives way to theoretical justifications of interest-taking in early capitalist Europe, which lead to advances in mathematics and business administration and represent one of the origins of modern economic theory. Other uniting themes include the relationship between metallic and paper money in Chinese and European experiences, and the cross-fertilisation of economic practices and ideas in the course of their pluri-millennial interactions. Differences emerge – the approach to the organisation of economic life was, and still is, more state-centred in China. The editors bring together these analytical threads in a final chapter, opening wider horizons for this new line of comparative economic research, which is important for an understanding of modern ideological turns.

This volume provides valuable reading for scholars in the history of economic thought, economic history and Chinese studies.

**Iwo Amelung** is Professor at Goethe University, Frankfurt am Main, Germany. His research interests are the history of knowledge of modern China, the bureaucracy and social history of the Qing period, and the emergence and development of scientific disciplines in modern China.

**Bertram Schefold** is Senior Professor at Goethe University, Frankfurt am Main, Germany. He teaches economic theory and the history of economic thought. His research interests are capital theory, and the history of economic thought and development.

# Routledge Studies in the History of Economics

**Foundations of Organisational Economics**
Histories and Theories of the Firm and Production
*Paul Walker*

**John Locke and the Bank of England**
*Claude Roche*

**Poverty in Contemporary Economic Thought**
*Edited by Mats Lundahl, Daniel Rauhut and Neelambar Hatti*

**Thomas Aquinas and the Civil Economy Tradition**
The Mediterranean Spirit of Capitalism
*Paolo Santori*

**The Macroeconomics of Malthus**
*John Pullen*

**Competition, Value and Distribution in Classical Economics**
Studies in Long-Period Analysis
*Heinz D. Kurz and Neri Salvadori*

**David Ricardo. An Intellectual Biography**
*Sergio Cremaschi*

**Humanity and Nature in Economic Thought**
Searching for the Organic Origins of the Economy
*Edited by Gábor Bíró*

**European and Chinese Histories of Economic Thought**
Theories and Images of Good Governance
*Edited by Iwo Amelung and Bertram Schefold*

For more information about this series, please visit www.routledge.com/series/SE0341

# European and Chinese Histories of Economic Thought

Theories and Images of Good Governance

Edited by
Iwo Amelung and Bertram Schefold

LONDON AND NEW YORK

First published 2022
by Routledge
2 Park Square, Milton Park, Abingdon, Oxon OX14 4RN

and by Routledge
605 Third Avenue, New York, NY 10158

*Routledge is an imprint of the Taylor & Francis Group, an informa business*

© 2022 selection and editorial matter, Iwo Amelung and Bertram Schefold; individual chapters, the contributors

The right of Iwo Amelung and Bertram Schefold to be identified as the authors of the editorial material, and of the authors for their individual chapters, has been asserted in accordance with sections 77 and 78 of the Copyright, Designs and Patents Act 1988.

All rights reserved. No part of this book may be reprinted or reproduced or utilised in any form or by any electronic, mechanical, or other means, now known or hereafter invented, including photocopying and recording, or in any information storage or retrieval system, without permission in writing from the publishers.

*Trademark notice*: Product or corporate names may be trademarks or registered trademarks, and are used only for identification and explanation without intent to infringe.

*British Library Cataloguing-in-Publication Data*
A catalogue record for this book is available from the British Library

*Library of Congress Cataloging-in-Publication Data*
A catalog record has been requested for this book

ISBN: 978-0-367-43448-9 (hbk)
ISBN: 978-1-032-10399-0 (pbk)
ISBN: 978-0-367-43449-6 (ebk)

DOI: 10.4324/9780367434496

Typeset in Bembo
by Newgen Publishing UK

# Contents

*List of figures and tables* ix
*List of contributors* x
*Preface* xiii
*Acknowledgements* xviii

**PART I**
**Chinese lines of evolution** 1

**Section 1 The agency of the state** 3

1 People's livelihoods and good governance in the past and for the future 5
R. BIN WONG

2 Justifying office-selling for famine relief in nineteenth-century Qing China 19
ELISABETH KASKE

3 The cost of security: Financing Yellow River hydraulics during the late imperial period 33
IWO AMELUNG

**Section 2 Land, interest and usury** 47

4 Outline of the institutions for land transactions in traditional China 49
DENGGAO LONG AND XIANG CHI

## vi  *Contents*

5  Loans and interest rates in traditional China  63
QIUGEN LIU

6  Foreign currencies in ancient and premodern China  77
YAGUANG ZHANG, YUE BI AND ZYLER WANG

## PART II
## European lines of evolution  89

### Section 1  From rationalisations of usury to deductive theories of interest  91

7  Theorising interest: How did it all begin? Some landmarks in the prohibition of usury in Scholastic economic thought  93
IRINA CHAPLYGINA AND ANDRÉ LAPIDUS

8  Merchants and the new Catholic view on the economy: Florence and Augsburg between the fifteenth and sixteenth centuries  106
MONIKA POETTINGER

9  From Kaspar Klock's "De aerario" (1651) and Leibniz's "Meditatio de interusurio simplice" to Florencourt's "Abhandlungen aus der juristischen und der politischen Rechenkunst" (1781): How calculus led from the logic of a device for circumventing the prohibition of usury to a modern theory of depreciation  119
BERTRAM SCHEFOLD

10  Interest on money, own rate of interest, the natural interest rate and the rate of profits: A short history of concepts ultimately emerging from the usury debate  133
VOLKER CASPARI

### Section 2  The spread of monetary relations and the transition from poor relief to the welfare state  143

11  Labour and poverty in medieval and early modern Europe  145
COSIMO PERROTTA

## Contents vii

12 After China, before Sweden and England: The circulation
of paper money in Naples 158
LILIA COSTABILE

13 European models and transformations of the welfare state 170
HANS-MICHAEL TRAUTWEIN

**PART III**
**Contact, comparison and interaction** 185

**Section 1 Before the revolutions** 187

14 Xunzi and Plato on the economics of totalitarianism:
A meeting of distant minds 189
TERRY PEACH

15 *Yantie lun* in the Pro-Legalist and Anti-Confucian Campaign 202
QUNYI LIU

16 A critical examination of Chinese influences on Quesnay 215
RICHARD VAN DEN BERG

**Section 2 The traces of the past in the transition
to modernity** 231

17 Rethinking traditional attitudes towards consumption in
the process of formation of Chinese economics (Late Qing
and republican periods) 233
OLGA BOROKH

18 China's ancient principles of price regulation through
market participation: The *Guanzi* from a comparative
perspective 246
ISABELLA M. WEBER

19 Confucian entrepreneurship and moral guidelines for
business in China 259
MATTHIAS NIEDENFÜHR

viii  *Contents*

**PART IV**
**Conclusions and perspectives**  275

20 Towards a systematic comparison of different forms of
  economic thought  277
  IWO AMELUNG AND BERTRAM SCHEFOLD

  *Index*  303

# Figures and tables

**Figures**

| | | |
|---|---|---|
| 2.1 | Authority in contribution campaigns | 26 |
| 2.2 | Disaster reports, 1840–1911 | 27 |
| 2.3 | Famine relief in three provinces and income of the Shanxi Contribution Campaign, 1877–79 | 28 |
| 4.1 | The relations between *dian*, *yazu* (rent deposit) and tenancy from the point of view of the land owner | 52 |
| 10.1 | Saving–investment mechanism | 139 |
| 13.1 | Targets and instruments in the Rehn-Meidner model | 178 |
| 13.2 | Inflation and unemployment in Sweden and Germany, 1973–98 | 180 |
| 15.1 | Estimated output and productivity, 1952–76 | 209 |
| 15.2 | A simplified governance framework of the new political economy in China | 212 |
| 16.1 | Reproductions of the divinatory hexagrams and the *Tableau* | 220 |
| 19.1 | 2016 campaign poster in Beijing with an *Analects* quote | 266 |
| 19.2 | The Neisheng-Waiwang principle in Confucian entrepreneurship | 271 |

**Tables**

| | | |
|---|---|---|
| 2.1 | Contribution campaigns, 1644–1840 | 22 |
| 3.1 | Revenue and expenses of river administrations | 41 |

# Contributors

**Iwo Amelung** is a professor at Goethe University, Frankfurt am Main, Germany. His research interests are the history of knowledge of modern China, the bureaucracy and social history of the Qing period, and the emergence and development of scientific disciplines in modern China.

**Yue Bi** is a PhD student at Peking University in Beijing, China. She majors in the history of Chinese economic thought. Her primary research interest is the history of economic thought.

**Olga Borokh** is a leading researcher at the Russian Academy of Sciences, Institute of Far Eastern Studies, Moscow. Her research interests are the history of Chinese economic thought since the early twentieth century and contemporary economic debates in China.

**Volker Caspari** is a professor emeritus (economic theory) at the Technical University Darmstadt, and since 2019 has been a senior professor of economics at Goethe-University Frankfurt. His main fields of research are growth economics, the history of economic thought and macroeconomics.

**Irina Chaplygina** is an associate professor of economics at Moscow State University, Russia. She teaches the history of economic thought. Her research interests are the history of economic thought and methodology.

**Xiang Chi** is Assistant Professor at the Institute of Modern History, Chinese Academy of Social Sciences (CASS) and UCLA graduate of 2019. Her research interests encompass Chinese economic history, forest history and economy and environment in modern north-east China.

**Lilia Costabile** is a full professor of economics at the University of Naples Federico II, a fellow of the Royal Historical Society and a life member at Clare Hall, Cambridge. Her main research interests are monetary theory and history, and the history of economic thought.

**Elisabeth Kaske** is a professor in the society and culture of modern China at Leipzig University. She studies China during the nineteenth and early twentieth century, covering social, military, fiscal and intellectual aspects.

*List of contributors* xi

**André Lapidus** is an emeritus professor of economics at PHARE, University Paris 1 Panthéon-Sorbonne, France. His research interests are the history of economic thought, decision theory and methodology.

**Qiugen Liu** is a professor of Chinese history at Hebei University, Baoding, China. His main research interest is Chinese economic history, and he has published extensively on credit and loans in imperial China.

**Qunyi Liu** is an associate professor at Peking University, Beijing, China. She teaches world economic history and the history of economic thought. Her research interests are the history of economic thought and East Asian economies.

**Denggao Long** is a professor at the Institute of Economics and chair of the Center for Chinese Entrepreneur Studies (CCES) at Tsinghua University, China. His research interests are the economic and social history of late imperial and modern China, including Jiangnan's market and economy, traditional Chinese institutions of land property and overseas Chinese business.

**Matthias Niedenführ** is a junior professor at Eberhard Karls University, Tübingen, Germany. Since 2016, he has been the vice director of the China Centrum in Tübingen (CCT). His research interests are business ethics in China and the Chinese diaspora.

**Terry Peach** is a professor of economics at Shanghai University of Finance and Economics, honorary senior research fellow at the University of Manchester and chair of the UK History of Economic Thought Society. He teaches and researches on the history of Western economic thought and comparative ancient Chinese and Greek thought.

**Cosimo Perrotta** is a full professor of the history of economic thought at the University of Salento, Italy. His research interests are economic thought about wealth and labour, and production and consumption from antiquity to the present day.

**Monika Poettinger** teaches economic history and the history of economic thought at Bocconi University and at the University of Florence. Her research comprises a decennial work on foreign entrepreneurship in Milan and its role in the industrialisation of Lombardy, and on international merchant networks operating between the eighteenth and the twentieth centuries.

**Bertram Schefold** is a senior professor at Goethe University, Frankfurt am Main, Germany. He teaches economic theory and the history of economic thought. His research interests are capital theory and the history of economic thought and development.

**Hans-Michael Trautwein** is a professor at Carl von Ossietzky University, Oldenburg, Germany. His research interests are macroeconomics, monetary integration, international financial markets, regulation and the Chinese economy.

**Richard van den Berg** is an associate professor at Kingston University Business School, London. He writes about economic thought during the Enlightenment, especially in France and Britain. Besides publications in the main history of economic thought journals, he has edited the writings of Richard Cantillon and Achilles Nicolas Isnard.

**Zyler Wang** is a history PhD student at Harvard University, Boston. Her research interests are economic concepts and their application in twentieth-century China.

**Isabella M. Weber** is Assistant Professor at the University of Massachusetts Amherst, USA. Her research interests are economic theory, economic history, China studies and the global political economy.

**R. Bin Wong** is a distinguished professor of history at the UCLA Asia Institute. His research interests are Chinese patterns of political, economic and social change compared with European patterns.

**Yaguang Zhang** is an associate professor at Peking University in Beijing, China. He teaches the history of economic thought. His research interests are monetary history and the history of economic thought.

# Preface

China is a rapidly rising rival of the Western powers, and purports to be a model for all other countries. The resulting tensions will probably persist for many years. They are not only political and economic, but also cultural; as the ideologies are being confronted, each side tries to defend its views as the legitimate outgrowth of past intellectual developments and its own history, and strives also to rationalise the position of the other side in historical terms. Differences in the histories of economic thought obviously must be part of the explanation of the divergence; however, surprisingly, the history of economic ideas is a generally neglected subject, although it is being taught in universities in both the East and the West, and very little has been done to compare the respective traditions. The editors of this volume undertook a project, "Chinese and European Economic Thought in Comparison", as Fellows of the Institute for Advanced Studies in the Humanities (Forschungskolleg Humanwissenschaften) in Bad Homburg, which is associated with Goethe University, Frankfurt am Main. We were convinced from the start that it would not do to look at modern history alone. Whereas Europe took up the rationality and the achievements of antiquity only in the Renaissance, there is a high degree of continuity in premodern China over 2000 years from the unification under the Qin and Han empires to the turbulences and shocks of the nineteenth century, and the subsequent revolutions of the twentieth century. Although China was split into different political entities several times, and even conquered and ruled by non-Chinese ethnic groups, it always preserved a dominant Chinese culture and basically used only one language, Mandarin, and Classical Chinese in writing. Compared with this, European history was and is much more complicated, dominated by fragmentation – a multiplicity of languages, ethnicities and nationalities. Both China and the West often refer to the middle of the first millennium BC as a historical divide, identified by Karl Jaspers (1949) as the *Achsenzeit*, the turning point, when thinkers and philosophers began to reflect systematically on the social conditions and the moral duties of humanity. There were the itinerant intellectuals who migrated to the archipelago of the Greek islands and similarly to the archipelago of the territorial states, ruled by princes, which constituted China in the Spring and Autumn and the Warring States periods. Thus one can compare Socrates and Confucius, Aristotle and Mencius, who philosophised about the nature of man, the organisation of societies, the roots of justice, the process of cognition and education that would lead to a virtuous and happy life. It was clear to all of them that the economic conditions, as we call them today, mattered as soon as the ideas were to be realised in more concrete terms. Here, however, we can distinguish broad differences. The Chinese thinkers, beginning with Confucius, tend to be resolutely pragmatic, as far as practical life is concerned, while the Greek philosophers must struggle with the multiplicity of constitutions and forms of government that can be observed in the city states and their colonies. They see citizens who must organise themselves, defend their community and form their political intercourse. The Chinese thinkers advise princes on how to govern the different strata of their subjects. We believe it is still true that Chinese economic thought is more pragmatic and starts from the problem of good economic government, which must overcome the centrifugal forces in the economy and set goals for economic development, while the European economic thought starts from the autonomy of the economic actors who use the market and political imperatives to form their community from below. Comprehensive theories of the market were not yet developed and, despite capitalistic elements in commerce, mining, shipbuilding and similar industries, causal economic analysis was not invented in antiquity, but originated in the West only in the eighteenth century, apart from some forerunners.

We therefore come to the questions: How was it possible that, in China, the fundamental characteristics of its economic thought could be preserved for over 2000 years up to the time of the revolutions, and transformed by modernisation and Western influence even beyond? No such direct continuity can be observed in the West. The question there becomes: How did the economic theory of the autonomous forces in the market and in capitalist development originate, how were these forces transformed by the Romans and Christianity, and how could they regenerate thereafter? These questions are old, and answers exist in the form of separate Western and Chinese histories of economic thought, but they have not often been confronted. There are not many comparisons (exceptions will be mentioned in the book) – not so much because of negligence, but because there is a systematic difficulty, which should be understood from the start. The periods are few in which the political and economic situation in China and in Europe was sufficiently similar to warrant a broad and systematic comparison. Such a comparison could concern the Roman and the Han empire because of the similarity of the general political and economic conditions, but these were more different in other eras. Comparisons can concern specific authors or periods, which are not contemporaneous. These must be based on special analogies – as, for instance, in direct comparisons such as between the conceptions of monarchic rule and administration in two philosophers (see Chapter 14 by Terry Peach) or between mercantilist ideas and the Guanzi (see Chapter 18 Isabella M. Weber). The reader will find a number of other comparisons and can use the insights gained from the chapters in this book to make their own. Such comparisons can be challenging and illuminating, but the main point we want to make with this book is different, for the book intends to show how the fundamental characteristics mentioned above came about. In order to make that possible, we here offer an overview of some specific developments.

On the one hand, we study in Part I how the idea formed in China that the state should elevate the livelihood of the population and how the success of good governance in this sense has remained the measuring rod for the ruling elite even until today (R. Bin Wong in Chapter 1). This is then exemplified by looking at the sources, which inform us how specific policies were seen, like office-selling for famine relief (Elisabeth Kaske in Chapter 2) and financing river management (Iwo Amelung in Chapter 3). China was an economy in which agriculture was dominant, and the primacy of agriculture played an important role in economic thought. The interpretation of land transactions according to the older doctrines of Sino-Marxism started from the assumption that there were small-scale peasants and landlords, with tenants who were obliged to pay rents in kind or in money. The peasants were miserable because they were poor, and the tenants were unhappy because they were oppressed by debts and were thus even more exploited than if they had been serfs. Chapter 4 by Denggao Long and Xiang Chi offers a more modern interpretation of the facts and analyses the relationships as those of a market economy, in which both peasants and tenants are entrepreneurs. The chapter thus sheds indirectly light on the ongoing shift of the economic thought on the matter.

The monetary institutions formed the other great domain in which the state regulated the economy; it is here represented by Chapter 5 on credit and interest in traditional China by Qiugen Liu and Chapter 6 on the perception of foreign monies by Chinese interpreters by Yaguang Zhang, Yue Bi and Zyler Wang. The chapters show how these monetary institutions worked and how they were understood, how interest rates were high and how, nonetheless, the state saw fit to pursue policies to avoid excessive indebtedness, without engaging in a general critique of usury – in fact, the state itself was an important lender and not a borrower, as in the West. This too was explained in terms of the duty to provide good governance.

Part II traces European lines of evolution. Here, the first focus is on interest-taking and the role of the prohibition of usury in the Jewish, Greek, Roman and Christian traditions. Chapter 7 by André Lapidus and Irina Chaplygina expounds the sophisticated scholastic discourse on interest-taking and explains how the borderline between licit and illicit interest-taking was to be drawn. The Reformation was not generally associated with a more modern view on this matter, as in Calvinism; Chapter 8 by Monika Poettinger shows that Luther's opponents were more moderate critics of usury than he was himself. These debates and their sequels compelled contemporaries to reflect on why certain forms of interest-taking were regarded as illicit and others not. Hence these debates created a need to analyse the phenomenon of interest-taking theoretically, and soon mathematical models to calculate interest and amortisation in different credit relationships arose, which were then used in business administration (see Chapter 9 by Bertram Schefold). Chapter 10 by Volker Caspari shows how the concepts formed in the debate eventually became the roots of modern general equilibrium economics. What had seemed one of many customary rules of the Jewish tradition – that one should not lend to one's Jewish partner against interest but rather assist him – thus became, in a very indirect manner, one of the reasons why a theoretical analysis of interest seemed useful in the West, while one lived without it perfectly well in China. Only the complications of a more modern economy much later turned this theoretical knowledge into knowledge that was also useful and contributed to the great divide in the development of East and West.

The second section of Part II shows that what is traditionally good governance in China by and large corresponds to the set of measures successively introduced in the West to alleviate the lot of the poor, to organise the workforce and, in more modern times, to secure employment, with all the policies that are conducive to full employment, particularly wages policies. Chapter 11 by Cosimo Perrotta and Chapter 13 by Hans-Michael Trautwein show this with historical detail and by differentiating between countries. Some nations were more successful than others in organising the labour force under mercantilism; today, it is a question of whether one has, and wants to have, a welfare state, or whether the policies of assistance could be based on the principle of subsidiarity. In between these chapters is Lilia Costabile's Chapter 12 on money creation in the West, as exemplified by the origin of paper money in Naples – a little-known fact of economic history, to be seen in contrast with the earlier creation of paper money in China, which reflects a change in the understanding of the functioning of monetary systems and credit relationships.

Part III offers more direct comparisons and examples of contact between Eastern and Western economic thought and some intertemporal comparisons. Chapter 14 by Terry Peach presents Plato (in his role as author of the dialogue *The Republic*) and Xunzi as advocates of totalitarian forms of government. In Chapter 16, Richard van den Berg traces the origins of Quesnay's famous views on China as an ideal physiocratic state by critically analysing his sources. A leading example of the continuity in Chinese economic thought is given by the debate on salt and iron *(Yantie Lun)* in Chapter 15 by Qunyi Liu. Continuity does not mean that the same ideas are carried from one millennium to the next, but rather that there is continuity in the controversy; the same type of antagonism is discussed in the first century BC and in the twentieth century AD during the Cultural Revolution.

We then have three intertemporal comparisons relating to China, which the reader can easily connect with comparisons to the West. The persistence of Chinese traditional thought is evident in the latest phase of the empire and also in the republican period, when Confucian ideas about frugality had to be confronted with the then emerging influences of Western economic thought, as discussed in Chapter 17 by Olga Borokh. Surprisingly, recent Chinese pricing policies in the spectacularly successful transition of China from a planned to a market economy can be related to a tradition of the analysis of pricing, which goes back right to the Guanzi, more than 2,000 years earlier, as Isabella M. Weber relates in Chapter 18. Part III concludes with Chapter 19 by Matthias

Niedenführ, which discusses the principles and realities of the attempts to reintroduce Confucian moral standards into modern business in China.

Part IV presents the editors' conclusions. They may be read also as an introduction. Chapter 20 by Iwo Amelung and Bertram Schefold is first an attempt to synthesise the individual contributions to generate a general comparison of economic thought in East and West. The chapter then argues that the history of Chinese economic thought will become more important in the Chinese intellectual discourse in the future as the idea of a specific Chinese way of development, in accordance with old and oldest Chinese traditions, gains ground and is promoted by President Xi Jinping.

## Reference

Jaspers, K.: Vom Ursprung und Ziel der Geschichte. Munich: Piper, 1949.

# Acknowledgements

We should first like to thank the directorate and the staff of the Institute for Advanced Studies in the Humanities (Forschungskolleg Humanwissenschaften) in Bad Homburg, which financed an international symposium and an international conference that formed the background for this book and in which most of the contributors participated. We would also like to thank the publisher, Routledge, and their staff for their helpful collaboration in the production of this book. We thank three anonymous referees for their valuable advice (the responsibility remains ours) and we thank Mrs Erna Jeganathan, Ines Balta, Birgit Herrmann, Anna Mogilevskaja and Johanna Kleensang who successively helped with the production of the manuscript. We are relieved that the publication could take place despite the perturbations caused by the COVID-19 pandemic.

# Part I
# Chinese lines of evolution

# Section 1
# The agency of the state

# 1 People's livelihoods and good governance in the past and for the future

*R. Bin Wong*

China's rapid economic growth over the past four decades, which has resulted in the country's economic strength in today's global economy, has prompted a mix of anxiety and approval among other countries. Missing from most accounts is an account of some major and very different features of reform-era economic change. I will introduce three of these and suggest why they are hard for many observers to consider within a common conceptual frame of understanding. When we add some historical perspectives on the Chinese political economy and its guiding principles, we can recognise resonances with reform era efforts that minimally pose the possibility that they helped guide Chinese leaders' choices about how to pursue economic development. Such perspectives at least make possible a coherent understanding of motivation for policy choices taken, and we have statements by no less a figure than Deng Xiaoping, the Chinese leader who is credited with fostering the general direction during its initial years of transition to replace a Soviet-style planned economy. In clarifying his view of the socialist rather than capitalist nature of Shenzhen, the PRC's first special economic zone established in May 1980, he said in 1992, "Failing to adhere to socialism, to carry out reform and opening up, to develop economy and to improve people's livelihood can only lead us up a blind alley. The basic line governs one hundred years and must not be shaken" (Deng, Xiaoping 2002). The stress placed on people's livelihoods is one shared by Chinese governments of earlier centuries as well.

By the early twenty-first century, three impacts on standards of living of China's economic growth, beginning in the 1980s, had become very visible. First, at the beginning of the economic reform era in the 1980s, China had a developing economy, with 65 per cent of its population (652 million people) estimated to be at or below the absolute poverty line in 1981. By 2004, that fraction had dropped to 10 per cent (135 million people) (World Bank 2009, p. iii). Second, as a global economic powerhouse, Chinese growth had created an urban middle class. Gustafsson, Sicular & Yang (2020, p. 124) estimate that:

> In absolute numbers China's middle class in 2013 stood at approximately 250 million people. This was roughly two-thirds the contemporaneous size of the EU's middle class of 370 million people… in 2013 China's middle

DOI: 10.4324/9780367434496-3

class was equal in size to 80 percent of the total US population of 316 million. We have projected that by 2018 China's middle class had grown to over 450 million people, which would make it the single largest segment of the global middle class.

Third, as standards of living have risen among the absolute poor and for a new middle class, there has been increasing social inequality between urban and rural populations (Rozelle & Hell 2020). State policies have deliberately aimed to achieve the first two impacts and have also aimed to reduce the third impact, which has proven very difficult, since it is largely the result of the first two impacts. Yet we tend to view the two impacts, which are achievements, and the third impact, which is a serious problem, separately. The first impact demonstrates China's success among the world's countries with large amounts of absolute poverty. The second impact makes China the world's largest middle-income country. The third impact sounds an alert; according to Piketty, Yang and Zucman's research on the distribution of wealth and income in China between 1978 and 2015, "China's inequality levels used to be close to Nordic countries and are now approaching US levels" (Piketty, Yang & Zucman 2019, p. 2469). Thinking of the international contexts with which China is compared for each of these impacts of growth, we end up with three very different juxtapositions: alongside the world's poorest societies, middle-income countries and the United States, respectively.

If we turn to Chinese history, we can better understand the policy approaches enabling the two successes highlighted above, as well as reasons for combatting the problems spawned by economic growth. Not surprisingly, we do not look for what is reasonably assumed to be irrelevant features of bygone eras to explain contemporary changes, yet we might want to consider that the state policies creating the first two impacts and addressing the third can all be related to the concept of "people's livelihood and wellbeing" (*minsheng* 民生), a term in use today that is also found in ancient Chinese texts. Viren Murthy (2000) has made a related argument about the democratic potential of the classical concept of "people as the root" (*minben* 民本). While Murthy stresses the relevance of *minben* to contemporary politics, I am highlighting the connection between *minsheng* as a historical concept creating a particular logic of connecting people's economic abilities and successes to the ruler's political efforts. A ruler's attention to people's livelihood and wellbeing was central to one of the ancient Chinese approaches to governing because of the ruler's political success and security. According to this view, his abilities to foster social order required him to strengthen the abilities of the people to achieve material security in a decidedly insecure natural world that was subject to the shocks of floods, droughts and disease. Remarkably, such a formulation of political objectives emerged in China's Warring States era (475–221 BCE), a time when the unstable natural world was made even more dangerous due to violent competition among ambitious power-hungry individuals seeking to rule more territory and garner more wealth. The political logic stressing people's livelihoods and wellbeing reasoned that rulers could attract people to live under their rule by assuring their material security, and that security would in turn enable these people to become more productive; the more productive they became, the more they could afford to support the ruler's needs, including making war on his competitors. The ruler's success relative to that of his rivals would come from his good treatment of the people, which in turn would better enable them to support him. The ruler's interest in people's security demonstrated the legitimacy of his rule. As political theorist Loubna El Amine (2016, p. 73) explains, in classical era Chinese political thought, "the aim of these policies is to promote the state's productivity and thus provide for the common people's basic needs. Only when this is achieved can the ruler be successful at winning the loyalty of the common people and thus at maintaining political order." By strengthening the material foundation for people's lives, the ruler could make moral claims for what we can term his good governance and legitimacy.

When European rulers faced a similar situation of intense political competition and violence some fifteen centuries later, they too cared about gaining resources for their needs and for the people becoming more productive to make this possible. But the processes to achieve these partially similar political desires were quite different. Under the rubric of mercantilism, early modern European rulers wanted their subjects to produce and export more goods than they bought from abroad, creating more wealth flowing into the country, which the ruler could tap to satisfy his appetite for resources needed for making war.

The challenges of ruling relatively large spaces in the third century BCE encouraged the translation of earlier Chinese political principles for securing social order into economic policies. Beyond the agrarian empire, serious political competition came from nomadic or semi-nomadic peoples, whose approaches to wealth and power were different from those of both early modern European rulers and the Chinese imperial state. Applied across far greater demographic and territorial scales than any individual early modern European or modern European state could imagine, Chinese approaches to achieving social order were repeatedly deployed, albeit not constantly sustained, for nearly two millennia. For the last five centuries of imperial rule, the political principles for achieving economic governance became crucial elements of the state's strategies to maintain or recover social order. Some of those principles are invoked by today's leaders to explain the motivation for their policies.

During the Qing dynasty (1644–1911), the Chinese state promoted both agricultural and handicraft production, supported commercial exchange across the empire and paid special attention to people's dependence on the natural world. The expansion of agricultural production meant extending production to land not being cultivated and intensifying land use through irrigation where it was feasible. Officials organised compendia of information about crops and their cultivation (Deng, Gang 1993). The Yongzheng emperor in particular pushed the expansion of paddy rice cultivation into areas of North China (Brook 2005, p. 88). More generally, officials undertook projects to dredge rivers when silt build-up had slowed water flow, often compounded by the diversion of river and stream waters to rice paddy fields. In some situations, land reclamation reduced water flows of rivers used to move people and goods, causing officials to halt additional land reclamation (Perdue 1982;Will 1980, 1985, 1998). By the sixteenth century, commercial handicrafts that initially were deemed a household activity to complement crop cultivation entered widespread commercial circulation; most prominent were cotton textiles (Zurndorfer 2011).

In general, after the thirteenth century the state promoted the commercial circulation of goods, approving the principle of market transactions as positive. There were only two major exceptions in the eighteenth century: salt and grain. Salt circulation was legal only for merchants who paid for state licences; some of these merchants amassed considerable wealth at the same time as the state received a source of revenue. Grain trade was in private hands, with the most commercialised parts of the empire in the lower reaches of the Yangzi River basin (near modern-day Shanghai) dependent on grain imports from rice-rich areas further upstream (Wong 2014, pp. 132–36). The state also maintained a civilian granary system made up of several kinds of granaries managed by both officials and local elites; these granaries sold or lent grain in the lean spring season and, after the autumn harvests, bought or received grain in compensation for what had been disbursed the previous spring (Will & Wong 1991). This system was also a first line of defence against more severe harvest failures to which were added other more extraordinary efforts to face famine possibilities through lifting transit taxes on commercial shipments into areas in need, official purchase and transport of commercial grain in other locales for transport back to their grain-short jurisdictions, setting up rice-gruel stations, and more generally organising broader social efforts to combat dire conditions (Wong & Perdue 2008). Taken together, state economic policies were intended to support people's livelihoods (民生 *minsheng*), a term with classical antecedents and a basic component of Chinese good governance during the early modern era. In his biography of Chen Hongmou, William Rowe goes so far as to suggest that while *minsheng* was probably never absent from official discourse through the imperial era, "*minsheng* may never have been more prominently featured than in the mid-eighteenth century"; he goes on to explain:

> Chen invokes the interests of *minsheng* as legitimation for initiatives in what might seem a surprising range of areas, from reforms in tax collection and in processing civil litigation to suppression banditry and gambling, even to streamlining channels of bureaucratic governance.
> 
> (Rowe 2001, p. 188)

For activist eighteenth-century officials such as Chen, *minsheng* could inspire multiple initiatives that make up a Chinese view of good governance.

Chinese good governance began with the commitments and capacities of the state to conceive and implement policies intended to support people's livelihoods and wellbeing through bureaucratic action. China in the tenth and eleventh centuries was certainly unusual, if not unique, for developing a rule-governed bureaucracy with many officials who passed civil service exams and served outside the locales where they could have exploited family connections for illicit gain. However, given the spatial and demographic scales of the empire, the bureaucratic capacities so created were insufficient to achieve social order. Officials relied on local elites whose efforts complemented official statecraft, *jingshi* ("ordering the world"). Chinese statecraft in subsequent centuries also included major mobilisations of capital and labour for large-scale projects such as expanding granary reserves and dredging rivers, which were examples of supporting people's livelihoods. These were not routine bureaucratic actions, but recurring – similar to modern era attention to infrastructure that can be expanded and requires maintenance (Wong 2001, pp. 401–07).

During the nineteenth century, the central government's capacity to address people's livelihoods diminished. The state was unable to maintain some institutions, such as the granary system, and less able to finance major maintenance expenditures, such as those required for the Grand Canal or by the Yellow River Administration. At the same time, the state did meet new expenditure demands brought forth by the pressure to respond to foreign challenges and threats. Together, these changes made up a clear shift in priorities for state efforts and an expansion of fiscal capacities to achieve "wealth and power" (*fuqiang* 富强) (Halsey 2015; Wong 1997, pp. 155–56). By the late nineteenth century, there was a visible expansion of the "wealth and power" aims from those intended to strengthen the state to calls for people to produce more goods for export in order to compete with foreign sources of wealth. At the same time, some officials came to consider the term "industry" (工业 *gongye*) to include not only conventional factory production, but also craft production of rural households that used iron-gear looms for cotton textile weaving (Wong 2015, p. 384). Industry, in other words, came to have a place in "people's livelihoods" at the same time as it remained basic to the pursuit of wealth and power.

The term "people's livelihood" (*minsheng*) made a prominent and extended appearance in 1924 when Sun Yat-sen, the first provisional president of the Republic and leader of the Nationalist Party, articulated the "three principles" he considered desirable for building the Chinese state: nationalism, democracy and people's livelihood. Neither democracy nor people's livelihoods proved very visible for several decades. For the Nationalist government of the 1930s, "industry" no longer included rural household craft production, and some officials went so far as to imagine the state establishing plans for state-led industrialisation (Kirby 1990, pp. 125–28). While the state's plans were often little more than that, what new factory-based industrialisation did take place largely featured light industries for consumer goods (e.g. cotton cloth, food oil, cigarettes, matches, flour) based in treaty ports, especially Shanghai. In the 1940s, faced with wartime conditions, the Nationalists directly took control of many industries (Hou, Chi-ming 1977, pp. 203–41; Rawski 1989). The Communist victory over the Nationalists after World War II allowed them to develop industry in many of the ways previously desired by the Nationalists. In the first half of the 1950s, the state stressed heavy industry development deemed necessary for the state to defend itself against a new round of foreign threats brought on the by the Korean War. By the mid-1950s, Mao Zedong recognised the need to develop both light and heavy industries, and thus acknowledged people's needs for light industrial consumer goods. However modest or major the rebalancing actually would be, such changes mattered far less than the Great Chinese Famine that accompanied the Great Leap Forward (1958–61). This colossal human catastrophe costing tens of millions of deaths exacerbated the impacts of widespread natural disasters on China's still largely rural population (Mao, Zedong 1977, pp. 61–62; Wu, Jinglian 2005, pp. 43–56; Zhao, Zhongwei & Reimondos 2012).

It is little wonder that the episodic and largely modest appearance of concern for linking social order to the material wellbeing over much of the twentieth century, despite its importance to earlier Chinese economic thought and good governance, seems no longer relevant (Wong 2012). But while the principles I sketched above are certainly foreign to the far more familiar patterns found in European history, we need not fail to recognise the possibility that principles deemed desirable and expressed through diverse economic policies and social practices over several hundred years preceding the twentieth century might still matter when China became a national state – the only national state able to claim sovereignty over a huge population and vast territory roughly the size of the empire it succeeded. Certainly the late twentieth and early twenty-first century Chinese state has appealed to principles and practices of good governance similar to those present centuries earlier, within which "people's livelihoods" are often mentioned.

Recent Chinese publications on the concept of "people's livelihoods" include studies by historians, as well as efforts by people looking at contemporary challenges to compare traditional ideas about people's livelihoods with current concerns regarding sustainability (Guo, Jinping 2020; Guo, Ruipeng 2015; Su 2012). The recognition of the concept "people's livelihoods" having a lexical history dating back to more than two millennia does not mean, of course, that many contemporary discussions of the term invoke historical meanings or practices, any more than statements about contemporary democratic political principles and policies refer back either to Athenian direct democracy or the election of representatives in the Roman Republic. Today's leaders are far more concerned about the place of the principle of "people's livelihoods" within their political system (中国制度) and governance structure (治理体系) (Zheng, Gongchen 2019).

Consider an example of people's livelihood and wellbeing fitting into economic development approaches at the same time as these approaches embrace concerns more familiar to international observers. The relevance of *minsheng* to development is explicit in the title of economist Hu Angang's work *Zhongguo: minsheng yu fazhan* ("China: People's livelihood and development") (Hu, Angang 2008). *Minsheng* gives economic development a set of purposes and priorities that resist acceptance of widespread disparities in society as the state seeks to enable the people to thrive due to their hard work and effort. Hu

Angang has been better known outside China in recent years for what some observers within and beyond China consider his trumpeting of China's emerging status as a superpower in a nationalistic rhetoric. At the same time, he has been a major advocate for China aggressively addressing climate change as part of international efforts with the European Union and the United States (Hu, Angang 2009; Hu, Angang & Guan, Qingyou 2017; Li, Cheng 2011). When taken together, Hu sees economic development's links to concerns the Chinese have had from several periods of Chinese history – since ancient times (people's livelihoods), since the late nineteenth century (the pursuit of wealth and power) and since the late twentieth century (environmental impacts of economic growth). None of these themes precludes the others, but only the second two are at all familiar to most foreign observers of China. We thus fail to take the measure of how one prominent intellectual conceives contemporary challenges and responsibilities, much as analysts routinely have little to say about the use of "people's livelihoods" by Chinese leaders and policy-makers. We therefore miss some of the motivating logic for Chinese economic development in this century.

I suggested at the beginning of this chapter that the economic development responsible for China's two quite distinct social achievements – lifting poor rural people out of absolute poverty and creating an urban middle class – indicates the importance of people's livelihoods. When we reflect upon the state's targeted efforts to reduce disparities caused by economic development, also noted in the opening paragraph of this chapter, an historian familiar with earlier periods of Chinese history can hear echoes of early modern Chinese state efforts to improve people's livelihoods across an empire through a combination of balancing population and resources, spreading agricultural and craft technologies, supporting widespread commercial exchange and creating institutions and policies intended to address harvest instabilities that could cause serious subsistence insecurities (Wong 2019). I argue that all these efforts mattered to the ways in which principles for political intervention in the economy created political legitimacy through good governance.

The Chinese state's broad approach to economic development since the 1980s has repeatedly drawn links between economic growth and political legitimacy without explicitly noting how the conceptual link is fashioned, at least in part, out of ideas about good governance and people's livelihoods conceived in ancient China and implemented through a variety of institutions and policies through Chinese history. While historians have dramatically widened and deepened the scholarship we produce on world regions outside Western Europe and North America, the histories that continue to inform what policy-makers, officials and entrepreneurs imagine as possible and desirable for economic development today, and the kinds of states that can achieve the good governance deemed necessary to ensure broad participation in the fruits of development, all come out of Western developments of democratic political order and capitalist societies. Even as historians have expanded our understanding of diverse pasts, the knowledge of past political priorities and practices in world regions beyond

Europe and its white settler societies has not encouraged adequate consideration of the different paths from those pasts to the present that at least some of those non-Western regions may have followed.

As an alternative to explaining Chinese economic changes in terms of social theories designed to explain Western-style success stories, I suggest that China is a former territorial empire that became a modern national state capable of economic development in part by utilising approaches to governance formulated in its own past. This helps explain why the Chinese state has, for the past 40 years, formulated policies to improve people's livelihood and well-being. These have meant different kinds of efforts to address social inequalities. The spatial and demographic dimensions of social inequalities amidst the past four decades of Chinese economic development span a geographical space as large as Europe, where unequal economic development began more gradually in the early nineteenth century. The rapid emergence of inequality in China makes it an easy target of criticism without considering how inequalities emerged more slowly in Europe to persist into the present; however, because some of these inequalities are between European countries, they do not appear as visible as differences between Chinese provinces, which are often the demographic and territorial size of larger European countries. Foreign evaluations of China's economic changes often identify emulation of Western practices as a positive source of development, and assert that the scale of social inequality in China is due to flawed Chinese policies. It may be that some of the reasons for China's social inequality include its recent common economic traits with Western societies at the same time as the reasons for its development include economic governance practices consonant with earlier Chinese governance principles. In other words, China's economic problems and possibilities may both be understood best by identifying those already present historically and those created by China's dramatically expanded connections with the West, which began, episodically, to occur by the fourth decade of the nineteenth century.

To observe the potential relevance of principles in those earlier Chinese approaches to later periods of history, we need to understand the broader set of political and social propositions within which any particular principles, such as seeking to support people's livelihoods, exists. As I have explained above, state policies to underpin people's livelihoods entailed the performance of deeds enabling the ruler to claim political legitimacy – a moral achievement resting upon affirming people's material interests. It thus should be understandable that a similar form of reasoning could be present today. Instead, contemporary Chinese efforts to support people's livelihoods through economic growth are often seen as a Communist Party strategy to prevent popular demands for democracy in order to remain in power. Such an approach is deemed impractical by scholars believing that modern political legitimacy depends on democratic principles, in part because no state's economic policies can guarantee continuous economic growth (Tsang 2009). In 2019, for instance, Beijing University law professor He Weifang called on China to meet its WTO obligations for reform, arguing that, "If there is no structural reform, China cannot sustain its economic growth and the economic downturn will fundamentally shake the legitimacy of the Communist Party's regime" (Tsang 2009; Zhou 2019). In fact, Chinese responses to the 2019 pandemic make it clear that the state is less committed to economic growth than it is to sustaining people's livelihoods. By April 2020, the Chinese state had formulated its general strategy toward reopening the economy. President Xi Jinping stressed "six guarantees" regarding the people's employment, basic livelihood (基本民生), market order, food and energy security, the stability of supply chains and the operation of local government functions (Niewenhuis 2020). None of these guarantees speaks about economic growth. At a State Council executive meeting on 13 May 2020, associated with the 13th National People's Congress, Premier Li Keqiang stressed six priorities in a State Council English-language statement available two days later:

> Six priorities, namely, employment, people's livelihoods, the development of market entities, food and energy security, and stable operation of industrial and supply chains, as well as smooth functioning at the community level, are positive measures against difficulties and challenges because they address prominent contradictions and risks faced by the current economy and require a lot of effort, the Premier added.
>
> (State Council 2020)

Li went on at a press briefing for foreign journalists on 28 May to reiterate explicitly that the state was not setting any economic growth target (*China Daily* 29 May 2020). Clearly, the Chinese state has been able to frame the issue of people's livelihoods without making it dependent on achieving economic growth.

As a final example of the relevance of the pursuit of people's livelihoods to Chinese economic governance, consider the concept's presence in water governance reform, a key component of the Chinese response to climate change consistent with the United Nations' 2030 Sustainable Development Goals. "People's livelihood" is the first principle stated to guide water governance reforms and development presented in the state's major water governance document, providing the initial framework for water governance efforts since 2011: "First, persist in giving priority to people's livelihood" ("一要坚持民生优先" *yi yao jianchi minsheng youxian*) What people's livelihood means as a principle for water management locates the issue in terms of relationships between economic and environmental governance (UN Water 2018). This Chinese policy approach incorporates scientific knowledge of human impacts on the environment to create boundary conditions within which economic decision-making involving water should promote sustainable development – motivated first and foremost by the principle of people's livelihoods.

We can also see that the ways in which people's livelihood and wellbeing in the context of a contemporary pressing challenge are addressed at least partly use strategies resembling those of China's early modern era. The last paragraph of the document citing people's livelihood as the first principle for water governance reform efforts states:

> Step up efforts to increase the public awareness of national conditions in respect of water resources, increase the public sense of flood, saving water and water resource protection and mobilize broad-based efforts in water conservancy development. Water-related education shall be included in the national quality education system and the primary and secondary education system, and designated as a crucial element in training and education of government officials and civil servants. Water conservancy shall be included in public service advertising to create a favorable public atmosphere for sound and rapid development of water conservancy. Governments at all levels shall commend and reward entities and individuals who have delivered outstanding contributions to accelerating water conservancy reform and development. Accelerating water conservancy reform and development is a glorious mission, and also a considerable challenge and great responsibility. We must unite closely under the CPC Central Committee with Comrade Hu Jintao as its general secretary, stay current, keep forging ahead and strive to turn a new page in the water conservancy drive.

The paragraph opens with a call to make more efforts to expand public awareness of water issues with subsequent calls for public service advertising. It calls for education in schools and especially for officials, much as the early modern state sought to influence social behaviour and educate officials to understand important subjects. Those who make major efforts and achieve major contributions to improving water governance at local, provincial or higher levels, whether as organisations or individuals, should be recognised publicly by the government with symbolic recognition echoing the kinds of symbols of official recognition granted by the early modern Chinese state and also used at the end of the Qing dynasty to encourage private capital investments into industry. The importance of improving water governance is underscored by exhorting people to organise under the Communist Party leadership and its general secretary in rhetoric resonating with language used in earlier Communist political campaigns, however hollow such language sounds when translated into English. The 2011 Document No. 1 presents a policy vision that calls on the state's many bureaucracies and society's many organisational actors, as well as people as individuals, to mount a campaign motivated by their material interests and persuaded by the moral appeals of leadership to improve water governance. While the particular form of organisation, the Communist Party, is historically recent, the logic of political campaigns they deploy for major concerns is not (CPC Central Committee and the State Council 2010, p. 20).

The major document introducing the major priority placed on water governance reform in 2011 was followed in the next decade by more specific policy decisions and laws to implement the standards for water quality, water use efficiency and total quantities used for different purposes. The No. 1 Central Document itself lays bare key principles motivating Chinese approaches to sustainable development and the practices they deploy to achieve their goals, in this case specifically for water governance reform. Both principles and practices clearly echo those of earlier centuries, even as they are expressed through a political ideology and enacted through institutions quite different from those of the past. Both historically and today, these principles and practices pose ideals of good governance conceived quite distinctly from those identified in Western economics and political science scholarship. Whether we look at Chinese or Western notions of good governance, we can see how each was crystallised over time through historical processes of change. This is not to say that either Chinese or Western countries consistently achieve their principles of good governance; however, it does alert us to these principles posing different criteria for judging success. The strengths of Western principles of good governance are well understood; those of Chinese good governance are far less so.

Good governance in the Chinese political tradition depends on establishing social order, which in turn depends at least partly upon addressing people's material security; this captured the notion of people's livelihoods and wellbeing. *Minsheng* is one of the purposes for developing the Chinese economy over the past four decades, amidst policy responses to climate change. We see people's livelihood stressed by Chinese leaders and policy-makers; the Chinese have had both in water governance reform and the state's responses to the COVID-19 pandemic. However desirable Western principles of good governance continue to be in the future, the practical governance challenges of facing global pandemics threatening human life and achieving sustainable development to enable the planet's longer-term future have to be met as well. This chapter has briefly introduced the importance of people's livelihoods to Chinese good governance in the past, and confirmed its durable presence today, suggesting that it may well continue to motivate Chinese responses to our shared global challenges of sustainable development. This possibility makes it important for people more generally to discover how China's past principles and practices regarding its economy could well matter in terms of what good governance in the future might mean.

## References

Brook, Timothy: *The Chinese State in Ming Society*. London: Routledge 2005.
China Daily: Premier Li Keqaiang Meets the Press: Full Transcript of Questions and Answers. *China Daily*, http://english.www.gov.cn/premier/news/202005/29/content_WS5ed058d2c6d0b3f0e9498f21.html (retrieved 4 November 2020), 2020.
CPC Central Committee and the State Council: *Decision from the CPC Central Committee and the State Council on Accelerating Water Conservancy Reform and Development* [official English translation of No. 1 Central Document for 2011], 2010.
Deng, Gang: *Development Versus Stagnation: Technological Continuity and Agricultural Progress in Pre-modern China*. Westport, CT: Greenwood Press, 1993.

Deng, Xiaoping: Records of Comrade Deng Xiaoping's Shenzhen Tour. *People's Daily Online*, http://en.people.cn/200201/18/eng20020118_88932.shtml (retrieved 4 November 2020), 2002.

El Amine, Loubna: *Classical Confucian Political Thought: A New Interpretation*. Princeton, NJ: Princeton University Press, 2016.

Guo, Jinping: *Minsheng xingfu shi zhongguo gongchandang de genben jiazhi zhuiqiu* (The Chinese Communist Party's fundamental pursuit of value is the happiness of people's livelihoods) [民生幸福是中国共产党的根本价值追求]. *Shehui kexue luntan*, 1, pp. 152–57, 2020.

Guo, Ruipeng: *Jiaqi minsheng yu richang shenghuo de qiaoliang* (Support bridging people's livelihoods and daily life) [架起民生与日常生活的桥梁]. *Zhongguo shehui lishi pinglun*, 16(2), pp. 187–91, 2015.

Gustafsson, Björn, Sicular, Terry & Yang, Xiuna: Catching Up with the West: Chinese Pathways to the Global Middle Class. *The China Journal*, www.journals.uchicago.edu/doi/pdfplus/10.1086/708752 (retrieved 28 June 2020), 2020.

Halsey, Stephen: *Quest for Power: European Imperialism and the Making of Chinese Statecraft*. Cambridge, MA: Harvard University Press 2015.

Hou, Chi-ming: Economic Development and Public Finance in China, 1937–1945. In: Paul K.T. Sih (ed.): *Nationalist China During the Sino-Japanese War, 1937–1945*. Hicksville, NY: Exposition Press, pp. 203–41, 1977.

Hu, Angang: *Zhongguo: minsheng yu fazhan* (China: people's livelihood and development [中国：民生与发展]). Beijing: Zhongguo jingji chubanshe, 2008.

Hu, Angang: "I Openly Call for Emission Cuts" (1) & (2). *China Dialogue*, 6–7 August 2009.

Hu, Angang & Guan, Qingyou: *China: Tackle the Challenge of Global Climate Change*. London: Routledge, 2017.

Kirby, William: Continuity and Change in Modern China: Economic Planning on the Mainland and on Taiwan, 1943–1958. *Australian Journal of Chinese Affairs*, 24, pp. 121–41, 1990.

Li, Cheng: Introduction. In: Hu Angang: *China in 2020: A New Type of Superpower*. Washington, DC: Brookings Institution Press, 2011.

Mao, Zedong: On the Ten Major Relationships. *China Quarterly*, 69, pp. 221–38, 1977.

Murthy, Viren: The Democratic Potential of Confucian Minben Thought. *Asian Philosophy*, 10(1), pp. 33–47, 2000.

Niewenhuis, Lucas: Xi Says Back to Work, Back to School, Back to Consumption to Revive Struggling Economy. *SupChina*, 23 April, https://supchina.com/2020/04/23/xi-says-back-to-work-back-to-school-back-to-consumption-to-revive-struggling-economy (retrieved 23 April 2020), 2020.

Perdue, Peter C.: Official Goals and Local Interests: Water Control in the Dongting Lake Region during the Ming and Qing Periods. *Journal of Asian Studies*, 41(4), pp. 747–765, 1982.

Piketty, Thomas; Yang, Li & Zucman, Gabriel: Capital Accumulation, Private Property, and Rising Inequality in China, 1978–2015. *American Economic Review*, 109(7), pp. 2469–96, 2019.

Rawski, Thomas: *Economic Growth in Pre-War China*. Berkeley, CA: University of California Press, 1989.

Rowe, William: *Saving the World: Chen Hongmou and Elite Consciousness in Eighteenth-Century China*. Stanford, CA: Stanford University Press, 2001.

State Council: Premier Stresses Priorities in Six Areas, http://english.www.gov.cn/premier/news/202005/15/content_WS5ebdd4ebc6d0b3f0e9497aee.html, 2020.

Su, Yiping: *Chuantong minben sixiang yu shengtaixing minshengguan de xiangrongxing ji qishi* (The compatibility and lesson of an ecological model traditional thinking about people as the root and the concept of people's livelihood) [传统民本思想与生态型民生观的及启示]. *Journal of Guizhou Radio and TV University*, 20(4), pp. 62–65, 2012.

Tsang, Steven: Consultative Leninism: China's New Political Framework. *Journal of Contemporary China*, 18(62), pp. 865–80, 2009.

UN Water: *UN World Water Development Report 2018 Nature-Based Solutions for Water*. New York: UNESCO, 2018.

Will, Pierre-Etienne: Un cycle hydraulique en Chine: la province du Hubei due XVIe au XIXe siècles. *Bulletin de l'Ecole française d'Extrême Orient*, 68, pp. 261–87, 1980.

Will, Pierre-Etienne: State Intervention in the Administration of a Hydraulic Infrastructure: The Example of Hubei Province in Late Imperial Times. In: Stuart Schram (ed.): *The Scope of State Power in China*. SOAS and Chinese University of Hongkong, Hong Kong, pp. 295–347, 1985.

Will, Pierre-Etienne: Clear Waters versus Muddy Waters: The Zheng-Bai Irrigation System of Shaanxi Province in the Late-Imperial Period. In: Mark Elvin and Liu Ts'ui-jung (eds): *Sediments of Time: Environment and Society in Chinese History*. Cambridge: Cambridge University Press, pp. 283–343, 1998.

Will, Pierre-Etienne & Wong, R. Bin with Lee, James and contributions by Oi, Jean C. and Perdue, Peter C.: *Nourish the People: State Civilian Granaries in China, 1650 1850*. Ann Arbor, MI: University of Michigan Press, 1991.

Wong, R. Bin: *China Transformed: Historical Change and the Limits of European Experience*. Ithaca, NY: Cornell University Press, 1997.

Wong, R. Bin: Formal and Informal Mechanisms of Rule and Economic Development: The Qing Empire in Comparative Perspective. *Journal of Early Modern History*, 5(4), pp. 387–408, 2001.

Wong, R. Bin: Taxation and Good Governance in China, 1500–1914. In: Bartolomé Yun-Casalilla & Patrick K. O'Brien with Francisco Comín (eds): *The Rise of Fiscal States: A Global History, 1500–1914*. Cambridge: Cambridge University Press, pp. 353–77, 2012.

Wong, R. Bin: China Before Capitalism. In: Larry Neal & Jeffrey Williamson (eds): *Cambridge History of Capitalism Vol. 1: The Rise of Capitalism from Ancient Origins to 1848*. Cambridge: Cambridge University Press, pp. 125–64, 2014.

Wong, R. Bin: Self-strengthening and Other Responses to the Expansion of European Economic and Political Power. In: John McNeil & Kenneth Pomeranz (eds): *Cambridge World History*, Cambridge: Cambridge University Press, 7(2), pp. 366–94, 2015.

Wong, R. Bin: Coping with Poverty and Famine: Material Welfare, Public Goods, and Chinese Approaches to Governance. In: Masayuki Tanimoto & R. Bin Wong (eds): *Public Goods Provision in the Early Modern Economy: Comparative Perspectives from Japan, China, and Europe*. Berkeley, CA: University of California Press, pp. 130–44, 2019.

Wong, R. Bin & Perdue, Peter C.: Famine's Foes in Ch'ing China. In: *Chinese Economic History Up to 1949. Vol. 1*: 80–106. Leiden: Brill. [originally published in *Harvard Journal of Asiatic Studies* 43.1 (1983): 291–332], 2008.

World Bank: *China From Poor Areas to Poor People: China's Evolving Poverty Reduction Agenda, An Assessment of Poverty and Inequality in China.* Geneva: World Bank, 2009.

Wu, Jinglian: *Understanding and Interpreting Chinese Economic Reform.* Stamford, CT: Thomson, 2005.

Zhao, Zhongwei & Reimondos, Anna: The Demography of China's 1958–61 Famine: A Closer Examination. *Population (English Edition)*, 67(2), pp. 281–308, 2012.

Zheng, Gongcheng: *Minsheng jubian yu Zhongguo zhidu ji zhili tixi de shishi luoji* (The factual logic of great changes in people's livelihood and China's political institutions and governance system) [民生巨变与中国制度 及治理体系的事实逻辑]. *Zhongguo dangzheng ganbu luntan,* 12, pp. 6–13, 2019.

Zhou, Cissy: China Risks "the Legitimacy of the Communist Party's Regime" Without Changes, Says Law Professor. South China Morning Post, www.scmp.com/economy/china-economy/article/3002866/china-risks-legitimacy-communist-partys-regime-without, 2019.

Zurndorfer, Harriett T.: Cotton Textile Manufacture and Marketing in Late Imperial China and the "Great Divergence". *Journal of the Economic and Social History of the Orient*, 54, pp. 701–38, 2011.

# 2 Justifying office-selling for famine relief in nineteenth-century Qing China

*Elisabeth Kaske*

Food security as a public good has been high on the agenda of Confucian governance for millennia. The chapters in this section discuss the main tenets of this notion as it played out in the Qing dynasty: government investments in flood control and irrigation; the maintenance of a network of granaries; and famine relief in times of dearth. Of course, the Qing was far from a modern welfare state. As Bin Wong (2019) argues, famine relief required campaign-style activity from imperial institutions, small and with limited reach in normal times, as well as considerable input from local elites who saw the provision of food security as a shared responsibility. At the same time, the respective roles of local government and elites showed considerable variation, and how to calibrate private donations and relief management was a question that vexed officials for much of the Qing period. There was, to be sure, a tradition of local private famine relief, with its repertoire of donations, gruel kitchens, refugee accommodation and distribution of seeds and draught animals for post-disaster rebuilding. What interests me here, however, is an equally old tradition of drawing private funds and grain into the state-led relief effort by rewarding "contributions" (used below without quotation marks as a technical term) with degrees, honorific titles, brevet rank and even full official rank. These rewards were expressions of social status, but since social status was highly bureaucratised, they could amount to a *de facto* sale of official rank and even office-holding. Office-selling was a common phenomenon of the early modern period, not just in China, though it was gradually outlawed in Europe from the end of the eighteenth century. In China, however, contributions exploded in the nineteenth century, partly (but not exclusively, as we will see) due to the deteriorating fiscal conditions of the empire. My initial question was: What happens when, in times of a rapid expansion of office-selling, one ideal of Confucian governance – meritocratic recruitment of bureaucrats – clashes with another – the provision of food security? What I found instead was a whole array of conflicts that played out on different levels: state vs. elite, centre-province-local governments, and various purposes of appropriation. This made me rethink the system of office-selling in China and develop a model for the nineteenth century.

The chapter begins by briefly outlining the history of office selling in China compared with Europe. It then develops a model. I will argue that office selling

DOI: 10.4324/9780367434496-4

was an expression of the Qing notion of sovereignty. The Qing emperor as sovereign (in theory) holds monopoly over "the totality of the traffic in honours to which 'gentlemen' may lay claim" (Bourdieu 1994), but is not free to commodify these honours as he pleases. Office-selling was highly bureaucratised and limited to what I call the "sovereign tasks of empire" – that is, security (war), river conservancy, maintaining the court, and famine relief. The goal of these tasks was imperial survival – in other words, military, hydraulic, dynastic and agricultural security. While there was no fundamental rejection of the system of office selling prior to the Sino-Japanese War of 1894/95, criticism expressed frequently in the sources reflects fissures between different prerogatives of Qing governance. Finally, the chapter will examine one of the conflicts inherent in the system: that between various agents to whom sovereignty was in fact delegated, in this case the central government and the provinces. I will show that famine relief contributions became one element in an increasing fiscal autonomy of the provinces that went hand in hand with shifting the focus of public goods provision from the central to the provincial governments.

## Office-selling in China

The idea of bestowing rank and office as a reward for donating grain to the state can be traced back to the Legalist thinker Shang Yang in the fourth century BCE (Shang, Yang 1928, pp. 64–65, 236, 253, 304). This makes for a dubious legitimacy within the context of Confucian theories of governance. Consequently, Shang Yang (or his alleged Han-dynasty follower, Chao Cuo, 200–154 BCE) was almost never directly evoked in any of the discussions concerning office-selling,[1] although it continued to be discussed in similar meritocratic terms in official sources. Replenishing the granaries and relieving famines were considered particularly worthy causes, even as military causes and payment in money often reaped greater rewards. Under the Song dynasty (960–1279), the Neo-Confucian thinker Zhu Xi (1130–1200) praised office-selling as a means to raise grain for famine relief. This vindication of office-selling helped to legitimise the practice in nineteenth-century Korea, but I have found no references to Zhu Xi in pertinent Qing debates (Karlsson 2007; Lo 1987, pp. 70–71). Lists of prices that matched amounts of grain with rewards are already mentioned for the Song dynasty. By the Yuan (1279–1368), grain was commutable in paper money (YS 1979, juan 82, p. 2053). By the Ming (1368–1644), the system was fully bureaucratised and began to use the terminology common until 1911, from "paying grain for appointment to office" *(nasu buguan)* to "contributing for an office" *(juanguan)* (Wu, Yue 2006). The payment in silver was first suggested in 1479 (though subsequently suspended until 1508) (MS, juan 186, p. 4921). Xiang Jing (2006) shows that Ming dynasty famine relief campaigns rewarded contributors with honorific titles and brevet rank rather than full official rank. However, since brevet and full official rank formed a continuum, this did not prevent awardees from seeking paths into government employment, aside from the other privileges that came with the brevet, such as exemption from corvée labour. Thus, the history and rational of office-selling differs from Europe where, according to Wolfgang Reinhard (1974), office-selling was a phenomenon of the early modern era, when an inherited notion of an office (and its benefice) as private property of the office-holder clashed with new economic realities: the monetisation of the economy, increased financial needs of the state due to mercenary warfare and an under-developed capital market. Some elements of Reinhard's definition are, however, applicable to China, especially in the nineteenth century.

Under the Qianlong emperor (r. 1735–96), whose reign is considered the heyday of imperial munificence, contributions became more systematised. Qianlong introduced an important distinction between full official rank, which qualified for actual official appointment, and mere status awards – brevet rank, honorific titles and imperial academy degrees (the entry ticket into gentry status). While both were hitherto sold during short-term campaigns, to be stopped each time the emergency had ended, the latter were now sold on a regular basis. A contribution office *(juanna fang)* was established in the Board of Revenue, which reserved for itself the monopoly of silver contributions for all regular status awards as well as full official rank, which was only sold during short-term campaigns. The provinces, in turn, were only allowed to award degrees for grain contributions to the local granaries (Xu, Daling 1977, Kaske 2011).[2]

An office-selling "campaign" was not a random activity, but an administrative act based on legal statutes *(shili)* put in force for a limited period of time. Qianlong made serious efforts to reduce office-selling campaigns: among other measures, he decreed that they should be opened only when extraordinary government expenditures exceeded 3–4 million taels, a substantial amount that was hardly reached in famine relief situations (QSL, QL 18.8.29., 800–01). The moratorium also limited a special type, so-called gratitude contributions *(baoxiao)* by officials, as well as chartered salt and foreign trade merchants, which were in fact a tax on privilege similar to the *augmentation des gages* of Ancien Regime France. In China, as in France, office and rank were in high demand. Qianlong rebutted repeated requests from both his bureaucrats and the chartered merchants to open office-selling campaigns under various pretexts.

Qianlong's restraint in selling offices was up-ended by his successor, Jiaqing (1796–1820), who faced the exploding costs of a guerilla war waged by the White Lotus rebels and several large floods of the Yongding and Yellow Rivers. However, fiscal emergency was not the only reason to expand office-selling. The Qing faced a legitimacy crisis. Keeping taxes low while offering the local elites paths to honour and advancement and promoting their involvement in the provision of public services were among the strategies employed to regain public confidence (Han 2016a; Kaske 2018; Zhang 2013). The genie was never returned into the bottle. While office-selling went out of fashion in Europe, it thrived in China during the nineteenth century. By the time of the Opium War (1839–42), the right to sell full official rank was delegated to the provinces. During the first half of the nineteenth century, office-selling campaigns had been frequent; following the Taiping Rebellion (1851–64), they became permanent until 1901 (with a short break from 1879 to 1885). This was the legal environment under which the debates about office-selling discussed in the following sections took place.

## Office-selling and state sovereignty

The nature of office-selling in China is insufficiently understood. There is little if any theorising or attempts at a philosophical justification in contemporary Chinese accounts compared, for example, with Korea. Chinese and Western critics since the Qing era have tended to emphasise two aspects: the deficiency of office-selling as an instrument of emergency finance and the deleterious effects of office-selling on bureaucratic recruitment and official morale.[3] Only recently historians have begun to reassess office-selling and explore its meaning for the reproduction of the elites (not in competition, but complementary to the civil service examinations) and for their involvement in public affairs (Han 2016; Wu, Yue 2011; Zhang 2013).

Despite this reassessment of office-selling in recent scholarship, there was plenty of criticism even during the Qing dynasty, even including suggestions of abolitionism, although the latter remained marginal until the Sino-Japanese War of 1894/95 fomented more fundamental value change (Xiao, Shouku 2006). The following is an attempt to locate office selling as a bureaucratic practice within the conceptual world of Qing governance and gain a more systematic understanding of the conflicts and criticisms of the practice. As stated above, office-selling was highly regulated in Qing administrative law. I argue that the practice was tied to the Qing notion of sovereignty and the sale of full official rank was limited to what I call "the sovereign tasks of empire" – war, river conservancy, the supply of the capital and treasury of the Board of Revenue, and famine relief. With one exception – Yongzheng's innovative (but never repeated) use of contributions as incentives for land reclamation in 1726 – all the 55 statutory contribution campaigns until 1840 found by Jiang Shoupeng (1985, p. 47) fell into one of the four tasks (Table 2.1).[4]

Before more fundamental attacks were levied against office-selling at the end of the nineteenth century, conflicts mainly arose in three areas: first, over which of the four sovereign tasks to prioritise; second, between various paths

*Table 2.1* Contribution campaigns, 1644–1840

| Type of campaign | No. of campaigns |
| --- | --- |
| Military | 15 |
| Famine relief | 14 |
| River conservancy | 11 |
| National treasury | 10 |
| Other | 5 |
| Total | 55 |

to official appointment; and third, between the various agents (central, provincial, local governments, military headquarters) to whom imperial authority was delegated. The bureaucratic system was able to fine-tune these conflicts of interest by manipulating the status awards themselves. There were four basic categories in the Qing reward system: full official rank; personal status awards (brevet rank, title, degree); military honours (esp. plume decorations); and minor embellishments (door inscriptions, ceremonial arches). Within full official rank, the distinction was between seal-holding rank (magistrates, prefects and circuit intendants, all with access to a treasury) and auxiliary rank. Priorities were sold to fast-track actual appointment. The decision of which imperial agent was allowed to sell which status award for which purpose determined the priority of tasks, as well as the hierarchy of imperial agents.

A conflict over the priority of sovereign tasks shows in the remark of a foreign observer on the translation of a call for grain contributions to supply the capital Beijing posted in 1848 Shanghai:

> It is worthy of notice that two proclamations should appear at the same time, one detailing the disasters of famine and making provision for the relief of the distressed, and the other calling for purchasers of rank, when this rank is to be obtained by contributions of grain, the product of the same soil, to be carried away from the very doors of the starving people to Peking.[5]

Famine relief had been downgraded in the hierarchy of sovereign task since the Qianlong reign. Full official rank could no longer be sold in relief campaigns unless linked to river conservancy – that is, repairs to the Yellow River and Grand Canal. The proclamation gives priority to the supply of the capital Beijing over local famine relief. It reflects Beijing's increasing dependency on office-selling for both grain and revenue. In 1814, Grand Councillor Yinghe decried a plan of his fellow high ministers to fight the government deficit with another contribution campaign, arguing that contributions could not ensure stable government revenue. He failed to convince the Jiaqing emperor that to lift the ban on gold and silver mining and to tax confiscated land would be more prudent fiscal policy (Ni, Yuping 2013, pp. 136–37; Xu, Daling 1977, pp. 52–53).

Qianlong's concern that purchase officials could crowd out examination graduates, the second major conflict of interest, was not shared by his successors. In 1793, the Qianlong emperor declared that meritocratic recruitment was crucial for good governance and denounced officials who requested office-selling campaigns for war or river conservancy as "profit-talkers" (*yan li zhi chen*, a Mencian anathema to good governance) (QSL, QL 58.11.20, 244a-b). Jiaqing turned his father's words on their head by exclaiming in 1811: "That WE have broadened the channels of communication *(yanlu)* does not mean that we have broadened the channels to talk profit. I will not employ any official who advocates heavy taxation" (QSL, JQ 16.11.21., 382a–383b). The expansion of

24  *Elisabeth Kaske*

office-selling in the early nineteenth century was a political choice, not a necessity: it was the payoff for a low-tax policy in a state that did not rely on government debt. Reinhard's concern that office selling was in fact a sort of crooked government loan repaid by the people was not absent in China. In 1874, already under the impression of foreign military superiority, Zhu Cai complained that:

> For every million taels that the Board of Revenue earns from the sale of offices per year, there will be hundreds or thousands of expectant officials more in the provinces, which will cost several hundred thousand taels of revenue. Over thirty years the state pays ten times more than it has received. This is like a middle-income family that fails to live parsimoniously and instead relies on high-interest loans for sustenance. After several years it will end in bankruptcy.
> 
> (Zhu 1957, pp. 340–41)

But Zhu was a low-ranking official at the time, and his warnings went unheard.

The impact on bureaucratic recruitment was obvious. After a century of office-selling and civil wars, success in the highly competitive civil service examinations ("regular path", *zhengtu*) was no longer the main path into office, purchase *(juanna)* had become as important as military service *(jungong)* and recommendation for distinguished service *(laoji)*. In 1897, the later "father of the Republic", Sun Yat-sen (1897, pp. 425, 436), while plotting revolution in London, derided the Qing's "universal and systemic corruption … [as] directly responsible for famine, flood, and pestilence". He observed that, "The fourth method of entering public life, i.e., by purchase pure and simple, is quite recognised by law, and is becoming more common every year." But Sun also had to admit that "my early years were spent in intimate association with members of the Chinese official class, and … my friends were anxious for me to purchase an entry into public life, as very many of my acquaintance have done within the last ten years". Office-selling was popular among the elites. Literati criticism was hardly motivated by concern for meritocracy, but rather betrays the status anxiety of the landed gentry as men lacking good pedigree *(liupin hunza)* entered the competition for official positions. An indictment of 1864 includes expletives against merchants and the lower rungs of administrative employment (private secretaries, clerks, sedan chair bearers) (QSL, TZ 2.5.21., 364a–365a; cf. Wright 1966, p. 86).

This was also the main complaint of the famous indignant Confucians, a coterie of low-ranked but influential court officials who dominated public opinion with their memorials until the 1880s. They matter for this chapter thanks to their activity during the Great North China Famine of 1877–79, where they emphasised the Confucian role of the ruler to feed the people and supported contribution campaigns, including office-selling (Edgerton-Tarpley 2008). At the same time, they rallied against the modernising governors for squandering money for shipyards and arsenals, and ganged up against officials whose pedigree was deemed suspicious or who mingled across class boundaries with merchants and rank purchasers. China's first modern newspaper, *Shenbao*, quipped:

> Since the wars increased military expenses, office-selling campaigns were widely opened which accepted grain or money at greatly diminished prices. As a result, the pedigrees *(liupin)* of office purchasers have become diverse and men of all professions have risen into the ranks of officialdom. Peasants, artisans and merchants are generally considered as "pure" *(qingbai)*, of course more dignified than menial laborers and servants. But the graduates of the civil service examinations still harbor the feeling that they are not their peers. The "pure stream" *(qingliu)* must not spoil itself *(zizhuo)*.[6]

"Pure stream" *(qingliu)* became the name under which this group is still known today.

Office-selling thus united imperial prerogatives of benevolent low taxation and elite demands for rank and status. It was a policy geared to win over large landowners, who literally became "gentrified" as office purchase bought the legal status of gentry *(shenshi)* even if they did not gain appointment, a strategy that paid off in the suppression of the mid-century rebellions (Kuhn 1970, pp. 205–06).

The civil wars gave rise to a third force that kept office-selling alive – and potentially created friction – namely, provincial governors. Seunghyun Han (2016b) has shown that as early as under Jiaqing, the throne used the contribution reward system to prevent local governments from extracting additional funds from taxpayers under the pretext of famine relief or public welfare. Even for symbolic embellishments such as inscriptions and ceremonial arches, contributors had to report to the provincial government and eventually to the throne through the routine memorial system. (More important status awards were reported through priority "secret" memorials not investigated by Han.) The mid-century rebellions further strengthened the power and autonomy of provincial governors, who profited not only from newly established commercial taxes but also directly from office-selling, which had been delegated to the provinces in the Fund-Raising Statutes, the administrative law that regulated contributions between 1851 and 1879. The provinces each ran their own campaigns, creating a family of provincial regulations *(zhangcheng)* under the licensing power of the statutes *(shili)*. The latter defined the price lists, while the former included a more limited choice of status awards but could offer discounts. The newly formed triangular relationship between provinces, central government and purchasers are depicted in Figure 2.1. The central government—the throne was occupied by child emperors after 1862 and retained a largely symbolic function—maintained the power to license both the right of a province to collect money by contributions and the status award thus obtained by the purchaser. The revenue was shared in the way explained above. Buying an office was not a simple straight-forward affair, but required the purchase of several status awards, the degree, the office, certain bureaucratic requirements,

26  *Elisabeth Kaske*

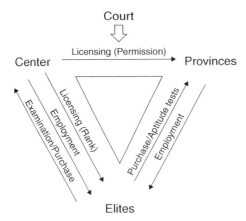

*Figure 2.1* Authority in contribution campaigns

a priority, etc. Which status awards were sold by the province or the Board of Revenue was negotiated for each specific campaign. The real novelty was that the provinces created new employment opportunities outside the statutory bureaucracy. Sprawling provincial bureaucracies of bureaus (ju) for military supply, foreign affairs, law, army expenses, post-war reconstruction, or famine relief needed to be staffed. The contribution bureaus themselves provided career opportunities for junior staff members, since successful solicitors could be promoted further. Therefore, contributions not only generated revenue but also created a tool in the hands of provincial leaders to provide patronage for their expanding networks. The army of "expectant officials" in the employ of the provinces outgrew the tiny number of appointed officials in the statutory bureaucracy which tenaciously clung to the ideal of small government. These provincial opportunities fueled enduring demand for office purchase, but also became alarming to the conservatives in court, especially after the Great North China famine of 1877–1879.

## Centre–province conflicts in famine relief contributions

With the last of the rebellions gradually suppressed by the 1870s and post-war reconstruction well underway, the governors faced a problem: war disappeared, and with it the very *raison d'être* for provincial control over contribution campaigns. Li Hongzhang, one of the most powerful former militia leaders and newly coined governor-general of the capital province of Zhili, found a way out in 1871. Famine became the new war.

Famine relief contributions, long discriminated against in the list of sovereign tasks, had been superseded during the rebellions by military forces getting directly involved in civil reconstruction and relief tasks. As seen

*Justifying office-selling for famine relief* 27

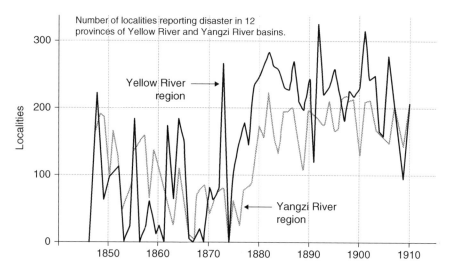

*Figure 2.2* Disaster reports, 1840–1911

above, a provincial contribution campaign was an administrative act requiring regulations *(zhangcheng)* that was approved by the central government. In 1871, following severe flooding in the Tianjin region, Li Hongzhang converted the old provincial wartime campaign-styled Tianjin Rice Contribution into the Tianjin Relief Contribution, offering the same conditions, a 40 per cent discount on the list prices of the Fund-Raising Statutes for full official rank (but not seal-holding offices) and a 20 per cent discount for other status awards (Li, Hongzhang 2008, vol. 4, p. 401). According to one of the major historians of famine in China, Lillian Li (2007, p. 268), Li Hongzhang managed to revive famine relief "to a surprising extent". He even coined a new term, *zhenjuan* (relief contribution, modifier+noun) instead of *juanzhen* (contribution [for] relief, verb + object) used before.

This is not a minor detail, as it may in fact change our assessment of the incidence of disaster in nineteenth-century China. Environmental historians have observed a steep increase in famine reports shortly after 1870 and especially after 1877 (Davis 2017, p. 370) (Figure 2.2). We need to consider the possibility that, rather than assuming more disaster, the expansion of relief contribution campaigns created an incentive for provinces to report famines. Li Hongzhang's campaign model was widely copied, especially after the epic Great North China Famine of 1877–79. There were 14 famine relief campaigns during the 200 years until 1849, but at least 143 between 1875 and 1908 (Xia, Minfang 2010, p. 38).

During the North China Famine, governors of several provinces collaborated to obtain relief funds by selling offices. Tianjin became a hub that provided half of the funds for the most severely hit province of Shanxi. The success was not based on the Tianjin regulations alone. Shanxi governor Zeng Guoquan

28  Elisabeth Kaske

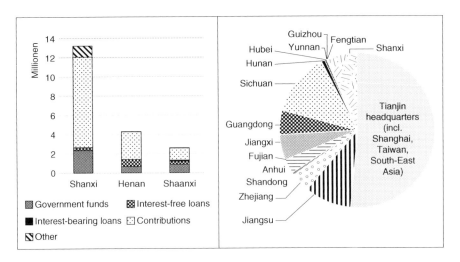

*Figure 2.3* Famine relief in three provinces and income of the Shanxi Contribution Campaign, 1877–79

Sources: JLZ, 03-5590-8, 11, 12; 03-5585-72-74; 03-5589-12; GXSTZ, 353-354.

managed to gain even more concessions from the central government with the permission to copy another more prestigious wartime contribution campaign for remote Guizhou province (see Kaske 2011). Shanxi bureaus opened in many provinces, and even overseas, and sold the full range of status awards, including the most coveted seal-holding offices and plume decorations, a very expensive military honour consisting of a peacock feather. "If the goal of the military is to pacify the region," wrote Censor Guo Congju, who requested permission to sell them, "then relief efforts are equally protecting the lives of the people … If people voluntarily donate to support the relief effort, their merit is no less than supporting military funds." (*Shenbao*, 9 February 1878; Zeng, Guoquan 2006, vol. 1, pp. 211–12). Shanxi consequently profited most from the contribution campaign. The province received 9.5 million taels from contributions alone between 1877 and 1879, an amount equal to its total statutory land tax during this period (Figure 2.3).

In 1879, however, the central government put a sudden stop to the Fund-Raising Statutes. This meant that the sale of most status awards was discontinued. Provinces with famine relief contributions were only allowed to sell brevet rank and honorific titles, and could no longer offer discounts on the list price. Even Imperial Academy degrees were banned. As a result, revenue fell steeply. The reasoning of the Board of Revenue for the ban reflects the pounding of the "pure stream" faction decrying the increased social mobility created by office selling. It also shows discomfort with the market forces unleashed by the provincial competition for contributors:

> Since the start of contributions all provinces have established contribution bureaus and have reduced prices by discounting and converting [silver into other kinds of payment] … the prices of offices in the various regulations have been reduced so much, that contributors find it relatively easy to collect the money. Once approved, they are appointed [by the Board of Civil Office] or assigned [to an unsalaried probational position], and quickly become real officials. Among these contributors, the able and inapt cannot be immediately distinguished. Moreover, contribution bureaus have grown like a forest, they compete with each other with different prices, so that it is also difficult to prevent clever people from looking for the cheapest way.
>
> (JSWXB, juan 31, 1b-4b)

This conflict is also expressed in the criticism by Zhang Peilun, one of the most famous of the indignant Confucians. Aside from the usual diatribe against the putative low (social) quality of contributors, the main target of his memorial written four years after the stop of the sale of full official rank was to crack down on the army of expectant official staffing the provincial bureaus (GXSTZ 9.1.16, JLZ, 3-132-6535-32; Kuhn 2003, p. 121). This was a direct attack on the newly won provincial autonomy, and shows that the conservative faction in court was concerned about provincial independence.

When a central office-selling campaign returned during the Sino-French War of 1884–85 in the form of the Maritime Defence Contribution *(Haifang shili)*, the centre banned provincial relief contributions altogether, hoping that the provinces would remit all funds collected by office-selling to Beijing only (Li, Hongzhang 2008, vol. 11, p. 39). The ploy failed. Governors bombarded Beijing with requests for contribution campaigns. Li Hongzhang was in a strategic position to retaliate against the ban, and at least twice threatened to confiscate the grain tribute destined for the capital (Li, Hongzhang 2008, pp. 11, 184, 456). By the end of 1886, provincial famine relief campaigns were back and price discounting continued unabated (Li, Hongzhang 2008, vol. 11, p. 539; vol. 12, p. 453). The central government won a partial victory by keeping full official rank off limits for the provinces. This step reclaimed sovereignty for the centre and downgraded famine relief – which by now had completely become a task of provincial governments – in the hierarchy of sovereign tasks. It was a revenue-sharing arrangement rather than a limit on office selling, because contributors purchased brevet rank in provincial famine relief contributions at the discounted price and counted them at nominal price against full official rank in the Maritime Defence Contribution run by the Board.[7]

## Conclusion

In 1901, in an edict signed by the Empress Dowager, the throne again tried to outlaw the sale of full official rank, this time for good. The move followed another expansion of office selling for an ostensible famine relief campaign for Shaanxi province, which but was aggravated by the presence in the province of the imperial court exiled from Beijing by the foreign occupiers (Chao, Xiaohong 2009). That this ban was slightly more successful than the previous one was less due to a stronger central government; rather, the fiscal crisis caused by the Boxer Indemnities had removed all ideological limits to tax increases, thus giving the provinces ample alternative ways to generate revenue. Administrative and educational reforms would soon admit new educational careers, and thus dampen the demand for official rank.

Qing-style office- and rank-selling belongs to the political economy of a society that rations status using strict sumptuary laws (Douglas 1967). In our assessment of the Qing ideal of small government, benevolent taxation and campaign-style crisis solutions, we need to consider its pay-offs and inconsistencies. In the first half of the nineteenth century, the Qing could only maintain its ideal at the expense of expanding office-selling, which the Qianlong emperor would not have approved. Nonetheless, the symbolic power of rank and status continued to keep the state and elites united, even as it became increasingly venal. After 1850, the court clung to the ideal of small government, but it became an empty shell as the provinces expanded their extractive capacities and governments' footprints in society. Once the administrative reforms after 1905 shattered the hegemony of rank and status, the dynasty soon fell apart.

## Notes

1 Modern newspapers took licence and pointed out the origin in Chao Cuo's writings in an article cheering the abolition of office selling in 1901: see 'Lun yong ting juanna shi' 論永停捐納事 *Shenbao* 1901.09.14.
2 The famous corruption scandal in Gansu of 1782 was all about illegal acceptance of silver contributions by the provincial authorities.
3 One early Western example to decry office selling as corruption is Robert M. Martin (1847), treasurer of Hong Kong 1844–45.
4 Four of the five "other" contributions concern shipping grain for the army or the supply of the capital during the breakdown of the Grand Canal.
5 The Sale of Official Rank, Adopted by the Government of China for Increasing Its Revenue; Translation of a Proclamation Calling on the People to Come Forward and Make Purchases, in: *The Chinese Repository*, 18, pp. 207–09, 1849.
6 Zhong Shang Lun 重商論, *Shenbao* 1879.10.13.
7 Hubu fuzou heshi zhenjuan zhe 戶部覆奏核實賑捐摺, *Shenbao* 1898.04.11.

## References

Anders, Karlsson: Famine Relief, Social Order, and State Performance in Late Choson Korea. *The Journal of Korean Studies*, 12(1), pp. 113–41, 2007.
Bourdieu, Pierre: Rethinking the State: Genesis and Structure of the Bureaucratic Field. *Sociological Theory*, 12(1), pp. 1–18, 1994.
Chao, Xiaohong 鈔曉鴻: Qingmo Feizhi Juanna Shiguan Kaoshi 清末廢止捐納實官考實. *Zhongguo Jingji Shi Yanjiu* 中國經濟史研究, 4, pp. 25–34, 2009.

Davis, Mike: *Late Victorian Holocausts: El Niño Famines and the Making of the Third World.* New York: Verso, 2017.

Douglas, Mary: Primitive Rationing. In R. Firth (ed.): *Themes in Economic Anthropology*, pp. 119–47. London: Tavistock, 1967.

Edgerton-Tarpley, Kathryn: *Tears from Iron: Cultural Responses to Famine in Nineteenth-Century China.* Berkeley, CA: University of California Press, 2008.

GXSTZ: Zeng Guoquan 曾國荃 et al. (eds): Guangxu Shanxi Tongzhi 光緒山西通志, juan 82. *Xuxiu Siku Quanshu* 續修四庫全書, 643, 1995.

Han, Seunghyun: *After the Prosperous Age: State and Elites in Early Nineteenth-Century Suzhou.* Cambridge, MA: Harvard University Asia Center, 2016a.

Han, Seunghyun: Changing Roles of Local Elites from the 1720s to the 1830s. In: Willard J. Peterson (ed.): *The Cambridge History of China: Volume 9 – The Ch'ing Dynasty to 1800.* Cambridge: Cambridge University Press, 2016b.

Jiang, Shoupeng 姜守鵬: Qingdai Qianqi Juan Na Zhidu de Shehui Yingxiang 清代前期捐納制度的社會影響. *Dongbei Shida Xuebao* 東北師大學報, 4, pp. 47–54, 1985.

JLZ: Junjichu lufu zouzhe 軍機處錄副奏摺, held by the First Historical Archives, Beijing.

JSWXB: Huangchao jingshi wenbian xubian, ed. Ge, Shijun. Shanghai: Guangbaisong Zhai, 1891, cited from Scripta Sinica database, Academia Sinica, Taiwan.

Kaske, Elisabeth: Fund-Raising Wars: Office Selling and Interprovincial Finance in Nineteenth-Century China. *Harvard Journal of Asiatic Studies*, 71(1), pp. 69–141, 2011.

Kaske, Elisabeth: Austerity in Times of War: Government Finance in Early Nineteenth-Century China. *Financial History Review*, 25(1), pp. 71–96, 2018.

Kuhn, Philip A.: *Rebellion and Its Enemies in Late Imperial China: Militarization and Social Structure, 1796–1864.* Cambridge, MA: Harvard University Press, 1970.

Kuhn, Philip A.: *Origins of the Modern Chinese State.* Stanford, CA: Stanford University Press, 2003.

Li, Hongzhang: Li Hongzhang quanji 李鴻章全集. Gu, Tinglong 顧廷龍 & Dai Yi 戴逸. Hefei (eds.): *The Complete Works of Li Hongzhang.* Beijing: Anhui jiaoyu chubanshe, 2008.

Li, Lillian M.: *Fighting Famine in North China: State, Market, and Environmental Decline, 1690s–1990s.* Stanford, CA: Stanford University Press, 2007.

Lo, Winston W.: *An Introduction to the Civil Service of Sung China: With Emphasis on Its Personnel Administration.* Honolulu: University of Hawai'i Press, 1987.

Martin, Robert M.: *China, Political, Commercial and Social: In an Official Report to Her Majesty's Government*, Vol. 1. London, 1847.

MS: Yang, Jialuo 楊家駱 (ed.) & Tingyu Zhang 張廷玉: *Xin jiao ben Ming shi i*新校本明史. Taipei: Dingwen shuju, 1975, cited from Scripta Sinica edition.

Ni, Yuping 倪玉平. *Qingchao Jiadao Caizheng Yu Shehui* 清朝嘉道財政与社會. Beijing: Shangwu yinshuguan, 2013.

QSL: Qing Shilu, cited from Scripta Sinica database, Academia Sinica Taiwan. (QL: Qianlong, JQ: Jiaqing, DG: Daoguang; chapter and page reference point to the edition for the respective reign period).

Reinhard, Wolfgang: Staatsmacht Als Kreditproblem. Zur Struktur Und Funktion Des Frühneuzeitlichen Ämterhandels. *Vierteljahrschrift Für Sozial- Und Wirtschaftsgeschichte*, 60(3), pp. 289–319, 1974

Shang, Yang: *The Book of Lord Shang: A Classic of the Chinese School of Law.* Translated by J.J.L. Duyvendak. London, 1928.

Sun, Yat-sen: China's Present and Future: The Reform Party's Plea for British Benevolent Neutrality. *Fortnightly Review*, 61(363), pp. 424–40, 1897.

Wong, R. Bin: Coping with Poverty and Famine: Material Welfare, Public Goods, and Chinese Approaches to Governance. In: Roy Bin Wong & Masayuki Tanimoto, (eds): *Public Goods Provision in the Early Modern Economy: Comparative Perspectives from Japan, China, and Europe*. Berkeley, CA: University of California Press, pp. 130–44, 2019.

Wright, Mary Clabaugh: *The Last Stand of Chinese Conservatism: The T'ung-Chih Restoration, 1862–1874*. New York: Atheneum, 1966.

Wu, Yue 伍躍: Mingdai juanna zhidu shitan 明代捐納試探. In: Zhu, Chengru 朱誠如 & Wang, Tianyou 王天有 (eds): *Ming Qing Luncong* 明清論叢, 7. Beijing: Zijincheng chubanshe, pp. 55–80, 2006.

Wu, Yue 伍躍: *Chūgoku No Ennō Seido to Shakai* 中国の捐納制度と社会. Kyōto: Kyōto Daigaku Gakujutsu Shuppankai, 2011.

Xia, Mingfang 夏明方: Jiuhuang Huomin: Qingmo Minchu Yiqian Zhongguo Huangzhengshu Kaolun 救荒活民: 清末民初以前中國荒政書考論. *Qingshi Yanjiu* 清史研究, 78(2), 2010.

Xiang, Jing 向靜. Mingdai de Yiguan Yimin 明代的義官義民. *Ming Qing Luncong* 明清論叢, 7, pp. 81–101, 2006.

Xiao, Shouku 肖守庫: Jiawu Zhanzheng Qianhou Juanna Yulun de Hongguan Qingshi 甲午戰爭前後捐納輿論的宏觀情勢. *Hebei shifan daxue xuebao: Zhexue shehui kexue ban*, 4, 2006.

Xu, Daling 許大齡: *Qingdai Juanna Zhidu* 清代捐納制度. Taibei xian: Wenhai chubanshe, 1977.

YS: Yang, Jialuo 楊家駱 (ed.) & Song Lian 宋濂: *Xin Jiaoben Yuanshi* 新校本元史. Taipei: Dingwen shuju, 1979, cited from Scripta Sinica edition.

Zeng, Guoquan: *Zeng Guoquan Quan Ji* 曾國荃全集, Haoming Tang (ed.). Changsha Shi: Yuelu shushe, 2006.

Zhang, Lawrence: Legacy of Success: Office Purchase and State–Elite Relations in Qing China. *Harvard Journal of Asiatic Studies*, 73(2), pp. 259–97, 2013.

Zhu, Cai 朱采: Haifang Yi 海防議. In: *Yangwu Yundong* 洋務運動. Shanghai: renmin chubanshe, 1957.

# 3 The cost of security

Financing Yellow River hydraulics during the late imperial period

*Iwo Amelung*

Karl August Wittfogel (1896–1988) first developed his concept of the so-called "hydraulic society" in his *Wirtschaft und Gesellschaft Chinas* (Wittfogel 1931). While he particularly stresses the supposed necessity and ability of the Chinese state to mobilise large numbers of corvée workers, Wittfogel also goes to considerable lengths to highlight the capability and willingness of the state to commit a large part of its fiscal resources for maintaining hydraulic services. Based on a rather limited number of figures, mainly gathered from translations of the *Beijing Gazette*, he also shows that the amount of money remained considerable but decreased in absolute but especially in relative terms during the very late imperial period (Wittfogel 1931, p. 443).[1] It actually is a considerable challenge to obtain reliable figures for the amount of silver the Chinese state was willing to spend for river control during the late imperial period. One source used by a number of scholars is Wei Yuan's 魏源 (1794–1857) "Chou He pian" 籌河篇 (Opinions on Planning the River), which was written in 1842. Through his official connections, Wei had comparatively reliable figures on the expenditures of the Qing government. He points out that the amount of money spent on river works had greatly increased since the Yongzheng period. As an official inclined to reform, he does not see this as an indicator of the ability of the state to mobilise large amounts of money for useful hydraulic projects, but rather the contrary: for him, the ever-increasing amount of money needed was an indicator of a state that was unable to reform its basic institutions and that was therefore heading for demise (Wei, Yuan 1968).

Contrasting the ideas of a Marxist sinologist historian of the 1920s with the writings of a Qing reformer roughly a hundred years earlier appears to be a rather risky business; however, the contrast is telling not only with respect to the evaluation of the necessity of spending for hydraulic work, but also for highlighting that the money provided by the state needed to be employed in a sensible and appropriate way in order to have the expected effects.

In this chapter, I discuss the dynamics of financing river control during the late imperial period. I am less interested in figures than in the ideas and the fiscal (and at times economic) thought, which guided the actions of the relevant actors – officials, scholars and the emperor himself. I adopt the notion of "river works" (*hegong* 河工) as it was understood by Qing officials – that is, as relating

DOI: 10.4324/9780367434496-5

to the Yellow River and the Grand Canal, which was administered by a special administrative body under the control of the general directors of the waterways (*hedao zongdu* 河道總督).[2]

## Early Qing

The early Qing system of controlling the Grand Canal and the Yellow River was a continuation of that of the predecessor dynasty, the Ming. This means that part of its rationale was to guarantee the shipping of the grain-tribute (*caoliang* 漕糧) – grain levied as a tax in kind in eight southern and south-eastern provinces – to the capital of Beijing, for which a transport surcharge of about 17 per cent had to be covered by the taxpayers in the provinces in question. The transport of this large amount (about 280,000 tons) of grain was done by means of the Grand Canal, since sea transport was considered risky (Hinton 1956). This meant that the provision of the imperial family, the central administration and the large number of troops stationed around Beijing depended on the Grand Canal. To keep the Grand Canal usable, it was necessary to establish control over the Yellow River, especially at Qingjiangpu 清江浦, where the Grand Canal crossed the Yellow River. In order to enable the Grain Tribute barges to cross the river, it needed to be deep enough, which was achieved by a complex engineering solution, involving the water of the Hongze Lake, which was located directly at the crossing. The Yellow River and the Grand Canal thus required extensive engineering care, which could become very expensive. Financing the control of the Yellow River and the Grand Canal was frequently justified as taking care of the "economic needs of the state and the livelihood of the people" (*guoji minsheng* 國計民生) (Edict, Kangxi 47/7, QSL j. 205, 2). The Kangxi Emperor also said:

> Since I am administering the court, I consider suppressing the "Three Feudatories", the Control of the Rivers and the transport of the Grain Tribute as the three great issues of my administration and I am concerned about them by day and night. I also wrote this down [on a scroll], which I hung in the palace.
>
> (Edict, Kangxi 31/2, QSL J. 154, 7)

What did this mean in terms of expenses for river hydraulic in the early Qing? During the Kangxi reign, the most important official in charge of river works was Jin Fu 靳輔 (1633–92), who directed extensive efforts of dredging the river, restoring the Grand Canal and erecting stone embankments along the Hongze Lake. In 1677, he wrote that during the ten years prior to his appointment to office, construction work had been executed that in total amounted to about three million tael silver (Jin, Fu 1967, j. 1), which means an average of about 300,000 tael a year. During this time also for the first time a budget of 200,000 tael was fixed, which could be used for "annual repairs" (*suixiu* 歲修) and "emergency repairs" (*qiangxiu* 搶修) and for which rather elaborate regulations regarding accounting existed.³ During the next five years, Jin Fu continued to work on the river and the Grand Canal, and spent another 2.5 million tael – most likely not including the afore mentioned 200,000 tael for annual repairs. At this time, the annual revenue available to the government was about 35 million tael. (Vries 2015, p. 121). Monetary expenses for river control thus were limited, mainly because the early Qing state continued to use corvée and levies. Peasants were employed as workers and the crucial issue of material – in the first place, wood, reeds and stalks for construction the giant fascines, which were necessary to protect the banks of the river – were levied from the people living in the districts along the river. The details of how this system worked at the local level are hard to grasp. We know that all districts had quota of how many able-bodied men had to be sent to the river for annual repairs and for so-called "great works" (*da gong* 大工) – extraordinary works such as repairs that went beyond the fixed budget (Qinding da Qing huidian, 1976, j. 60, 228). These quota were set according to the area of agricultural land of the single districts. For some of his endeavours, Jin Fu employed as many as 200,000 conscripted workers (Hu, Ch'ang-t'u 1954, p. 141).

Twenty-five years after Jin Fu's death, in 1718, the Kangxi Emperor, always proud of this thriftiness, compared the expenses for maintaining his residences during his famous Southern Tours – 10,000 to 20,000 tael silver to the more than 3 million tael annually spent for river control (QSL, j. 275, 7a). How can this remarkable rise in expenses be explained? The most important aspect apparently was the shift from corvée labour to hiring workers, especially for executing earthworks. The corvée system worked by exacting a certain number of labourers according to the cultivated area from the districts through which the Yellow River and the Grand Canal were flowing. According to the government's view, those who profited most from the protection from floods should shoulder the largest burden:

> The workers (*fu* 夫) of the districts in Henan province are calculated according to the amount of tillable land near [to the River], the number of *mu* are the basis for sending workers. It should be considered that [workers] from areas, which are a little bit further away are used as assistance.
> 
> (Zhu, Zhixi 2002, p. 618)

In Henan in 1645, this meant that for every 45 *qing* 頃 (30 hectares) of arable land, one worker was to be used; in those areas that frequently suffered from disaster, this was reduced to one worker for every 90 *qing*.⁴

When more workers were needed, however, the basis of assessment could shrink, and the administration also expected that for "great works, assistance will come from neighbouring provinces, for middle works assistance will come from neighbouring prefectures, for small works, assistance will come from neighbouring districts" (Guan, Jiezhong 1695, j. 6, "Hefang"). Such a system was difficult to enforce, since the further away people lived, the less willing they were to work effectively, so in Henan in some cases, the burden became larger and there were cases in which, for every four *qing*, one worker had to be sent (Guan, Jiezhong 1695, j. 6 "Hefang"). This burden, according to some sources, was much heavier than the regular taxation; as a consequence, some districts resisted as a whole, while in others workers absconded (Xue, Fengzuo 1987, J. 8, 372). Many peasants busied themselves with their fields rather than working on the dykes. They thus hired workers who would stand in for them (Ji, Yuan 1992). Some of these men were quite useless, and in some cases – knowing that they depended on the necessity of work at the dykes – even went so far as to damage the dykes (Wang, Min 1892, j. 1 "Hefang").

For this and other reasons, the governor of Henan 1673 proposed to replace the system of exaction by a system of hiring workers. Beginning in 1677, this was applied for the southern part of river administration as well (*Qingchao wenxian tongkao* 1936, j. 22, p. 10). It is clear that this move was beneficial for the people, since it allowed peasants to concentrate on farming and at the same time provided job opportunities for those who did not have any land to farm. While certainly increasing the agricultural productivity of the areas in question, it also fits into the general approach of the Kangxi Emperor, driven by Confucian paternalistic considerations to lighten the burden for the common people. This had a price, however, which was substantially increasing the financial burden of the central government. It is clear, moreover, that larger landowners profited from the change more than the smaller ones, since they originally had to provide a larger number of labourers. However, once the system was introduced, it was quickly extended to all aspects of river work and in the First Year of the reign of the Yongzheng Emperor (1723), corvée was abolished for the annual repairs of the river, which soon resulted in the build-up of a specialised workforce of so called "river-troops" (*hebing* 河兵), who took care of guarding the dykes along the river and maintaining them. Employing an institutionalised workforce to control the river according to the Qing state's fiscal logic required fixed sources from which the money was drawn and transferred. This was done mainly from the provinces affected – via land-taxes and customs duties – but also from salt monopoly, a rather stable course of revenue for the Qing-state (*Qinding da Qing huidian shili* 1976, j. 104, p. 435). The shift from corvée to river troops, of course, also needs to be seen in relation to the increasing commercialisation of the Qing economy.

## Material problems

As we just have seen, a large part of the money used for controlling the Yellow River (and the Grand Canal) during the Qing period was spent on labour. On the one hand this meant earthwork (such as building dykes, excavating canals, etc.) and on the other hand maintenance work, especially building and replacing the gigantic fascines, which were employed in order to protect the dykes of the river from erosion. Fascines originally had been produced mainly from wooden twigs and grass, but during the late Ming, due to the scarcity of these materials, a shift began to employ reeds in those areas where they were available and stalks – especially millet-stalks (*jie* 秸) – mainly in Henan province. Reeds and stalks were also necessary to repair dyke breaches, along with other materials such as wood, hemp and so on. The amount of this material was large – at times constituting as much as half of the expenses for repairing a breach in the dykes (Amelung 2000, pp. 297–98). The material was inefficient for protecting the dykes, but it was not until the very late nineteenth century that it was replaced by stones. The provision of stalks is thus of great importance in order to understand the costs of security of the Yellow River during the high Qing.

Not all details are completely clear, but apparently in the southern part of the administration material was paid for according to an official statute, which was titled *Caoyun chenggui* 漕運成規 (Regulations for Transporting the Tribute Grain) and local regulations.[5] From 1732 on, centrally fixed prices emerged through the practice of precedent-setting, which was common within the Qing administration.[6] Apparently from early on some of these prices were lower than the market prices, one reason being that they included the transport of material to the places where they were needed (Qinding da Qing huidian shili 1976, j. 907, 465, Hedong hegong wuliao jiazhi n.d., p. 7). This is reflected by the expression used: *pai mai* 派買 ("assigned buying"). "Assigned buying" was a means to make use of the resources of the nearby population in order to provide security; at the same time, it allowed for a considerable number of abuses and lacked the flexibility necessary to adapt it to changed conditions. This basically forced officials to deal with it in "creative" ways, which in the long run meant that a system created to obtain and maintain control over material procurement resulted in an increasing loss of control.

Millet was a popular grain all over north China. The prices for millet stalks, fixed in the statutes, varied from district to district. The need for large amounts of millet stalks actually seems to have contributed to a high degree of specialisation in growing millet in many districts along the Yellow River and the Grand Canal (Gao, Yuanjie 2019, p. 67). It is clear that in larger construction or repair projects, the price of stalks grew rapidly. Particularly when stalks needed to be shipped over a longer distance – at times from places as far away as 500 kilometres – the price tended to raise fiercely, sometimes to three to four times the price in normal times.[7] This, however, only partially benefited the sellers. In fact, we know about a considerable number of abuses in which the abhorred and despised sub-officials (*lixu* 吏胥) used their power to make the lives of the population miserable. Since in the end it was them who had to issue receipts for the stalks, they were in a powerful position. The use of manipulated scales, for example, made it possible to pocket some of the money provided by the government. Most abuses, however, were related to the question of transport. Especially for smaller households living far away from the river, this could constitute a large problem, since it was impossible for them to stay away from their fields for a as long as was required to transport the stalks to the construction sites. They thus were forced to use professional agents (*baolan* 包攬), who demanded a much higher price (Chen, Fa 1935) for their services.

38  Iwo Amelung

Another common complaint was that the officials refused to accept the stalks on delivery, so those delivering them at times had to wait for a long time until the material was weighed and the certificate of acceptance was issued, which could mean disaster for a poor peasant during the agricultural high season. Especially when several dyke breaches happened, the demand for stalks could become so pressing that officials even forced the peasants to harvest their not-yet-ripe grain in order to obtain the necessary stalks (Edict QL 51,7, QSL, j. 1260, 23). A system of fixed prices thus meant an improvement over a system of requisition, as one would expect.

From the perspective of the central administration, however, the compilation of regulations for river works helped to rationalise accounting practices. The older rules no longer matched the changed conditions. For example, old rules still referred to reeds and other material, and not to stalks, now commonly used along the river in Shandong and Henan – these were "empty names" (*xu ming* 虛名), as the preface to the new regulations called it (Hedong hegong wuliao jiazhi n.d., p. 5a).

The regulations fixed the prices for both materials and labour. Local officials would report about the costs for necessary work on the basis of the prices fixed in the regulation. The Board of Works (*gongbu* 工部) in the capital would approve them, and only then would the construction work be taken up. After the completion of the work, the responsible director generals would prepare accounting lists, which were to be checked by the Board of Works – and either approved or rejected. The regulations thus were of the utmost importance in order to prevent fraud and abuses within the administration, and it certainly is no accident that the first set of new regulations was compiled during the reign of the energetic Yongzheng Emperor (Amelung 2005). The problem was that the new regulations quickly became outdated since there was no mechanism to accommodate secular trends such as inflation or an increased demand – as, for example, in the case of concurrent dyke breaches. For "engineers" and administrators, it became increasingly difficult to deal with the question. A certain amount of flexibility was brought about by two categories of accounting, namely "great works" mentioned above and, more importantly, "extraordinary works" (*ling'an* 另案), which were also not covered from the regular budget – they thus had to be applied for individually, although accounting had to be done according to the statutes and regulations. Even this was not enough in all cases, so that deficits were quite often made up by additional exactions from the nearby population. This practice was referred to as "Helping the price" (*bangjia* 幫價).[8] When in 1781 the Yellow River broke its dykes at Qinglonggang (青龍崗) in Henan, the costs of repairing the dyke breach, which took three years, became extraordinary high – 10 million tael were covered from the state revenue, and another 11 million had originally been exacted from the population living nearby and was to be levied together with the regular taxes during the next few years. Wei Yuan relates that:

> In the 47th year of the Qianlong reign, however, when the great work at Qinglonggang at Lanyang was carried out and it took three years to repair

the breach, except for the more than 10 million tael, which were mobilized from the state treasury, there still was the additional price of more than 11 million tael, which should be exacted over a period of several years. At that time the state treasury was overflowing, so an exceptional exemption was granted, and this later on became a fixed rule. Exaction *(tanzheng* 攤徵) from this time on became an empty title.

(Wei, Yuan 1968, pp. 4037–4038)

Indeed, the Qianlong Emperor during the 57th year of his reign explicitly again confirmed his former decision, making the governor of Henan responsible for not tolerating such practices in order to "not the least burden the population" (*bu de sihao pailei minjian* 不得絲毫派累民間) (Edict Qianlong Emperor, QL 57, Qinding da Qing huidian shili 1976, j. 904). Here the same mechanism was at work as we have already observed with respect to the Kangxi Emperor. As long as there was enough money available, emperors tended to reduce the burden of the population in a rather generous way.

It was around the same time, however, that the fiscal practices of the Qing dynasty began to create serious problems. Since it had become increasingly difficult to do accounting according to the regulations for river work, which had been valid since Yongzheng times, officials were forced to engage in "creative bookkeeping". This basically meant that officials reported larger dimensions of dykes, gave wrong distances for the transport of materials, reported larger dyke-breaches and so on. A considerable number of documents refer to "flexible" 通融 (*tongrong*) accounting practices, which apparently were considered common practice. It was a memorial of the newly appointed Director General Dai Junyuan 戴均元 (1746–1840), which was written in 1806, that alerted the emperor to the problems. Dai inquired about accounting practices after having received his seal of office. His subordinates and colleagues acquainted him with the fact that "flexible" accounting was not only common but even necessary in order to guarantee the working of the administration. Since Dai basically refused to continue these practices, as "knowing about them and not to speak about it is resigning into deceiving, and being burdened with an even greater guilt", he forced the emperor into taking action (Memorial Dai Junyuan, JQ 11, 7th month; Li, Shixu; Pan, Xi'en 1970, j. 34, 727). Dai Junyuan's critique was, of course, entirely justified – practices like this completely erased the differences between legitimate and corrupt behaviour. Interestingly enough, the emperor did not mete out any punishments, but indeed initiated a revision of the regulations used for accounting. The prices fixed in the new regulations now were in some instances four and a half times the price included into the old regulations. This, of course, also made an adoption of the budget for annual and emergency repairs necessary, which in the case of the southern part of the administration was raised from the old 600,000 tael silver to first 1.5 million tael in 1807 and then in the next year to 2 million tael.

Early in the Jiaqing reign, some officials became aware that the financial situation was getting serious. In 1799, Wu Jing 吳璥 (1747–1822), who had just been appointed director-general for the Eastern River, proposed to raise additional money by means of exaction, by levying a surtax in the localities affected by the floods of the river (*guidi tanzheng* 歸地攤徵). The emperor's reaction, based on a memorial of the household ministry, was extremely negative. If the proposal was followed, the whole population of Henan would suffer: "If one holds high the people, how can one tolerate this?" (*wei min shangzhe qi ren chu ci?* 為民上者豈忍出此). Even though the proposed sum was rather small, the ministry was of the opinion that the petty officials in the districts, once they were involved, would use it as a pretext to continuously add exactions. Moreover, once it had been agreed to levy this additional tax, it would be impossible to diminish it again. It thus was not a means to solve the problem temporarily but instead would lead to eternal suffering of the people. Referring to the decision of the Qianlong Emperor several years earlier, Wu Jing's case was transferred to the Ministry of Personnel for severe punishment (Edict JQ4, 6, QSL j. 46, 9–10). When Wu Jing made a similar suggestion several years later, he again was punished using the same argumentation (Edict JQ11, 12, QSL j. 170, 30).

## Spinning out of control

During the Daoguang reign, the fixed cost for annual repairs and emergency repairs continued to amount to about 4 million tael for the complete administration (Wu, Tongju 1970, j. 149, p. 3915). This means that the statutory costs for river control at that time constituted about one-tenth of the total revenue controlled by the central government in 1812.

On top of that, there was a tendency to shift expenses for the control of the river to the category of "extraordinary cases", the number of which started to expand greatly. Shortly after he had ascended the throne, the Daoguang Emperor reminded his officials that it was inappropriate that, alone in this year, the eastern part of the administration had asked for a sum as high as 1 million tael:

> The situation along the banks of the River is different from year to year. This means, that if there are years in which the cost increase, there also should be years in which the costs decrease. If we only witness increases every year, where will this all end?
> 
> (Qingding da Qing huidian shili 1976, j. 906, 451)

Interestingly enough, the emperor in the same year allowed the raise of the "danger-work funds" (*xian gong* 险工), which were part of the "emergency funds" for another 50,000 tael (Qinding da Qing huidian shili 1976, j. 906, 451–52).

These numbers do not include the costs for repairs when major breaches of the dykes happened. During the late Daoguang period, these became very serious, starting with the Xiangfu flood in Henan, which even threatened the provincial capital of Kaifeng in 1841, and shortly afterwards the Zhongmou breach in 1844. On its own, the repair of the Zhongmou breach, which was successful

Table 3.1 Revenue and expenses of river administrations

| Year | Revenue and expenses of the whole country | | Expenses for "extra-ordinary cases" for both river administrations | | |
|---|---|---|---|---|---|
| | Revenue | Expenses | Eastern river | Southern river | Combined |
| DG 25 (1845) | 40,612,380 | 38,815,891 | 2,058,007 | 3,304,808 | 5,362,815 |
| DG 26 (1846) | 39,222,630 | 36,287,159 | 1.947.123 | 2.953.524 | 4,900,647 |
| DG 27 (1847) | 39,387,316 | 35.584.467 | 1,798,987 | 2,785,000 | 4,583,987 |
| Yearly average | 39,740,775 | 36,958,390 | 1,934,705 | 3,014,444 | 4,949,149 |

Source: Wang Qingyun 1985, j. 3, pp. 144–149.

only after a failed attempt, had cost more than 12 million tael, the repair of the Xiangfu breach had amounted to more than 6.5 Million Tael (Dodgen 2001, p. 103). But even in years in which no major breaches happened, the costs remained very high (Table 3.1).

To the already quite high costs for the "extraordinary cases", the statutory expenses for "annual repairs" and "emergency repairs" need to be added. At this time, they were running at about 4 million tael a year for both parts of the administration (Shen, Bing 1970, p. 281), so that even in years without dyke breaches, the expenses for the control of the river and the Grand Canal amounted to more than 20 per cent of the total revenue of the central government.

## Demise and devolution

Already prior to the Daoguang reign, Chinese bureaucrats and scholars were divided into two schools of thought explaining the rising costs of hydraulics. One argued with environmental and hydraulic dynamics – basically the large amount of sediments carried by the Yellow River and the need to guarantee the working of the crossing of river and canal. It could not, however, offer any solutions – or if it tried to, as Bao Shichen did by attempting to finance river control by taxing agricultural land that had been produced by river-sediments, it met with fierce resistance from the emperor. The other school blamed the southern course of the river, which was considered non-canonical and wasteful, and promoted a northern course for the Yellow River. This was not a disinterested move: it would make sea transport of the Grain Tribute necessary, and discontinue – or at least reduce – the hated grain surcharge. Wei Yuan, however, mainly stressed the additional advantage:

> When the River shifts to the north, the several hundred superfluous officials of the Southern and Eastern River administration which have caused millions of superfluous costs would be wiped out from the century old rat-hole in which they had found their home.
>
> (Wei, Yuan 1968, p. 4047)

Such considerations – as well as the Taiping and the Nian Rebellions – did indeed play a role when the court finally decided not to repair the Tongwaxiang dyke breach of 1855, which had resulted in a northern course of the Yellow River, mainly affecting the western part of Shandong province. While the change of course resulted in serious flooding of a large area in south-west Shandong, in terms of expenses for the central government, it seemed to work. For the new course of the river in Shandong, the central government managed to pay almost nothing for almost 20 years, when it was forced to regularly provide money to the newly emerging control structures in Shandong province. Starting with a yearly budget of 50,000 tael in the late 1870s, in 1880 the sum of 320,000 tael was reached, which soon needed to be raised to 600,000 tael.

A late Qing report made an estimate of the costs for Shandong province in the following way:

a) Flood defence fund: 600,000 tael
b) Emergency repair cost: 50,000 or 100,000 tael
c) Dyke-strengthening cost ca. 150,000 tael
d) Changing dyke protection to bricks or stones: 65–75,000 tael (Shandong diaocha ju 1910, pp. 44b–45a.)

The flood defence fund supported a civil and military administration, which at the end of the Qing dynasty consisted of about 5000 men. Different from the old administration, this administration was completely "extra-statutory", although large parts of it were paid for by the central government. The crucial aspect was the establishment of *ju* 局 "offices", staffed by personnel who did not have substantial offices. The costs for hydraulic security in Shandong, however, were not limited to this administrative and military structure, with court-provided funds rising to 1.5. to 2.4 million tael for the costs of building dykes and repairing dyke breaches in the 1880s and 1890s in several cases. However, no repair project along the new course of the Yellow River cost as much as the repair of the break at Zhengzhou in 1887/88; after one failed attempt, the court spent a total of 12 million tael on this project (Zhou, Fu 1992, j. 10).

Xia Mingfang has attempted to calculate the total expenditures for river control for the period between the second and the 25th year of the reign of the Guangxu Emperor (1876–99) and arrives at a figure of slightly more than 52 million tael. While this probably is a low figure, it would suggest an average yearly expenditure of about 2.2 million tael (Xia, Mingfang 1995). This is clearly much less than before the northern shift of the river, but still a considerable amount (and incidentally much higher than the numbers provided by Wittfogel). Xia's main point, however, is to show that the total sum of expenditures for the Yellow River was rising during the late Qing – and this certainly is true. The devolution of the administration thus did not have – and this is not particularly surprising – a lasting money-saving effect.[9]

The devolution of the administration and the difficulties for the local and regional administrators to mobilise funding created opportunities for private organisations, and thus foreshadowed developments that would come to the fore during the 1910s and 1920s. This actually implied the government's gradual loss of influence in an area deemed crucial for the Chinese state. It is interesting to note as well that, as late as in the Guangxu era, the problems of how to provide and account for material had not been solved conclusively. The volatility of prices made accounting according to fixed regulations a farce. It certainly is no accident that even in 1910, Shandong administrators still referred to Dai Junyuan's proposal to account for on the basis of "real prizes" (*shijia*) from the Jiaqing-era as model for dealing with the problems in Shandong (Shandong diaocha ju 1910, p. 45b).

## Some preliminary conclusions

Karl August Wittfogel's idea of a "hydraulic society" has been correctly dismissed by generations of researchers. It is still clear, however, that there was a very high degree of state involvement in hydraulic problems with regard to the Yellow River and the Grand Canal. This was because the control of the river and the canal indeed had a great impact on "the interest of the state and the welfare of the people". While engineering and environmental dynamics clearly are of great importance for understanding the problem of river control in late imperial China, I have tried to show that a fiscal approach is useful as well. The large amount that the Chinese state was willing to spend is a reminder of the centrality of river engineering in late imperial China. Activist emperors such as the Kangxi and the Qianlong Emperors were aware of the engineering nightmare; however, it is also clear that their approach to the river was guided by fiscal considerations that were deeply rooted in Confucian paternalism – "taking the people as root" or "putting the people at peace". While this might have been due partly to their efforts to claim legitimacy for the ruling dynasty, the historical records suggest that there was more to it. In the very moment that they suspected the common people were suffering from corvée or because of the exaction of building material, both emperors did not hesitate to greatly increase spending for hydraulic measures. Certainly, the favourable fiscal situation during the eighteenth century played a role in allowing them to do so. It is significant, however, that both emperors failed to point out fixed sources of revenue from which the additional expenses would be covered in the long run. This behaviour corroborates von Glahn's notion of the Qing state as a *provisioning state* dedicated to improving the people's livelihood through famine relief, flood control and so on (von Glahn 2016, p. 313). Both the Yongzheng and the Jiaqing Emperors, as the successors of the generous Kangxi and Qianlong Emperors respectively, tried to regain control over the expenditures and to rationalise accounting practices.

This, however, did not suffice to prevent the complete loss of financial and engineering control, which happened during the latter part of the Daoguang reign. In fact, the adopted accounting practices might have aggravated some of the environmental and engineering problems.

Accepting the change of course of the river after 1855 had environmental, engineering and administrative motives and consequences. It is important to stress, however, that it followed a fiscal logic as well. It allowed the reduction of expenditures and the devolution of the administration, and thus at least temporary reverse trends, which had been initiated by the policies of the Kangxi and the Qianlong Emperors. The fact that private organisations began to influence hydraulic engineering in Shandong in the 1880s neatly corresponds to this trajectory, which can also be observed in other areas – notably famine relief. There is, however, some irony involved as well, since all of this happened at the very moment when the Chinese state began to greatly expand its extractive capacity by means of Likin and the revenue from the maritime customs (von Glahn 2016, p. 381).

## Notes

1 Wittfogel's numbers are total expenditures of the state prior to 1850 –31,522,800 tael silver; prior to 1900 – 52,500,000 tael; 1905 – 102,454,000 tael for hydraulic concerns and 3,800,000, 1,500,000, 1,389,000 respectively. This is a decrease from 12 per cent over 3 per cent around 1900 to a mere 1.38 per cent.
2 The administrative body did not have a Chinese designation: the term "Yellow River administration", often found in Western literature, is *post-factum* and does not have any correspondence in the Chinese sources (cf. Hu, Ch'ang-t'u 1954).
3 The different categories are defined in the *Statutes*, cf. *Qinding da Qing huidian* (1976), j. 60, p. 634.
4 It is hard to come up with average arable area per household. Later data (especially the Mantetsu surveys for the north of China), suggest about 120 hectares of arable land per village, consisting of about 100 households.
5 There are references to the *Caoyun chenggui* in later publications as well as in several local gazeteers, I have failed, however, to locate the original book.
6 The mechanisms of how something became a precedent were quite complex. On this issue, see Metzger (1973).
7 My example here refers to the very late imperial period, however – namely the repair of the breach at Zhengzhou in 1887/88 (cf. Wu Yongxiang 1930, j. 14, 2a–3b).
8 The term *bangjia* also was used with a different meaning, namely as a subsidy in cases where the statutory price was too low.
9 Given the fact that reimbursement for labour and materials was done with *cash*, the rising price for cash actually should be taken into account when trying to figure out the "costs of security". This, however, is beyond the scope of this preliminary chapter.

## References

Amelung, Iwo: *Der Gelbe Fluß in Shandong. Überschwemmungskatastrophen und ihre. Bewältigung im China der späten Qing-Zeit* (Opera Sinologica 9). Wiesbaden: Harrassowitz, 2000.

Amelung, Iwo: Preliminary Observations on "Regulations and Precedents for River Works" (*Hegong zeli*) During the Qing Dynasty. In: Christine Moll-Murata, Jianze

Song & Hans Ulrich Vogel (eds): *Chinese Handicraft Regulations of the Qing Dynasty: Theory and Application*. München: Iudicium, pp. 285–305, 2005.

Chen, Fa 陳法: *Dingzhai hegong shudu* 定齋河工疏牘 (River works documents from the Ding-studio) (Qiannan congshu bieji), Guiyang, 1935.

Dodgen, Randall: *Controlling the Dragon: Confucian Engineers and the Yellow River in the Late Imperial China*. Honolulu: University of Hawai'i Press, 2001.

Gao, Yuanjie 高元杰: Huanjingshi shiye xia Qingdai hegong yong jie yingxiang yanjiu 環境史視野下清代河工用秸影響研究 (Research on the influence on stalks for River works during the Qing from an environmental history perspective). *Shixue yuekan*, 2, pp. 60–74, 2019.

Glahn, Richard von: *The Economic History of China: From Antiquity to the Nineteenth Century*. Cambridge: Cambridge University Press, 2016.

Guan, Jiezhong 管竭忠, Zhang Shu 張沐 (comp.): *Kangxi Kaifeng fu zhi* 康熙開封府志 (Gazeteer of Kaifeng prefecture from the Kangxi reign), 1695.

*Hedong hegong wuliao jiazhi* 河東河工物料價值 (ed. Gongbu 工部) (Material price for river works in the Eastern part of the River administration), n.p., n.d.

Hinton, Harold C.: *The Grain Tribute of China 1845–1901*. Cambridge, MA: Harvard University Press, 1956.

Hu, Ch'ang-t'u: The Yellow River Administration in the Ch'ing-Dynasty. PhD dissertation, University of Washington, 1954.

Ji, Yuan 紀元: He gongfu shiliao jia yi 河工夫食料價議 (Opinions on rations of river workers). In: He Changliang & Wei Yuan (comp.): *Qing jingshi wenbian*. Beijing: Zhonghua shuju, j. 103, pp. 2519–20, 1992.

Jin, Fu 靳輔: *Jin Wenxiang gong (Fu) zou shu* 靳文襄公(輔)奏疏 (Memorials submitted by Jin Fu) (Jindai Zhongguo shiliao congkan 143). Taibei: Wenhai chubanshe, 1967.

Li, Shixu & Pan, Xi'en 黎世序, 潘錫恩: *Xu Xingshui jinjian* 續行水金鑒 (Continued mirror for the regulation of the rivers) (*Zhongguo shuili yaoji congbian* 2). Taibei: Wenhai, 1970.

Metzger, Thomas A.: *The Internal Organization of Ch'ing Bureaucracy. Legal, Normative, and Communication Aspects*. Cambridge, MA: Harvard University Press, 1973.

*Qinding da Qing huidian* 钦定大清会典 (*Guangxu*) (Imperially mandated statues of the Great Qing dynasty). Taibei: Xin wenfang chubanshe, 1976.

*Qinding da Qing huidian shili* 钦定大清會典事例 (Guangxu) (Cases and precedents of the Imperially mandated statutes of the Great Qing dynasty). Taibei: Xin wenfang chubanshen, 1976.

*Qingchao wenxian tongkao* 清朝文獻統考 (Encyclopedia of the historical records of the Qing dynasty). Beijing: Shangwu yinshuguan, 1936.

QSL: *Qing Shilu* 清實錄 (Veritable Records of the Qing-dynasty). Beijing: Zhonghua shuju, 1987.

Shandong diaocha ju 山東調查局: *Shandong hewu xingzheng yanxi libi baogaoshu* 山東河務行政沿習利弊報告書 (Report on the customs of the river administration in Shandong), 1910.

Shen, Bing 申丙: *Huanghe tongkao* 黃河通考 (Comprehensive investigation of the Yellow River). Taibei: Taiwan Shuju, 1970.

Vries, Peer: *State, Economy, and the Great Divergence. Great Britain and China 1680s–1850s*. London: Bloomsbury, 2015.

Wang, Min 王枚: *Xuxiu Suizhou zhi* 續修睢州志 (Continuation of the Gazeteer of Suizhou district), 1892.

Wang, Qingyun 王慶雲: *Shiqu yuji* 石渠余記 (Additional records from the court). Beijing: Beijing guji chubanshe, 1985.

Wei, Yuan 魏源: Chou he pian 籌河篇 (Opinions on planning the river). In: Wu Tongju (ed.): *Zaixu xingshui jinjian*. Taibei, j. 154, pp. 4037–48, 1968 [1942].

Wittfogel, Karl August: *Wirtschaft und Gesellschaft. Versuch der wissenschaftlichen Analyse einer grossen asiatischen Agrargesellschaft.* Leipzig: C.L. Hirschfeld, 1931.

Wu, Tongju 武同舉 (comp.): *Zaixu xingshui jinjian* 再續行水金鑒 (*Zhongguo shuili yaoji congbian* 21). Taibei: Wenhai, 1970.

Wu, Yongxiang 吳詠湘 (comp.): *Yuhe zhi* 豫河志 (Records on the Yellow River in Hena). Henan: Hewu gongzhu, 1930.

Xia, Mingfang 夏明方: Tongwaxiang gaidao hou Qing zhengfu dui Huanghe de zhili 銅瓦廂改道後清政府對黃河的治理 (The Qing Government's policy of Yellow River control after it changed course at Tongwaxiang). *Qingshi yanjiu*, 4, pp. 40–51. 1995.

Xue, Fengzuo 薛鳳祚: Liang He qing hui 兩河清匯 (The confluence of the two rivers at Qingjiangpu). In: Ji, Yun (ed.): *Siku quanshu*. Shanghai: Shanghai guji chubanshe, 579, 1987.

Zhou, Fu 周馥: *Zhishui shuyao* 治水述要 (Describing the importance of regulating the Waters). In: *Zhou Queshen gong quanji, Vols 1–10*, Beijing, 1992.

Zhu, Zhixi 朱之錫: Hefang shulüe 河防述略 (A description of river defence). *Xuxiu siku quanshu*. Shanghai: Shanghai guji chubanshe, 493, 2002.

# Section 2
# Land, interest and usury

# 4 Outline of the institutions for land transactions in traditional China

*Denggao Long and Xiang Chi*

As the primary source of production in an agricultural society, land and its related institutions underlie the processes of resource allocation and of business operations. To analyse them is the first and most fundamental task if one wants to understand the transformation of China from a traditional society to a modern one. Such understanding is also key to the current agricultural reform, and is of special theoretical value for world economic history. While previous understanding and assessments of this fundamental issue have been anything but uniform, dealing with the difficulty has been especially fruitful and new breakthroughs have been made over the last two decades.[1]

This article reconstructs China's traditional land property rights and its transaction system by examining primary sources, especially land transaction deeds and the land disputes in the "routine memorials on criminal matters of the Board of Law" (*xingke tiben* 刑科題本). It offers an in-depth analysis of the institutional legacies of China's land system, as well as of its transformations. On this basis, I try to provide a comprehensive analysis and explanation of the processes of resource allocation and of business operations in the land tenure system, based on economic principles and tools. I also offer a systematic framework for understanding and explaining the historical transformation of the traditional economy, which revolves around land rights (or land tenures) and has an impact on the economic reform of modern China.

## The theoretical reconstruction of forms of land tenure

Private (family and private) property rights, corporate property rights and state property rights in land coexisted in traditional China. Among them, private property forms were much more mature and demonstrated an innovation of Chinese origin, based on the conceptual definitions and the theoretical reconstructions of the system of China's traditional land property rights.

First, land rights can exist independently, and can be traded in the market at different levels and at different times, thus forming forms of property rights such as ownership, possession and usage rights, as well as their corresponding forms of transaction, which constitute the land rights transaction system. Second, all these different levels of realisation of various forms of property rights can be

DOI: 10.4324/9780367434496-7

acquired through investment and trade. This results in rules that are universally accepted by society, licensed by the government and regulated by the legal system, thus giving them the force of law. Third, documents of property rights and transactions expressed through contracts have a long history in civil practices and have been recognised and regulated by successive governments through laws. Fourth, property rights of legal persons (corporate property rights) were derived and developed from private property rights.

There has been a long-term sentiment – which still remains influential today – that, historically, China lacked the idea of property rights and had failed to develop a spirit of contract. In fact, a simple idea of property rights and a related legal system existed in traditional society, and both were deeply rooted in people's hearts. Both private and corporate land was titled and traded by deed, and different levels of land rights could be acquired through investment capital (in addition to inheritance, etc.). Non-landowners also could obtain a corresponding disposition of land rights by investing and controlling land yields and the appreciation of land, and they could thus share land rights with the landowners. One instance is the so-called surface right of land (*tianmianquan* 田面權). It coexisted with the subsoil right (*tiandiquan* 田底權) as a property right, and was different from the regular tenancy right (*dianquan* 佃權). Similarly, the *dian* 典 (conditional sale) right resembled the surface right, and both were distinctive forms of land tenure and of a sale of property right.

Corporate property rights are derived by extension from private property rights, reflecting the degree of development of the private property rights system. For example, clans, temples, academies of classical learning and private schools, non-profit organisations, charity organisations and various associations (*hui* 會) and societies (*she* 社) in the industrial, commercial, financial, cultural, sports and entertainment industries could form a property unit, a transaction unit and a taxing unit, with features such as integrity, indivisibility and exclusivity, and developed an efficient management model based on the independence of property (Long, Denggao; Wang, Zhenghua & Yi, Wei 2018). They were recorded as "public properties" (*gongchan* 公產), as opposed to "governmental properties" (*guanchan* 官產) owned by the government, and "private properties" (*sichan* 私產) owned by private individuals.

State land has existed for generations, and was usually not tradable. It could be traded only when privatised. At that time, its character had been changed to private or corporate property, and that did not happen in every dynasty. There was, however, a general tendency of the share of state land to diminish gradually.

## A systematic discussion of the land transaction system

### *The* dian 典 *right and its transaction*

There has been a strong concentration on studying *dian* (conditional sale), since it is the form of land property right and transaction with the "most traditional Chinese characteristics", but many controversies have continued to surround it.

Some regarded *dian* as the transaction of usage rights, while others argued that there was no difference between *dian* and the practice of "live sales" or "living sales" (*huomai* 活賣).[2]

Based on my analysis of original deeds and employing economic theory, I find that *dian* refers to a transaction regarding the management of land with all its profit and interest in an agreed period, and not to the "balancing of rent and interest" (*zuxi xiangdi* 租息相抵), as claimed by some scholars.[3] A "conditional sale" (*dian*) is a property right in the form of a possessory right, and can assume the function of a security interest; the land becomes a collateral. In other words, the *dian* practice is a transaction between the right to occupy land and interest on capital. It is different from both the sale and purchase of ownership and that of a tenancy as a transaction of the usage right, thus clarifying previous misunderstandings. The *dian* seller (*chudianren* 出典人) actually realises the future interest on the value of the land to obtain a loan, while the *dian* buyer (*chengdianren* 承典人) receives the possession for the agreed term and could choose between either operating income (self-farming), investment income (leasing) or realising future income (*dian* transfer), depending on their own preferences and needs. Moreover, the *dian* buyer could rent out the *dian* land, even to the landowner and *dian* seller. It reflects a pattern of shared land rights constructed by landlords, *dian* owners and tenant farmers relying on market transactions, and sheds light on the characteristics and orientation of the traditional land rights market (Long, Denggao, Lin, Zhan & Peng, Bo 2013).

## *An analysis of various land transaction forms*

In different time periods, different levels of land rights could be transacted, forming a diversified regime of land transactions such as sales, conditional sales (*dian*), rent deposit (*yazu* 押租), tenancies, mortgages (*di* 抵) and loans through land as collateral (*taijie* 胎借). The system became mature during the Ming and Qing dynasties. Depending on the order of usage right, possession, and ownership, the greater the rights to the land, the higher the returns and the higher the transaction price.

The multi-layered land rights and diversified forms of land rights transactions were quite complicated in reality. Ambiguities, disputes and misunderstandings related to them in the past were due mainly to the lack of a theoretical explanatory framework. I therefore offer an analytical framework regarding the different levels of land rights as well as regarding the development of regulations across the time, distinguishing between the roles of the different land rights transactions and paying attention to differences and interconnections.

*Dian* (conditional sales) originated from sales. In the Tang and Song Dynasties (618–1279), the term *dianmai* 典賣 was used, and both transaction rules and tax payment procedures were not clearly separated. The main distinction between a "conditional sale" (*dian*) and a "sale" (*mai* 卖) was made by the contractual form and by the fact that, although even for a "conditional sale" the tax-duty was transferred to the new owner, the administration continued to consider the original owner as possessing the "field bone" (*tiangu* 田骨). In the Qing dynasty, the two were further clearly separated. On the one hand, the "sale" (*mai*) of ownership was broken down into a "living sale" (i.e. a not-finalised sale) (*huomai* 活賣) and "finalized sale" (*juemai* 絕賣). The nature of a "living sale" is an ownership transaction. In a "living sale", the title to the land can be redeemed, but only as a right of first refusal. In a *dian* transaction, on the other hand, the redeeming of land ownership signifies the conclusion of the transaction.

Tenancy is a transaction of the usage right. A regular tenancy is a post-rental payment, while a rent deposit (*yazu*) is a partial pre-payment. There is a progressive relationship between tenancy and *dian*. When a rent deposit is maximised (C in Figure 4.1), it gets close to *dian* from the point of view of the landowner, but a partial rent deposit cannot create a security interest (full collateral). If the rent deposit is considered as an investment and as purchase of land usage rights, then in a case of rent deposit, the tenant can acquire the right to field surface in a similar way as the *dian* right. At this point, the surface right of land is also a right of possession with property attributes.

Both *dian* and mortgages can constitute security interests (represent collaterals). However, land mortgages are usually short-term loans with a high risk of title transfer, whereas *dian* transactions effectively buffer the eventual transfer of land ownerships. Therefore, the *dian* practice was popular and recognised by the government. This is one of the reasons for the long prevalence of *dian* in the market of land rights. As institutions of *dian* and *huomai* have effectively reduced the transfer of land ownerships and acted as hedge factors against the concentration of land ownership rights, they helped peasants to weather the storm and restore and re-establish independent farming. Practices such as "add-on" (*zhaojia* 找價) and "joyous-gift silver" (*xiliyin* 喜禮銀)[4] could also be seen, to

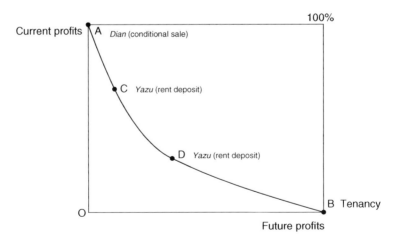

*Figure 4.1* The relations between *dian*, *yazu* (rent deposit) and tenancy from the point of view of the land owner

some extent, as relief for landless peasants. Thus, the customary practices and legal provisions of *dian* have protected the vulnerable while preserving peasants' ownership rights and therefore contributed to the socio-economic stability of traditional Chinese society.

The above differentiation and analyses have revealed the interconnection and logical relations among various land rights transaction forms (Long, Denggao & Wen, Fangfang 2018). The land rights transaction system thus meets the different preferences and demands of factor market actors and reduces the systemic risks of land rights transactions, especially ownership transfer.[5] The development of a market for land rights on this basis is conducive to the strengthening of the ability of individual farmers to operate independently, and contributes to the stability and development of the traditional economy and society.

## *The transmutation process of land rights system*

Since the Warring States period and the Qin and Han dynasties (471 BCE–220 CE), the forms of land rights transactions have gradually multiplied, and the forms of land property rights have become more varied, including the *dian* rights in the Tang and Song dynasties, the permanent tenancy system in the Song and Yuan dynasties, and the emergence of surface rights, rent deposit and not-finalised sales in the Ming and Qing dynasties. The transformation of land rights from the Song to the Qing dynasty and their differentiation reflect the process, in which the land-right transaction rules developed from spontaneous generation to gradual improvement and standardisation. Social perceptions and government management also changed along the way.

The Song dynasty was at the beginning of the development of the *dian* right. It was relatively easy to apply, and for this reason it was easy to grasp the original nature of *dian*. In the Qing dynasty, the development of the *dian* right led to complex and diverse forms and manifestations, and the rights derived from it gradually became explicit and were no longer forbidden, as during the Song dynasty. Nevertheless, they also contributed to obscuring and distorting the original nature of *dian*.

First, regarding the origin of *dian*, in the Song dynasty the fundamental norm was "*dian* selling the land off the property" (*diantian liye* 典田離業). The control of the land and the transfer of all business income during the agreed period were the origin and core of the *dian* right. Second, the derived rights and the manifestation of diversity of *dian* are highlighted by the different ways to transact land in *dian* sales. Misconceptions of *dian* in the Song and Qing dynasties are also related to these different transaction procedures. For example, the practice of the *dian* buyer renting out land to the original landowner was not recognised in the Song dynasty, while in the Qing dynasty this form was widely popular.

Third, the different policies and regulations of the Song and Qing dynasties regarding *dian* transactions were also compatible with the rules mentioned above. In the Song dynasty, the transaction of *dian* fields required the transfer of the tax obligation of land tax and corvée, and payment of a transaction tax. The form of the deed was correspondingly contractual – that is, the deed consisted of two parts, which would be put together at the date of redemption, a practice referred to as *heqi tongyue* 合契同約. In the Qing dynasty, the management of *dian* fields was simplified and the tax was exempted for a long time, so there was no need to go through the procedure of transfer of farm tax. The contractual deeds of *dian* land also changed into single deed form, which was adapted to the increase of subsequent transactions or related transaction forms in the Qing Dynasty. On the original deeds and agreements, people could record and practise *dian* transfer, *dian* add-on and other additions.

These phenomena and differences cannot be understood in isolation, but are interrelated and corroborate each other according to an internal logic; thus, they constitute an explanatory framework. The differences in the stages and characteristics of the development of the *dian* rights reflect the transformation of the rules of land rights transactions, thus enabling us to understand more fully the pattern of land property rights and transactions in traditional China (Long, Denggao, Wen, Fangfang & Qiu, Yongzhi 2016).

## Land rights markets, family farms and characteristics of the traditional economy

### *The connection and influence of land tenure markets and individual family farms*

The markets for land rights and individual family farms were interrelated and constitute two of the most fundamental features of China's traditional economy and its unique path of development. The two promoted and reinforced each other, improved economic efficiency and land output, contributed to the stable development of the traditional economy, and inhibited its transformation and change into modern economic forms. This helps to explain the difference in the evolution of the Chinese and Western economic forms, and is one of the most important reasons why China's traditional economy was not able to move towards an industrial revolution spontaneously and powerfully.

Self-employed, semi-employed and tenant farmers established individual family farms by virtue of their ownership, possession and usage rights, and produced and reproduced with the help of a combination of market factors and resources. A multi-layered land rights transaction system enabled peasant households to make choices according to market prices and risk appetites, and to cater to their own needs; it also helped to achieve regulation between current and future profits, thereby facilitating the combination of land circulation and productive factors and improving economic efficiency (Long, Denggao 2009, 2012). The redemption mechanism, which included the use of *dian*, *huomai* and *yazu*, effectively preserved the willingness of peasant households to secure and resume their land ownerships and made less complex, but potentially usurious, property transfers such as finalised sales or mortgages more unlikely.

The land rights market that supported individual family farms was characterised by a low threshold, separability and easy replication. Farmers could support their families even when encountering natural and human-made disasters, and members of an increasing population coming from existing families and villages were able to establish their own independent farms. Since the Chinese used to have a system of equal inheritance among sons (*zhuzi junfenzhi* 諸子均分制), rather than a system of primogeniture, people's family members, land and individual farms were constantly divided and regenerated.

The self-regeneration and dynamism of individual family farms, however, also inhibited the growth of large-scale and capitalist operations. As a result, it was difficult for new factors to emerge while the original essence of the Chinese agricultural economy was continuously reinforced. The changes in pre-modern Western Europe came mainly from new forces outside the manorial system. Because of the weak capacity of individual farmers to operate independently, farmers were dependent on the estate. At the same time, the estate was integral and inseparable, which was related to its property rights attributes and the estate's combined farming operations. As a result, the additional population of the estate, or younger sons under the primogeniture system, found it challenging to establish their own independent agricultural operations, to exist and develop outside the estate and to promote the growth of new factors, and thus qualitative change.

## *Reconstructing share tenancy: A reflection on the "optimal owner-peasant"*

Tenancy and land-rights transactions enabled the owners of factors with different endowments to cooperate effectively, increased the mobility and efficiency of the factors of production, brought about changes in different classes and changes in management, and thus reflected the social mobility of the time. With regard to tenant peasants, previous studies have generally considered them to be the landowners' labour, similar in nature to hired labour, and remunerated on a par with hired labour, a stereotype that has led to a misconception of economic interpretation and historical understanding (Jing, Su & Luo, Lun 1978). In fact, during the Ming and Qing dynasties, tenant farmers already managed their businesses independently. Through the channels of personification and marketisation, they combined different factors of production from the family, the landlord and the market to create wealth and used diversified methods of farming. Moreover, they dominated the residual claims, reaping under uncertainty the rewards and risky returns that only an entrepreneur can earn; the future benefits of his investment in the land and farm can be realised through trade. In all these cases, the hired farmers had no connection to them, just like today's entrepreneurs, who do not own capital, land, labour or technology, but rather integrate these factors of production and resources through the market to build enterprises that create wealth. The economic efficiency and land output are driven by the transfer, selection and allocation of factors of production under the system of land rights transactions, and the tenancy is an important source of dynamism for tenant farming and the smallholder economy (Long, Denggao & Peng, Bo 2010).

The dominant traditional myth that peasant farming is fair and efficient, while under the tenancy the tenant farmer is exploited by the landlord and is less efficient, has been challenged both historically and theoretically. In a free market situation, the structure of land rights depends on the transaction costs and the level of the total surplus of the system. Drawing on the theory of optimal ownership structure to analyse the total institutional surplus of owner-farmers, tenant farmers and hired labourers, I argue that the optimal scale of land management, level of technology, land endowment, market conditions and so on will affect the choice of the structure of tenure, and owner-farmers are not necessarily optimal. By examining the impacts of the degree of marketisation of agricultural products, transportation costs, the scale of land management and the degree of dispersion of land rights on tenancy rates, using statistical methods, and by comparing the scale of production and profits of modern owner-farmers with those of tenant farmers, it was found that the tenant economy exhibited advantages in many respects. The explanation lies in the fact that tenancy separates the asset function of land from the factor of production function, makes the area of land management independent of the area of land ownership and leads to a meritocracy of the cultivators (Zhao, Liang & Long, Denggao 2012).

## *Corporate property rights, civil organisation and grass-roots order*

If the right to private ownership of land is the cornerstone of the independent operation of peasants, then the right to corporate ownership is the basis for the independent development of civil society organisations, which together constitute the organic system of the private and public spheres of traditional society.

Non-governmental and non-profit micro-objects, represented by various civil society organisations, are prevalent in grass-roots society and the public sphere. They have independent property, especially estates and funds (*huijin* 會金), with future value-added income for long-term operation. Such separate property is a corporate property right, exclusive, integral and indivisible, and is guaranteed by the government and the law. Corporate property rights existed not only in "bridge societies" (*qiaohui* 橋會) and "voluntary ferry" societies (*yidu* 義渡), but also in water conservancy societies (*zhahui* 閘會), industrial and commercial societies, guilds and secret societies, and more generally in families, temples, schools, and charitable and relief institutions. They became the basis for the independence and sustainability of any such social organisations, which developed and existed over time, independent of the power of government and administration.

The micro subjects of corporate property rights formed an effective organisational system and governance structure. They operated in an open and transparent manner, were accountable to society and stakeholders, had clear regulations and institutional safeguards, and were able to embark on the path of sustainable development. Their effective incentive and discipline mechanisms were not only directly related to their economic interests but were also compatible with the prevailing religious, ethical and moral values. The directors of social organisations were willing and committed, and their employees worked hard. Meanwhile, strict regulations and public supervision prevented them from being able to take advantage of the situation and from being passive, thus rent-seeking and corruption were overcome effectively.

In short, independent property rights of corporate entities, clear statutes and rules, effective governance structures, open and transparent operations, incentives for social and economic interests, and supervision and restraint by the public all constitute the institutional arrangements of traditional Chinese civil organisations. The government manages grass-roots society indirectly through social organisations and social elites, which become the dominant force in the public sphere and provide public goods, services, and services to the grass-roots (Chen, Yueyuan & Long, Denggao 2020; Long, Denggao, Wang, Zhenghua & Yin, Wei 2018). The grass-roots private and public spheres, provided by independent and autonomous micro-entities, allow the governmental authorities to achieve and maintain unity at a low cost.

## The transformation of the modern land rights system and cognitive misunderstandings

In modern times, the system and order of China's land rights have been undermined by power and violence, and this deterioration led to the socio-economic upheaval and decline in the late Qing dynasty and the early Republican era. People often blame it on the private property system itself, and in particular they infer that free trade in land rights leads to land appropriation and concentration. However, the cutting edge of economic historians' scholarship over the last two decades has shown that this traditional view has been significantly exaggerated.

### *An examination and analysis of land holdings*

The amount of land held by wealthy landowners and peasants is an important indicator of the distribution of land rights in modern times after 1949, and fundamental for judging the land tenure system and the modern economy, yet there has been a lack of convincing basic data. A detailed nationwide census was conducted on land reform and, although accurate national data were not published, it laid the foundation for statistical work. Based on the land reform census data from 1949 to 1952, I was able to establish that the proportion of land held by the top 10 per cent of the rural wealthy on the eve of land reform was around 30 per cent ($\pm 5$ per cent) in the southern provinces, much lower than in the north. This figure should be lower if the occupancy status of land rights such as surface rights, permanent tenancy rights and public land is taken into account (Long, Denggao & He, Guoqing 2018). In other words, the rural rich held about 30 per cent of land ownership, but their land rights and benefits were shared with the rest of the population.

Land concentration phenomena and trends are exaggerated. Another important reason lies in the notion that this is an inevitable consequence of free trade. The lack of convincing academic analysis has led to the neglect of the negative feedback mechanisms that inhibit and hedge against land ownership concentration.

Apart from the well-known system of equal inheritance rule among various sons, there were other important factors hedging against the concentration of land rights and the causes responsible for the fragmentation of land rights. First, the more diverse the forms of transactions, the more likely they are to reduce systemic risk, such as redemption mechanisms to protect the rights of vulnerable groups, and also to delay the transfer of land rights, providing the possibility for farmers to weather the storm, recover and rebuild their farms, and operate independently. Second, with regard to land tenure, it is not just about ownership but also about possession. It is a fact that a vast number of middle-and-lower-class farmers had the right to the surface of the land and the right to sell the land in a conditional sale, which was also a property right. Third, the land of corporate property rights, such as family-owned lands (*zutian* 族田), temple fields, school fields, various association fields and community fields, had to some extent reduced the unevenness of private land occupation. For example, the proportion of public land (*gongtian* 公田) in Guangdong and Fujian could reach about 30 per cent. These institutional arrangements made it possible for individual farmers to gain ongoing competitiveness and vitality, and inhibited land concentration and mergers to some extent.

## *Equalisation of land rights: A reflection on history and reality*

Sun Yat-sen's political slogan, "equalisation of land rights" (*pingjun diquan* 平均地權), has been the dominant ideological trend in China and was put into practice nationwide in the mid- to late twentieth century. The Land Reform Movement of 1949–52 was a compulsory change to equalise land ownership, whereas the Collectivisation Movement since the late 1950s and the 1981 Family Contract Responsibility System were about equal distribution of land usage rights.

The initial equalisation, whether of ownership or use rights, was quickly disrupted under the influence of factors such as female marriage, changes in household composition, population mobility and farming capacity . Therefore, the dynamic combination of land and labour was difficult to maintain when combined with other variables. In the twenty-first century, the shift in national policy towards encouraging land transfers meant a shift from government allocation of agricultural land to an enhanced role for the market (Long, Denggao 2018).

From an academic perspective, it is extremely rare to find economic "experiments" and research materials on how the tenure status changed after the initial measures of tenure equalisation, so what does exist is of irreplaceable value. Although there are many results on equal land rights and each land system reform, there are limited systematic studies on a coherent basis. In reality, each change has had a profound impact on the economy and politics of China and provides inspiration and lessons for the current land system reform so as to grasp its orientation and basic ideas. The transformation as a whole helps to understand fundamental characteristics of Chinese society and economy.

In fact, the one-sidedness of the mainstream thinking of the twentieth century, such as the theory of optimal self-farming, the theory of unfairness and inefficiency of tenancy and the theory of equal land rights, is due to the lack of market mentality. It was all static thinking, based on the premise of the immobility of land and other factors of production. It became mainstream thinking under the strong influence of China's economic backwardness and the quest for a strong state, able to resist foreign imperialism in the modern era.

## *Dilemmas and perceptions of the transition from traditional to modern economies*

Owning landed property and trading it to create wealth can be said to be deeply rooted in the nature of traditional Chinese people. But in modern times, it has lost importance due to the chaos created by backwardness, and economic and military aggression by foreign powers. People sentimentally attribute poverty and backwardness to the concentration of land rights due to private ownership of land, which led to bankruptcy, migration and poverty of peasants, and the disorder of the economy due to factor and commodity markets. They believed that China could break out of the chaos and attain the goal of becoming a rich and strong country only through governmental control of the allocation of resources. This became the dominant ideological strain during most of the twentieth century. However, the main external cause of the economic decline of modern China was in fact the incessant wars, while the fundamental internal cause was the failure of the transition from a traditional to a modern economy (or the industrialisation of the agricultural economy).

Many scholars have hypothesised that if China had been able to generate an industrial revolution on its own, as Britain did, it would have been able to avoid being left behind and beaten. Similarly, many scholars have discussed why France, Spain, India and the Muslim world did not have a spontaneous industrial revolution. In fact, all other regions industrialised by learning and imitating the "British model". The absence of a spontaneous industrial revolution does not indicate the stagnation and lack of dynamism of the traditional Chinese economy, nor does it entirely negate the traditional Chinese system and culture.

On the one hand, comparing the forms of property rights and business operations between China and Western Europe in the pre-modern period, we find that the characteristics of traditional China – individual farming based on private property rights of land and market transactions, with low threshold, divisibility, replicability and easy recovery – created a substantial middle class of peasants in the agricultural era and achieved relative economic and social stability. On the other hand, this stability and the self-reinforcement of essential attributes inhibited the emergence of factors such as the alienation of land of poor peasants – as, for example, in Britain – which then would constitute the workforce in newly emerging factories. Here we can observe some of the essential characteristics of the traditional Chinese economy, which were at least partially responsible for a path of economic development different from that of Western Europe.

## Conclusion

Through systematic investigation of the traditional land property rights system over the past millennium, this chapter has re-examined the land rights system and the traditional economy, and reflected on some deeply influential existing theories in order to form a new understanding. Meanwhile, the all-round excavation of this irreplaceable institutional heritage, as well as the in-depth investigation of land property rights and the diversified forms of transactions, has resulted in new academic discoveries and theoretical innovations, and contributed to forming a systematic understanding and explanatory framework.

In this chapter, we have reflected on the established theories; however, we do not intend to create new ones, but rather to base our own perspectives on the explanatory framework of a self-contained logical system. The interpretation of the relevant issues is not based on the deduction from some theories or models, but rather on new insights based on the restoration of historical facts. The unique heritage of the traditional land tenure system has reference value for the current market-oriented reform of the agricultural land system. The recent construction and development of a market economy rests on specific traditional institutional and cultural foundations. However, these institutional legacies have not been properly explored for a long time in the past; on the contrary, they have been neglected or even presented in a distorted way by historical research (Li, Bozhong 2018). This chapter has aimed to present these valuable legacies to enable a better understanding of the market economy system with "Chinese characteristics" and highlight its theoretical value for further research.

## Acknowledgement

This chapter is a synthesis of a major project of the National Social Science Foundation of China (Grant No. 10&ZD078, principal researcher Long Denggao) entitled "Zhongguo tudi zhidu biange shi" (History of Land System Changes in China), and of the author's series of publications.

## Notes

1 Over the last two decades, Zhao Gang 趙岡, Fang Xing 方行 and other senior scholars of the older generation, such as Qin Hui 秦暉, Gao Wangling 高王凌, Luan

Chengxian 欒成顯, Cao Shuji 曹樹基, Li Deying 李德英 and others have made new explorations. See Zhao, Gang (2000a, 2000b); Fang, Xing (2001); Gao, Wanling (2005a; 2005b); Cao, Shuji (2007a); Cao, Shuji & Li, Feiqi (2008); Cao, Shuji & Liu, Shigu (2014); Li, Deying (2006).

2 Dai Jianguo (2011) and others have argued that *dian* is a transaction of usage rights. Quite a few scholars, on the other hand, have argued that *dian* is a not-finalised sale (*huomai*), which means that *dian* is a transaction of ownership. For example, Ye Xiaoxin (1999, p. 249) holds that *dian* "can also be called as *huomai*". Chen Zhiying (2006, pp. 140–47) clarified the meaning of *dian* and the difference between *dian* and sale, especially finalised sale (*juemai*), but still customarily thought of *dian* as "a not-finalised sale (*huomai*)". Li Li (2006) claims that, during the Qing, people saw *dian* as a sale. However, the deeds that his article used were all deeds of sales.

3 Some scholars, such as Wu Xianghong (2009, Ch. 7) have misunderstood the core rule of *dian* practices. I characterise their misunderstandings as "balancing of rent and interest" (*zuxi xiangdi*) because they ignored the differences between different categories of *dian*.

4 When a current landowner sold his land, the original landowner asked for and usually received "joyous-gift silver" from the buyer. This custom was widespread, and more than 20 cases were recorded in a collection of routine memorials on criminal matters from the Qing period (Zhongguo diyi lishi dang'anguan 1988, vol. 2)

5 Some scholars today question the efficiency or rationality of pawn transactions, which is actually a misinterpretation, cf. Long, Denggao & Wen, Fangfang (2014). In the traditional period, the opposite was true: the "conditional sale" (*dian*) was regarded as the "correct *dian*" and the mortgage was subject to moral attack. In fact, each transaction method has its own advantages and should not be viewed in isolation, but should be embedded in the trading system, so it is understood that the coexistence of trading methods with different preferences can reduce systemic risk.

## References

Cao, Shuji 曹樹基: Su'nan diqu "tianmian quan" de xingzhi 蘇南地區「田面田」的性質 (The nature of surface land rights in southern Jiangsu province). *Qinghua daxue xuebao (Zhexue shehui kexueban)*, 22(6), pp. 59–71, 2007a.

Cao, Shuji: 曹樹基, Liangzhong "tianmian tian yu Zhejiang de 'er'wu jianzu" 兩種「田面田」與浙江的「二五減租」(Two kinds of permanent tenancy and rent reduction in Zhejiang province). *Lishi yanjiu*, 2, pp. 108–21, 2007b.

Cao, Shuji & Li, Feiqi 曹樹基, 李霏霽: Qing zhonghou qi zhenan shanqu de tudi diandang – jiyu songyang xian shicang cunde "dangtian qi" de kaocha 清中後期浙南山區的土地典當—基於松陽縣石倉村「當田契」的考察 (Land mortgage in mountainous regions of Southern Zhejiang during the mid- and late Qing: A study based on "land mortgage contracts" from Shicang Village, Songyang County). *Lishi yanjiu*, 3, pp. 40–54, 2008.

Cao, Shuji & Liu, Shigu 曹樹基, 劉詩古: *Chuantong zhongguo diquan jiegou jiqi yanbian* 傳統中國地權結構及其演變 (Traditional Land Property Rights Structure and Its Transformation). Shanghai: Shanghai jiaotong daxue chubanshe, 2014.

Chen, Yueyuan & Long, Denggao 陳月圓, 龍登高: Qingdai shuyuan de caichan shuxing jiqi shichanghua jingying 清代書院的財產屬性及其市場化經營 (The property attributes of Qing academies and their market-oriented operation). *Zhejiang xuekan*, 3, pp. 205–16, 2020.

Chen, Zhiying 陳志英: *Songdai wuquan guanxi yanjiu* 宋代物權關係研究 (A Study of Property Rights Relations in the Song Dynasty), Beijing: Zhongguo shehui kexue chubanshe, 2006.

Dai, Jianguo 戴建國: Songdai de mintian dianmai yu "yitian liangzhu zhi" 宋代的民田典賣與「一田兩主制」(The *dian* transactions of civil lands and the system of "one piece of land with two owners" in the Song dynasty). *Lishi yanjiu*, 6, pp. 99–117, 2011.

Fang, Xing 方行: Zhongguo fengjian shehui de tudi shichang 中國封建社會的土地市場 (The land market of China's feudal society). *Zhongguo jingjishi*, 2, pp. 8–22, 2001.

Gao, Wangling 高王凌: Zudian guanxi xinlun 租佃關係新論 (A new perspective on the tenancy relationship). *Zhongguo jingjishi yanjiu*, 3, pp. 15–24, 2005a.

Gao, Wangling 高王凌: *Zudian guanxi xinlun—dizhu, nongmin he dizu* 租佃關係新論——地主、農民和地租 (New Theory of the Tenancy Relationship – Landlords, Peasants and Land Rents). Shanghai: Shanghai shudian chubanshe, 2005b.

Jing, Su & Luo, Lun: *Landlord and Labor in Late Imperial China: Case Studies from Shandong*. Trans. from Chinese with an introduction by Endymion Wilkinson. Cambridge, MA: Harvard University, Council of East Asian Studies, 1978.

Li, Bozhong 李伯重: Xu 序 (Preface). In: Long Denggao 龍登高: *Zhongguo chuantong diquan zhidu jiqi bianqian* 中國傳統地權制度及其變遷 (China's Traditional Land Tenure System and Its Changes). Beijing: Zhongguo shehui kexue chubanshe, pp.1–4, 2018.

Li, Deying 李德英: *Guojia faling yu minjian xiguan: minguo shiqi chengdu pingyuan zudian zhidu xintan* 国家法令与民间习惯（民国时期成都平原租佃制度新探）(National Decree and Civil Customs: A New Probe into the Tenancy System of Chengdu Plain during the Republic of China), Beijing: Zhongguo shehui kexue chubanshe, 2006.

Li, Li 李力: Qingdai minjian tudi qiyue duiyu dean de biaoda jiqi yiyi 清代民間土地契約對於典的表達及其意義 (The expression and significance of Qing dynasty civil land deeds to the *dian*). *Jinling falü pinglun*, 1, pp. 111–18, 2006.

Wu, Xianghong 吳向紅: *Dian zhi fengsu yu dian zhi falü* 典之風俗與典之法律 (Customs and Laws of *Dian*). Beijing: falü chubanshe, 2009.

Ye, Xiaoxin 葉孝信: *Zhongguo fazhi shi* 中國法制史 (History of the Chinese Legal System). Beijing: Beijing daxue chubanshe, 1999.

Zhao, Gang 趙岡: Cong ling yige jiaodu kan mingqing shiqi de tudi zudian 从另一个角度看明清时期的土地租佃 (Viewing the land tenancy system of Ming and Qing dynasties from another perspective), *Zhongguo Nongshi*, 19(2), pp. 43–49, 2000a.

Zhao, Gang 趙岡: Lishi shang nongdi jingying fangshi de xuanze 歷史上農地經營方式的選擇 (The choice of agricultural land management mode in history). *Zhongguo Jingjishi Yanjiu*, 2, pp. 26–32, 2000b.

Zhao, Liang; Long, Denggao 趙亮, 龍登高: Tudi zudian yu jingji xiaolü 土地租佃與經濟效率（Land tenancy and economic efficiency). *Zhongguo jingji wenti*, 2, pp. 3–15, 2012.

Zhongguo di yi lishi dang'anguan 中國第一歷史檔案館 (ed.): *Qingdai dizu boxue xingtai – Qianlong xingke tiben zudian guanxi shiliao zhiyi* 清代地租剝削形態-乾隆刑科題本租佃關係史料之一 (Patterns of Exploitation Regarding Land-rent During the Qing Dynasty – First Collection from Routine Memorials on Legal Matters Regarding Tenancy Relationships from the Qianlong Reign), 2 vols. Beijing: Zhonghua shuju, 1988.

# 5 Loans and interest rates in traditional China

*Qiugen Liu*

## Introduction

When looking into interest rates in ancient and traditional China, it is possible to distinguish between two different types. On the one hand, there were the interest rates of profit-making lending operations, which quite often operated as money-lending shops, some of which were family businesses. Most loans were given by landlords, merchants, nobility and others, who owned some property. In some periods of Chinese history, however, there also were cases, in which governments directly provided profit making loans. On the other hand, there were non-profit loans, which – especially since the times of the Tang dynasty – were offered within a framework of "ever-normal granaries" (*changpingcang* 常平倉), "reserve granaries" (*yubeicang* 預備倉), "community granaries" (*shecang* 社倉) and "public granaries" (*yicang* 義倉) and were operated by the government or the society at large with the aim of stabilising prizes. They also functioned as a grain reserve system for disaster relief. The costs for organising and operating the system could amount to as much as 20 per cent of the loans provided. While all these institutions were intertwined, this chapter will focus mainly on the former aspect.[1]

## Development of interest rates in ancient China

The interest rates in traditional China developed in wave-line with ups and downs corresponding to the rise and fall of the commodity economy. From a long-term perspective, however, a trend to stabilisation and decrease can be observed. Looking into it in a more concrete way, it can be claimed that the interest rates from the Warring States period through to the Qin and Han dynasties remained at a comparatively low level. This can be seen from Sima Qian's 司馬遷 *Records of the Historian* (*Shiji* 史記), in which he relates the story of the political adviser Su Qin 蘇秦 who, during the Warring States period, realised that all the people in his hometown, regardless of whether they engaged in land transactions, commerce or handicrafts, were striving for a profit rate of 20 per cent (Sima, Qian 1982, j. 69, "Su Qin liezhuan", p. 2241). In his *Biographies of Merchants* (*Huozhi liezhuan* 貨殖列傳), Sima Qian confirms that for all

DOI: 10.4324/9780367434496-8

agricultural and commercial transactions there was the expectation of a profit of 20 per cent, or *shier* 什二 as he called it (Sima, Qian 1982, j. 129). The story of the rich merchant Huan Tan 桓谭, who during the Eastern Han dynasty could obtain an annual interest of 20 per cent, suggests a certain amount of continuity (Fan, Ye 1965, j. 58). The *Nine Chapters of Mathematical Arts* (*Jiuzhang suanshu* 九章算術) contains a reference to a monthly interest rate of 3 per cent during the later Han-dynasty (Jiuzhang suanshu 1990, j. 3, "shuai fen", p. 245) – this means an annual interest rate of 36 per cent. We also know, however, that in critical times the interest rates could raise to an alarming degree. It is also Sima Qian who says that during the time of the chaos of the seven countries, the feudal lord – who had been enfeoffed with the capital Chang'an 長安 – had to enlist an army and needed to borrow money from a money-lender, having to pay 10 times the normal interest rate (Sima, Qian 1982, j. 129, 3280). The book *Taipingjing* 太平經 (The Scripture on Great Peace), which was completed during the Eastern Han, notes that at that times, when poor people wanted to borrow money from rich people, they needed to pay an interest rate of more than 100 per cent; only then would the money-lenders be willing to provide a loan. At times, the interest rates were even higher (Taipingjing, 2002, j. 67).

During the Wei, Jin, and Northern and Southern Dynasties (c. 220–589), interest rates began to rise. Let us first examine this from the perspective of high-interest capital operated by the government. During the Wei and Jin periods, and during the period of the Southern and Northern dynasties, it mainly seems to have been local officials engaging in this business, or the different separatist regimes were operating their own high-interest capital lenders; however, records on their interest rates are rare. During the time of the 16 kingdoms (304–439), Prince Zhang Jun 張駿 of Liang 涼, in order to increase fiscal revenue, loaned all the grain and silk in his possession to the common people and received an annual interest rate of 100 per cent (*yi bei* 一倍, Wei, Shou 1974, p. 2195). During Sui and Tang times (581–907), courts and local governments at all levels set up lending institutions, which were called "office funds" (*Gongxie benqian* 公廨本錢). They were operated by local businessmen or entrusted to businessmen, and the interest rate was prescribed by the government. This interest rate was between 4 and 10 per cent monthly (Wang, Pu 1960, j. 93; Wang, Qinruo & Yang, Yi 1960, j. 506–08, 2114). This is corroborated by documents excavated in Dunhuang as well as records from the Otani Collection, which note a monthly interest rate of 5 per cent (Tang, Gengou 1985) to 7 per cent (Tang Feng jun zhu deng nali qian li 1987).

During this entire period, interest rates for private loans were rather high. One edict from the second year of the Heping reign of the Northern Wei period (461) pointed out that in order to collect the household taxes, regional governors often forced the ordinary people to borrow money from rich merchants and businessmen. For those months during which there was no harvest, the interest could amount to several times the original capital (Wei, Shou 1974, j. 5, 119). This, however, was an extreme case and may be exaggerated. Interest rates as high as 100 per cent are documented (Li,Yanshou 1974, p. 1092), while excavated documents from Dunhuang and Turfan for the Five Dynasties (907–979) have monthly interest rates of 10 per cent for money, and annual interest rates for in-kind borrowing such as grain, oil, food and cloth reaching 50 to 70 per cent. One page of an account book of a pawn shop from the Tang dynasty capital Chang'an shows that the interest rate for mortgaged loans there was about 5 per cent per month (Chen, Guocan 1983).

During most of the Song, private loans maintained a rather high interest rate. In the sources, we find many examples of annual interest between 50 and 100 per cent – the so called "double interest" (*bei cheng* 倍稱). The monthly interest could be higher – as high as 10 to 20 per cent; however, it almost never exceeded an annual interest of 100 per cent (Chen, Shunyu 1987, j. 5: "Zouxing qingiao xin fa zihe zhouzhuang"). On the whole, commodity loans (mainly grain) carried a much higher interest rate than currency loans.Yuan Cai points out that pawn shops were expected to make a three-year profit of 100 per cent, which would correspond to an annual interest rate of just over 30 per cent (Yuan, Cai n.d., j. 1, "Tongju bu bi sizing jinbao", j. 3, "Jiadai quxi gui de Zhong"). It is well known that it was the great influence of money lenders – whether specialised lenders or landlords – who demanded high interest that was the main reason for the reform measures initiated by Wang Anshi 王安石 (1021–86). The underlying perception was that high-interest money lenders incapacitated smaller households and thus had a very negative impact on the economy of the Song state, which was under high pressure due to the military defeats against the northern non-Chinese people.

## Interest rates during the Song and Yuan dynasties

In fact, early in Song times, a comparatively sophisticated system of granaries, consisting of "ever-normal-granaries" and "public welfare granaries", had come into being, which provided famine relief, loans and rice sales at reduced prices. Loans in kind – in this case, grain – were provided; the interest rate is unclear, however. During the second year of the Xining reign, 1069, Wang Anshi pushed through his reform and implemented the famous "green sprout law" (*qingmiaofa* 青苗法). According to this law, cash loans from the ever-normal granary funds were dished out in spring, and in autumn grain was taken back with a semi-annual interest rate of 20 per cent (Toqto'a 1985, p. 10544).

While well intentioned, the law – which had been contested from the outset – did not work as envisaged. While the 20 per cent interest had been introduced as a means to attain self-finance of the measures, it quite clearly was legitimated as being directed against the so-called "engrossers" (*jianbing* 兼並), which were held responsible for the credit squeeze from which the small-holding peasants were suffering:

> The reason people are burdened by deficits is because in that seasonal gap separating the old harvest from the new, engrossing households take

advantage of the crisis to demand interest rates of 100 percent. Consequently, would-be borrowers are often denied the funds they need.

(Xu, Song 2014, "Shihuo" j. 4, 16a)

In fact, Wang Anshi's reform extended to other areas as well, and it is quite easy to see that other measures employed, such as Wang's "State trade law" (*shiyifa* 市易法) also aimed – here by the means of mortgage – to bring down interest rates to 20 per cent annually.

It is hard to determine the extent to which these measures ultimately helped to reduce interest rates. However, it is clear that the imposition of interest, as in the green sprout loans, had the (intended) side-effect of greatly expanding state revenue. Both were in fact "high-interest loans". Given the extent of the empire and the vastly different economic conditions, the overall impact of such measures on the interest rates of private business is not easy to determine. During the Qiandao and Chunxi reigns of the Southern Song (1165–89), apparently the interest rates even in well-developed areas were higher, namely about 30 per cent (Yuan, Cai n.d., j. 1, "Tongju bu bi sizing jinbao"). During the period from the seventh year of the Chunxi reign to the seventh year of the Jiaxi reign (1180–1240), in the areas of Hunan and Hubei, peasants could borrow copper coins as strings with an interest rate of 30 and 40 per cent for 100 coins; the lowest rate was not less than 20 per cent (Minggong shu pan qing ming ji n.d., j. 9, "Huhun men", "Kuben", "Beizhu lai kuben qian"). It seems clear, however, that these measures contributed to the general tendency of the reduction of interest rates, which continued into Southern Song times.

During Yuan times (1271–1368), the interest rate of loans in general was quite high. In Mongolia and during the early years of the Yuan dynasty, when the people had to pay taxes and borrowed money to do so, the annual interest was 100 per cent and often compound interest was used by means of regularly exchanging loan contracts. Around the tenth year of the Zhiyuan reign (1273), when officers loaned money to the soldiers, the interest for three or five months was more than 100 per cent (Hu, Zhiyu 1987, j. 22, 42a-b). In the 19th year of the Zhiyuan reign (1282), the secretariat memorialised that those who had power and influence when giving out loans were not supposed to demand interest rates of higher than 50 per cent (Guo, Weicheng 1999, j. 28, 319–321). Around the 29th year of the Zhiyuan reign (1292), the normal practice in the villages was that if a family that did not have anything to eat borrowed money from the rich, for every *dan* 石 if the interest rate was light, they had to pay an interest of five *dou* 斗; if it was heavy, they had to pay 100 per cent (Yuan dianzhang n.d., j. 27). The Yuan dynasty law mandated an annual interest rate of 30 per cent; some usurers, however, issued "virtual deeds", which on the surface mandated an interest rate of 30 per cent, but in fact the interest rate was higher than 100 per cent (Yuan dianzhang n.d., j. 27). In the famous Yuan dynasty play *The Injustice to Dou E, Which Touched Heaven and Earth*, there is a passage in which the pharmacy owner and physician Sai Lu lends 10 tael silver to Granny Cai, and she is expected to re-pay 20 tael as capital and interest

(Zang, Maoxun 1616, j. 42). Loan contracts in Uighurian script from the Yuan dynasty, which were excavated at Turfan, as well as Chinese contracts from Chara-Choto, which document loans of sesame, oil, cotton, linen, grain seeds, barley, wheat and other objects as well as silver loans, paper money loans and other currencies, all have a monthly interest of 10 per cent or an annual interest of 100 per cent (Yang, Fuxue 1990; Li, Yiyou 1991; see also Yang, Xuandi 1996).

## Formal and informal credit-providing institutions

Before moving on, it is necessary to stress that the figures given so far reflect local conditions. While a comparatively great amount of market integration had been achieved during the Song, in general until far into the nineteenth century, interest rates differed vastly, not only related to economic cycles, but also for different regions. From the Ming on, when we have a growing corpus of source material – especially including more contracts – it becomes clear that loans were not always integrated into regional market systems. Intra-village loans were more widespread than is often assumed. This grew partially out of mutual help and kinship relations and was partially due to the fact that local landlords where familiar with the conditions, and thus could provide loans without collateral or guarantors. It should be noted that in kinship circles, short-term loans without interest can be observed. There also were local "rotating saving associations" (*hehui* 合會), which could help to solve temporary financial problems (Liu, Qiugen 2000, p. 68). Local credit services, moreover, could be tailored to the individual needs – they were offered in cash or in kind, with highly flexible terms.

While local loans – intra-village credit in the rural society – continued to play an important role, the market integration and the development of a commodity economy (in Chinese Marxist parlance, often called 'sprouts of capitalism' *zibenzhuyi mengya* 資本主義萌芽) made the development of new forms of credit and credit-giving institutions possible, if not necessary. It is possible to distinguish between "informal" and "formal" institutions. The informal credit market consisted of landlords who also operated beyond the boundaries of their own villages, professional money-lenders and merchants. It is important to see that the credit market during most of the Ming and Qing differentiated between loans in kind and cash loans. As a rule, the interest rate for cash loans was markedly lower than for loans in kind – especially grain.

There were, among the population, different reasons for taking out credit. Most important were consumptive loans for subsistence purposes because of a temporary shortage of funds. This quite often was related to unforeseeable crises, especially natural disasters. The second reason was the requirement to cover certain needs, such as marriages, burials, building of houses, religious needs or luxuries. There also was the inability to pay taxes.

The other large group of loans was related to agricultural reproduction, such as paying for seeds, fertiliser, cattle or agricultural implements. A certain drive for "development capital" can also be observed, such as investments into land or irrigation. Furthermore, there was cooperative investment into agricultural enterprises by landlords or merchants.

One important source of informal loans during most of the Ming and Qing periods were shops located in market towns. They would offer loans for consumption – important especially in areas that had switched to cash-crops – but also for seeds, fertiliser and so on. Credit services thus also were a way of keeping these shops in business. The second important group offering loans were merchants – sometimes roving merchants, but during the late imperial era also more specialised merchants, especially from Huizhou or Shanxi, who would open shops in market towns.

There were, of course, landlords as well, who realised that they could make larger profits. At the end of the Ming in Changshu 常熟 county near the Great South-Eastern bridge, there was a family Huang, which was of the opinion that tilling the field and collecting rents was not as profitable as giving out grain loans. For this reason, the family engaged in the high-interest loan business, because the profit was double and there was no pressure to pay taxes and provide corvée *(Yuyang shuoyuan jiabian "Guoxu zhigan")*. However, most landlords who offered loans did so in order to enable agricultural reproduction. Grain loans in most cases were provided on the basis of monthly interest, and were to be returned in kind. There were also situations in which loans and famine relief were intermingled. For example, the gentry-landlord Chen Longzheng 陳龍正 (1585–1645), in Jiashan in 嘉善 1630 when a famine struck, gave his tenants relief grain of 2 *dou* grain for every *mu*, but expected that this would be paid back in winter with an interest of 2 *sheng* 升 – that is, an interest rate of 20 per cent (Chen, Longzheng 1628, j. 4). Landlords giving loans to their tenants were therefore a quite common phenomenon, which made sense as well, since of course landlords residing in their localities were familiar with the local conditions and most likely the financial situation of their debtors/tenants. Grain loans, especially in the highly commercialised areas in the Yangzi delta, where peasants would specialise in cash crops, were also provided by long-distance grain merchants, who would offer loans in kind in spring, which needed to be paid back in autumn; these were locally known as *zhuandoumi* 轉斗米 (Ji, Lei & Shen, Meishou 1844, j. 2).

Except for these "informal" institutions that had existed since the early Qing, "formal" credit-providing institutions provided loans. These, on the one hand, were granaries, which actually had the function to provide relief in times of famine and to control the grain prices; however, due to the fact that they had to initially collect a large amount of grain for their operation, which needed to be replaced regularly in order to prevent damage, they were engaged in the loan-giving business as well. The second type of institution was pawnshops, which had existed in Buddhist temples, and during the early Qing had become the most important loan-providing institutions in the empire. In contrast to the informal institutions, the investment in pawnshops was huge. Most had a considerable capital basis of several thousand to several 10,000 tael silver. Many of them were cooperate investments by landlords and merchants. There were government-run pawnshops as well. In any case, pawnshops needed to be government approved – the application among others revealed the identity of the investors – and they had to pay taxes (although not very high ones). One tendency, which began during the Ming and became ever more widespread during the Qing, was for officials and military officers to invest in and even own pawnshops. He Shen 和珅 (1750–99) and his cronies, for example, had run a considerable number of pawnshops (Shiliao xunkan 1930/31, pp. 240–41) and many other examples could be given.

While most pawnshops were physically located in cities and market towns, most of their customers were peasants. Pawns could vary considerably: typical commodities were clothes, jewellery, calligraphies or paintings of prominent people, but also agricultural implements and even cattle. It was typical for peasants to pawn clothes in the spring and redeem them in the autumn. Interest rates were calculated on a monthly basis. During the Qianlong and Jiaqing periods (c. 1735–1820), in some areas of Hunan and Jiangxi, another form of pawnshop emerged; called "head-grain" (*tougu* 頭谷) or "pawn-grain" (*zhigu* 質谷), it was run by landlords and gave out loans in grain in spring, when the peasants' need was greatest, against objects such as clothes. These could then be redeemed with an interest of 30 per cent in the autumn (Wu, Minshu 1893, j. 2, j. 9). Not too surprisingly, cases of pawning persons – especially children, but wives as well – occurred, especially when pawnbrokers exploited peasants who were in dire straits. We know about cases of pawning wives in which male offspring – if they were born – served as "interest" (Hu, Yanyu n.d., j. 2, "Jin ninü dian fu"). The most common collateral, of course, was land; during the late Qing, there even were places in which the local "customs" prescribed that loan contracts needed to identify land, which would serve as collateral (*Qingdai tudi zhanyou guanxi yu dianong kangzu douzheng* 1988, vol. 1, p. 138, 142). The rather complicated situation of land rights – distinguishing between surface and "bone", subsoil, in some places – was reflected in such loan contracts as well (Liu, Qiugen 2000, pp. 165–68). Another common practice was to arrange loans through middlemen, who then would serve as guarantors (*baoren* 保人) as well and, in case the debtor was not able to repay loan and interest, would stand in for him (Niida, Noburu 1963).

## Loans for soldiers and officials

It is clear that loans and interest were a completely normal phenomenon in the rural society of late imperial China. It is actually possible to say that since it was so common, the complicated and sophisticated structures described above emerged. Loans played a role in the urban society as well, however. Most conspicuous here are loans provided for soldiers and officials, which were needed to cover expenses when waiting on official appointment – which could take months or years – or in order to travel to the place where one was stationed, of course accompanied by family, household employees and so on. While such loans are recorded for the Tang dynasty, these so called "capital loans" (*jingzhai* 京債)

in the early Qing "were extremely widespread" (Gu, Yanwu 1998, j. 28). Since the beginning of the Qing, they were provided mostly by an institution, which was called an "account office" (*zhangju* 賬局). During the early Qing, there were several attempts to discontinue the practice by way of imperial edicts, but to no avail. Giving such loans was risky from a legal point of view, but it could be because of other reasons as well: officials could die before having repaid the loans or they could be dismissed, among other possibilities. It is not surprising, therefore, that interest rates for these kinds of loans were very high. During the mid-Qing, Zhao Yi 赵翼 (1727–1814) suggested that the interest rate might be as high as 1000 per cent, without giving proof (Zhao, Yi 1990, j. 33). The main means to arrive at such high interest rates was to pay out only parts of the interest rate, at times 70–80 per cent but in extreme cases only 30–40 per cent (Zhao, Yi 1990, j. 33, 577). This was a common practice, which often is referred to as *duan piao* 短票 "shortened ticket" (*Qing shilu* 1986, Qianlong, j. 561, p. 108). There was also a practice that effectively invalidated the prohibition of compound interest, which was called "rolling interest" (*gunli* 滚利); this was achieved by regularly exchanging the loan contracts (Wei, Yijie 1985, j. 3, "Qing xing faping the lie shu", p. 69). Indeed, on the basis of archival material Jiang Xiaocheng has calculated that for *jingzhai*, very high interest rates could be realised (Jiang, Xiaocheng 2017, p. 100). There are also numerous stories of creditors accompanying officials who they had provided with loans to their new appointments and extorting money, not only from the officials indebted to them, but from other officials or the population: "They are really like tigers and wolves, considering the population as their meat and fish in order to satisfy their very deep desire for money" (Ouyang, Yu 1986, p. 48). The debtors "accompany [the newly appointed official] to the place he is stationed and recklessly demand compensation [of the loan], they hound the officials and Yamen runners, this really is bad behaviour" (Qinding da Qing huidian shili 1976, j. 764) or "when they arrive at their official position, they embezzle official funds, exploit the common people, trying to make up their expenses. All kind of abuses come from this" (*Qinding da Qing huidian shili* 1976, j. 764).

There are also cases where the state was not able to pay salaries, so soldiers or officials needed to take out loans, quite often with an interest rate of more than 100 per cent, as occurred during the Jiajing period (1521–67) of the Ming, for example (Zhang, Xuan 1940, j. 76). Finally, we should mention that there are cases of office sales in which loans played a role (Liu, Jinzao 2000, j. 93).

## Records of interest rates in legal texts

One approach to understanding interest and interest rates in traditional China is to look into legal texts. Observations regarding interest rates and suggestions on how to control them can be found in records as early as the *Guanzi* 管子 (Guan, Zhong 1996, "Qing Zhong", pp. 618–20) or the *Rites of Zhou* (*Zhouli* 周礼), although neither was a legal work in the strict sense (Zheng, Xuan 1999, p. 382).

There is no doubt that there were legally mandated interest rates during the Qin and Han dynasties; however, there are no documents available with accurate information. Beginning with the Tang code, we can see clearly how the state tried to prevent officials from providing loans in their own jurisdictions. There were other regulations as well, such as the prohibition of compound loans (*hui li zuoben* 回利作本) (Da Tang liu dian 1962, j. 6, 46a–b). An edict from 737 mandated that the monthly interest should not exceed 6 per cent of the principal, and the total debt was never allowed to exceed the total amount of principal lent (Niida, Noburu 1963, pp. 853–54). There were further regulations during the Song, which mandated that the rate of private loans should be 4 per cent monthly, while official loans had an interest rate of 50 per cent annually (Song xingtong 1984, j. 16, 413). During Yuan times, the monthly rate was reduced to 3 per cent (Yuan dianzhang n.d., j. 27, 5b). At the same time, it is clear that – especially during the Yuan – these regulations were in no way enforced: the monthly interest rate was higher and the regulations regarding compound interest were bypassed as well.

The paragraph "Illegal acquisition of interest and profit" (*weijin quli lüwen* 违禁取利律文) was first included in the Ming-code; in the Qing code it read, "Whoever lends money or accepts property in pawn shall receive no more than 3 per cent interest per month. No matter how much time passes, the total interest which accumulates shall not exceed the total amount of principal." The law also includes regulations about officials lending money, but contains regulations regarding the obligation to repay loans and the prohibition on the debtor pledging wives, concubines, sons or daughters.

There are, moreover, sub-statutes prescribing fines for debtors and creditors when abuses of capital uses were observed (*Da Qing lüli tongkao jiaozhu* 1992, pp. 522–26).

Certainly, what can be learned from this legal perspective is that there was a continuous decrease in interest rates. Yet successive dynastic governments allowed private and official lending, while at the same time making great efforts to regulate it – although not successfully in all cases.

## Conclusion

It is clear that by the Qing dynasty a sophisticated structure of loan-providing institutions had developed. Interest rates were rather high, especially compared with the experience of the countries of the West. At the same time the Chinese imperial state made great efforts to rein in this loan market through its own institutions and through sophisticated and far-reaching legal provisions. What can be observed, in any case, is an overall tendency to diminishing interest rates. I have undertaken some preliminary explorations, taking into account the development of the commodity economy and the restricting impact of government policies and law on interest rates.

First, under the premise of the development of the commodity economy, the producers could enter the market, which prompted them to develop a variety of business operations and increase their level of income. With respect to production, the traditional Chinese economy was dominated by a self-sufficient production, combining family handicrafts and agriculture, but at the same time needed to engage in commercial production. Under such circumstances, the realisation of the social reproduction process had to be more or less related to the market and commercial high-interest capital. For the purposes of reproduction and living, debt was relatively common, and a considerable part of it was permanent. As long as such a permanent need for credit capital persisted, it was not possible to expect the stabilisation of, or even falls in, interest rates – only the rise of interest rates and the shrinkage of reproduction. The situation was different, however, when there was a developed commodity economy – when producers could enter the market and sell their products.

In China's south-east cotton-spinning production area, for example, due to the increase in the commercialisation of cotton textiles and the development of the regional division of labour between textiles, and cotton and grain production, the share of handicraft industry income in the total income of small farmers increased, so even if the output did not increase, their individual income could increase. After the crops were harvested or the products were sold, they were able to effectively pay off their debts, successfully complete reproduction, maintain the family's food and clothing livelihoods, and pay government taxes, thus breaking free of the permanent chain of debt. From this we can observe that when the income level of the producers increased, the repayment rate also increased, which means that the risk of borrowing money decreased, and interest rates naturally tended to stabilise or even fall.

Second, the capitalisation process of social production that accompanied the development of a monetarised commodity economy also promoted the stability and decline of interest rates. If the possession of land is the most important feature of a traditional society, and the possession of capital of a modern one, then there necessarily needs to be a process in which land possession is transformed into the power of capital. Seen from the perspective of historical development, this transformation was roughly completed in two steps. First, on the basis of the small-scale mode of production, social production, circulation, distribution and consumption gradually became capitalised – that is, these processes gradually depended on capital (including commercial capital and high-interest loan-capital), so that the exchange value gradually became more important than the value in use. The second step was based on fundamental changes in production methods to transform capital into industrial capital. Following the emergence of new production methods (the mode of large-scale mechanised industrial production), which occupied all production areas of society, capital power finally became dominant over the power of land possession, and the capitalisation process was completed. Undoubtedly, traditional Chinese society was still in the first step – the second step was only reached in the Ming and Qing periods, when sprouts of capitalism emerged and a certain development ensued. Even so, its impact on the stabilisation of high-interest loan capital and on driving down the interest rate was also quite obvious.

One important indicator of capitalisation is the development of the credit system. And it was this development that increased the ability of business people and high-interest capital to control societal savings. The constant concentration of scattered funds and the extent to which they were used as high-interest-loan capital significantly drove down interest rates. The development of the deposit business after Song and Yuan times resulted in the investment of a large amount of idle capital in business and high-interest loan operations. This was of great benefit for the circulation of capital, the improvement of management and the reduction of material risk and thus the stabilisation of interest rate of high-interest capital, and especially their typical representatives: the pawnshops.

The development of financial credit services such as currency exchange and remittance – the two businesses in the Ming and Qing Dynasties were handled by specialised native banks (錢莊 *qianzhuang*) and native Shanxi-banks (票號 *piaohao*) – also gathered a large amount of funds, and a considerable portion was invested into high-interest loan operations. In addition, by means of partnership operation, a considerable portion of small monetary wealth-owners put their wealth into operations. This resulted in more complete operating rules, a more adequate supply of funds and a closer relationship with economic processes. It thus also resulted in lower interest rates, such as the loans of pawnshops and, since Ming and Qing times, private banks and money exchange shops, which had lower interest rates and were more stable than the occasional loans provided by ordinary landlords or officials, who were not specialised in the money business. For this reason, the development of the former naturally restricted and affected the interest rates as a whole.

When social production and circulation processes depended more on capital, a credit system gradually evolved and, in some regions with a more developed monetarised commodity economy, a capital market gradually formed. The development of such productive and management borrowings related to production and circulation necessarily stabilised and decreased interest rates because the level of interest of such loans was inevitably constrained by the profitability of the industry in which it operated. The decline in the interest rates after the Song-dynasty was due to this factor to a considerable extent.

In addition, successive governments stipulated special laws and policies regarding interest rates and the operation of high-interest loans, such as stipulating the upper limit of interest rates, stipulating the upper limit of the total amount of interest taken and forcing the exemption of all or parts of the total amount of interest when it amounted to 100 per cent or more.

Compound interest was legally prohibited and interest-reduction measures were implemented. Even if not all creditors obeyed these laws and policies, they of course had an impact on reducing interest rates.

In summary, under the influence of a series of factors such as the increase in the income level of small producers due to the development of the commodity economy, the gradual progress of the capitalisation process in society, and the constraints of laws and policies on the interest rate of high-interest capital in traditional China, showed a steady and declining trend.

In traditional China, there is no concept of "usury". The modern term 高利貸 *gao lidai* just means "loan of high interest"; it is, however, regularly used as a translation of "usury", which in the West is a highly laden concept. This is most conspicuous in the translation of Marx's (1970) *Capital*, in which 高利 *gaoli* was used as translation of "usury". We have seen that it was a widely accepted practice to pay interest for loans. While there was some suspicion for those who would gain profit (*li*) from money, there is little doubt that the need for loans was widely acknowledged. This becomes clear from an annotation of the Qing code, for example, which on one hand criticised the "illegal acquisition of profit", but in an annotation also notes "the function of making loans or accepting property in pawn is to aid people in distress, so that even in taking profit, there is the moral duty to help others". The question of where to draw the line between loan and profiteering is a difficult one. There is no doubt at all that on the basis of Marx, most loans in traditional China would be considered usurious. On the other hand, it is possible to show for most of the Qing dynasty that agricultural profits could be quite high as well. For peasants, it was thus possible to survive even if they had to pay an annual interest of 50 per cent for loans (Liu, Qiugen 2000, pp. 257–64). Researching interest and loans in traditional China thus needs to move beyond normative considerations and take the country's vastly differing local and temporal conditions into account. This only can be achieved by taking the great treasure of historical sources seriously.

(Translated by Iwo Amelung)

## Note

1 Note by translator: for a seminal treatment of the granary system during the Qing cf. Will & Wong (1991).

## References

Chen, Guocan 陳國燦: "Cong Tulufan chutu de zhiku zhang kan Tangdai de zhiku zhidu" 從吐魯番出土的質庫賬看唐代的質庫制度 (The Tang pawn-system as seen from the account-book of a pawnshop unearthed in Turfan). In: Tang Changru (ed.): *Dunhuang Tulufan wenshu chutan* 敦煌吐魯番文書初探, Wuhan: Wuhan daxue chubanshe, pp. 316–343, 1983.

Chen, Longzheng 陳龍正: *Jiting waishu* 幾亭外書 (Unofficial works of Chen Longzheng), 1628.

Chen, Shunyu 陳舜俞: *Duguan ji* 都官集 (Collected works of Chen Shunyu), (Qing Wenyuange Siku quanshu). Shanghai: Shanghai guji chubanshe, 1987.

*Da Qing lüli tongkao jiaozhu* 大清律例通考校注 (Annotated edition of the comprehensive examination of the Great Qing Code), comp. by Wu Tan 吳壇. Beijing: Zhongguo zhengfa daxue chubanshe, 1992.

*Da Tang liudian* 大唐六典 (The six statutes of the Great Tang-dynasty), comp. by Li Linfu 李林甫. Taibei: Wenhai chubanshe, 1962.

Fan, Ye 范曄: *Hou Hanshu* 後漢書 (History of the later Han). Beijing: Zhonghua shuju, 1965.

Gu, Yanwu 顧炎武: *Rizhi lu* 日知錄 (Records of Daily Knowledge). Xi'an: Shaanxi renmin chubanshe, 1998.
Guan, Zhong 管仲: *Guanzi xiaoshi* 管子校释 (Annotated edition of Guanzi) annotated by Yan Changyao 顏昌嶢. Changsha: Yuelu shushe, 1996.
Guo, Weicheng 郭成伟 (comp.): *Da Yuan tongzhi tiaoge* 大元通制条格 (Zhonghua chuanshi fadian). Beijing: Falü chubanshe, 1999.
Hu, Yanyu 胡衍虞: *Juguan guaguo lu* 居官寡過錄 (How an Office holder earns Few Demerits), n.p., n.d.
Hu, Zhiyu 胡祇遹: *Zishan da quanji* 紫山大全集 (Complete works of Hu Zhiyu)(Qing Wenyuange Siku quanshu). Shanghai: Shanghai guji chubanshe, 1987.
Ji, Lei; Shen, Meishou 紀磊，沈眉壽: *Zhenze zhenzhi* 震泽镇志 (Gazetteer of Zhenze), 1844.
Jiang, Xiaocheng 江曉成: Qingdai de jingzhai yu difang lizhi 清代的京債與地方吏治, *Qingshi yanjiu*, 2, pp. 94–105, 2017.
*Jiuzhang suanshu* 九章算術 (Nine chapters of Mathematical Arts) ed. by Guo Shuchun 郭書春. Shenyang: Liaoning jiaoyu chubanshe, 1990.
Li, Yanshou 李延壽: *Beishi* 北史 (History of the Northern Dynasties). Beijing: Zhonghua shuju, 1974.
Li, Yiyou 李逸友 (ed.): *Heicheng chutu wenshu (Hanwen wenshu juan)* 黑城出土文書（漢文文書卷）(Unearthed documents from Heicheng (Chinese documents)). Beijing: Kexue chubanshe, 1991.
Liu, Jinzao 劉錦澡 (ed.): *Qingchao xu wenxian tongkao* 清朝續文獻通考 (Sequel to the Comprehensive Examination of Qing documents). Hangzhou: Zhejiang guji chubanshe, 2000.
Liu, Qiugen 劉秋根: *Ming Qing gao lidai ziben* 明清高利貸資本 (High-interest loans of the Ming and the Qing). Beijing: Shehui kexue wenxian chubanshe, 2000.
Marx, Karl: *Das Kapital, Vol. 1*, MEW Vol. 23. Berlin: Dietz Verlag, 1970 [1867].
*Minggong shupan qing ming ji* 名公书判清明集 (A Collection of Enlightened Judgments by Famous Officials), n.p., n.d.
Niida, Noboru 仁井田陞: *Chūgoku hōsei shi* 中國法制史 (Chinese Legal History). Tokyo: Iwanami Shoten, 1963.
Ouyang, Yu 欧阳昱: *Jianwen suolu* 見聞鎖錄 (Trivial Records, Heard and Seen), Changsha Yuelu shushe, 1986.
*Qinding da Qing huidian shili* (Guangxu) 欽定大清會典事例(Cases and precedents of the Imperially mandated statutes of the Great Qing dynasty). Taibei: Xin wenfang chubanshe, 1976.
*Qing shilu* 清實錄 (Veritable Records of the Qing-Dynasty). Beijing: Zhonghua shuju, 1986.
*Qingdai tudi zhanyou guanxi yu dianong kangzu douzheng* 清代土地佔有關係與佃農抗租鬥爭 (Qing Dynasty Landownership Relations and Tenant Rent Resistance Struggles), ed. by Zhongguo diyi lishi dang'an guan, Zhongguo shehui kexueyuan lishi yanjiusuo 中中國第一歷史檔案館，中國社會科學院歷史研究所. Beijing: Zhonghua shuju, 1988.
*Shiliao xunkan* 史料旬刊 (Historical Material published every ten days), Beiping: Palace Museum, 1930/31.
Sima, Qian 司馬遷: *Shiji* 史記 (Records of the Historian). Beijing: Zhonghua shuju, 1982.
*Song xingtong* 宋刑統 (Criminal law of the Song dynasty) comp. by Dou Yi and Wu Yiru 竇儀，吳翊如. Beijing: Zhonghua shuju, 1984.

*Taiping jing jinzhu jinyi* 太平經今注今譯 (Modern translation and annotation of the *Scripture of Great Peace*), annotated by Yang Jilin 楊寄林. Shijiazhuang: Hebei renmin chubanshe, 2002.

Tang, Gengou 唐耕耦: "Tang wudai shiqi de gao lidai - Dunhuang Tulufan chutu jiedai wenshu chutan" 唐五代时期的高利贷——敦煌吐鲁番出土借贷文书初探 (High interest loans during the Tang and the Five Dynasties —A first exploration from excavated loan contracts from Dunghuang and Turfan). *Dunhuangxue jikan*, 12, pp. 11–21, 1985.

Tang Feng jun zhu deng nali qian li 唐馮君住等納利錢歷, *Tulufan wenji*. Wuhan: Wuhan daxue chubanshe, pp. 270–271, 1987.

Toqto'a (Tuotuo) 脫脫: *Song Shi* 宋史 (History of the Song-Dynasty). Beijing: Zhonghua shuju, 1985.

Wang, Pu 王浦: *Tang Huiyao* 唐會要 (Institutional History of the Tang). Beijing: Zhonghua shuju, 1960.

Wang, Qinruo; Yang, Yi 王钦若,杨亿: *Cefu yuangui* 册府元龟. Beijing: Zhonghua shuju, 1960.

Wei, Shou 魏收: *Wei shu* 魏書 (History of the Wei-Dynasty) Beijing: Zhonghua shuju, 1974.

Wei, Yijie 魏裔介: "Qing xing faping zhi lieshu" 請行發憑之例疏 (Memorial asking for establishing a rule for the reimbursement of official on their way to office). In: Wei, Yijie, *Wei Wenyi gong zouyi* 魏文毅公奏議. Beijing: Zhonghua shuju, p. 69, 1985.

Will, Pierre Etienne; Wong, R. Bin: *Nourish the People. The State Civilian Granary System in China 1650–1850*, Ann Arbor: Center of Chinese Studies the University of Michigan, 1991.

Wu, Minshu 吳敏樹: *Banhu wenji* 拌湖文集 (Collected works of Wu Minshu) (Xuxiu siku quanshu), 1893.

Xu, Song 徐松: *Song huiyao jigao* 宋会要辑稿 (Song Government Manuscript Compendium). Beijing: Zhonghua shuju, 2014.

Yang, Fuxue 楊富學: Tulufan chutu Huigu jiedai wenshu gaishu 吐魯番出土回鶻借貸文書概述 (Description of loan documents written in Uighur unearthed at Turfan). *Dunhuang yanjiu*, 1, pp. 77–84, 1990.

Yang, Xuandi 楊選第: Yuandai Yinaiji lu de minjian jiedai qiyue 元代亦集乃路的民間借貸契約 (People's loan contracts from Yuan-dynasty Chara-choto). *Nei Menggu shifa daxue (Zhexue shehui kexue ban)*, 3, pp. 98–103, 1996.

Yuan, Cai 袁采: *Yuan shi shifan* 袁氏世範 (Models for the world by Master Yuan) (Qing Wenyuange Siku quanshu), n.d.

Yuan dianzhang 元典章 (Statutes of the Yuan dynasty), n.p., n.d. Guangxu-era.

Yuyang shuoyuan jiabian 虞阳说苑甲编 (Garden of stories from Yuyang, first collection). In: Yu Hao (ed.).: *Ming Qing shiliao congshu xubian*, Beijing: Guojia tushuguan, vol. 16, 2009.

Zang, Maoxun 臧懋循: *Yuan qu xuan* 元曲選 (Selection of Yuan operas) 1616.

Zhang, Xuan 張萱: *Xiyuan wenjian lu* 西園聞見錄, Beijing 1940.

Zhao, Yi 趙翼, *Gaiyu congkao* 陔餘叢考 (Collection of Studies after Work in the Cultivated Fields). Shijiazhuang: Hebei renmin chubanshe, 1990.

Zheng, Xuan 鄭玄: *Zhouli zhushu* 周禮註疏 (Commentated edition of the "Rites of Zhou"). Beijing: Beijing daxue chubanshe, 1999.

# 6 Foreign currencies in ancient and premodern China

*Yaguang Zhang, Yue Bi and Zyler Wang*

## Introduction

In the preface to *The History of Chinese Currency* (*Zhongguo huobi shi* 中國貨幣史), Peng Xinwei (1958, p. 7) wrote:

> Considered as a form of culture, Chinese currency in the same way as Greek currency, was like a shining body, which had illuminated the surrounding world. However, the Greek's light was a borrowed one, borrowed from Lydia, while the Chinese "light" was an autochthonous one.

Scholars are generally of the opinion that ancient coins can be divided roughly into one of two systems: the oriental monetary system represented by ancient China and the occidental monetary system represented by ancient Greece and Rome. The two systems were not completely separate from each other, however. According to archaeological evidence, foreign ancient coins – including gold coins from the Byzantine Empire and silver coins from the Sassanid Empire – were unearthed in China. Likewise, Chinese ancient moneys, such as Wuzhu coins (五銖錢) of the Han and Tang dynasties and paper moneys of the Song and Yuan dynasties (宋元紙鈔), were discovered in other countries. This can serve as an indicator that there were diverse and frequent exchanges between the monetary systems of the ancient world, to some extent similar to those of today.

Browsing through the official histories, we can discover that already in Sima Qian's 司馬遷 *Shiji* (Records of the Grand Historian of China 史記), which was written during the Western Han dynasty (202 BCE to CE 9), there were records about foreign coins: "Parthia (*Anxi guo* 安息國) uses silver as money, which is designed with their king's face. When the previous king dies, they mint new coins with the present king's appearance" (*Shiji*, p. 3313) We find similar records in later standard histories, which followed the style of the *Shiji*. At the same time, records related to Chinese currency as well as economic and trade contacts were preserved in historical texts of Korea, Japan, Vietnam, Persia and other countries. They document a long history of currency interaction and

DOI: 10.4324/9780367434496-9

suggest a considerable degree of integration between the currency cultures of the Orient and the Occident.

## Dimensions of knowledge of foreign coins in ancient China

The different aspects and levels of understanding of foreign coinage developed by the Chinese of antiquity can be reconstructed from three types of historical texts. The first is the genre called "biographies of non-Chinese ethnics" in the standard histories – that is, non-Chinese people settling beyond China's borders. The second consists of specialised records of money and related comments based on textual research throughout history. The third consists of travel notes written by envoys or travellers who visited foreign countries. These three types of historical material are the main sources that can be used when exploring the history of economic thought on monetary matters in China.

### *Ancient and premodern Chinese numismatics*

The description of the shape and structure of foreign coins in ancient China can be divided into three aspects: basic shape, font and material. Furthermore, the oriental monetary system, represented by Chinese coins, is clearly used as a reference to observe and compare other coins.

Already in the *History of the Han Dynasty* (*Hanshu*), Ban Gu recorded the appearance of a kind of coin from the Central Asian regions in the second volume, "Biographies of the Western Regions" (*Xiyu zhuan*): "In Kophen (*Jibin guo* 罽賓國) coins are made of gold and silver, and the obverse of the coin is designed with a horsing-riding pattern, while the reverse is a human face." There also is a record in the *Biography of the Xirong* (*Xirong zhuan* 西戎傳) of the *Old Tang-history* (*Jiu tangshu*): "coins are made of copper without a perforation in the country of Licchavi (Nipoluo 泥婆罗国, a country to the west of Tibet in the Tang dynasty). The obverse of the coin is a portrait, while the reverse is the pattern of horse and cattle." This clearly shows that Chinese of antiquity quite accurately observed two important characteristics of coins from the Western regions: "whole patterns" and "no perforation". Since the Qin dynasty (221–207 BCE), Chinese currency had consisted of coins with a square hole and edge decorations, significantly differing from Western currency, which is full of portraits and animal patterns on the sides of coins. There are, moreover, a considerable number of records regarding the use of scripts and fonts on coins, especially during the Song dynasty. This most likely is due to the sophisticated status of calligraphy and calligraphic arts during the Song, and the frequent combination of cursive script (*caoshu* 草書), clerical script (*lishu* 隸書) and seal script (篆書). In Hong Zun's 洪遵 (1120–74) *Quanzhi* 泉志 (Monetary records) during the Song-dynasty, for example, both Japanese and Korean coins were described in some detail: "There are four types of Japanese coins with one-*cun* (1/3 decimeter) diameter. Each Japanese coin weighs five *zhu* (3,25 grams) with clerical-font characters." Most Tongbao (通寶) coins in Goryo (高麗), one of the ancient countries on the Korean Peninsula, were designed with "characters with seal or running fonts, and Zhongbao (重寶) coins have an obverse side with seal-font characters. Both types of coins have real workmanship" (Hong, Zun 2013, p. 190). The use of Chinese-style coins in Japan and Korea reflects that neighbouring countries in East Asia were deeply influenced by the Han culture and maintained close economic and cultural exchanges with the Song government. Most historical records detailing the materials used to produce coins were combined with characteristics of local metallic mineral deposits, including the records in *Datang Xiyu Ji* (Xuanzang's Record of the Western Region during the Tang Dynasty 大唐西域記), which contains some descriptions about Nepala (Niboluoguo 尼波羅國, the present-day Nepal): "The rose copper is the main mineral resource, and rose-copper coins are used in trade." During the Qing dynasty, Weng Shupei made a general assessment of foreign coins: "coins from the North-Western countries are usually made of silver, while those from southeastern countries are made of copper" (Weng, Shupei 1994, p. 1419). Special attention was accorded to foreign coins, which were minted from mixture or material, and there are rather detailed descriptions.

Furthermore, special attention and detailed descriptions mention foreign coins minted with a mixture of materials. Hong Zun, for example, described the coins in the Seljuq empire (Cengtanguo 层檀国): "coins used for transaction in the Seljuq empire are made of three metals, one third of gold, one third of silver and one third copper respectively. This is done in order to prevent counterfeiting" (Hong, Zun 2013, p. 228) Another case is Java (爪哇國), recorded in *Daoyi Zhilue* 岛夷志略 (Descriptions of Foreign Countries ) in 1350: "The habit here is to mix silver, tin, brass, and copper to mint coins. Coins are as big as the shell of a conch, called the silver coin, but they are used as copper coins" (Wang, Dayuan 1981, p. 159). The reason for mixed-alloy coins also may have been to prevent loss and corrosion during storage and transportation, or to issue undervalued currency in a coveted format. The concerns about materials used in foreign currencies may indirectly reflect the ancients' further considerations about convertibility of local to foreign currencies, as well as exchange rates among different types of currencies. Corresponding to the development of productivity and the deepening of Sino-foreign trade and economic exchange, the knowledge about the shape and structure of foreign currencies increased.

While overseas trade had reached a first peak during the Song dynasty, the scale and depth of trade still were rather limited. Browsing through Zhou Hui's description of Hong Zun's collection of ancient coins, one can discover that Hong, who lived during the Song dynasty, had a great interest in ancient coins, collected them with enthusiasm and was rigorous and precise in his historical research. At the same time, however, he was not able to see some foreign currencies first hand, and only could rely on the oral descriptions of others to record the shape and structures of these currencies. For this reason, one limitation of Hong Zun's *Quan zhi* is the illustrations. All illustrations in the 12th volume, "Foreign Genres" (*waiguo pinzhong* 外國品中), are almost identical, and all the pictures are of Chinese traditional round coins with squared holes. In fact, the pictures are quite different from the real external appearances of foreign coins.

By the Qing dynasty, illustrations in Ni Mo's 倪模 (1750–1825) *Gujin Qianlue* (古今錢略 Accounts of Ancient and Modern Currencies) (Ni, Mo 1992) had become exquisite and elaborate, and the shapes and structures of foreign coins were described in meticulous detail. The illustrations and descriptions suggest that Ni had seen the coins with his own eyes. He stated, for example, that on one side of a coin there was a man with a sword standing in the middle of the coin, which had been designed with foreign characters on the other side. He also recorded size and weight of other kinds of coins (Ni, Mo 1992, pp. 1698, 1714). Descriptions and illustrations of coins became more elaborate during the Qing dynasty. There are two explanations for this phenomenon: first, foreign currency-making skills were improved and more modern; and second, currency exchanges between China and other countries became more frequent.

## *Knowledge of exchange ratios and influences of foreign currencies in ancient China*

Knowledge of foreign currency exchange ratios in ancient China does not just extend to China and the exchange value between standard currencies and fractional currencies in a specific country, but also includes currency exchange ratios between China and other countries.

The exchange ratios between standard currencies and fractional currencies in a specific country were studied in ancient China, and Ferdinand Verbiest (Nan Huairen 南懷仁 1623–88), a Belgian missionary who was active during the early Qing dynasty and also served as tutor of the Kangxi Emperor, introduced some exchange ratios in his book, *Xifang Yaoji* (西方要紀 Key Elements of the Occidental World) (Bugli, Magalhaens & Verbiest 1985). Before the emergence of credit currency, the general rule was to take the intrinsic value of a metal as the basis of the currency ratio, which was also recognised and recorded in traditional China. A description of the exchange value of currencies in the *History of the Later Han-Dynasty* (*Hou Han shu*) reads as follows: "gold and silver are used as currencies in the Roman Empire (Da Qin 大秦), and the value of ten silver coins equals the value of one gold coin". Similar knowledge can be found in many later sources. One case appears in the book *Yingya Shenglanji* (瀛涯勝覽集 Overall Information of Foreign Countries: Information of 20 Countries along Zheng He's Voyages), first published in 1522:

> People in the country Kezhi (柯枝國, the present-day Cochin region of south-west India), used "gold or silver coins in transaction. The gold coins, called Fanan (法南), are with about 90% fineness and have a length of one *fen* and one *li*. The silver coin, called Da'er (荅儿) is just like the conch

dimple, with a length of four *li*. Fifteen silver coins can be exchanged for one gold coin.

Another case is related to Russian currency in the *Yiyu Lu* (異域錄 Records of Foreign Regions), published at the beginning of the eighteenth century: "There are different silver coins with varying denominations, calculated in Chinese denominations worth three, ten, fifty and one hundred cash. There are also large red copper coins, which have the same denomination as small silver coins" (qtd. in Weng, Shupei 1994, p. 1454). Some records only enumerate different currencies with different sizes, materials or denominations from countries, or add words such as "gold", "silver," "large-denomination" or "small-denomination", which are used to measure currency value. However, this method ignores the exchange value of currencies within one country or with other countries.

From the Song dynasty, the international influence of Chinese currency began to grow, and many countries established stable exchange ratios with the Chinese currency. During the Mongolian Yuan dynasty, for example, a kind of banknote called Yuanbao Chao (元寶鈔) could be used as "world" currency in long-distance trade during the heyday of its development, thus greatly reducing exchange risks in trade. Two other cases recorded in the *Daoyi zhilüe* (岛夷志略 *A Brief Account of Island Barbarians*), from the Yuan dynasty can be used to illustrate the phenomenon:

> Each silver coin weights two *qian* and eight *fen* (10.4 grams) in Wudie 乌爹 [the area around Udaipur in present-day Western India], and can be exchanged for a ten-liang[1] *Zhongtong chao* 中统钞, banknote ... In Jiaozhi 交趾 [the present-day Cochin region of north Vietnam], people use 67-qian copper coins to exchange a one-liang Zhongtong Chao-banknote.
> (Fei, Xin 1954, p. 34)

In his *Shuyu Zhouzilu* 殊域周咨錄 (Informative Records on Countries Far Away), Yan Congjian 嚴從簡 (fl 1560–74), introduced the situation in Sumatra, in today's Indonesia, where different materials – including metals and silks – could be used as money; he states that 192 gold coins from Sumatra equalled 9000 copper coins of China; as emphasised in a special note, this amount could buy one *jin* of spices (Yan, Congjian 1993, p. 311). However, although the exchange ratio of Chinese and foreign currencies stabilised in certain historical periods, this did not mean that foreign currencies could circulate freely in China.

Li Mingwei is of the opinion that with regard to the archaeological discovery of coins, compared with the tens of thousands of Chinese coins unearthed in batches in foreign countries, the number of foreign coins unearthed in China was rather limited (Li, Mingwei 1992); therefore, foreign coins were not circulating currency in China. The absolute domination of the natural economy in traditional China, especially in the border regions, resulted in a low degree of monetisation and even less momentum in establishing a credit system of foreign currencies. On the other hand, because oriental luxury merchandise items were major objects of long-distance trade in ancient times, foreign undervalued currencies could not be used as payment instruments. Luo Feng (2004) moreover, does not believe that gold coins of Byzantium or silver coins of the Sassanid Empire, which had higher values, could be used as domestic currencies. Judging from the fact that most unearthed gold or silver coins were processed or remoulded, people at that time might have regarded these foreign coins as precious merchandise or ornamentation. Archaeological findings suggest that many Spanish dollars, which flowed into the south-east coastal area during the Ming dynasty, had cut marks, and many of them were even fragmented. The fact that these Spanish dollars were processed indicates that such foreign coins were only "used to supplement differences after weighting in the circulation of the Chinese market" (Chen, Jianying 1994). Hosea Ballou Morse (1855–1934), who was working for the Imperial Customs Service of China during the late Qing dynasty, commented that:

> China is a country in which there is never any fixed exchange ratio between any of its currencies, even between two currencies of the same metal; but all exchanges are influenced by intrinsic value and by supply and demand.
>
> (Morse 1900, p. 204)

A lack of awareness of the independence of local and foreign currencies in ancient China meant that:

> Pieces of silver as well as dollars were shroffed and weighed before being deposited in the treasury. When that was done, dollars had no longer a distinct existence, for in commerce the Chinese treat silver and gold as they do lead, iron or copper.
>
> (Hunter 1882, quoted in Morse 1900, p. 56)

Therefore, even during the Ming and Qing dynasties, there was no public understanding of exchange ratios. Disputes about exchange ratios between Chinese and foreign currencies could not be separated from the theory of an economy controlled by the state, which had been prevalent since the *Discourses on Salt and Iron* (*Yantie lun*) in the Han dynasty.

## Knowledge regarding the management of foreign currencies in traditional China

China has a long history of maintaining the free flow of domestic and foreign currencies. According to the *History of the Sui-Dynasty* (*Sui shu* 隋書), "in each county of the Hexi Region [i.e. the area to the West of the Yellow

River, present-day Gansu Province], some people used gold or silver coins from the Western Regions (*Xiyu*) and local governments did not prohibit these usages". During the Ming and Qing dynasties, with the expansion of foreign trade, "the value of foreign silver dollars was calculated by the piece amount of coins, which was convenient for daily use; so the people welcomed this kind of currency very much" (Lin, Manhong 2011, p. 40). Therefore, foreign dollars circulated widely in China, especially in coastal areas: "In remote and isolated areas, people only knew foreign coins, instead of Yinliang (Chinese silver ingots)" (Zhongguo renmin yinhang zonghang canshi shi jingrong shiliao zu 1964, p. 47).

However, the Qing government usually acquiesced in the phenomenon of free circulation and exchange of domestic and foreign currencies spontaneously arising from the public. In 1829, an edict of the Daoguang Emperor stated that "foreign currencies are used in all sorts of circumstances, whether paying taxes or doing businesses" (Zhongguo renmin yinhang zonghang canshi shi jingrong shiliao zu 1964, p. 42). Richard von Glahn points out that:

> Unlike in Europe, Chinese officials paid little attention to the issues of international exchange and trade balances…the focuses of Chinese monetary policies were on how to regulate and control the balance between commodity and currency and how to stabilize the exchange value of different currencies.
>
> (Von Glahn & Wencheng 2012, p. 74)

These differences in monetary policy targets reflect the significant size and high self-sufficiency of the Chinese economic system and the dominance and relative closure of its monetary systems to the world. Based on the situation in China, only if the inflow of a foreign currency had reached a certain scale and become an important currency in circulation, or if a currency had enjoyed a similar status to the local currency and they had been used together in transactions, could these required conditions stimulate officials' awareness to establish policies for foreign currency management. Nevertheless, these assumptions were not true prior to the Ming and Qing dynasties. In general, the following points can be enumerated.

The first aspect is the management of representative foreign full-bodied moneys. In the second year of the Tianxi reign of Emperor Zhenzong of the Song dynasty (1018),

> the aide to the palace library (*mishu cheng* 秘書丞) Zhu Zhengcheng (朱正臣) addressed the Emperor Zhenzhong stating, "the previous controller-general of Guangzhou (*tongpan* 通判) has secretly observed a great number of foreign merchants coming to trade markets in Guangzhou with Lizi coins (黎字錢) or Shala coins (砂鑞錢),[2] disturbing Chinese laws and regulations.
>
> (Li, Tao 1986, p. 820)

This record shows that the local government started becoming vigilant towards the inflow of shoddy coins with impurities or executed through poor workmanship. Beyond that, though, there are few records about the government's restrictions on the inflow of foreign currency prior to the Ming dynasty.

In the second year of the reign of the Daoguang Emperor (1822), the censor Huang Zhongmo 黄中模 expressed concerns about a large inflow of foreign representative full-bodied silver coins and considered the inflow of these coins an important reason for the outflow of silver:

> the melted foreign silver dollars contain only 70 to 80 percent silver. However, when foreigners exchange their silver dollars with the people of non-Chinese ethnicity in our country for Chinese currency, these foreigners can get silver ingots with a high degree of purity.
> (Zhongguo renmin yinhang zonghang canshi shi jingrong shiliao zu 1964, p. 1)

Funi Yang'e 富呢揚阿 (1788–1845), the governor of Zhejiang Province, was of the opinion that the purity of foreign silver dollars was relatively low, so they were convenient for people to carry and use in daily life:

> When assessed value of foreign silver dollars was higher than that of Chinese silver ingots, this would be a reversed situation of expensiveness and cheapness for currency exchanges. Therefore, it is necessary to set up regulations to restrict exchange between foreign silver dollars and Chinese silver ingots. After reorganizing regulations of currency exchanges, the price of foreign silver dollars should be always calculated according to the current price of Chinese silver ingots; it cannot be higher than that of Chinese silver ingots. This regulation can lead to all kinds of public affairs being resolved without obstacles, and local people will have an advantage from this new regulation. Also, there will be no disadvantages caused by unfair treatment.
> (Zhongguo renmin yinhang zonghang canshi shi jingrong shiliao zu 1964, p. 19)

The considerations of Funi Yang'e were still subjected to economic thought, which postulated an "economy controlled by the state", but his proposition to adjust exchange rates based on the domestic silver price can be considered as historical progress.

The second aspect is the use of foreign currency to relieve the pressure of domestic liquidity shortages. Mu Tianyan 慕天顏 (1631–96), governor of Jiangsu Province, then submitted a memorial to the Kangxi Emperor requesting the discontinuation of the maritime ban policy (*Qing kai haijin shu* 請開海禁疏):

> Silver comes from two sources: from mining, or from inflow by foreign trade … Ever since the strict Imperial edict was issued, which mandated

to remove the population of the provinces along the South-Eastern coast inland 30 to 50 li, no ships have been allowed to go to sea. If both sources of silver were eliminated, the silver in circulation among provinces within the country would be the only silver that had already existed.

(He, Changling 1992, j. 26)

In addition, many officials suggested to maintain the circulation of foreign silver dollars at that time. As Li Hongbin 李鴻賓 (1767–1846), then governor-general of Guangdong and Guangxi Provinces, stated:

This kind of foreign silver dollars has been circulating and used in China for a long time. Indeed, as the Emperor said, it is hard to implement containment measurements suddenly. These foreign silver dollars should be allowed to continue circulating and being used as usual, so as to adapt the public usage habits.

(Zhongguo renmin yinhang zonghang canshi shi jingrong shiliao zu 1964, p. 5)

However, accelerating overseas trade and boosting silver inflow was still a new idea. Maintaining the traditional monetary system, which was self-sustainable and self-supporting, instead of the open monetary system, which was receptive to foreign currencies to supplement domestic circulation, was more in line with the general standpoint of the group of scholars and bureaucrats of that day, because of three needs. The first was to ensure a reasonable quantity of currency for stable circulation, because the inflow of silver was as difficult to control as illicitly minted copper coins. The second need was to prevent excessive mintage dependence on foreign countries. And the third, and most essential, need was to maintain central control over the monetary system and the highly self-sufficient economic system. Therefore, He Liangjun 何良俊 (1506–1573) stressed that the government's control was essential in order to maintain a stable circulation of currency (He, Liangjun 1997, p. 157); Huang Zongxi's 黃宗羲 (1610–95) proposal was to abolish gold and silver as currency; Gu Yanwu 顧炎武 (1613–82) proposed considering the weight of coins (Gu, Yanwu 1994, p. 76). These were common arguments based on the general standpoints of scholars and bureaucrats of that time.

It was necessary to imitate the implementation of a modern currency system on the basis of the practice of foreign currencies. After the middle of the Qing dynasty, imitating the implementation of standardised silver dollars was put on the government's agenda. This was not just because continuing to use copper coins instead of silver seemed difficult to adapt to the booming and changing domestic and foreign market systems, but also because of an awakening consciousness of national independence and sovereignty. Gong Zizhen 龔自珍 (1792–1841), a poet and reformer of the late Qing dynasty, expressed his worries about the circulation of foreign coins and his considerations about modelling China's own standardised pieces in one of his poems. Similarly, Wei

Yuan's 魏源 (1794–1857) idea was to copy the production of foreign coins but to suppress their circulation and use in China (Lin, Manhong 2011, p. 195). Lin Zexu 林則徐 (1785–1850) believed that if foreign coins were to be suppressed in China, the government should first mint its own standardised silver coins for public use (Zhongguo renmin yinhang zonghang canshi shi jingrong shiliao zu 1964, p. 15). The thought of scholars and bureaucrats in China, such as Wei and Lin, directly reflected the idea of "learning from foreigners and then mastering them" in the monetary field. The emphasis on the independence and sovereignty of currency, the maintenance of normal circulation and the effective exchange rate of local and foreign currencies are important signs of the deepening understanding of foreign currencies in ancient China.

## Conclusion

In traditional China, the local currency was highly developed, and the volume of economic transactions was impressive for centuries. Yet the influence of foreign currencies on China's economic operations was relatively limited. For this reason, descriptions of foreign currencies in ancient literature were focused more on visual impressions when people saw these coins. Ideas about other aspects, such as currency exchange ratios between Chinese and foreign currencies, and the influence of foreign currencies on the domestic situation, were much less developed and consequently the response to them was slow. The focus of Chinese monetary policies was not on the balance of international payments, but rather on regulating the balance between commodities and currencies and on the stability of exchange ratios between different currencies. These differences in monetary policy targets reflect the significant size and high self-sufficiency of the Chinese economic system, and the dominance and relative closure to the world of the monetary system. From the middle of the Ming dynasty, corresponding with the increased connectivity of domestic and foreign markets and related to the inflow of silver, the impact of foreign currencies on the domestic monetary system started to become part of public concern. At this time, the public understanding of the independence of monetary sovereignty began to be connected to the awakening consciousness of national sovereignty.

## Notes

1 Liang is a traditional Chinese weight unit; one liang is 37.3 gram in the old system of measurement.
2 A kind of coin made of an alloy of tin and lead.

## References

Bugli, Ludovic, Magelhaes, G. de & Verbiest, Ferdinand 利类思: *Key Elements from the Occidental World* 西方要纪. Beijing: Zhonghua Book Company, 1985.

Chen, Jianying 陈健鹰: Some Problems on the Inflow of Spanish Silver Coins to China 关于西班牙银币流入中国的若干问题. In *Proceedings of The Seminar Album of the 5th Historical Currency from Southeastern Asia and the Maritime Silk Road* 第五次东南亚历史货币暨海上丝绸之路货币研讨会专辑. Fuzhou: Numismatic Society of Fujian, 1994.

Fei, Xin 费信: *Key Issues During Zheng He's Voyages* 星槎胜览校注, collated and annotated by Chenjun Feng 冯承钧. Beijing: Zhonghua Book Company, 1954.

Gu, Yanwu 顾炎武: *Tinglin's Anthology: Vol. 1 Discussions of Money and Grain* 亭林文集·卷1·钱粮论上. Shanghai: Shanghai Classics Publishing House, 1994.

He, Changlin 贺长龄: *Collections of Articles about Economic and Politic Affairs in the Qing Dynasty*, Vol. 26 Household Policy 清经世文编·卷26·户政一, in *The Siku Quanshu* (Complete Library in the Four Branches of Literature. Wenyuange 《文渊阁四库全书本》 n.d.

He, Liangjun 何良俊: *He Hanlin's Anthology: Vol. 19 With Mr Wang, Huaiye* 何翰林集·卷19·与王槐野先生书. Jinan: Qilu Press, 1997.

Hong, Zun 洪遵: *Monetary Records: Vols 11 and 12 Foreign Genres* 泉志·卷·外国品中, compiled by Shengduo Wang 汪圣铎. Beijing: Zhonghua Book Company, 2013.

Hunter, William 亨特: *The Fan Kwae at Canton Before Treaty Days, 1825–1844* 广州番鬼录. Trans. by Shutie Feng 冯树铁 et al. Guangzhou: Guangdong People's Press, 2009.

Li, Mingwei 李明伟: *The Research on the Silk Road and Northwestern Economic Society* 丝绸之路与西北经济社会研究. Lanzhou: Gansu People's Press, 1992.

Li, Tao 李焘: *The Continuation of Comprehensive Mirror to Aid in Government*, Vol. 92 续资治通鉴长编·卷 92. Shanghai: Shanghai Classics Publishing House, 1986.

Lin, Manhong 林滿紅: Yinxian: shijiu shiji de shijie yu Zhongguo 銀線：19世紀的世界與中國, translated from *China Upside Down: Currency, Society, and Ideologies, 1808–1856* by Zhan Qinghua 詹慶華 et al. Nanjing: Jiangsu renmin chubanshe, 2011.

Luo, Feng 罗丰: *Between Hu and Han People: The Silk Road and Northwestern Historical Archaeology* 胡汉之间——"丝绸之路"与西北历史考古. Beijing: Cultural Relics Publishing House, 2004.

Morse, Hosea Ballou: *The International Relations of the Chinese Empire*, Vol. 1, New York: Paragon Books, 1917.

Ni, Mo 倪模, Guji qianlüe 古今錢略: *Accounts of Ancient and Modern Currencies: Vol. 19 Foreign Country* 古今钱略·卷19·外国下. Shanghai: Shanghai Classics Publishing House, 1992.

Peng, Xinwei 彭信威: *The History of Chinese Currency* 中国货币史. Shanghai: Shanghai People's Press, 1958.

Von Glahn, Richard & Wencheng, Wang 王文成: China's Currency and Monetary Policy in the 11th–18th Centuries 11–18 世纪中国的货币与货币政策. *Thinking*, 6, 2012.

Wang, Dayuan 汪大渊: *Descriptions of Foreign Countries* 岛夷志略校释, collated and annotated by Jiti Su 苏继提. Beijing: Zhonghua Book Company, 1981.

Weng, Shupei 翁树培: *Summaries of Ancient Money: Vol. 7 Foreign Country* 古泉汇考·卷7·外国. Beijing: Beijing Library Press, 1994.

Yan, Congjian 严从简: *Records of Neighboring Counties and Regions*, Vol. 9 殊域周咨录·卷 9, collated by Sili Yu 余思黎. Beijing: Zhonghua Book Company, 1993.

Zhongguo renmin yinhang zonghang canshi shi jingrong shiliao zu 中國人民銀行總行參事室金融史料組 (ed.): *Zhongguo jindai huobi shiliao, diyi ji* 中國近代貨幣史資料·第1輯 (Sources for the Monetary History of Modern China). Beijing: Zhonghua shuju, 1964.

# Part II
# European lines of evolution

# Section 1
# From rationalisations of usury to deductive theories of interest

# 7 Theorising interest

## How did it all begin? Some landmarks in the prohibition of usury in Scholastic economic thought

*Irina Chaplygina and André Lapidus*

## Introduction

The great period of the pre-classical theory of interest and of the associated doctrine of usury[1] took place in a long thirteenth century, beginning in the mid-twelfth century with the *Decretum* by Gratian and ending in the first years of the fourteenth century with the *Tractatus de Usuris* by Alexander Lombard. Historically, it might be viewed as one aspect of a broader history concerning the three great monotheisms (Ege 2014). Analytically, the problem of interest rests on an entanglement of its positive and its normative side: let us call them respectively the "theory of interest" and the "doctrine of usury".

Hereafter, we will try to not only separate positive and normative statements, but also explain how and why they were embedded. Our contention is that Schoolmen did have explanations of a possible difference between the amount lent and the amount paid back by the borrower to the lender: this is for the *theory of interest* side. However, on moral grounds, all these explanations were not equally acceptable: this stands for the *doctrine of usury* side. The resulting construction, from an economic theorist viewpoint, is made clear in the concluding section of this chapter.

During this long thirteenth century usually related to the Great Scholastic, the explanations given for the difference between the money lent and the money paid back looked like those with which we are familiar today: they favoured, for instance, time preference, technical productivity, risk-taking, liquidity preference and negotiation power. Nonetheless, on moral grounds, at least the last one – the use of greater power in negotiation in order to obtain this difference – was clearly not admissible. More generally, in other cases, the mere existence of such difference does not by itself show how it should be explained. Whereas the dismissal of the usual explanation based on the money loan itself, as presented by Thomas Aquinas in the *Summa Theologica*, deserves attention, alternative explanations, based on the existence of opportunity costs linked to a loan, gave rise to the emergence of extrinsic titles. But the moralist – that is, a priest or a judge at an ecclesiastical court – still ignores whether these, or their substitutes, do not depend on a greater negotiation power. It is this lack of knowledge

DOI: 10.4324/9780367434496-12

that gave rise to the search for an appropriate criterion, which ensures that the income perceived by the lender is non-usurious – hence the focus on property and risk-bearing. The various positions of the schoolmen regarding money loans can therefore be understood as so many attempts to avoid the committing of a major sin, and to obtain the relevant information on the actual interpretation of interest that should prevail.

## Allocating the surplus from exchange

Crucial elements in favour of a strict prohibition of interest could be traced back to Christian antiquity, to the Greek and Latin Church fathers who told, in various ways, the same instructive story: that of a consumption loan by a rich man who is widely provided for in all necessities, given to a poor man for whom obtaining the loan is a condition of survival (typical examples from the fourth century can be found in Gregory of Nazianzus or John Chrysostom). This story remained a reference point for centuries, and later most scholastic thinkers considered that in such a situation the voluntary agreement of both parties was not enough to prevent the loan from being usurious, even if the borrower could be cleared of the charge of usury (e.g. see the *De Usura* (17–19) of Robert of Courçon at the beginning of the thirteenth century): this voluntary agreement was called "absolute" for the lender, but "conditioned" for the borrower.

This distinction, concerning the nature of an agreement, rests on a positive statement: the money loan can be understood as a particular case of voluntary exchange. As such, it is mutually beneficent (see, for instance, Thomas Aquinas in *Ethicorum*, l.V, lect.9, c or in the *Summa Theologica* II$^a$–II$^{ae}$, q. 77, a.1, resp.), so that neither the lender's nor the borrower's situation can be worse. This is a way to argue that some kind of surplus arises from a money loan as it does from every more standard type of voluntary exchange. It also explains why interest is a withdrawal from this exchange surplus to the benefit of the lender. However, the story of the consumption loan has another consequence: it emphasises the difference between the negotiating power of the lender and of the borrower. The lender is supposed to be vested with a much greater power than the borrower, so they are able to appropriate most of the surplus emerging from exchange. The normative conclusion is straightforward: the condemnation of usury amounts to the condemnation of the appropriation of a part of the surplus arising from a loan.

Now, what is the proportion of the surplus above which a morally acceptable, licit transaction would turn into a usurious transaction? Curiously, the primary impression produced by the literature on usury suggests two different answers. The story of the consumption loan is one where the total amount of the surplus falls into the hands of the lender: the loan has not helped the borrower escape misery. His situation after the loan has not improved. Usury might therefore be viewed as a situation in which the negotiating power of the lender is high enough to allow him to appropriate the whole surplus. By contrast, both the severity of the church fathers and the popular knowledge based on the *exempla* to which Jacques Le Goff (1986) had devoted special attention suggest that even the slightest amount perceived above what is paid back would be usurious.

The contradiction is only apparent. The consumption loan story expresses constant suspicion of the lender, and the belief that his negotiation power usually gives him all that is possible under the condition of voluntary agreement by the borrower. The church shows such a strong aversion to this asymmetry of power that it finds it more appropriate to forbid any kind of supplement paid on a loan.

The basis of such suspicion against the lender comes from the fact that usury as a sin is a sin of intention; this means that, far from being self-evident from its factual existence, it depends on an intention that usually is not observable to the moralist. In the early thirteenth century, for instance, William of Auxerre defined usury as "the intention to receive something more in a loan than the capital" (*Summa Aurea*, t.48, c.1, q.1; see also Robert of Courçon, *De Usura*, 3, 13, 57, 61, and 78).

## Thomas Aquinas's classical argument

Thomas Aquinas's argument against usury provided a rigorous basis for its prohibition, in the sense of the payment of an income in reason of the loan itself. It might be considered as a development of three topics, coming from Roman law, from Canon law and from the Aristotelian tradition respectively. The first borrowed from the *Digesta* the contractual framework of the money loan; the second skilfully justified the choice of this framework by reversing the way the *Decretum* explains how an income is generated by a stock; the third draws on the Aristotelian analysis of the causes of exchange.

### *The contractual framework of the money loan: The* **mutuum**

Even before Thomas Aquinas, the legal framework for money loans was a free contract for fungible goods, the *mutuum* (see *Digesta*, 44, 7, f.1, n.2, 4). When the underlying contract for a transaction is a *mutuum*, the nature of this contract itself precludes any interest being paid. Robert of Courçon, for example, at the very beginning of the thirteenth century, explained the mechanism by writing:

> [T]he name of the mutuum comes, indeed, from that which was mine [*meum*] becomes yours [*tuum*] or inversely. As soon as the five shillings that you lent me become mine, property passes from you to me. It would then be an injustice if, for a good which is mine, you were to receive something; for you are not entitled to any return from that which is my possession.
> (*De Usura*, 15)

In the *mutuum*, the prohibition of interest is linked to the fact that the money lent and the money paid back is not, physically, the same object, so that the ownership of the lender has to be interrupted at the beginning of the loan. However, Roman law also acknowledged other contractual arrangements that would allow such a payment: the *locatio*, for instance, in which only the use of a thing is transferred from the lender to the borrower, its possession remaining unchanged; or the *foenus*, in which possession is transferred, but where such transfer is not free. So that what Thomas did, was to remove the possible arbitrariness of the choice of the *mutuum* as the contractual framework for money loans.

### *What can generate an income?*

This was made possible by reversing an argument concerning the reasons why a stock can be a source of income. This argument was presented in a well-known palea called *Ejiciens*, wrongly attributed to John Chrysostom and integrated by Gratian in Canon law. The author of *Ejiciens* asked whether "the one who rents a field to receive its fruits or a house to receive an income is not similar to the one who lends money at usury" (*Decretum*, dist. 88, can. 11). Among the reasons pointed out for a negative answer, the last one deserves our attention: "its use gradually exhausts the earth, deteriorates the house, whilst the money lent suffers neither diminishing nor ageing" (*Decretum*, dist. 88, can. 11).

In other words, *Ejiciens* asserts that a stock is a source of income from the moment the stock begins to depreciate. This income is then defined as the counterpart of this depreciation. Now, Thomas's great skilfulness was to reverse *Ejiciens*' position (see Noonan 1957, pp. 54–55). His argument was expounded in *De Malo* (q. 13, a.4c) or in the *Summa Theologica*:

> One must know that the use of certain things is identical with their consumption ... In such [exchanges], one must not count the use of the thing apart from the thing itself but, as a result of conceding the use, the thing itself is conceded. And this is why, for such things, the loan transfers property. Thus, if someone wanted to sell wine on the one hand and the use of wine on the other hand, he would sell twice the same thing or sell what is not ... Conversely, there are things the use of which is not their consumption. So, the use of a house is to live in, not to destroy it. Therefore, one can concede separately use and property.
> (*Summa Theologica*, II$^a$–II$^{ae}$, q.78, a.1, resp.)

As a result, interest as an income no longer proceeded from the depreciation of a stock but rather from the possibility of separating property and use – the sale of the latter producing the income. Therefore, a house or a field could – as in *Ejiciens*, but for another reason – be the source of an income, while bread, wine and of course money could not.

## *The material and the formal causes of exchange*

Far from being a consequence of a possibly arbitrary decision of a moralist or a lawyer, the choice of the *mutuum* for a money loan now came from the nature of the object of the transaction: this means that the nature of money itself, as a thing whose possession cannot be separated from its use, determined the nature of the contract. This conception of money was explained by Thomas Aquinas chiefly in his commentaries on Aristotle.

It was when commenting on Aristotle's *Politics* that Thomas stressed the conventional nature of money (*Politicorum*, I, 7; see Lapidus 1997, pp. 24–27), pointing out two functions of money, which he discussed at length in various writings. The first function of money stood in the Aristotelian tradition – it is a medium of exchange:

> But money, according to the Philosopher [Aristotle] in the *Ethics* (V, 5) and in the *Politics* (I, 3), was principally invented to facilitate exchanges: and so, the proper and principal use of money is to be consumed without diversion, because it is spent in exchanges.
> (*Summa Theologica*, II$^a$–II$^{ae}$, q. 78, a. 1, resp.)

In this regard, usurious activity is considered as distorting the nature of money (*Politicorum*, I, 8).

But when introducing the second function of money – the unit of account – Thomas was not so faithful to Aristotle:

> All other things have from themselves some utility: however, this is not the same for money. But it is the measure of the utility of other things, as it is clear from the Philosopher in the *Ethics* (V, 9). And therefore the use of money does not hold the measure of its utility from this money itself but from the things which are measured by money according to the various people who exchange money for goods. Hence, receiving more money for less seems nothing else than differentiating the measure in giving and receiving, which obviously brings inequity.
> (*Sententiarum*, III, dist. 37, a. 1, q. 16)

This contrasts with Aristotle's original position, according to which "money itself is submitted to depreciations, for it has not always the same purchasing power" (*Ethicorum*, V, 5, 14). However, such kind of emphasis on money as a unit of account meant that it could not give rise to any supplementary income.

Despite their discrepancies, the various sources of Scholastic thought continued along the same lines as Thomas's construction: the nature of money and the contractual framework thereby induced rendered impossible the charging of interest on a money loan. This impossibility is, first of all, a positive one: interest, as generated by the money loan itself, can simply not exist. So, if interest happens to be associated with a money loan, its amount must be explained on another basis than the money loan itself.

## Interest as a compensation of a harm from outside the loan: Extrinsic titles

The literature on usury shows that the range of analytically acceptable explanations of the existence of interest was limited. Each attempt to provide an alternative explanation therefore reveals to the moralist that the income perceived by the lender was only due to his negotiation advantage and had to be viewed as usurious.

The starting point was the widespread idea that for both the lender and the borrower, a present and a future good are not worth the same. "One harms one's neighbour," wrote Thomas Aquinas, "when preventing him from collecting what he legitimately hoped to possess. And then, the compensation should not be founded on equality because a future possession is not worth a present possession" (*Summa Theologica*, II$^a$–II$^{ae}$, q. 62, a. 4, resp. 2; see also his disciple, Giles of Lessines, *De Usuris*, c. 9). This was a way to say that although the legitimacy of interest paid on a loan does not depend on it, it might depend on the harm generated by this loan. Also, when interest compensates for the harm suffered by the lender, the operation is not usurious. Extrinsic titles aim, precisely, at identifying this harm.

Exterior to the loan contract and providing reasons for a compensating payment, the so-called "extrinsic titles" might be viewed as attempts to account for the harm suffered by the lender, according to its nature. These extrinsic titles, such as *poena conventionalis*, *damnum emergens* or *lucrum cessans*, existed separately from the *mutuum* and, for each of them, gave reasons for the payment received by the lender. A general problem linked to extrinsic titles is that although some of them became widely accepted, the harm often remained unobservable, so that the possibility of a usurious transaction could not totally be avoided. The level of acceptation or refusal of the extrinsic title therefore depended less on the nature of the alleged harm than on the trust or distrust on the effectiveness of this harm.

Designed to protect the creditor from a possible failure of the debtor to repay the loan in time, the *poena conventionalis* stipulated a daily indemnity in case the expiry date was not respected. Through the *damnum emergens*, the prejudice to the lender was described as his sacrifice, in terms of consumption, in order to keep his money available for lending. The *lucrum cessans* widened the perspective to the profitable operations that would have to be given up in order to carry out the loan, so that the prejudice was the sacrifice of a possibility of profit.

The *damnum emergens* and the *lucrum cessans* make obvious the working of the harm–compensation mechanism. As Noonan (1957, p. 116) points out, these two titles were not really discussed before the mid-thirteenth century (with the exception of Robert of Courçon, who condemned the *lucrum cessans*; *De Usura*,

61–63) since they needed, as a prerequisite, a general agreement about the use of the *mutuum* for a money loan. Despite showing a certain mistrust – chiefly aimed at the *lucrum cessans* – Thomas clearly stated the principles on which they were founded:

> In his contract with the borrower, the lender may, without any sin, stipulate an indemnity to be paid for the prejudice he suffers while being deprived of what was his possession; this is not to sell the use of money, but to receive a compensation. Besides, the loan may spare the borrower a greater loss than the one to which the lender is exposed. It is thus with his benefit that the first makes up the loss of the second.
> 
> (*Summa Theologica*, II$^a$–II$^{ae}$, q. 78, a. 2, ad. 1)

The principle of an interest that was both analytically and morally acceptable therefore appeared as an outcome of the discussions on the *mutuum* and the major extrinsic titles. The emphasis laid on the fact that the interest was a compensation for the specific harm suffered by the lender, and not a product of the loan itself, shows that it might be understood as the opportunity cost of the loan. This opportunity cost is the key to the distribution of the surplus of exchange between the lender and the borrower: after the payment of an interest equal to the cost of opportunity of the loan, the respective situations of the lender and the borrower have improved.

Naturally, this requires the credibility, for the moralist, of the harm alleged by the lender. In case the fear of a mortal sin was not sufficient to move the latter away from a usurious transaction, this might constitute an evident weakness of the system. This explains the importance granted, in the discussions between Schoolmen, to the nature of the harm associated with each extrinsic title. For instance, it justifies the quite general mistrust about the *lucrum cessans* (when compared with the *damnum emergens*): not because this kind of prejudice was inexistent but because, by nature, it concerns professional merchants who are always suspected of taking advantage of their superior power of negotiation. This also explains the poor confidence, even during the sixteenth century, in a loan where the interest paid is supposed to compensate an insufficiently specified harm stating only that the lender suffers from a lack of money: the late extrinsic title called *carentia pecuniae*.

## Substitutes for an interest loan

Whereas the extrinsic titles added something more to the main loan contract, a complementary possibility for a potential lender to draw an income was to replace the interest money loan by another intertemporal operation for which it would be a close substitute. The difficulty of the problem faced by the moralists came from the ability of the merchants to construct such close substitutes: credit sale, anticipated payment, *census*, *societas*, triple contract, *mohatra*, mortgage, *foenus nauticum*, bank deposit and so on.

The typical solution for separating usurious from legitimate transactions in the presence of these kinds of substitutes was to find among them a characteristic that would allow such a separation. *Property* could be viewed as such a characteristic: in the *mutuum*, the interruption in property made impossible the receipt of an income by the lender; continuous property might, on the contrary, support a claim for such income. However, the institutional arrangements of the transaction can conceal the reality of the ownership. The *societas* illustrates this point. In Roman law, this is an association between persons who engaged their labour, money or goods in a profitable operation. The income of each member of the *societas* depends, naturally, on the issue of the operation. Every modality of sharing was allowed. However, in the Middle Ages, this excluded the modality in which one partner would bear the entire responsibility in case of loss (see Robert of Courçon, *De Usura*, 73).

This shows that, in turn, the claim for property was not enough to ensure its reality, and that beyond its formal existence, a supplementary characteristic of this property was required in order to consider it as able to produce non-usurious income for the owner. This supplementary characteristic, based on risk-taking, was stated by Thomas as follows, again regarding *societas*:

> The one committing his money to a merchant or a craftsman by means of some kind of partnership does not transfer the property of his money to him, but it remains his possession; so that at his [the lender's] risk, the merchant trades or the craftsman works with it; and he can thus licitly seek a part of the profit as coming from his own property.
> (*Summa Theologica*, IIa–IIae, q.78, a.2, obj.5)

The importance of risk for assessing the legitimacy of a transaction appeared clearly in the debates concerning the sea loan, the *foenus nauticum*, especially through the interpretation of the well-known decretal *Naviganti* by Pope Gregory IX:

> Somebody lending a certain quantity of money to one sailing or going to a fair in order to receive something beyond the capital, for he takes the risk upon himself, is to be thought a usurer. Also the one who gives ten shillings to receive after a certain time the same measure of grain, wine or oil, though it is then worth more, when one really doubts whether it will be worth more or less at the date of delivery, must not, for that, be considered a usurer. Because of this doubt again, the one who sells bread, grain, wine, oil or other commodities so that he receives after a certain period of time more than they are worth then, is excused if, in lack of a forward contract, they would not have been sold.
> (*Decretales*, l5, tit. 19, c. 19, *Naviganti*)

This decretal is highly questionable (see McLaughlin 1939, pp. 103–04 or Noonan 1957, pp. 137ff). At first glance, it seems to adopt successively two opposite positions concerning the effects of risk: the first sentence condemns the sea loan while the concluding sentences allow a reduction in price in the case of anticipated payment – and an increase in the case of a credit sale – if the future value of the sold commodity is uncertain.

However, a careful examination suggests more consistent interpretations. The first rests on the expression "is to be thought a usurer" (*usurarius est censendus*). Usury being a sin of intention, this means that, in the *foenus nauticum*, receiving an income is not in itself usurious, but an external observer will be far from certain that the lender is not overestimating the risk of the operation to disguise a usurious benefit as a legitimate income.

Besides this "moral hazard" interpretation of *Naviganti*, it may also be noticed that the *foenus nauticum* is not such a simple operation, where only two possibilities can occur: the freight either arrives safe and sound or perishes at sea. Actually, if the freight is intact, the merchant will run another risk when selling it. This last risk is not taken into account in the contract between the lender and his borrower. Thus, in the event of the ship not sinking, one party has to assume the entire responsibility if a loss occurs. As the possibility of selling overseas is submitted to the advance of capital that belongs to the lender for the duration of the crossing, there is no reason for this ownership to be transferred to the borrower during the second phase of the operation. In spite of its name, the *foenus nauticum* is clearly not a loan, but rather similar to a kind of partnership (a *societas*) that allows common ownership of money invested in a presumably profitable operation. This strictly forbids any partner from escaping, at any moment, from the risk of loss.

This shows the utmost importance of risk-bearing as sign of a lender's continuous property during an intertemporal operation, therefore allowing the payment of a non-usurious income. Nonetheless, this did not nullify the suspicion concerning the lender's intention, and it justifies the typical medieval solution of the resort to an expert, a wise man, already advocated by William of Auxerre in the *Summa Aurea* (De Usura, c. 3, q. 2).

## Conclusion: An economic theorist's view on what happened

The general context of the treatment of interest loan, exemplified by authors such as Thomas Aquinas in his *Summa Theologica*, can be regarded as a special application of a theory of justice. This has an outstanding and obvious consequence: understanding interest rests on the coexistence of a norm which satisfies the requirements of justice, and of a departure from this norm which explains actual behaviour. The outcome is a rather sophisticated device in which explanations of interest are interwoven with moral assessments and policy choices. This device might be accounted for as a construction whose steps make sense from an economic theorist viewpoint. It is described hereafter and it is deliberately that historical evidence which gives support to it, as shown in this chapter, is left aside.

The five first steps correspond to the developments of the section above on the "allocation of the surplus of exchange" (see pp. 94–5):

1. The basis is the understanding of intertemporal transactions as giving birth to a surplus, potentially advantageous for both the lender and the borrower. Interest, as an income of the lender, depends on the way such surplus is allocated.
2. The loan is perceived through a bilateral relation, so that the amount of the interest perceived by the lender depends on the respective negotiation power of the lender and the borrower.
3. Now, the loan is usually viewed as a consumption loan, in which the negotiation power of the lender and the borrower is asymmetric, at the benefit of the first and at the expense of the latter. In such case, interest is viewed as usurious and gives rise to a clear condemnation.
4. A special difficulty depends on the non-observability, in general, of the respective negotiation powers of the lender and of the borrower – such information remaining private and unavailable to the moralist.
5. In case the moralist has a strong aversion against usury, it is consistent to forbid any interest – not because it is necessarily usurious, but because it might be and this very possibility should be avoided. But if the moralist's aversion is weaker or if what he thinks should be avoided is the condemnation of non-usurious transactions along with usurious ones, a reliable criterion to separate licit from usurious loans is required.

The following four steps constitute the classical argument against usury (*supra*, pp. 95–8). They are the result of attempts to find a clear criterion for non-usurious loans – that is, to give a solution to the problem open at step 5. As a consequence of an analysis of the relations between stock and flow, it is argued that property might be such a criterion:

6. Any stock is clearly understood as able, in principle, to give birth to a flow of income, either through produces which are to be sold or through services which are to be rent. This might of course concern a stock of money.
7. But, from a normative viewpoint, the right to sell a flow of services generated by a stock rests on the property of this stock at the very moment when it is generating such flow. And because of the nature of money, property is interrupted during the loan.
8. Therefore, a money loan cannot give birth to a non-usurious income for the lender *in reason of the loan itself*.
9. An immediate consequence is that asking for an income for no other reason than the loan itself cannot be supported by reason. Claiming the opposite is therefore the sign of a usurious intention which shows that the lender is abusing his negotiation power. But this does not cancel out every possibility of obtaining an income on the occasion of a loan: the analytically and

morally acceptable allocation of the surplus of the intertemporal exchange between the lender and the borrower is not "nothing for the first and the whole surplus for the second".

The next two steps, related to extrinsic titles (*supra*, pp. 98–9), explore the ways in which harm, and the corresponding opportunity cost, might be compensated:

10. Whereas a money loan cannot generate a flow of income for the lender because of itself, it can do so indirectly, because of the opportunity cost of the loan. A lender is entitled to ask for a compensation of a non-consumption or (to a lesser degree) of a non-investment during the duration of the loan or if it is not repaid at maturity.
11. Yet, the harm suffered by the lender because of the loan is also widely private information. And this casts doubt on the legitimacy of interest resting on an extrinsic title.

The last four steps are related to the section on substitutes for an interest loan (*supra*, pp. 99–101) aim at finding conditions that might help to distinguish licit and usurious loans, thus showing when interest is both analytically understandable and morally acceptable:

12. An appropriate response from the lender to the prohibition of usury is to resort to some close substitute for a money loan: a transaction involving the productivity of non-money stocks. In such case, the question is again of knowing whether this transaction is licit or usurious.
13. A first solution is again to resort to propriety as a criterion: if the lender remains the owner of the productive stock which stands for a substitute to a money loan, then the income he might receive would be non-usurious.
14. But ownership in turn appears as private information, possibly different from what is legally argued.
15. In this case, risk becomes the criterion for propriety, which stands for the criterion for a licit substitute to a simple money loan. And risk-bearing is much more observable, since it involves the possibility of a material, visible loss from the lender.

Concealed behind seemingly contradictory statements about the moral acceptability of such money loan or its substitutes, the device described above shows how Schoolmen had come to an intellectual construction in which we find the ingredients of a sophisticated conception of interest:

- It allows identifying the origin of interest in the surplus from intertemporal exchange.
- It leads us to view its amount as depending on the allocation of this surplus between a lender and a borrower.

- It acknowledges the role of the respective power of negotiation of the lender and the borrower, in order to determine the share of the surplus which might be presented as interest on a loan.
- It shows what kind of explanation of interest should be dismissed – a monetary one, in which interest arises from the loan itself.
- Symmetrically, it shows what kind of explanation is admissible, on both analytical and moral grounds – interest as the compensation for the cost of opportunity of giving up consumption or investment.
- It makes obvious the existence of close substitutes for money loans.
- It draws the consequences from the usually private character of relevant information on the possibility of a usurious intention for a loan.
- It finds successively in property and in risk-bearing a way to make concealing this information less obvious.

We could discuss over and over again the question of knowing whether interest on money loans was actually restricted and on the consequences of this possible restriction on the development of trade and on the emergence of new financial instruments. But it remains that all the elements allowing the construction of a genuine theory of interest were already present from the thirteenth century, in the writings of the Schoolmen.

## Note

1 Within the wide bibliography on interest and usury during the Middle Ages, see, among others, Chaplygina & Lapidus (2016a, pp. 27ff); Chaplygina & Lapidus (2016b); De Roover (1967); Langholm (1984); Lapidus (1987, 1991, 1992); Le Bras (1950); McLauglin (1939); Noonan (1957) (which is an impassable reference).

## References

Aquinas, Thomas: *De Malo*. In: P. Mare & S.E. Frette (eds): *Opera Omnia, Vol. 13*. Paris: Vivès, 1871–80.
Aquinas, Thomas: *Sententiarum*. In P. Mare & S.E. Frette (eds): *Opera Omnia, Vol. 10*. Paris: Vivès, 1871–80.
Aquinas, Thomas: *Politicorum*. In: P. Mare & S.E. Frette (eds): *Opera Omnia, Vol. 26*. Paris: Vivès, 1871–80.
Aquinas, Thomas: *Ethicorum ad Nichomachum*. In: P. Mare & S.E. Frette (eds): *Opera Omnia, Vol. 25*. Paris: Vivès, 1871–80.
Aquinas, Thomas: *Summa Theologiae*, 8 vols. Lander, WY: Aquinas Institute, 2012.
Aristotle: *Ethics*. London: J.M. Dent, 1934.
Aristotle: *Politics*. Harmondsworth: Penguin, 1981.
Chaplygina, Irina & Lapidus, André: Economic Thought in Scholasticism. In: Gilbert Faccarello & Heinz Kurz (eds): *Handbook on the History of Economic Analysis*, Vol. 2. London: Routledge, pp. 20–42, 2016a.

Chaplygina, Irina & Lapidus, André: Economic Thought in Medieval Europe [in Russian]. In: Aleksandr Khudokormov & André Lapidus (eds): *Economic Theory from an Historical Viewpoint* [in Russian]. Moscow: Infra-M, pp. 32–86, 2016b.
De Roover, Raymond: The Scholastics, Usury, and Foreign Exchange. *Business History Review*, 41, pp. 257–71, 1967.
*Decretum*. In: *Corpus Juris Canonici*, vol. 1. Leipzig: B. Tauchnitz, 1879–81.
*Digesta*. In: *Corpus Juris Civilis, Vol. 1*. Zürich: Weidmann, 1968.
Ege, Ragip: La question de l'interdiction de l'intérêt dans l'histoire européenne: un essai d'analyse institutionnelle. *Revue Economique*, 65(2), pp. 391–417, 2014.
Giles of Lessines: *De Usuris*. In: Thomas Aquinas: *Opera Omnia, Vol. 28*. P. Mare & S.E. Frette (eds.) Paris: Vivès, 1871–80.
Langholm, Odd: *The Aristotelian Analysis of Usury*. Bergen: Universitetsforlaget, 1984.
Lapidus, André: La Propriété de la Monnaie: Doctrine de l'Usure et Théorie de l'Intérêt. *Revue Economique,* 38(6), pp. 1095–1110, 1987.
Lapidus, André: Information and Risk in the Medieval Doctrine of Usury During the Thirteenth Century. In: William Barber, (ed.): *Perspectives in the History of Economic Thought, Vol. 5*. Cheltenham: Edward Elgar, pp. 23–38, 1991.
Lapidus, André: Introduction à la Pensée Economique Médiévale. In: Alain Béraud & Gilbert Faccarello (eds): *Nouvelle Histoire de la Pensée Economique, Vol. 1*. Paris: La Découverte, pp. 24–70, 1992.
Lapidus, André: Metal, Money, and the Prince: John Buridan and Nicholas Oresme After Thomas Aquinas. *History of Political Economy*, 29(1), pp. 21–53, 1997.
Le Bras, Gilbert: La Doctrine Ecclésiastique de l'Usure à l'Epoque Classique (XIIème-XIVème siècles). In: A. Vacant, E. Mangenot & E. Amann (eds): *Dictionnaire de Théologie Catholique, Vol. 15(2)*. Paris: Letouzey and Ané, pp. 2336–72, 1950.
Le Goff, Jacques: *Your Money or Your Life: Economy and Religion in the Middle Ages*. New York: Zone Books, 1986.
Lombard, Alexander (Alexander of Alexandria): *Tractatus de Usuris*. In: Alonzo M. Hamelin (ed.): *Un Traité de Morale Economique au XIVe Siècle*. Leuven: Nauwelaerts, 1962.
McLaughlin, Terrence P.: The Teaching of the Canonists on Usury (XIIth, XIIIth and XIVth Centuries), Pt 1. *Mediaeval Studies*, 1, pp. 81–147, 1939.
Noonan, John T. Jr: *The Scholastic Analysis of Usury*, Cambridge, MA: Harvard University Press, 1957.
Robert of Courçon: *De Usura*. In: G. Lefevre (ed.): *Le Traité 'De Usura' de Robert de Courçon, Travaux et Mémoires de l'Université de Lille*, Vol. 10, m. 30. Lille: University of Lille, 1902.
William of Auxerre: *Summa Aurea*. Paris: CNRS, 1986.

# 8 Merchants and the new Catholic view on the economy

Florence and Augsburg between the fifteenth and sixteenth centuries

*Monika Poettinger*

### Law systems and the emergence of economic rationalisation

Between the eleventh and fifteenth centuries, the economy changed profoundly in Continental Europe. The so-called commercial revolution[1] implied demographic growth, increased agricultural production, acceleration of interchange and urbanisation. The development also involved the realm of ideas, changing the world view of philosophers, theologians, jurists and even merchants (Armstrong 2016, p. 12). Man, who had entered the middle ages as part of a mystical or political body, subject to dictates imposed by God's representatives, became the norm that ruled the world. Historiography variously speaks of humanism and laicisation or rationalisation of the world. The emergence of the spirit of capitalism can thus be pre-dated to the late Middle Ages (Kerridge 2002).

One way to highlight this phenomenon is by registering the subtle changes that affected laws on contested economic issues like the legitimacy of interest rates on loans of any kind. In Western Europe at the time, various sources of law and prescriptions coexisted, representing different views on the morality and acceptability of economic actions (Armstrong 2007, p. 43). The menace of eternal damnation was, indeed, one of the most effective measures of law enforcement and theology, based on the scriptures and the recurrent councils of bishops; it represented one of the main guides to human action.[2] In the twelfth century, canonical law emerged from the incorporation of Roman law procedures (Hartmann & Pennington 2008) – as summarised in Justinian's *Corpus iuris civilis* – and Aristotelian rationale into Papal decrees and in the legal textbooks that were produced in monasteries and ever more often in the newly founded universities.[3] Next to theology and canonical law, secular law systems existed: the *ius commune*, the legal foundation of the Holy Roman Empire, that was formed by the Justinian code, its glossae and summae and the decrees of the Emperor; and the *iura propria* emanated by local institutions. These normative systems coexisted during the commercial revolution, creating many conflicts, particularly in the economic sphere. Inevitably, a process of adaptation to the diffused mutations in economic practices set in – but at different paces. In theology, the change was brought about by penitential handbooks. These guides for priests and

DOI: 10.4324/9780367434496-13

penitents spread massively after the fourth Lateran Council of 1215 that made an annual confession to the parish priest compulsory (Langholm 2003, pp. 7–8). Confession brought the church into close contact with everyday life. Inductively, the changes caused by the processes of urban and economic development made their way up into the moral realm. Canonical law was another way through which empiricism and rationalisation entered the relationship between the church and Christians. By incorporating Roman law and other secular sources, Canonists construed a positive law that had less to do with God's dictates than with objective and rational rules. On economic questions, Canonical law could clash with the writings of the Church Fathers or even Papal decrees (Armstrong 2007, pp. 44–45). Secular law systems suffered a similar fate and, while Roman law in general was more open to the requirements of commerce than church law, novelties in favour of merchant practices were often introduced via *jura propria*. Oscar Nuccio (1984) convincingly argues that, in the late Middle Ages, the struggle between powers was mainly fought in this legal arena between Canonical law, Roman law and communal law. The increasing interference of the church in economic matters, culminating at the end of the Middle Ages in a last momentous effort of Scholastic creativity, should be interpreted as a reaction to the perilous sprouting of communal independence that undermined the theocratic vision of universal order that the church had tried to impose on the world from the ninth to the fifteenth centuries, while extending its control over more than one-third of Continental Europe (Nuccio 1984, p. 513).[4] Aside from being a mirror of the power struggle between secular and religious institutions, the prevalence of one or the other of these varying set of norms would also be a key feature in justifying rational economic action, igniting economic growth and the development of a systematic economic thought (Quaglioni, Todeschini & Varanini 2005).

## The new Catholic view on the economy: Italy

In the case of Italy, Oscar Nuccio underlines how, between 1050 and 1450, the first step towards a new understanding of economic interaction[5] came from secular law and the work of jurists (Nuccio 1984, pp. 258–60). Commentators and annotators painstakingly retrieved the origin of Roman law in the rationality and the natural inclinations of man. In consequence, the rules that governed man in his political and private life became detached from religious norms (Nuccio 1984, p. 681). This new Aristotelian jurisprudence transformed the depersonalised individual, subject to the *utilitas publica*, into a citizen – *civis* – who actively participated, among other things, in setting up the law system. The sets of norms that mostly reflected this new conception of man were the *jura propria*. These free communal judicial systems, as the internal regulations of merchant guilds and associations, comprised economic regulations that opposed or neutralised both Canonical and Roman law prescriptions, generating veritable zones of trade free from God's condemnation and even church taxes – the infamous *decime*.

The prohibition of interest was a main point of dispute. Neither the Bible nor the Patristic writings univocally expressed a condemnation of the charging of interest on loans. The negative judgement was reserved to an excessive interest, mainly in defence of the poor (Nuccio 1984, p. 427). Only with the Council of Reims (1049) was the charging of any kind of interest on loans prohibited to laymen as well as to clergymen. Yet the canonist Henry of Susa, in his *Summa* written in the middle of the thirteenth century, still justified the legitimacy of interest in Justinian's Codex for economic and social reasons (Armstrong 2007, p. 45). The climax of the condemnation of usury would only be reached under Pope Clement V in the Council of Vienne (1311). Reacting to the extending jurisdiction of *jura propria* and the increasing autonomy of cities, Clement V decreed that, in the communities where usury was allowed by local laws, not only should the usurer be excommunicated but so should all officials who legitimised and guaranteed the usury loan. In the world of the baptised subjects of the church, the desire for profit – *lucrum* – and whatever exceeded the necessities of life became a reason for heresy and eternal condemnation (Friedberger 1967) and avarice substituted pride – the major sin of the feudal world – as the origin of all evil (Nuccio 1984, p. 439). Therefore, many different justifications were found by Canonists and theologians to prohibit interest payments (Nuccio 1984, p. 450). While theologians appealed to the scriptures and the writings of the Church Fathers, Canonists sought a natural explanation, an intrinsic character of money that excluded the payment of interest. One condemnation, dating to Aristotle and appropriated by Thomas Aquinas, underlined the sterility and fungibility of money. Money was considered a consumption good: its ownership could not be separated from its use. In consequence, to ask for interest on a monetary loan would imply a double payment and had to be condemned (Johnston 1953; Langholm 1992, pp. 236–44). With various refinements, namely by Gerard of Siena and Giovanni d'Andrea, this argument against usury dripped down into the work of the Canonists of the fourteenth century (Armstrong 2007). The idea of a natural and unchangeable value of money and other fungible goods, based on number, measure and weight, found a theological counterpart in the doctrine of the "just price" (Baldwin 1959; De Roover 1958) that opposed the liberal dictates of the *Corpus Juris Civilis*, extending the tribal exchange moral to the whole of Christianity. Notwithstanding the injection of natural law and empirical analysis through the work of Canonists (Schumpeter 2003 [1954], pp. 119–27), in the fourteenth century the Christian front against usury appeared compact (Armstrong 2007, pp. 57–58).

The main source of innovation came from the minor orders that operated near markets and fairs, and in bustling cities, confessing merchants and usurers. To appease the conscience of their devotees, pastors like the Dominican Friar Antoninus Pierozzi (1389–1459), Archbishop of Florence, closely examined all trading intercourses pronouncing their legitimacy or not.[6] The case of Florence is exemplary of the complex solutions caused by the clashing of the theocratic view of the church and the emerging merchant society (Poettinger 2012, pp. 49–72). Florence never openly disputed the predominance of the church in its statutes (Nuccio 1984, p. 621) and the civil life of the city was regulated by a strict collaboration of the merchant class and the monastic orders that represented church and doctrine. Antoninus, protégée of Cosimo de Medici, preached no more of money as *res quae usu consumuntur*, sterile and unproductive, but instead *"per modum capitalis, ut scilicet in persona tradentis emptionibus et mercationibus deputetur"* (Antonino da Firenze 1740–41, pars II, tit. I, cap.VII, par. XVI).

In the wake of the Franciscan Friars Pèire de Joan-Oliu and Saint Bernardino of Siena (Bazzichi 2011; Spicciani 1990; Todeschini 1980), Antoninus affirmed that paying interest on capital invested in merchant ventures was acceptable to church doctrine. The justification was that of *lucrum cessans*, according to which money, in the hands of the merchant class, became productive capital and produced fruit, so that renouncing to it for a given amount of time deprived its owner of an income that had to be replaced by the payment of an interest. In practice, all society contracts and trading contracts escaped the accusation of usury (De Roover 1970, p. 18). The case of banking was slightly different. Lending money against interest *per se* remained sinful. The solution in this case was to transform money lending into money changing, a minor sin that could be counterbalanced by practising the virtue of *magnificentia*, the use of riches in order to transform Florence in the image of the celestial Jerusalem (Howard 2004).[7] Antoninus clearly stated that *"duas esse virtutes circa pecuniam vel usum ejus, scilicet liberalitatem et magnificentiam"* (Antonino da Firenze 1740–1741, IV:III:IV, col. 80D). The morality of economic action thus shifted from the way riches were acquired to the way they were spent (Poettinger 2012, pp. 54–59).

The legitimacy of an interest payment on loans concerned not only private merchants, but also public entities (Kirshner 1970). To finance the increasing public expenses connected with the defence of the cities, some communes built up a reserve of capital, imposing extraordinary taxations or compulsory loan schemes. Florence did so in 1343–45, creating a *mons communis* out of the *prestanze* – loans – exacted from its citizens. The municipality paid a rent of 5 per cent on the *prestanze*, while a secondary market emerged for the titles of debt emitted by the *mons* (Barile 2010, p. 3). Obviously, the titles sold well under their nominal value, given the uncertainty about the capability or willingness of the municipality to repay its creditors. While no one blamed the original retainers of the public debt, Dominicans and Augustinians accused the buyers of the titles of debt of usury. Instead, the legitimacy of the original interest payment and of eventual successive selling contracts was invoked by the Franciscan Friar Francesco da Empoli, who had studied at or visited Oxford in the mid-1340s and successively lived in the convent of S.Croce in Florence, becoming the reference person of the Order in Tuscany. He made his case in favour of the public debt market through an empirical case study, depicting an exacted citizen, Petrus, and the buyer of his public debt title, Johannes. According to Francesco, no usury was involved in the transaction, given that Johannes only acted against the municipality in substitution of Petrus, without being a creditor himself. The legitimacy of the discount on the nominal value of the title bought by Johannes was further justified by Francesco as a risk premium with an analogy with maritime insurance policies.

The interpretation of Francesco da Empoli on the legitimacy of the market for public debt became prevalent in Florence exactly as the doctrine of Pèire de Joan-Oliu on usury was finally accepted and divulged by Antoninus, which was an indication of a general shift of local theological thought in favour of merchant activities. The case of Florence in the fifteenth century, here briefly recounted, is an example of how Italian cities reconciled public welfare, defined by religion, with the private vice of avarice typical of the new emerging merchant class. The *jura propria* – communal statues, merchant tribunals and local legislations – created a space for the individual venture to flourish, while empirically oriented theologians and preachers of the minor orders defended the new economic practices from the condemnation of usury. Members of the Medici family, bankers and merchants, could ascend to the government of the city of Florence, to the throne of France and even to the papacy with no fear of burning in Hell for their economic actions.

## The new Catholic view on the economy: Johann Eck and southern Germany

The holy alliance between merchants and the church, so effectively at work in Florence, did not extend north of the Alps. Whereas the alliance of Saint Antoninus and Cosimo de' Medici nurtured a cultural and artistic renaissance in Florence, the same did not happen in Augsburg.[8] The 'new Catholic view on the economy' (Obermann 1981), nurtured at the University of Tübingen, could not prevail despite the attempts made by Jacob Fugger (1459–1525) and Johannes Eck (1486–1543).

Johann Maier von Eck[9] obtained his Master's degree in 1501 at the university of Tübingen, where he studied theology under Johann Jakob Lempp while acquiring knowledge in business ethics from Konrad Summenhart (Ott 1966). After some years in Freiburg, in 1510 Eck obtained a theological chair at the university of Ingolstadt. Two years later, he was elected pro chancellor at the university and, thanks to this position, transformed Ingolstadt into a fortress of Catholicism against the Reformation. Of interest in the present study are the early years of Eck's activity (Schlecht 1915), in which he dedicated his efforts to the question of usury (Wurm 1997). His writings on the issue are preserved as manuscripts in the library of the University of Munich.[10] A first essay, the *Tractatus de contractibus usurariis*, was dedicated to usury contracts and repeated many arguments that were in wide circulation across Europe.[11] The *Tractatus de contractu quinque de centum* instead analysed the legitimacy of the contract that, in southern German states and cities, was widely used to circumvent the prohibition of interest. The pact consisted of three separate contracts: a society contract in which a capitalist provided capital to a merchant for a common venture; a contract through which the capitalist forfeited his profit share in exchange of the payment of a fixed rate of profits (for example 7 percent); and a third contract through which the capitalist insured his capital in exchange for the cession of further 2 or 3 per cent of his profit share, in the end maintaining the right to 5 per cent of profits. Such a baroque solution, as the Italian recourse to *lettere di cambio* and various society contracts, had been the response of the merchant class to the stricter rules against usury emitted by the church in the fourteenth century.

The rhetoric of Eck's writing is typically scholastic, but the arguments presented contradict the official stance of the theologians and Canonists of his time. Albeit professing a *via media*, typical of the university of Tübingen, Eck adhered to the *via moderna*.[12] Also known as nominalism, this doctrine stated the respective independence of philosophy and theology, while basing knowledge on empirical observation and experience. Nominalism also favoured new dialectical tools and a more precise and rigorous use of language. A proof of the modernity of Eck's writing is the continuous reference to the reality of his time to further prove his points. "The usury loan, wrote Eck, "drains out the debtor. The *contractus trinus* instead improves the wealth of the entrepreneur. Wherefrom would otherwise stem the richness of our merchants?" (Schneid 1891, p. 479). In general, Eck's essay is full of enthusiastic descriptions of the wealth of Augsburg. "Since the last century," he wrote, "possibly with the exception of Cosimo de' Medici, there were no merchants more famous than those of Augsburg" (Schneid 1891, p. 572). Enumerating the positive consequences of the *contractus trinus*, Eck boasted:

(a) the contract favours the merchants: the capitals they receive allow them to start grand enterprises and so gain the wealth that the whole world envies us
(b) The contract favours the lenders of the money. Thanks to this contract their capital and an interest rate of 5% are guaranteed. They must only fear the bankruptcy of the merchant, but this risk can be limited by investing solely in solid enterprises
(c) The contractus trinus is an act of mercy because it helped youngsters not yet of age and widows and many a worthy citizen to overcome their financial problems, increasing the welfare of the state
(d) It increases public welfare by creating a rich bourgeoisie as we can plainly see in Augsburg.

(Schneid 1891, pp. 480–81)

Finally, Eck ventured to demonstrate the validity of the contract by referring to its diffusion. "For more than 40 years," wrote Eck, "the contract has been used by the most noble men and women, scholars and burghers. This habit speaks in favour of my thesis and cannot be challenged by my adversaries" (Schneid 1891, pp. 480–81).

Eck's arguments are a clear demonstration of the *via moderna*. The goodness of an institution – an economic contract – was proved simply by referring to its positive effects on the general welfare, and such effects were measured by observation. Eck also underlined in his argumentation how the economic reality evolved; he concluded that the moral judgement of the church had to change accordingly: "We forcefully deny that everything that is unusual should be presumed bad. Where would the consequences of such an assumption lead us?" (Schneid 1891, p. 485). Furthermore, "Is everything new also bad?" (Schneid 1891, p. 492).

As "modern" as the views expressed by Eck on usury may appear today, and as revolutionary they were in the ears of his contemporaries, friends advised Eck not to stir such a question openly – not when social unrest plagued the south of Germany.[13] Pietism and humanism moved the consciences of scholars and people alike against the wealth displayed by the merchant class, particularly in Augsburg, and their defence could well cause the young theologian many troubles (Schneid 1891, pp. 573–76). However, even if he did not publish his manuscripts, Eck did not abandon the question of usury, and intended to defend his theses in public debates. At the end of his manuscript, he wrote:

> I'm used to speak freely and to call things by their names. I am convinced that the *contractus trinus* is permissible and I speak openly about it. I even consider it a moral obligation to express my belief openly and loudly, considering the practical diffusion that this contract has. That many priests assert that the truth about the *contractus trinus* should not be diffused among the population is curious ... They are priests and diffuse the Word of God, but at the same time they allow their followers to believe that something is an obligation or a prohibition, while in reality it is nothing of the sort. Only the truth will make us free.
>
> (Schneid 1891, p. 494)

True to his word, with the backing of Jacob Fugger's wealth and influence, Eck set out to defend his theses in Augsburg itself. It was not an easy feat. In the same 1514 in which Eck wrote his work on the legitimacy of *contractus trinus*, Jacob Fugger had taken from the archbishop of Mainz, in exchange of his outstanding debts, the right to collect the indulgencies, renovated by Pope Leo X, for the construction of the Dome of St Peter's in Rome. The indignation against the merchants and against the church could not have been higher, and *Fuggerei* soon became synonymous with usury: "The reformation obtained here many followers" (Roth 1901, p. 45).

Humanists, who formed the cultural elite of southern German cities, contrary to their Italian forefathers,[14] repudiated the social and economic changes caused by the spreading of trade and formed the backbone of the opposition to Eck and his theses.[15] While Tübingen and Ingolstadt would always support Eck, Nürnberg, Eichstätt and Augsburg obstructed him in every possible way (Schneid 1891, p. 578). Pirckheimer, Kress and Cochlaeus in Eichstätt, Adelmann in Augsburg and von Scheurl in Nürnberg erected a front against Eck that did not shy away from personal offences and ridicule, openly and through anonymous writings, and even resorted to slander and defamation, spreading lies through false recounts about Eck's achievements in his disputations.[16] In 1513, Willibald Pirckheimer himself had provoked all the renewed debates on usury, by translating from the Greek to Latin and publishing the essay of Plutarch, 'De usura vitanda'. Jacob Fugger's request for a scholarly counsel and Eck's writing on *contractus trinus*, completed in May 1514, were a consequence of this provocation. By the autumn of 1514, Eck could defend in Augsburg his ideas in a *disputatio de licitis usuris,* following the invitation of the Carmelites Stephanus Federicus Brixiensis and Genesio Rosano. Nothing is known about the scholarly outcome of the debate, but the reaction of the public could not be overseen. Many of those in the merchant class applauded Eck's initiative; however, many more from other classes condemned him, often with unjust and personal accusations. Since one of the falsehoods spread about this first dispute was that he had chosen Augsburg because of the cultural insignificance of the city, avoiding his own university for fear of more valiant opponents, Eck reacted by nailing down his theses in Ingolstadt in October 1514. The uproar of the public, both in favour and against Eck, was so relevant that the bishop of Eichstätt, Gabriel of Eyb, ordered to postpone the question without a date. Both the Duke of Bavaria and the university questioned the decision of the bishop and the bishop himself sought out the counsel of the universities of Mainz,[17] Wittenberg and Erfurt on the debate (Schneid 1891, pp. 661–64). Neither of the universities took the side of Eck, and Mainz openly advised against a public disputation on the question of usury. In consequence, the bishop definitively prohibited to hold the dispute at the university of Ingolstadt.

In the meantime, the question had reached Rome. The prior of the Dominican cloister of Ulm had asked the counsel of his superior in Rome, Tommaso De Vio (1469–1534), known as Thomas Cajetan or Gaetanus, on the thorny issue. On the same day that the question of the mounts of piety was resolved in favour of their legitimacy, against his opinion, Gaetanus wrote his answer on the admissibility of the *contractus trinus*. The *contractus* was acceptable, stated the famed theologian, so long as the three contracts were not stipulated at the same time.[18] Also positive was the judgement of the University of Paris, directly asked by Eck to comment on the *contractus trinus*. Given these encouragements, Eck decided to dispute his theses in Bologna, the oldest and most famous university for the studies in jurisprudence.[19] He published, in form of a letter, a recount of his journey to Italy from 19 June to 6 July 1515: a vivid testimony of the extension and functioning of the scholarly *universitas* of the Middle Ages (Eck 1515). Held on 12 July "in the temple of St Petronius in presence of the Rectors of the Theological and Juridical faculties, of the Bishop, theologians and jurists and many students" (Schneid 1891, p. 670), the debate was decided in favour of Eck and his theses were accepted by the theological faculty.

In Italy in 1515, evidently there was no difficulty in admitting the legitimacy of the *contractus trinus*, allowing the payment of interest through an easy *escamotage,* and the capabilities of Eck as a theologian were praised and appreciated. In Germany, on the contrary, humanists and theologians could not accept either Eck's views or his charisma. Surely his fellows at the University of Ingolstadt and Tübingen welcomed him warmly (Oberman 1981, p. 129). Instead, humanists in the person of Johannes Cochlaeus spread false recounts of Eck's disputation in Bologna, claiming that he had performed poorly and had been bested by his adversaries. Only the nailing down of the certificates obtained in Bologna and the intervention of Willibald Pirckheimer could dampen the polemics.[20]

Eck was still not appeased by the scarce recognition he had obtained *in patria* for the validity of the *contractus trinus*. In the summer of 1516, he travelled to Vienna to dispute the same question. The horror that the announcement of his visit instilled in the local university and all obstacles posed to an open dispute constrained Eck to change the subject of the proposed discussion so that it contained no reference to trading contracts and their legitimacy (Schneid 1891, p. 797). While, in the end, the debate brought Eck a measure of success and the respect of the local faculty, the question of usury was ignored. The Vienna disputation was the last act of Eck concerning usury and the *contractus trinus*. He further dedicated his efforts to the questions raised by Martin Luther and the defence of the Catholic Church. Yet his adversaries in the humanist camp did not cease their attacks. The booklet by Pirckheimer and Cochlaeus, *Eckius dedolatus*, printed anonymously in 1520, is a perfect example of the personal offence and ridicule that Eck was subjected to. Amidst questions about his character, the accusation was always that of defending the interests of merchants and usurers in exchange for personal gain. The stance of German universities against interest payments would not change, also, not even after the Reform. Luther and Melanchthon maintained the condemnation of usury in both their universities, Wittenberg and Erfurt. Only Calvin defended the legitimacy of interest, by using many of the same arguments as Eck.

The question remains open regarding the different outcomes resulting from the question of usury in Florence and Augsburg. Given the limited scope of this research, answers can only be tentative. While the virtues of *liberalitas* and *magnificentia* reconciled the governing merchants of Florence to the representatives of the church, this miraculous equilibrium – typical of Renaissance thought – was alien to German cities and states. The new Catholic view on the economy could not unite the interests of the different and opposing factions. Excessive taxation, corruption and the greed that seemingly united priests and merchants fuelled a widespread hatred against the Roman Church. The story of Eck is, in this sense, exemplary. His attempt to modernise the theological stance towards usury, adapting it to the changing economic reality of the commercial revolution, would be accepted and appreciated only abroad. In southern Germany, instead, he incurred in the wrath of humanists, canonists and theologians alike. Some historians blame Germany's excessive pietism for such harsh rebuke (Oberman 1981, pp. 8–9), but the explanation, as Summenhart had realised, lay more probably in the excessive taxation levied by the church on the German population over which it wielded an extensive secular power. The expansion of communal statutes had liberated Italian cities from the payment of the tithes and had granted a certain measure of freedom that was still unknown north of the Alps. The rupture there thus had to be more profound – a Reform instead of a Renaissance.

## Notes

1 The same phenomenon has also been called "the rise of capitalism" (Schumpeter 2003 [1954], pp. 97–98).
2 The first coherent theological textbook was the *Sentences*, written down in the middle of the twelfth century by Peter Lombard (Rosemann 2007). From then on, the most important theologians published commentaries on this work.
3 A first example of a comprehensive canonical textbook is the *Decretum Gratiani*, written in the first half of the twelfth century. Different versions of this text exist, showing that, in time, Roman law became part of the different canons discussed and reconciled in this fundamental legal textbook (Winroth 2004).
4 According to Nuccio, the church, as the major landholder in Europe and the greatest rentier, through its law system and moral impositions intended to maintain a society based on three orders of men: clergymen, noblemen and labourers: respectively, head, torso and inferior limbs of the *corpus societatis*. No space was reserved in this society for merchants. An English preaching book of the fourteenth century went: "God made the clergy, knights, and labourers but the Devil made burghers and usurers" (Owst 1961, pp. 553–54).
5 The case of Italy has been studied in depth in the recent past. Aside from Nuccio, see Spicciani (1990) and Todeschini (1980).
6 Schumpeter considered Saint Antoninus the first man to have had a comprehensive view of the economic process (Schumpeter 2003 [1954], p. 117); a similar opinion was expressed by Edgar Salin (2007, p. 24) and Amintore Fanfani (1933, p. 112).
7 "*Nam, ut dictum est, ad magnificentiam pertinet aliquid facere magnum, habito respectu ad res divinas vel communes, quibus debet magnificus intendere*". (Antonino da Firenze 1740–41, IV:III:V, §II, col. 86 A–B).
8 On the Fugger family and Augsburg, see Häberlein (2012).
9 The most recent and complete historiographic assessment of Johannes Eck is to be found in Bärsch & Maier (2014); see also Iserloh (1988).
10 *Tractatus de contractibus usurariis* and *Tractatus de contractu quinque de centum*, Codex manusc. N. 125. See Schneid (1891, p. 321). Versions of these manuscripts circulated widely. See, for example: Johannes Eck, *Consilium in casu quinque de Centenario*, Universitätsbibliothek Freiburg, i. Br., Hs. 601 [1r–28r], http://dl.ub.uni-freiburg.de/diglit/hs601
11 A summarisation and translation of Eck's manuscripts was written at the end of the nineteenth century by Joseph Schneid, mainly to defend Eck from the negative judgements of the historian Leopold Ranke and the economist Gustav Schmoller, who accused him of having unjustly defended the usurer (Schneid 1891).
12 The *via moderna*, started by William of Ockham (1287–1347), was introduced in German universities one century later, in the middle of the fifteenth century. There it coexisted with the *via antiqua* canonised by St Thomas.
13 See, for example, the letter written by Willibald Pirckheimer to Johannes Eck (n.d.): Nürnberg StB Pirckheimer-Papiere 234, http://ivv7srv15.uni-muenster.de/mnkg/pfnuer/Eckbriefe/N027.html

14 On the stance of early Italian humanism in respect to the new society of the commercial revolution, see Dotti (2011). Dotti himself, however, underlines how even in Italy humanism retreated from civil engagement into courtliness at the beginning of the sixteenth century.
15 Notable the exception of Konrad Peutinger (Welborn 1939). Peutinger would be the one to ask Eck, on behalf of Jakob Fugger, for an official position on the question of the legitimacy of a 5 per cent interest rate on loans. On the relationship between Eck, Peutinger and Fugger, and their common intent see the letter written by Peutinger to Eck on 19 December 1514: München BSB, Oefeliana 209 (Autograph), http://ivv7srv15.uni-muenster.de/mnkg/pfnuer/Eckbriefe/N017.html
16 Even his long-time friend Ulrich Zasius, famed jurist and humanist, would not subscribe the theses of Eck on the *contractus trinus*. He still considered it a form of usury. See the letter of Zasius to Eck of 28 February 1515, München BSB Clm 1470, fol 197r-199v, http://ivv7srv15.uni-muenster.de/mnkg/pfnuer/Eckbriefe/N020.html
17 Eck also wrote to the theological faculty of the University of Mainz to ask for an opinion on his treatise and the legitimacy of the Bishop's denial to discuss it in Ingolstadt. On the *contractus trinus* the answer was non decisive (Letter of the Theological Faculty Mainz to Eck of 10 January 1515, http://ivv7srv15.uni-muenster.de/mnkg/pfnuer/Eckbriefe/N018.html). Eck wrote similarly to the University of Tübingen: see letter by Johannes Eck to the Theological Faculty of the university of Tübingen of 10 February 11515: Tübingen UA 12/14 Nr 16 Autograph, http://ivv7srv15.uni-muenster.de/mnkg/pfnuer/Eckbriefe/N019.html
18 In opposition was the stance of the Prior of the Dominicans in Augsburg, Johann Faber, who disputed the legitimacy of the insurance part of the *contractus trinus*. Johann Faber decided to defend his positions in Bologna, and Eck followed suit.
19 See the letter by Johannes Eck to the Theological Faculty of the University of Bologna of 1 May 1515: "*Magnum semper fuit mihi desiderium, venerandi patres et praeceptores, Italiam tantopere celebratam invisere, quamvis commode votorum meorum hactenus compos fieri nequiverim. At cum modo Ioannes Faber vicarius apud nos Sancti Dominici, vir sane eruditus, propositiones quasdam publicaverit apud praestantias vestras in Iulio disputandas, occasionem nactus videor commodiorem, quo mea fruar sententia. Itaque decrevi me eo tempore velle ad Bononiam studiorum matrem conferre*" (Eck 1515, http://ivv7srv15.uni-muenster.de/mnkg/pfnuer/Eckbriefe/N021.html
20 See the letter by Willibald Pirckheimer to Johannes Eck (n.d.).

# References

Antonino da Firenze: *Summa theologica*, I–IV. Verona: Typographia Seminarii, 1740–41.
Armstrong, Lawrin: Law, Ethics and Economy: Gerard of Siena and Giovanni d'Andrea on Usury. In: L. Armstrong, I. Elbl & M.M. Elbl (eds): *Money, Markets and Trade in Late Medieval Europe: Essays in Honour of John H.A. Munro*. Leiden: Brill, pp. 41–58, 2007.
Armstrong, Lawrin: *The Idea of a Moral Economy: Gerard of Siena on Usury, Restitution, and Prescription*. Toronto: University of Toronto Press, 2016.
Baldwin, John W.: The Medieval Theories of the Just Price: Romanists, Canonists, and Theologians in the Twelfth and Thirteenth Centuries. *Transactions of the American Philosophical Society*, New Series, 49(4), pp. 1–92, 1959.

Barile, Nicola: Credito, usura, prestito a interesse. In: *Reti Medievali Rivista*, 11(1), pp. 475–505, 2010.
Bärsch, Jürgen; Maier, Konstantin (eds): *Johannes Eck 1486–1543: Scholastiker – Humanist – Kontroverstheologe*. Regensburg: Friedrich Pustet, 2014.
Bazzichi, Oreste: *Dall'usura al giusto profitto. L'etica economica della scuola Francescana*. Roma: Effatà, 2011.
De Roover, Raymond: The Concept of the Just Price: Theory and Economic Policy. *The Journal of Economic History*, 18(4), pp. 418–34, 1958.
De Roover, Raymond: *Il banco Medici dalle origini al declino (1397–1494)*. Firenze: La Nuova Italia Editrice, 1970.
Dotti, Ugo: *La rivoluzione incompiuta*. Torino: Aragno, 2011.
Eck, Johann: *Avdi Lector Joannis Eckij orationes accipe tres non inelegantes*. Augsburg: Miller, 1515.
Fanfani, Amintore: *Origini dello spirito capitalistico in Italia*. Milano: Vita e Pensiero, 1933.
Friedberger, Walter: *Der Reichtumserwerb im Urleil des Hl. Thomas von Aquin und der Theologen im Zeitalter des Frühkapilalismus*. Passau: Passavia, 1967.
Häberlein, Mark: *The Fuggers of Augsburg: Pursuing Wealth and Honor in Renaissance Germany*. Charlottesville, VA: University of Virginia Press, 2012.
Hartmann, Wilfried & Pennington, Kenneth (eds): *The History of Medieval Canon Law in the Classical Period, 1140–1234: From Gratian to the Decretals of Pope Gregory IX*. Washington, DC: Catholic University of America Press, 2008.
Howard, Peter: Preaching Magnificence in Renaissance Florence. Renaissance *Quarterly*, 61(2), pp. 325–69, 2004.
Iserloh, Erwin (ed.): *Johannes Eck (1486–1543) im Streit der Jahrhunderte*. Münster: Aschendorff, 1988.
Johnston, Herbert: On the Meaning of "Consumed in Use" in the Problem of Usury. *The Modern Schoolman*, 30, pp. 93–108, 1953.
Kerridge, Eric: *Usury, Interest and the Reformation*. Aldershot: Ashgate, 2002.
Kirshner, Julius: From Usury to Public Finance: The Ecclesiastical Controversy Over the Public Debts of Florence, Genoa and Venice 1300–1500. PhD thesis, Columbia University, 1970.
Langholm, Odd: *Economics in the Medieval Schools: Wealth, Exchange, Value, Money and Usury according to the Paris Theological Tradition, 1200–1350*. Leiden: Brill, 1992.
Langholm, Odd: *The Merchant in the Confessional: Trade and Price in the Pre-Reformation Penitential Handbooks*. Leiden: Brill, 2003.
Nuccio, Oscar: *Il pensiero economico italiano: le fonti (1050–1450). L'etica laica e la formazione dello spirito economico*. Sassari: Gallizzi, 1984.
Oberman, Heiko Augustinus: *Masters of the Reformation the Emergence of a New Intellectual Climate in Europe*. NewYork: Cambridge University Press, 1981.
Ott, Hugo: Zur Wirtschaftsethik des Konrad Summenhart ca. 1455–1502. *Vierteljahrschrift für Sozial- und Wirtschaftsgeschichte*, 53(1), pp. 1–27, 1966.
Owst, Gerald Robert: *Literature and Pulpit in Medieval England: A Neglected Chapter in the History of English letters and of the English People*. London: Basil Blackwell, 1961.
Poettinger, Monika: *Mercante e società: riflessioni di storia comparata*. Lugano: Casagrande, 2012.
Quaglioni, Diego, Todeschini, Giacomo & Varanini, Gian Maria (eds): *Credito e usura fra teologia, diritto e amministrazione: linguaggi a confronto (sec. XII-XVI)*. Roma: École française de Rome, 2005.

Rosemann, Philipp W.: *The Story of a Great Medieval Book: Peter Lombard's "Sentences"*. Toronto: University of Toronto Press, 2007.
Roth, Friedrich: *Augsburgs Reformationsgeschichte*. München: Theodor Ackermann, 1901.
Salin, Edgar: *Geschichte der Volkswirtschaftslehre*. Berlin: Springer Verlag, 2007.
Schlecht, Joseph: Dr. Johann Ecks Anfange. *Historisches Jahrbuch,* 36, pp. 1–36, 1915.
Schneid, Joseph: Dr. Johann Eck und das kirchliche Zinsverbot. *Historisch-politische Blätter für das katholische Deutschland*, l(108), pp. 241–59, 321–35, 473–496, 570–89, 659–81, 789–810, 1891.
Schumpeter, Joseph A.: *Storia dell'Analisi Economica, Vol. I*. Torino: Bollati Boringhieri, 2003 [1954].
Spicciani, Amleto: *Capitale e interesse tra mercatura e povertà nei teologi e canonisti dei secoli XIII-XV*. Roma: Jouvence, 1990.
Todeschini, Giacomo: *Un trattato di economia politica francescana: il "De emptionibus et venditionibus, de usuris, de restitutionibus" di Pietro di Giovanni Olivi*. Roma: Istituto Storico Italiano per il Medio Evo, 1980.
Welborn, Mary Catherine: An Intellectual Father of Modern Business. *Bulletin of the Business Historical Society*, 13(2), pp. 20–24, 1939.
Winroth, Anders: *The Making of Gratian's Decretum*. New York: Cambridge University Press, 2004.
Wurm, Johann Peter: *Johannes Eck und der oberdeutsche Zinsstreit*. Münster: Aschendorff, 1997.

# 9 From Kaspar Klock's "De aerario" (1651) and Leibniz's "Meditatio de interusurio simplice" to Florencourt's "Abhandlungen aus der juristischen und der politischen Rechenkunst" (1781)

How calculus led from the logic of a device for circumventing the prohibition of usury to a modern theory of depreciation

*Bertram Schefold*

### Economic knowledge: A factor of development?

Economic knowledge is a factor of economic development not only in modern times; it has also been one in the past (Schefold 2017). We here consider the example of interest-taking. Debtors could be crushed by the obligation to pay interest, and so authorities tried fixed ceilings on interest rates, forbade compound interest (charging compound interest was called *anatocism*) or, earlier, tried to eradicate what was felt to be usury altogether. But, as I shall now try to demonstrate, the result was paradoxical in that the discussions surrounding the prohibition of interest led to conceptual advances that, in the end, proved fruitful both for theory and practice. Similar observations could be made regarding the discussions of monopoly and competition, and especially taxation. I here concentrate on interest because of the paradoxical nature of the example. Elsewhere (Schefold 2011b), I have traced the path from late medieval discussions on usury via the scholastic discourse, especially of the School of Salamanca, to mercantilism and cameralism. When contractual loans replace the help by relatives and friends in emergencies, social tensions arise – but so do opportunities for investment. Often, as in old China, the gentry tends to look down on money-making as a private business. But the Abrahamite religions, the ancient Greeks and the Romans were not content with a disdain for merchants and their kind; they denounced usury in particular and Aristotle attempted to prove that it was unnatural. The early church associated usury with greed, but Gregory IX, Pope

DOI: 10.4324/9780367434496-14

from 1227 to 1241, defined it more narrowly (Corpus Iuris Canonici 1881; V, xix, 19) and Thomas (Aquinas 1968, quaestio 78) synthesised the biblical and the Aristotelian philosophical arguments at a time when the credit economy was on the rise in the Italian cities. Of the arguments then found to show why interest could be licit after all, in a discussion that culminated in the writings of the School of Salamanca and with Lessius, we here mention only *periculum sortis* (risk) and *lucrum cessans* (profit foregone, opportunity cost). Both evolved over the centuries. Risk, which for Gregory had not counted as an excuse, became an element of insurance costs (Goetzmann 2017) and opportunity cost led to the view that capital was productive of a profit (Olivi 2012 [1293]). It prepared for the insight that there is a rate of profit tending to uniformity. While the continuity is difficult to establish in the case of mercantilism (De Roover 1955), it is easy to prove in the case of cameralism (Schefold 2018b). Hence our focus will be on Kaspar Klock, a major representative of the older cameralists, for Klock documented how well he was acquainted with the writings of the School of Salamanca. As a conscientious person he still pondered the traditional arguments against usury, but as a lawyer he had to consider the legal limits on interest taking. We thus observe a new departure within cameralism. "Calculating jurists" appeared – here we take the examples of Leibniz and Florencourt – who used the conceptual framework created in the usury debate not to denounce interest-taking, but to calculate problems of valuation that occur in business, such as determining depreciation. The ethical and normative evaluation of interest-taking was thus replaced with a positive analysis that would – and eventually did – serve development.

## Kaspar Klock on usury

Klock (1583–1655) is considered as the main founder of the economics of public finance in the German realm in the first half of the sixteenth century (Mann 1937; Stein 1884; Vecchiato 1977). His vast *De aerario* (Klock 2009 [1651]) was widely read all over Europe; it contained a world survey of the relationships between the economy, public finance and the natural, social and historical conditions in major nations and colonies on the known continents, combined with a textbook of cameralist teachings of these matters. Mercantilism and cameralism meant state building, according to Schmoller (1967 [1884]), but a specific contribution of cameralism was to create the language for the new sciences of the state (Krauth 1984; Tribe 1988). Klock in particular used scholastic teachings to identify which forms of taxation were instrumental at which stage of development (Schefold 2009, pp. lxxix–lxxxvii).

He was a Protestant – not a Calvinist, but a Lutheran. The prosperity of the Netherlands impressed him, and is often mentioned in his work. He lived under more primitive conditions in Germany, devastated by the war and almost ruined. Usury is dealt with in Chapter 19 of his second book. It is an evil ("*malum*") to be contained and prohibited, but the usurers always find new techniques ("*artes novas*", book two, XIX, 1) to circumvent prohibitions. Interest-taking is clearly against the law of nature, for nothing originates from nothing ("*foenerandi ratio ... planè contra naturae regulam, cùm ex nihilo nihil gignatur*", book two, XIX, 5). The primary new techniques are the purchase of rents ("*venditiones redituum*"), anticipated purchases ("*locationes fructuum*" – the merchant buys the fruits of agriculture prior to the harvest) and contracts to buy and resell ("*venditiones cum pacto de retrovendendo*" – the creditor provides money to the debtor by buying something from him and agreeing on the spot to resell the good to him after some time at a higher price, the higher price reflecting interest). Klock, who is progressive on taxation – for example, by anticipating Adam Smith's saying that indirect taxes are an imposition on income – is conservative on usury. He complains that for every law prohibiting usurious techniques, there is a new fraud. But usury is to be demanded from one's enemy, not from one's neighbour. The belief is that helping the helpless by giving them credit is like giving wine to the sick: the sick will get some immediate relief, but will soon feel worse.

Klock argues his critique of usury at three levels. There is the level of tradition. As elsewhere in his book, he takes up the heritage of antiquity and the Middle Ages. There is no need for us to follow him in this and to repeat his quotations from Cato and other Roman authors. The second level is sociological. The usurer is described as one sitting at home (book two, XIX, p. 19), waiting for the calamities that must befall others so they will need his money. The usurer is anxious to lend out all his fortune. If he succeeds, he lives – like the Apostles – without money in his hands, but not for altruistic reasons. At the third level, Klock returns to the sources and restates that the Bible commands to provide loans without demanding interest (the well-known "*mutuum date nihil inde sperantes*", book two, XIX, pp. 49–51). The distinctions made by the scholastic authors, like "*damnum emergens* and *lucrum cessans*" (book two, XIX, p. 66), are mentioned – Klock knows them well – but they are vain. What now ultimately matters is the law: there are legally accepted rates of interest of 5 per cent or 4 per cent, which have been defended by different authors, among them the School of Salamanca. To this extent, interest-taking must be tolerated. If more is demanded, the prince must intervene.

In order to demonstrate that his approach is manageable, Klock derives criteria when a contract involving selling and reselling is to be regarded as usurious. It is likely to be usurious if the difference in price is large. A suspicion arises if the creditor has customarily acted as usurer. The most interesting case seems to be the antichretic contract, to which we shall return when we discuss Florencourt. Instead of paying interest, the borrower of a sum of money gives a pawn to the lender that bears fruit, like a field or cattle. The lender retains what he can get from using the pawn and returns it in the end, if it has not been used up, while the borrower returns the capital, if it has not yet been amortised through the revenues from the pawn. (The antichretic contract can be combined with a contract for selling and reselling, the "*pactum de retrovendendo*", mentioned above.) Klock introduces several variants of the contract. Is the profit of the lender legal, even if it exceeds what would correspond to legal interest? That is a nice problem, says Klock ("*pulchrae indaginis quaestio est*", book two, XIX, p. 41). There has to be a just price for the pawn. The rate of interest implied by the return derived from the use of the pawn (and possibly from the difference in the prices at which the pawn is exchanged) should not exceed the legal rate. It is also an indication of usury if the creditor can demand to resell at a given date or at his pleasure, and Klock's final conclusion is that antichretic contracts are not really licit, even if they are legal, because the implied interest rate is sufficiently low.

In substance, therefore, Klock insists on the simplicity of the Christian command not to take interest. He tolerates moderate interest, accepts legal interest from the legal point of view and deplores forms of usury that seem to him predatory. Eventually, he seeks practical solutions in the context of a book that is concerned mainly with taxation. He therefore warns against introducing draconic laws against usurers, as has often been done, and advises fining usurers for the benefit of the treasury. Practical proposals in later chapters then also include the introduction of state pawnshops ("*montes pietates*"), and a discussion of state borrowing – to introduce new borrowing is simpler than to impose new taxes. It does not occur to him to calculate the interest rate implied by the antichretic contract – that would be achieved only later by Florencourt. The German jurist David Mevius, Swedish councillor and high judge in Wismar, acknowledged half a century later that the *Contractus antichreticus* was not usurious as such, that it had become very frequent and legitimised (Mevius 1710, p. 51), provided that "der Abnutz die Zinnsen gar zu weit nicht übertrifft" ("the use does not exceed the interests too much", translated by Bertram Schefold). Such vague distinctions could be developed into precise criteria only by interdisciplinary work. We shall see in the next section how the outstanding genius of interdisciplinarity of the seventeenth century did this for a related problem.

## Leibniz: The anti-critique of usury in mathematical disguise

The great Leibniz (1646–1716), two generations younger than Klock, was a truly universal scholar – philosopher, scientist, mathematician, historian, jurist. He is so well known that it seems superfluous to insert a biographical note about him, but Roscher's (1874, pp. 329–39) characterisation of Leibniz's cameralist activities shows his potential as an economist, and it may be recalled in this book that he was also a great admirer of China (Li & Poser 2000). Leibniz still operated with the terminology created by theologians and jurists in the usury debate, but he used it to quantify complex problems so as to defend tools that eventually would serve business transactions. He wrote a *"Meditatio juridico-mathematica de interusurio simplice"* (Leibniz 1962 [1863, 1683]). *Interusurium* meant a rebate: the borrower is supposed to pay a debt (D) a year from now. If the debtor pays today, with the consent of the creditor, he can demand a rebate, which we would calculate as follows, given an interest rate (i): the unknown sum to be paid (R) could be lent at interest and would increase to D after one year, if $R(1+i) = D$. Hence the rebate is the present value of D, discounted at interest i, and

$$R = D/(1+i).$$

But Leibniz proceeds as follows: If the debtor now did not pay R, but the full D, he really would have paid too much, insofar as the creditor could now get interest on D for one year. The creditor therefore would, at the end of the year, owe iD to the debtor, but both want to settle the matter now. Therefore, if iD is paid by the creditor to the debtor now, the creditor has compensated the debtor, but by too much, since iD was due only after one year but is paid now, hence the debtor in turn owes $i^2$ per unit of the debt to the creditor. And so the two can go on paying each other what would be due in a year, anticipating that by paying now and paying compensation for the anticipation. As a result, the sum owed now is equal to $D(1-i+i^2-i^3+i^4...)$, a geometric series, which is equal – as is obvious to us and as Leibniz shows mathematically – to $D/(1+i)$.

What is the point of this excessively complex exercise? It looks even more bewildering to the modern reader, since Leibniz's notation is different from the one here employed; the inverse of the interest rate is used and the abstract reasoning is mixed with numerical examples. Leibniz himself, after having made these calculations and having extended them to several years, with the result that the infinite series get considerably more complicated, admits that one could also have started from the consideration with which we began: one treats the rebate as an unknown, and R is determined from $(1+i)R = D$. Leibniz says that he prefers his more complicated calculation because it avoids unknowns. This does not seem convincing to the modern reader, and it may be that Leibniz simply wanted to display his skill at operating with infinite series, especially in the case of several years. Leibniz was not the first to analyse the *Interusurium* mathematically – for a historical account of his predecessors, see Bortkiewicz (1907), who takes great care to verify Leibniz's formulas for the discounting over several years that involve combinatorial computations of coefficients, at which Leibniz was a master. Unusual is the sophistication of this derivation. But the historical significance seems to me in the fact that Leibniz thus bypasses traditional obstacles in the usury debate.

Suppose that the entire sum D is paid now without rebate. Then the creditor gets in effect more than what is due to him and the debtor has lent to the creditor. Interest therefore is not a one-sided exaction by which the creditor impoverishes the debtor, but a rebate means that both must compensate each other mutually and can demand interest from each other; the one-sided relationship becomes bilateral and symmetric. The repeated compensation also seems to be a step towards the recognition that compound interest here is licit. Finally, Leibniz explicitly says that interest paid becomes capital in this process of compensation, and this, too, is – or can be interpreted as – a move against the prohibition of compound interest (*anatocism*): the repeated mutual granting of simple interest amounts to the same thing.

But Leibniz surprises us and asserts explicitly that compound interest is not involved: "*Itaque usurae exactae ... non nisi vocabulum commune habent cum usuris usurarum non salutarum, quae legibus prohibentur*" ('So the interests obtained … have nothing except the word in common with compound interest, which is unsound and prohibited by law', translated by Bertram Schefold). The laws against the taking of compound interest have varied since Roman times.[1] They traditionally have one purpose in common: that the debtor shall be protected from a crushing accumulation of debt. Now this problem simply does not apply here, since it is the creditor who gets less in the form of the advanced payment.

Knobloch (2017, p. 23) thinks that Leibniz's method to discount over several years does not reveal why the objection that compound interest is involved should not be justified, and he quotes from a manuscript by Leibniz himself: 'It is therefore a question why I can demand interest on interest payments that I make before the debt is due and why I cannot demand interest on interest that you did not pay to me in time' (translated by Bertram Schefold). In other words, why is compound interest licit if the debt is paid ahead of time, but not if the debt is paid late? Leibniz does not provide an explicit answer to this question in his published paper, but he eliminates the asymmetry with his infinite series of alternating anticipated payments. Leibniz's paper on the rebate thus is a nice piece of early modern mathematics, but the interpretation is unclear.

An answer can be found in the splendid publication *Gottfried Wilhelm Leibniz: Hauptschriften zur Versicherungs- und Finanzmathematik* (Leibniz 2000). Leibniz's paper is presented together with more than 20 drafts, letters and notes by him, most of which are here printed for the first time. They prove that Leibniz was concerned with the mathematical problem of finding the correct formula for the rebate and with the juridical puzzles that arose simultaneously in this context. Rebates mattered not only when a personal debt was paid before it was due, but also in the context of auctions. Who had won, if one bidder offered a certain sum of money now and another a bigger sum, but promised for a later date in a public auction? Leibniz polemicises in the drafts against authors who used patently erroneous formulas for the rebate and admits:

> Hence it is obvious that the rebate does not flow together out of the interests of the postponed sum, as some believe, but out of the interests of the sum which is to be paid instead, if one anticipates it into the present. It is also clear that the latter sum is equal to the anatocism – if I may put it that way – of its present value.
> Translated by Bertram Schefold (Leibniz 2000, p. 160)

This means that the debt owed is equal to the present value plus the compound interest on it. But Leibniz hesitates to introduce this denomination. Most drafts contain a defence of the prohibition of compound interest, as he understands the phenomenon: "*anatocismus legibus prohibitus est proprie in odium creditorum et in favorem debitorum*" (Leibniz 2000, p. 162). "*Anatocism* is properly forbidden to the disfavour of the creditors and in favour of the debtors" (translated by Bertram Schefold).

For otherwise the interest owed by the borrowers would accumulate and the creditors could live in idleness. The borrowers "fall asleep" because of the silence of the creditors. It is in the interest of the state to induce the creditors to disturb the borrowers and to collect the interests regularly, so the borrowers feel the discomfort of being in debt and try to get rid of it gradually. Here, Leibniz returns to a quasi-theological discussion, for the earlier prohibition of usury was not strict, but a matter of degrees (compare p. 248 for an explicit reference to the Fathers of the Church). The poor borrower, who is in need of financial support, should be seen with compassion; that is why pawnbroking shops have been introduced and are publicly supported. The case of the rebate is quite different. Compound interest here favours the borrower, not the creditor. This seems to me the main insight that has been missed by later interpreters like Bortkiewicz, who were interested in the mathematical logic but not in the moral and juridical justification of Leibniz's position.

Leibniz further defends his point of view in a letter to Christoph Pfautz (Leibniz 2000, p. 242), written after the publication. He clarifies that it would suffice to say that traditional jurisdiction (*"jura recepta"*) only prohibits "later" interests, while the prohibition of the "later case" cannot be extended to the "earlier" case unless a reason is provided for the extension. Leibniz thus denies that the mathematical derivation of the rebate involves compound interest in this proper sense of the term (Leibniz 2000, p. 254), and he discusses the problem that words and definitions for this distinction are missing (Leibniz 2000, p. 243). The social and ethical norms here involved are much the same as in the earlier drafts. He deplores that Justinian prohibited compound interest in too broad terms, without adequate distinctions, which he believes now to have made (Leibniz 2000, p. 298).

## The mathematical jurists and Florencourt

Carl Chassot de Florencourt (1756–90), student of mathematics, later professor of philosophy in Göttingen, author of a book on mining in antiquity, of French descent, was employed in the German mining industry (Dukedom of Braunschweig) as Kammer- und Bergrath (councillor for financial matters and mining). His book (Florencourt 1781) contains numerous applications of mathematics to legal and economic problems, including population, probability theory and insurance, and it is interesting because it links problems typical for mercantilism (which, as we saw, in turn had medieval roots) with the then modern approach. And so Florencourt defends Leibniz's treatment of *Interusurium*. He mentions the prohibition of compound interest (Florencourt 1781, p. 8), but he also reports that the discounting formula (Florencourt 1781, p. 10) has been made legal in the Electorate of Saxony (Florencourt 1781, p. 18). He refers to Leibniz's paper, which we discussed in the preceding section, with his reasoning for the present value R of a debt D:

$$R = D\left(1 - i + i^2 - i^3 + i^4 \ldots\right) = D / \left(1 + i\right),$$

however calculating, like Leibniz, with the inverse of the rate of interest i (p.11).

Like Leibniz, he regards the use of compound interest in the case of the rebate as something different from *anatocism* (Florencourt 1781, p. 10). He finds cases where the law actually prescribes the use of compound interest (e.g. if a tutor manages the inheritance of a ward). His brilliant ability at transforming practical problems into calculations of compound interest and compound growth rates (e.g. of population) let him translate the traditional theological and juridical conceptions into practical economic notions. An example is the following text, which leads us back to the antichretic contract:

> *Antichretischer Vertrag … Er ist dann vorhanden, wenn der Schuldner dem Gläubiger, eine nutzbare Sache, auf eine gewisse Zeit übergiebt, sie gehörig zu nutzen, damit der Gläubiger, wegen des Verlustes am Nutzen seines Capitals, den der Schuldner zieht, entschädigt werde* (p. 35).
>
> English translation: Antichretic contract. … An antichretic contract exists, if the borrower delivers a useful thing to the lender for a certain time, so that the lender may use it to compensate the loss of the utility of his capital, which the borrower gets in his place.

As we saw, this was much discussed by scholastic and cameralist authors; we studied the example of Kaspar Klock above. Today, the antichresis might be called a "swap" or a "lease". The antichresis was discussed often in late scholasticism as one of the constructs in order to bypass the prohibition of usury. Since the swap can take place without an explicit and open calculation of interest taking on either side, usury could here be concealed perfectly.

In fact, such swaps may have existed long before the concept of interest rates was developed. Florencourt, by contrast, being a self-conscious pioneer of enlightenment, calculates openly with interest and compound interest. He assumes at first that the yearly revenue S derived from the useful thing in the hand of the lender is constant; the capital lent is C. The contract lasts n years. The lender gets S at the end of each year; the "utility", as Florencourt puts it, then is (using modern notation)

$$\left(1+(1+i)+\ldots+(1+i)^{n-1}\right)S = \frac{(1+i)^n - 1}{i}S,$$

while the capital lent C "has risen to" $(1+i)^n$ C. Hence what one gets from the other is

$$(1+i)^n C - \frac{(1+i)^n - 1}{i}S = M.$$

And Florencourt adds (Florencourt 1781, p. 35): "If M is positive, the lender gets it; if it is negative, the borrower." The transfer of M renders the swap just and licit at the legal interest rate. Although compound interest appears in the calculation, "many jurists assume that no forbidden *anatocism* here is involved" (Florencourt 1781, p. 37).

Florencourt discusses various applications. One can ask how long the contract should last if M is zero. One then gets the formula for the amortisation of a debt in n years:

$$S = \frac{i(1+i)^n}{(1+i)^n - 1} C \quad (F)$$

and, using logarithms, one can solve for n, as Florencourt does (Florencourt 1781, p. 37). In another application, the pawn provided in the swap for capital borrowed is land, but then the annual return S is perhaps not constant. Florencourt suggests taking averages in this case. He regards an "arithmetical average" as "fairly sure" (Florencourt 1781, p. 36).

A modern reader here feels to be on familiar ground: (F) then represents not bank credit, not land, but a machine of constant efficiency and a finite lifetime n which depreciates. S is the amortisation of the machine; it comprises the interest on the value of the machine as capital and depreciation.

The formula (F) had been known as an expression for the capital value of a series of yearly monetary payments S at rate of interest i, but the connection with depreciation and amortisation of equipment – Florencourt stands in between – seems not always to have been understood even in the early twentieth century. Passow (1912, p. 367), in a survey of accounting of 1912, was content with the vague statement: "In the calculation of rates of depreciation the desire is decisive to distribute the costs deriving from the depreciation of the corresponding equipment as equally as possible over all periods during which this equipment is used" (translated by Bertram Schefold). Sraffa (1960), when discussing (F), refers to the "handbooks of commercial arithmetic" as texts in which amortisation is explained in the case of constant efficiency and, we may suppose, in financial contexts. Apparently,[2] Sraffa primarily had two books in mind: the *Doctrine of Interest and Annuities* by Francis Baily (1808) and *Arithmetical Books* by de Morgan (1847). Baily's book is much less varied and less sophisticated in the applications than the earlier Chassot de Florencourt. Many numerical examples render it more difficult to identify the underlying theoretical ideas. The other book is a rich collection of references to books on commercial arithmetic, published in Great Britain and on the continent, but Chassot de Florencourt is missing.

Schneider (2001, p. 132) classifies Florencourt's book as political arithmetic of the eighteenth century. The book contains an introduction by Abraham Gotthelf Kästner, astronomer and professor of geometry in Göttingen. He was the teacher of Friedrich Gauss and is still known as a historian of mathematics.

He recommends Florencourt's book as a piece of *"juristische Mathematik"* ("juridical mathematics"). He uses the opportunity to praise Leibniz's achievement and mentions other works in this field. Today, many jurists profess to abhor mathematics. It seems to us that juridical mathematics were, if not necessary, then at least a useful and logical step in the development that brings together theoretical and practical reasoning in the cameralist period.

Schneider (1981, p. 337) shows that formula (F) was used (in an older notation) in 1822 by von Oeynhausen in an industrial application, based on a consistent observation of Leibniz's method to calculate compound interest. An increasing rationalisation in the consideration of depreciation was furthered by the experiences of railway companies with the wear and tear of rails in the course of the nineteenth century (Littleton 1933, pp. 223–41; see also Pollard 1963). Max Weber regarded accounting as an essential trait of modern "rational" capitalism, but he did not really grasp how competition determines the value of "capital" (Schefold 2011a).

## An intercultural comparison and conclusion

We thus have found that there is a continuity between the seemingly only ideological discussions of the Middle Ages and the formation of elements of modern economic theory, which has led us from the scholastic discussion between theologians and jurists to cameralism. Whereas the precursors of British mercantilism in late mediaeval thought are difficult to identify in the case of the British mercantilists, the continuity is obvious and striking in the case of continental cameralism, where ample quotes show that cameralists learnt about matters of theory and policy from the major figures of the School of Salamanca. We showed this by means of the work of Kaspar Klock. There resulted a structuring of problems of usury by jurisprudence such that the expression "mathematical jurist" – today a rather rare species – seems to have been a common expression. With the help of mathematics that had advanced in the natural sciences, tools were now forged for business accounting that helped to render the discussion about interest-taking more objective. These same techniques were also used in the theory of value in the classical period, and were inherited by neoclassicals. This continuity finally may also help to convince us that the development of economic knowledge is not indifferent for economic history. The systematic use of these commercial techniques is an expression of that growth of rationality which, at least according to Max Weber (esp. Weber 1924) constitutes the essence of modern capitalism and caused it to originate in Western Europe.

This was not the case in other countries, however, where other rationalities prevailed. Weber spent the last years of his life on their study; we can present an example. So, we end with an intercultural comparison. Traditional China was an agricultural country where the family possession of land was divided between the sons so that small-scale holdings prevailed, as in France, where there was no primogeniture either. Small-scale proprietors are the typical victims of usury. The money-lender, who does not easily find new customers ready to borrow at high interest rates, will wait and let the unpaid interest accumulate until he feels that the total debt approaches the value of the remaining property of the debtor, then he will try to seize it. We may interpret the prohibition of compound interest in Europe, following Leibniz, as an attempt to limit the accumulation of debts so as to give a chance to the debtor to recover. The bankruptcy laws are there to complement the precautionary prohibition of *anatocism*. The antichretic contract also led to such concerns. Was in this case not the lender in danger of consuming his capital, if he received a yearly amortisation? Florencourt (1781, p. 39) remained unmoved by this argument; he regarded both the lender and the borrower as responsible for their actions.

Now for the intercultural comparison. Jamieson (1921, section 149) renders the law on the maximum rate of interest and limitations on interest-taking at the time of the Qing dynasty as follows:

> The interest on borrowed money or on loans made by Pawnbrokers on goods pledged shall not exceed 3 per cent per month, and arrears of interest cannot be recovered to an amount exceeding the principal ...
>
> If debts are not paid at the stipulated period the defaulter is liable according to the amount to a penalty not exceeding 100 strokes, and shall still be required to repay the money. If the creditor instead of applying to the Court proceeds to seize the cattle or property of the debtor he shall be liable to 80 strokes, but if he has not seized more in value than the amount due for principal and interest, he may redeem the penalty by the corresponding fine. If he seizes more in value than is due, the surplus shall be deemed malversation and will subject him to the corresponding penalty up to 100 blows and 3 years banishment. He shall also be required to refund the amount misappropriated ...

These paragraphs illustrate beautifully how Chinese criminal law circumscribes, as by a circle, everything that is allowed inside by prohibiting what is illegal outside, and the details of the criminal law reduce the needs for having prescriptions of civil law apart from custom and mores. The maximum legal rate of interest had to be high on account of the risks involved. John Francis Davis, once Governor of Hong Kong, described these risks, comparing Chinese and British legislation on interest on the basis of direct observations in the 1830s. Instead of the rule of forbidding compound interest, we here find another: that the total of accumulated interest debts shall in no case exceed the principal. "The offspring must not be greater than the mother" (Davis 1836, p. 396). It is left to debtor and creditor to decide how much debt may accumulate with interest remaining unpaid up to those limits, but if they are exceeded, it is no longer a matter of private judgement, as the state intervenes with punishment. Beating the culprits is cheaper than keeping them in a prison maintained at public expense. It is interesting that the creditor here is punished as well if he fails to intervene once the debt becomes excessive, and further regulations state that he is also to be penalised if he takes the relatives of the debtor in some form of bondage.

The clarity and simplicity of such prescriptions may have helped to let the Chinese empire appear as wisely ordered to European observers in the seventeenth or eighteenth centuries, but less admiration was expressed in the nineteenth century, when it was felt that these foundations were inadequate for modernisation. Instead of denouncing interest in principle, the Chinese limited the accumulation of debt by simple means that allowed pre-modern prosperity to develop. Interest appeared as something more problematic and complex in the European agrarian and artisan economy for entirely spiritual reasons. More thought then had to be devoted to legitimising interest-taking, where the prohibitions were based on prejudice, and that led to more complex constructions, such as the idea that capital, and not just labour, might be productive. There followed a progressive separation of morals, based on theology, from civil law. Finally, specific applications such as the *Interusurium* or rebate and amortisation were developed and the normative discourse on interest-taking was transformed gradually into a founding stone of economic theory. Ethical norms imposed by authority became equilibrium conditions controlled by the market.

## Notes

1 There is still a law against compound interest in Germany (BGB § 248). One of the exceptions involves an asymmetry: banks pay compound interest on deposits, while an ordinary debtor does not. The commentators say that compound interest is excluded when a contract is made in order to render the obligation of the debtor clear (MüKoBGB/Grundmann, 4th ed. 2003, BGB 248 Rn1). This cryptic explanation probably refers back to a more archaic explanation of the prohibition of compound interest, which we shall discover in an earlier version of Leibniz's paper.
2 I owe this information to Heinz Kurz.

## References

Aquinas, Thomas: *Sancti Thomae Aquinatis Ordinis Praedicatorum Summa Theologiae III, Secunda secundae, cura fratrum eiusdem ordinis*. Madrid: Biblioteca de autores cristianos, 1968.

Baily, Francis: *The Doctrine of Interest and Annuities Analytically Investigated and Explained, Together with Several Useful Tables Connected with the Subject*. London: John Richardson, 1808.

Bortkiewicz, Ladislaus von: Wie Leibniz die Diskontierungsformel begründete. In: G. Adler et al. (eds): *Festgaben für Wilhelm Lexis zur siebzigsten Wiederkehr seines Geburtstages*. Jena: F. Fischer, pp. 59–96, 1907.

Corpus Iuris Canonici, Pars Secunda: In: Emil Ludwig Richter & Emil Friedberg (eds), *Decretalium Collectiones. Decretales Gregorii papae IX*. Leipzig, 1881.

Davis, John Francis: *A General Description of the Empire of China and Its Inhabitants, Vol. 2*. New York: Harper, 1836.

De Roover, Raymond: Scholastic Economics: Survival and Lasting Influence from the Sixteenth Century to Adam Smith. *The Quarterly Journal of Economics,* 69, pp. 161–90, 1955.

Florencourt Chassot de, Carl: *Abhandlungen aus der juristischen und politischen Rechenkunst*. Altenburg: Richterische Buchhandlung, 1781.
Glück, Christian Friedrich von: *Ausführliche Erläuterung der Pandecten nach Hellfeld. Ein Kommentar*. Ein und zwanzigsten Theils erste Abtheilung, 2nd ed. Erlangen: Palm, 1845.
Goetzmann, William N.: *Money Changes Everything. How Finance Made Civilization Possible*. Princeton, NJ: Princeton University Press, 2017.
Jamieson, G.: *Chinese Family and Commercial Law*. Shanghai: Kelly and Walsh, 1921.
Klock, Kaspar: *De aerario*. Hildesheim: Olms, 2009 [1651].
Knobloch, Eberhard: Finanzen und Versicherungen – Leibniz' mathematisches Modell des menschlichen Lebens. In: *Gottfried Wilhelm Leibniz (1646–1716) Akademievorlesungen Februar–März 2016*. Hamburg: Hamburg University Press, pp. 13–40, 2017.
Krauth, Wolf-Hagen: *Wirtschaftsstruktur und Semantik. Wissenschaftliche Studien zum wirtschaftlichen Denken in Deutschland zwischen dem 13. und 17. Jahrhundert*. Berlin: Duncker & Humblot, 1984.
Leibniz, Gottfried Wilhelm: Meditatio juridico – mathematica de interusurio simplice. In: V. C: Gerhardt (ed.): *G. W. Leibniz: Mathematische Schriften*, VII. Hildesheim: Olms, pp. 125–32, 1962 [1863, 1683].
Leibniz, Gottfried Wilhelm: In: V. Eberhard Knobloch & J.-Matthias Graf von der Schulenburg (eds): *Hauptschriften zur Versicherungs- und Finanzmathematik*. Berlin: Akademie Verlag, 2000.
Li, Wenchao & Poser, Hans: *Das Neueste über China. G. W. Leibnizens Novissima Sinica von 1697*. Stuttgart: Steiner, 2000.
Littleton, Ananias Charles: *Accounting Evolution to 1900*. New York: American Institute, 1933.
Mann, Fritz Karl: *Steuerpolitische Ideale. Vergleichende Studien zur Geschichte der ökonomischen und politischen Ideen und ihres Wirkens auf die öffentliche Meinung 1600–1935*. Jena: G. Fischer, 1937.
Mevius, David: *Von wucherlichen Contracten*. Erffurth, 1710.
Morgan, Augustus de: *Arithmetical Books from the Invention of Printing to the Present Time, Being Brief Notices of a Large Number of Works Drawn Up from Actual Inspection*. London: Taylor & Walton, 1847.
MüKoBGB/Grundmann: *Münchener Kommentar zum Bürgerlichen Gesetzbuch*. 4th ed. München: C.H. Beck, 2003.
Olivi, Pierre de Jean: *Traité des contrats*, édition de Sylvain Piron. Paris: Les belles lettres, 2012 [1293].
Passow, Richard: Bilanzwesen. In: Leopold von Wiese (ed.): *Wirtschaft und Recht der Gegenwart*, 2 vols. Tübingen: J.C.B. Mohr (Paul Siebeck), pp. 359–72, 1912.
Pollard, Sydney: Capital Accounting in the Industrial Revolution. *Yorkshire Bulletin of Economical and Social Research*, 15(2), pp. 75–91, 1963.
Roscher, Wilhelm: *Geschichte der Nationalökonomik in Deutschland*. München: Oldenbourg, 1874.
Schefold, Bertram (ed.): Das *De aerario* von Kaspar Klock. Eine Einführung in Leben und Werk. In: *Klock*, pp. vi–cxiii, 2009 [1651].
Schefold, Bertram: A Contribution to Weber's Theory of Modern Capitalism. Amortization According to Sraffa as a Rational Substitution of Missing Markets. In: Neri Salvadori & Christian Gehrke (eds): *Keynes, Sraffa and the Criticism of Neoclassical Theory. Essays in Honour of Heinz Kurz*. London: Routledge, 2011a.

Schefold, Bertram: Cameralism as an Intermediary Between Mediterranean Scholastic Economic Thought and Classical Economics. In: Heinz D. Kurz & Tamotsu Nishizawa (eds): *The Dissemination of Economic Ideas*. Cheltenham: Edward Elgar, 2011b.

Schefold, Bertram: The Significance of Economic Knowledge for Welfare and Economic Growth in History. Contribution to the AISPE Conference, 2017.

Schefold, Bertram: Thomas von Aquin, Petrus Johannes Olivi und Antoninus von Florenz. Mittelalterliche Kapitalkritik und die Weberthese. *Historisches Jahrbuch*, 138, pp. 92–118, 2018.

Schmoller, Gustav von: *Merkantilsystem in seiner historischen Bedeutung: The Mercantile System and Its Historical Significance*. New York: Kelley, 1967 [1884].

Schneider, Dieter: *Geschichte der betriebswirtschaftlichen Theorie*. München: Oldenbourg, 1981.

Schneider, Dieter: *Geschichten und Methoden der Betriebswirtschaftslehre*. München: Oldenbourg, 2001.

Sraffa, Piero: *Production of Commodities by Means of Commodities. Prelude to a Critique of Economic Theory*. Cambridge: Cambridge University Press, 1960.

Stein, Lorenz von: Zur Geschichte der deutschen Finanzwissenschaft im 17. Jahrhundert. *Finanz-Archiv*, 1, pp. 1–44, 1884.

Tribe, Keith: *Governing Economy: The Reformation of German Economic Discourse, 1750–1840*. Cambridge: Cambridge University Press, 1988.

Vecchiato, Francesco: *Note sul cameralismo tedesco. La dottrina economico-finanziaria di Caspar Klock*. Verona: Palazzo Giuliani, 1977.

Weber, Max: *Wirtschaftsgeschichte. Abriss der universalen Sozial- und Wirtschafts-Geschichte aus den nachgelassenen Vorlesungen,* eds V.S. Hellmann & M. Palyi, München: Duncker & Humblot, 1924.

# 10 Interest on money, own rate of interest, the natural interest rate and the rate of profits

A short history of concepts ultimately emerging from the usury debate

*Volker Caspari*

## Introduction

Peter John Olivi (c. 1248–98) was a French Franciscan and a pupil of Bonaventura. His *Tractatus de contractibus* contains a subtle discussion of the pricing of risks and probabilities in connection with valuing compensation due for compulsory requisitioning of property.

Looking back into the history of European economic thought reveals that during the Middle Ages scholastic scholars discussed usury and the conditions under which interest payments in a borrower–lender relation should be allowed or banned. The Dominican tradition represented by Albertus Magnus and Thomas Aquinas argued rather strongly for a ban on usury while the Franciscans Duns Scotus and William of Ockham followed Peter John Olivi's work *On Contracts*; they discussed the pricing of risks in connection with trade and interest in a subtle way as a compensation due to compulsory requisitioning of property. In addition, according to Olivi, *capital* has a certain *"quandam racionem seminalem lucri"*, a seed-like property to generate profits (Olivi 2012, p. 232).

It is a merit of these scholastic authors that they took up themes from different historical traditions – Aristotlian and Christian ethics and Roman law – and reflected on notions such as interest, credit, profits and capital.

In the usury debate, the scholastic authors reviewed different cases of contractual relations. They describe situations of intertemporal exchange, although not by using economic notions – which, in fact, were developed much later in a then-emerging discipline called political economy and later economics. Credit contracts existed long before the Middle Ages and interest payments were made in units of the commodity borrowed. When metal – very often silver – became the medium of exchange, the silver rate of interest was relevant. These commodity rates of interest are nowadays called own rates of interest. Even the money rate of interest can be regarded as an own rate of interest of money. During the Middle Ages, when merchandising and trade were growing, the case of an actual loss (*damnum emergens*) or a loss of profit (*lucrum cessans*) in these

DOI: 10.4324/9780367434496-15

trading activities became a theme. They were actually rediscovered cases, which Roman law already knew. *Damnum emergens* is "positive damage". Analysing the problem of usury, Thomas Aquinas raises and answers this objection:

> *Objection:* Now sometimes a man suffers a loss through lending money. Therefore, he may lawfully ask for or even exact something else besides the money lent.
>
> *Answer:* A lender may without sin enter into an agreement with the borrower for compensation for the loss he incurs of selling something he ought to have; for this is not to sell the use of money but to avoid a loss.
> (Aquinas 1947, q.78, 2)

A lender could charge not because of the loan of money itself, but for the economic loss incurred due to the circumstances in which the loan was made. That is the *damnum emergens*.

*Lucrum cessans* is a loss of profits (plus interest). If one could have made a profit with one's money instead of lending it (and can prove it!) then this becomes a legitimate title for interest. If I actually planned to buy a taxi car, but made the loan instead, the lender might also owe me the profit, which I lost from not owning the taxi car. Thomas Aquinas and other scholastic authors did not regard either *damnum emergens* or *lucrum cessans* as usury.

On the other hand, misgotten profits of merchants were viewed as sinful loot and were lumped together with usurers. This aversion toward merchants and trading changed, particularly during the late scholastic era, which is overlapping with the Late Middle Ages. People began to appreciate the services of the merchants. According to San Bernardino (of Siena), three types of merchants promote the general welfare:

(1) *mercantiarum apportatores* (exporters – importers)
(2) *mercantiarum conservatores* (transporters of goods through time)
(3) *mercantiarum immutatores seu melioratores* (they organise and finance the transformation of goods in precious goods) (Kaufer 1998, p. 105).

There was a change in attitude from disapproval, then tacit approval to eventual approbation of merchants. However, one aspect remained unchanged: the condemnation of exploiting people and trying to make profits as an end in itself.

With the emerging putting-out system in the Late Middle Ages, the third type of merchant became more prominent and the calculation of costs and profits required more complex methods, and not only because of the moral hazard problems at each stage of the manufacturing process. Calculations were confined to the value of the circulating capital (wool, cotton, flax, etc.) because fixed capital (i.e. weaving loom, spinning wheel) was the property of the subcontracting households and not of the merchant. However, that changed considerably with the introduction of the factory system in which the capitalist entrepreneur now owned both types of capital: circulating and fixed capital. He had to advance (finance) both types of capital, which again led to a more sophisticated calculation of costs and the rate of profits and called for a system of accounts that allowed all monetary transactions as well as the stock of inventory to be recorded.

At the beginning of the Industrial Revolution, the financial means needed for investment into machines and materials were not very large, but they increased considerably in the second stage of that process, when steam power was widely used to mechanise production processes. The other example is the expansion of the railway system, which needed enormous amounts of capital advances – something even a quite wealthy capitalist entrepreneur could not provide. Banks or capital markets developed where the savings of many people were pooled and then channelled either by credit or by securities into investments. In the late nineteenth century, the relationship between savings and investment moved into the focus of monetary economics. First Swedish economist Knut Wicksell and, some decades later, John Maynard Keynes used the savings–investment relationship to explain movements of the price level and of output and employment. Wicksell identified the bank rate of interest in relation to the *natural* rate of interest as the main variables that influenced savings and investment. The concept of the *natural* rate of interest has been revitalised very recently in a discussion on the secular stagnation hypothesis (Summers 2014a, 2014b; Weizsäcker 2013).

In the remainder of this chapter, I will explicate the theoretical ideas behind these notions, which emerged at different stages of economic history.

## Commodity rates of interest

Borrowing and lending – or, in modern economic terms, a credit relationship – is well known in economic history. We know that credit contracts existed already in ancient Babylon of Hammurabi. The famous Codex of Hammurabi allowed interest up to 4 per cent. If credits were not paid back, debt servitude loomed. Those credit contracts were very often contracts in terms of a commodity – that is, wheat or barley. The background of such an intertemporal contract was often that a family had an accident or a bad harvest, and thus risked dying of hunger. Another family was lucky and had a good harvest with a surplus. The family with the bad harvest borrowed a certain amount of, say, wheat, which had to be given back to the lending family. If the amount that had to be given back was larger than the amount that was borrowed, interest was included. Interest is the difference between the quantity in period t+1 minus the quantity period t. The interest rate is defined by dividing this difference by the amount borrowed in period t.

$$\text{wheat interest rate} = \frac{\text{wheat}_{t+1} - \text{wheat}_t}{\text{wheat}_t}.$$

It is a relation between quantities "today" and quantities "tomorrow", which may be understood as the exchange value of wheat today in terms of wheat tomorrow.

In general, a quantity of commodity i at date t is exchanged against a quantity of commodity i at date t+1:

$$\frac{p_{i,t}}{p_{i,t+1}} = \frac{q_{i,t+1}}{q_{i,t}}.$$

This equals the price of commodity i at date t+1 in relation to the price of commodity i at date t. While the left hand of that equation is called the value in exchange, the right hand is called the relative price.

The *own rate of interest* of commodity i at date t, $\rho_{i,t}$, is, according to Irving Fisher (1896, pp. 88ff) defined as:

$$\frac{q_{i,t+1}}{q_{i,t}} - 1 = \frac{p_{i,t}}{p_{i,t+1}} - 1 = \rho_{i,t}.$$

## Money rate of interest

The money rate of interest, $i_t$, is the own rate of interest of the numéraire if money is used as the standard of value or the numeraire. Of course, any other commodity could be chosen as numeraire:

$$\frac{€105 \text{ in } t+1 - €100 \text{ in } t}{€100 \text{ in } t} = i_t.$$

If we express all prices in terms of the numeraire – that is, money – then we get money prices.

Now, imagine a person who today will buy a certain amount of wheat and borrows money today. They need to know the present money price of wheat and the quantity they want to borrow. This means $p_{w,t} \, q_{w,t} = €_t$. Assume a year later the person has to pay back the money loan in terms of $€_{t+1}$. Given that the money rate of interest, $i_t$, is 5 per cent, they know they will have to pay back €105 tomorrow. Whether our wheat-borrower will gain or lose tomorrow depends on how they will use the wheat. If they eat it, no further calculation is necessary, because they know they have to pay back €105. However, if the wheat is taken as seed, then the first question is: How much wheat will the person have after the harvest in t+1? The second question is: What will be the money price of wheat tomorrow? Similar questions would occur if our person baked bread with the borrowed amount of wheat. In that case, the amount of baked bread and its money price tomorrow become relevant. A third possibility is that our person stores the wheat. Then the question is: What

## Concepts emerging from the usury debate  137

did they lose within a year and how did the money price of wheat change? We realise that our person may gain something, although they have to pay a money rate of interest of 5 per cent, if the wheat own rate of interest plus the change in money prices of wheat together come to higher than 5%.

As an example, we assume our person is storing the wheat. They lose 1 per cent (100 kg – 1 kg = 99kg) because of damage done by mice. During the year, the money price of wheat has risen by 10 per cent (€1 → € 1.1). Selling the wheat tomorrow leads to a sum of €108.9. Paying back their loan of €105, a surplus of €3.90 remains. In relation to the invested capital of €100, interest of 3.9 per cent accrues, while in relation to capital costs (€105) it is 3.71 per cent.

$$\frac{€1}{kg} \cdot 100 \text{ kg} = € 100$$

$$\frac{€1.1}{kg} \cdot 99 \text{ kg} = € 108.9$$

The change of prices from period to period is called appreciation if $p_{t+1} > p_t$ and it is called depreciation if $p_{t+1} < p_t$.

Amazingly, Scholastic writers must have known commodity rates of interest without defining them explicitly, because they discussed contracts that allowed paying back a loan either in terms of money or in units of the commodity borrowed. Such a situation could be confusing, because in terms of money, usury could be at hand while in terms of the commodity, the own rate of interest could be negative (Schefold 2018a).

After the period of Scholasticism and the demise of the usury discussions, commodity rates of interest mercantilists as well as classical economist lost track of the own rates until Sraffa and Keynes used the concept of own rates of interest in their 1932 critique of Friedrich A. von Hayek's (1928) theory of the business cycle, which he had presented in his *Prices and Production*. Already in the late 1920s, Hayek had developed the notion of intertemporal equilibrium, where own rates of interest emerge in connection with forward trading in future markets. To illustrate forward trading, I slightly modify an example used by Keynes (1936, p. 223) in his *General Theory*. Suppose that the spot (present) price of wheat is €100 per 100 kg and that the price of the future contract for wheat delivered a year later is €107 per 100 kg, and that the rate of money interest is 5 per cent. What is the wheat rate of interest? €100 spot will buy €105 for forward delivery and €105 for forward delivery will buy 105/107 x 100 (= 98) kg for forward delivery. Therefore, 100 kg of wheat for spot delivery will buy 98 kg for forward delivery. From this, it follows that the own rate of interest on wheat (or wheat rate of interest) is *minus 2 per cent* per annum. Obviously, own rates of interest can be negative – even some money rates of interest can become negative, as has become apparent recently, which to some extent is due to monetary measures used by the FED and then by the central banks.

An obvious question is: What are the factors that lead to positive or negative rates of (own) interest? According to Keynes (1936, p. 223), we may distinguish three factors: the yield of a capital good, its carrying costs and its liquidity premium. All are measured in terms of itself. Switching to money as numéraire, one has to take appreciation or depreciation of the capital good and of the carrying costs into account. The liquidity premium also has to be expressed in terms of money:

> It is characteristic of instrumental capital (e.g. a machine) or of consumption capital (e.g. a house) which is in use that its yield should normally exceed its carrying costs, whilst its liquidity-premium is probably negligible; of a stock of liquid goods or of surplus laid-up instrumental or consumption capital that it should incur a carrying cost in terms of itself without any yield to set off against it, the liquidity-premium also being virtually negligible as soon as stocks exceed a moderate level…; and of money that its yield is nil, its carrying costs negligible, but its liquidity-premium substantial.
>
> (Keynes 1936, p. 226)

Keynes wanted to emphasise the fundamental property of deposits and cash, and that they do not have a yield at all, while both have a highly positive liquidity-premium. On the other hand, invested instrumental capital usually has a yield and definitely no liquidity premium. Keynes' idea was that since the liquidity premium could never be negative, this liquidity premium is a barrier, which prevents the own rate of interest on money to fall below that premium, while other own rates of interest could become negative.

## Natural rate of interest

Knut Wicksell (1851–1926), a Swedish economist, developed in his book *Geldzins und Güterpreise* [*Interest and Prices* (Wicksell 1898) the concept of a "natural" rate of interest. According to Wicksell, the "natural" rate of interest is "a certain rate of interest on loans which is neutral in respect to commodity prices and tends neither to raise nor to lower them". This concept is based on Eugen von Böhm-Bawerk's (1961) capital theory, also known as the Austrian theory of capital. Wicksell rethought Böhm-Bawerk's ideas and, where he detected logical flaws, he revised his approach. Briefly, the theory of the natural rate states that savings (S) at the full employment level and investment at the full employment level (I) determine the "natural" rate. If the natural rate rules, then the price level of the GDP is stable; there is no inflation or deflation. The institutional background of this theory was the European continental type of financing investment via a banking system, and not via capital markets as this was usual in the Anglo-Saxon and Dutch financial system.

The narrative is that the savings of the households are "collected" by the banks, which lend this money to firms to finance their investments. Planned investments of firms give rise to the demand for credit, while savings provide credit supply. Savings are, according to Wicksell's theory, positively related to the rate of interest of loans, i, whereas investment demand is negatively related to the internal rate of interest. The internal rate of interest, r, is the rate that makes the capital value (CV) of a sequence of discounted future profits equal to zero:

$$0 = I - \sum_{0}^{T} \frac{P_t}{1+r^t}.$$

Now, if r = i, savings are equal to investment and the "natural" rate rules. Why is that a situation without inflation or deflation? Because if the loan rate is lower than the internal rate of interest, additional investment would be profitable and therefore investment is stimulated and demand for commodities increases. Given that there is full employment, this leads to rising prices (inflationary pressure). If the loan rate is higher than the internal rate of interest, investment is reduced and demand for commodities declines. That leads to a falling price-level (deflationary pressure) (Figure 10.1).

Keynes had a different view on the saving–investment mechanism. He showed that savings can equate investment at different rates of interest if there is unemployment. Therefore, unemployment may even exist if savings are equal to investment, a situation he called "under-employment equilibrium".

Very recently Wicksell's theory of the "natural" rate has been revived by some economists (Summers 2014b; Weizsäcker 2013), who argue that the "natural" rate has become very low or even negative due to a savings glut and very low rates of investment. The central banks have to consider the low or negative "natural" rate and adjust their interest policy so that the money rate of interest, which rules on the money market, has approached the zero lower bound.

## Rate of profits

The rate of profits is mainly associated with an economic system called capitalism, but the notion of "profits" appeared much earlier and in connection with trade and its risks. Historically, profits as an economic notion emerged as "trading profits", the income of medieval merchants. The traded commodities

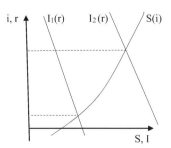

*Figure 10.1* Saving–investment mechanism

formed a large part of the capital of these merchants, while the other part consisted of houses, trading posts and sometimes even ships. The production of commodities was organised by merchants in the form of the putting-out system. Under this system, merchants owned the circulating capital, whereas the fixed capital was property of the different households, which were "subcontractors" of the merchants. Gradually, the merchants became entrepreneur-capitalists. They advanced all means of production and employed workers in their factories. Profit then emerged as the proceeds minus the costs of all means of production and minus the costs for the workers.

Ricardo clarified the fundamental feature of the rate of profits in the corn–corn model. In this simple world, output is produced only with circulating capital and labour. We have corn as gross output and corn (seeds) and labour as inputs. Assume that the workers get their wages in terms of corn and these wages are at the subsistence level. If we subtract the amount of corn that goes to wages and the amount of corn, which is reinvested from gross output of corn, we get the net product. Division of the net product of corn by the amount of corn for seeds defines the rate of profits. A positive rate of profits emerges if the net product is positive, which says that the production process is productive because it creates a surplus. If we do not assume that the real wage is at its subsistence level, then the rate of profits is defined as gross output minus seeds (capital) minus the real wage fund divided by seeds (capital).

I do not want to discuss the case of more than one capital good, which leads to questions and problems on which Ricardo was working until a few days before his unexpected sudden death. The main point of Ricardo's physical definition of the rate of profits highlights that profits are due to a productive production process, which means that, given the technology at hand, the production process allows production of a physical surplus. Without a surplus, there is no profit. Of course, the special distribution of the property rights – private property of the means of production – is a necessary but not a sufficient condition for profits being positive.

In a world with more than one capital good, a purely physical definition of a surplus and a profit is not possible because we can only add up "chalk and cheese" if we know the prices for both goods. The goods, which were advanced as capital goods to start a production process, are usually called advanced capital. The capitalist advances a capital value, which he might have invested in another branch or industry or might have lent it to the government for a bond that provides a relatively secure interest payment. Therefore, he wants at least a similar payment for his capital advances. If there is a surplus in production, this payment can be realised.

Marx (1970) provided a different answer to the question of why the rate of profits is positive. He assumed that all labour is productive and that the worker creates a surplus value (theories of absolute and relative surplus value) that, due to the property rights, he cannot acquire because the capitalist appropriates it. This surplus value emerges because the worker works more hours than he needs to earn his wage. That is the reason why Marx described the situation as exploitation. Exploitation follows logically from the assumption that labour is productive and that a worker needs only a fraction of the total labour time he spends earning his wage.

Sraffa remained on Ricardo's side. Sraffa showed that a positive rate of profits requires an economic system, which is capable to produce a surplus and this surplus is distributed between wages and profits according to the ruling property rights (Sraffa 1960, pp. 6ff.).

Neoclassical economics does not employ the concept of the rate profits. Böhm-Bawerk and other Austrians use the notion of capital interest (Kapitalzins) while followers of John Bates Clark relate the rate of interest on loan capital to the marginal product of capital. Neoclassical economics mentions profits only in connection with markets where monopolistic competition rules or a monopoly exists. Monopoly profit is in fact a monopoly rent or in Marxian terms a surplus profit. Under perfect competition and technologies that display constant returns to scale, profits are zero.

Böhm-Bawerk (1961) argued that a positive rate of capital interest is due first to a technological feature that roundabout methods of production are always productive, and second that people have a positive rate of time preference, which means they prefer present consumption to future consumption. The rate of interest in relation to the rate of time preference regulates the supply of savings of the households, while on the demand side, the rate of interest regulates the degree of roundaboutness. The higher the rate of interest, the lower is the degree of roundaboutness, which means that capital demand decreases.

## References

Aquinas, Thomas: *The Summa Theologica of St Thomas Aquinas* [Fathers of the English Dominican Province]. New York: Pinnacle Press, 1947 [1265–73].
Böhm-Bawerk, E. von: *Kapital und Kapitalzins*, 3rd ed. Stuttgart: Gustav Fischer Verlag, 1961 [1888].
Fisher, Irving: *Appreciation and Interest*. New York: Macmillan, 1896.
Hayek, F.A. von: Das intertemporale Gleichgewichtssystem der Preise und die Bewegungen des "Geldwertes". *Weltwirtschaftliches Archiv*, 28, pp. 33–76, 1928.
Kaufer, Erich: *Spiegelungen wirtschaftlichen Denkens im Mittelalter*. Innsbruck: Studien Verlag, 1998.
Keynes, John Maynard: *The General Theory of Employment, Interest and Money*. London: Palgrave Macmillan, 1936.
Marx, Karl: *Das Kapital*, Vol.1, MEW Vol. 23. Berlin: Dietz Verlag, 1970 [1867].
Olivi, J.P.: *Tractatus de contractibus*. In: Sylvain Piron (ed., trans.): *Traité des contrats*, Paris, Les Belles-Lettres, 2012. English translation: A Treatise on Contracts, Ryan Thornton & Michael Cusato trans. Saint Bonaventure, NY: Franciscan Institute, 2016 [1293–95].
Schefold, Bertram: Die Bedeutung des ökonomischen Wissens für Wohlfahrt und wirtschaftliches Wachstum in der Geschichte. In: *Sitzungsberichte der Wissenschaftlichen Gesellschaft an der Johann Wolfgang Goethe-Universität Frankfurt am Main, Vol LV, No. 2*. Stuttgart: Steiner, 2018a.

Schefold, Bertram: Thomas von Aquin, Petrus Johannes Olivi und Antonius von Florenz. Mittelalterliche Kapitalkritik und die Weberthese. In: Thomas Brechenmacher & Christoph Campmann (eds): *Historisches Jahrbuch*, Jg. 138. Freiburg i. Br.: Herder, pp. 92–118, 2018b.

Summers, Larry: U.S. Economic Prospects: Secular Stagnation, Hysteresis, and the Zero Lower Bound. *Business Economics*, 49(2), pp. 65–73, 2014a.

Summers, Larry: Reflections on the "New Secular Stagnation Hypothesis". In: *Secular Stagnation: Facts, Causes and Cures,* London: Centre for Economic Policy Research, pp. 27–38, 2014b.

Sraffa, Piero: *Production of Commodities by Means of Commodities*. Cambridge: Cambridge University Press, 1960.

Weizsäcker, C.C. von: Public Debt and Price Stability. *German Economic Review,* 15, pp. 42–61, 2013.

Wicksell, Knut: *Geldzins und Güterpreise [Interest and Prices]*. Jena: Fischer, 1898.

Section 2
# The spread of monetary relations and the transition from poor relief to the welfare state

# 11 Labour and poverty in medieval and early modern Europe

*Cosimo Perrotta*

## Premise: Labour in ancient society and the Dark Ages

Ancient societies were ruled by the landed and wealthy classes. Labour was delegated to the lowest classes: slaves, freedmen, manual workers and retail traders. This usually led to contempt for labour and the technical arts. The working classes were usually associated with the idea of poverty, in the sense of involuntary scarcity of goods and money.

On the contrary, voluntary frugality was praised by most thinkers. Socrates and his followers, up to Aristotle, highly commended the man who was content with what he possessed and did not strive to acquire ever more.[1] Along the same lines, the Stoics preached indifference towards wealth and material things.[2] All these authors stated the primacy of spiritual goods over material satisfactions, and of cultural activity over labour. This aristocratic attitude implied, again, that labour was to be despised.[3]

On the other hand, especially in the Hellenistic period, the custom of providing food to the poor or civic infrastructures spread among the rich who sought public appointments. This practice – called Evergetism – declined when the Christian church created its social network and took on the task of assisting the poor.

However, there is no continuity between the ancient and Christian culture on this issue. There was a sharp change in the attitude towards the poor, especially in the fourth and fifth centuries. The supply of slaves was dwindling because conquests were coming to an end (Weber 1909). The cities of the late Roman Empire were organised around the guilds of artisans, which were the sinews of the post-slave economy. Thus labour was no longer despised, and workers were no longer categorised as the poor.

The poor were by then marginal members of society who did not possess sufficient means for survival. For the Christian fathers, involuntary poverty was not desirable, while goods and wealth were seen as gifts of God.[4] On the other hand, voluntary poverty was a virtue practised by the most fervent followers of Christ (Viner 1978, p. 16).

The fathers were keen to define the new attitude towards involuntary poverty. First, as sons of God, the poor had the same dignity as all the other men.

DOI: 10.4324/9780367434496-17

In addition, the poor deserved special care, being the image of Christ and of his apostles, who were poor – albeit voluntarily. Thus a practice of assiduous relief of the poor was implemented. But the rich had the moral duty to help the poor.[5] During the Patristic era, it was proclaimed – later repeated by the Scholastics – that the rich who refused alms or relief to the poor were murderers.

During the Dark Ages, further fundamental developments occurred that led to a revaluation of labour. The slow recovery of agriculture promoted by the monastic orders employed both the labour of the monks themselves and hired labour, provided by the rare peasants. The labour contracts with the latter were usually based on emphyteusis, which implied a shared responsibility for the labourer. Finally, the Rule of St Benedict, unlike the oriental hermit culture, conferred upon labour the same importance as prayer. *"Ora et labora"* (Pray and work) was the motto of the order.[6]

All these elements converged in definitive transition from the ancient slave economy to an economy based on the labour of free men. When, in the ninth century, feudalism was introduced, many peasants became serfs – or, in other words, quasi-slaves. However, the feudal system could not destroy free labour (Kula 1972, pp. 68–85). Indeed, in the eleventh century, many serfs started fleeing to the old Roman cities, where they called on the protection of the bishops. The latter constituted the only power – inherited from the ancient society – that was independent of the feudal structure. The bishops protected the fugitives and favoured the revival of artisans' guilds after 500 years.

## The Middle Ages: Poverty as a positive value

In the eleventh century, a new and radical change occurred in attitudes towards poverty and the poor. It came about thanks to the new rising economy, which caused a rapid transformation of the cities and led to a new social structure.

In this period, agricultural productivity was increasing in many European regions thanks to the introduction of new techniques, which allowed for a growing number of workers to be displaced to commerce and handicrafts in the cities. The Hanseatic League in the Northern Sea, Flanders, Provence, Barcelona and Northern and Central Italy were the poles that saw the growth of the new economy (Little 1978, pp. 35–41).

To begin with, this economy was based on the independent labour devoted to commerce and handicrafts, with the workers organised into guilds. Soon, however, these kinds of activities found the support of corporate companies, which employed hired labour. The revived commerce and the new production generated a steady growth of wealth in the above-mentioned areas.

In turn, the steady increase in wealth led to further social division of labour. New specialisations and professions were born, and the traditional ones became more numerous and differentiated, generating new skills. Gradually, an increasing number of people were able to devote themselves to public administration and public services (Cipolla 1965, p. 412).

Throughout the entire ancient era, the authors had a vision of society as polarised between the rich and the poor. However, from the year 1000, social hierarchies became much more complex. The bipolar society, already undergoing erosion in the cities of late antiquity, no longer existed. The middle classes started growing, and never ceased to grow along with capitalist development.

The steady increase in wealth was an absolutely new phenomenon in human history. In pre-modern societies, big business depended on the rich landowners, who sold their agricultural surplus, or on limited companies that sold handicraft products. In the fifth century BC, in Athens, there were even companies that sold shares to collect their capital. This was the premise for the birth of a capitalist economy, although this never actually came about for reasons beyond our scope here.

As a matter of fact, the capitalist economy that was born in the core of European feudalism had no precedents. The social and cultural earthquake it generated was a real shock for the men of the time. None of the previous social analyses – from Plato to St Augustine – were able to explain what was happening.

The intellectuals were at the same time both fascinated and disconcerted by these processes. The transformation seemed to threaten many of the certainties of Christian philosophy. Not only voluntary poverty as a model of perfection, but also the poor as image of Christ, no longer seemed to be unquestioned values. The new economic activities jeopardised detachment from worldly things and relationships based on solidarity. New reference points were needed.

Hostility to the new economy was not only growing among intellectuals and religious people; it increased even more among the privileged categories of the old society – that is, the landlords and other representatives of the feudal hierarchy at all levels as well as the men of the church who concentrated power and riches in their own hands. These people understood very well that the new economy tended to marginalise them and to transfer power to the new classes, no longer dependent on them.

In this changing society, the church felt the need to strengthen its internal customs and discipline. During the eleventh century, a series of Popes, culminating in Gregory VII, waged a fierce battle against the corruption of the clergy, increased central control and reinforced discipline. They were supported by the Patarines from Milan, one of the first pauperistic movements. But soon the relationship between these movements and the institutional powers, both ecclesiastic and secular, deteriorated.[7]

In the eleventh and twelfth centuries, the pauperistic movements waxed scathingly critical of the traditional establishment. They preached a revival of the Gospel's message in praise of poverty ("apostolic poverty"), against the corruption and greed of the current society. Apparently, these movements opposed the new economy based on commerce, but their real nature was much more complex.

Diverse and even contradictory tendencies converged in these movements, in the person of representatives of the new economy, commerce and handicrafts;

the brutally exploited hired workers of the first textile manufactures; and people seeking a more heartfelt, less formal religious life. All these categories were unified by opposition to the old establishment and the radical revival of voluntary poverty.

Merchants and artisans expected wealth to be linked to labour, not to the rent and power possessed by the church and the feudal landlords. Hired workers stood in favour of poverty to defend their dignity and censure the rich. They were caught in the usual utopian trap: the conviction that the only way to abolish social inequalities was to make all people poor.[8] Religious people and intellectuals were interested in voluntary poverty as the only way to spiritual perfection.

These movements distrusted the Christian fathers' balanced vision of poverty (which was accepted by Thomas Aquinas). It seemed to them more like lip service than genuine adherence to the evangelical values. The need for a more radical attitude was so pressing that new religious orders were founded, called mendicant orders, which took on a social mission and rejected the possession of great wealth.

Although contradictory, the different factors that gave birth to the pauperistic movements were intertwined. Peter Waldes, from Lyon, and Francis of Assisi were both repented merchants who preached extreme poverty. The former was eventually declared a heretic, while the latter became a saint. The Cathars (or Albigenses) in Southern France, while representing an opulent society in which commerce and manufactures flourished, at the same time preached apostolic poverty. This was a consequence of the dualistic view that the Cathars inherited from certain oriental heresies (Vasoli 1983, pp. 392–96).

Innocent III, the same Pope who excommunicated the Cathars and instigated their massacre in 1209, in the same year approved – although in a mitigated version – the Rule of Francis of Assisi for his order. A few years after, Peter Olivi, born in Provence – the Cathars' region – joined the Franciscan order and re-proposed a pauperistic vision of religious life. Franciscan dualism made a sharp distinction between common life and the life of perfection, which implied voluntary poverty. The pursuit of wealth was condoned for the non-religious.

A different path was taken with the Aristotelian and Thomistic approach (supported by the Dominicans), endeavouring to maintain the unity of moral teaching. As a consequence, Thomism – which soon became the official doctrine of the church – found it more difficult to understand the needs of commercial society.

By contrast, Peter Olivi – although an extreme pauperist – was the first brilliant analyst of money investment. Contrary to the official church teaching, he even rejected the Aristotelian condemnation of monetary interest. Interestingly enough, Olivi was condemned and persecuted even after his death, not for his theory of interest but rather for his extreme pauperism.[9]

The Dominicans, too, were a mendicant order. Their founder, Dominic of Guzman, had taken part in the massacres against the Cathars (1209–29). With some reason, the Dominicans accused the Franciscans of putting their friars' lives in danger, given that their rule forbade them even to keep food in the drawers, and to accept as alms money or things not strictly necessary. The precept of the Franciscans was "Naked, follow the naked Christ".[10]

The Franciscan attitude to voluntary poverty was so extreme that, quite soon, the order started to quarrel and then to split between moderates and radicals. In extremist movements, there are always some who aspire to more perfect purity than the others, and divisions are very frequent.

## The fourteenth and fifteenth centuries: Poverty discredited – both voluntary and involuntary

In the European medieval universities, the dispute over voluntary poverty was so keen and persistent that it left the issue of involuntary poverty – that is, of the real poor – in the shade. However, Thomas Aquinas reflected the balanced vision of the Christian Fathers on this issue. He saw the poor as an essential element in the divine salvation plan. The poor oblige the rich to be charitable. This precept is the crucial way to salvation for the rich. The church, too, had the duty to relieve the poor.

On the other hand, for Thomas goods were not negative objects, as the pauperist movements maintained. They were gifts of God, and were to be respected and used, although a certain spiritual detachment from worldly things was always expected of the Christians.[11]

In the late medieval period, society had the task of supporting the involuntary poor. The convents saw their major task as giving food and alms to the poor. Convents and cities all over Western Europe were crowded with beggars and pilgrims.

The long process of privatising feudal lands ("enclosures") was growing during the fourteenth and fifteenth centuries. This was due to the increase in manufactures in the commercial regions mentioned above. Flanders and Florence in particular needed a great deal of raw wool for their manufactures and paid handsomely for it. Above all, in England and Spain – which produced the most valuable wool – landlords were set on extending their pastures ever more, to the detriment of cultivated land. They did not even stop when it came to the common land that the feudal system granted to the peasants' villages for their survival.

Meanwhile the serfs' economy was rapidly decaying, due to the flight of great numbers of serfs to the cities, where they could become free workers in handicrafts and enjoy the protection of the guilds. The disappearance of the common land drove away from the countryside a multitude of labourers, peasants and petty artisans, who became beggars in the cities, calling on convents, parishes and families for alms. The practice grew so rife that the cities became unsafe.

Thus, towards the end of the Middle Ages, attitudes towards the poor changed sharply, due to both the spread of begging and the increasing circulation of wealth in the cities Censure of begging increased in the fourteenth century. Jean de Meun criticised it,[12] but also Nicole Oresme, Pierre d'Ailly and many others. The anonymous *Le Songe du Vergier* (written shortly after 1372) was severely critical of monks, including the new orders, for feeding parasitism through indiscriminate charity, and indeed for practising begging themselves. Coming under particular attack were the Franciscans and the Beguines (Mollat 1978, pp. 305–10). Poverty now took on sordid overtones.

The mood set in even more firmly in the fifteenth century. In his dialogue *On Avarice* (1428–29), Poggio Bracciolini, the great humanist who explored monasteries throughout Europe to discover a great number of manuscripts containing fundamental ancient texts, was most decidedly critical of the traditional condemnation of greed. He maintained that if people were content with the mere necessities, as philosophers had always repeated since Aristotle, civilisation would die: there would be no cities, no activities, no trade. Cities and kingdoms are simply the fruit of avarice (Bracciolini 1952 [1428–29], pp. 248–301). His thesis is very similar to the point made by Mandeville in *The Fable of the Bees* three centuries later.

In this context, (Bracciolini 1952 [1428–29], p. 267) scathingly attacked and even insulted the mendicant friars for begging instead of earning their bread with work, and for "preaching to others poverty and disdain for possessions while they themselves make generous earnings". Only 80 years had passed since the death of the great philosopher William of Ockham, persecuted for his pauperism to the very end.

The same contempt for poverty and praise of wealth was also shown by other great humanists, such as Salutati, Alberti, Valla, Manetti, Pontano and Ficino, to name but a few. Together with praise of wealth, these humanists also praised labour and man's creativity. Work is a duty and a right, upon which human dignity is founded; and it is a free choice of the individual, like the pursuit of wealth. Liberty and dignity make man autonomous. Man is self-made. He is no longer an element subject to the universal plan of providence. Thus the poor, too, cease to be a factor in the plan of providence.[13]

Hostility towards poverty and begging waxed strongest among the Protestants, who even destroyed convents and expelled the monks. For them, wealth and success, far from being despised, became a sign of virtue and divine favour. Such was the Protestant ethic, so acutely analysed by Max Weber (1930 [1904]).

Meanwhile humanistic culture in Italy was petering out, in parallel with the gradual decline of the Italian economy. It became a rhetorical and indeed hypocritical vehicle to reaffirm the privileges of the old establishment (which included intellectuals). Claudio Tolomei was one of the most emblematic examples of this involution. He declared poverty an imaginary malaise (Tolomei 1565 [1547], pp. 161–79). Tolomei's highly successful book was a concentration of empty rhetorical stereotypes.

Of course, among the late humanists there were also authors who perceived and approved the advent of modern economy, but by then the centre of the new culture had shifted to other countries – the countries of rampant capitalism.

## The system of productive assistance in sixteenth- and seventeenth-century England

Nearly all the cities and regions that had led the way in economic development (soon after the year 1000) slowed down their race at the beginning of the modern era. The cities were by then too small to support the continual growth of the economy. Even the regional dimension was too narrow. Commerce was fast assuming an international dimension, bypassing the silk road and the Mediterranean, and supplanting them with the oceanic routes. Development could only be vouchsafed by national dimensions and state support.

Holland, France and England, above all, implemented projects for national development with the support of strong state policies. They built up big naval fleets, networks of roads, bridges, ports and canals; encouraged the spread of manufactures for the processing of national production; protected their merchants abroad and their national markets at home; regulated the artisans' guilds, strengthened their discipline; brought in improvements in training; and, finally, organised the poor and vagrants, setting them to work.

This complex governance of economic development constituted the core of what we now call mercantilism. Organisation of the poor was a basic element in this policy. It showed a radical shift from the medieval praise of poverty and begging, but it also put an end to the 15th-century contempt for the poor.

While embracing the view of man expressed by the first humanists, the mercantilists saw the poor not in terms of providence, but of potentiality. Thus, the poor merited neither praise nor blame; they needed to be organised and to make their contribution to economic development. From being images of God or dangerous vagrants, they were now simply unemployed, and ready to become workers.

The countries of the new capitalism had different dynamic trends. In the sixteenth century, two opposite models emerged in policy for the poor. One was best exemplified by Spain, the other by England. From the thirteenth to the fifteenth centuries, these two countries had been the main exporters of raw wool, the processing of which was the driving force of emerging capitalism.

In England, the cloth industry was already seeing substantial development in the fifteenth century; the Flemish and the Italian cities were gradually losing their grip on English raw wool. Finally, the Tudors' policy overthrew England's traditional submission in foreign trade and drove English capitalism to take off. The new policy found strong support in the acute analysis of an Oxford philosopher Thomas Starkey.

Around 1530, Starkey made a series of simple points. First, why should we go on enriching our neighbours with our raw materials? Not only do they take our resources but, after working them, they re-sell them to us at greatly increased value. Moreover, he added, while they put their poor to work, we fail to employ ours (Starkey 1989 [1529–32], pp. 24, 60–62, 113–17). In these few arguments is encapsulated the entire mercantilist strategy for development.

152  Cosimo Perrotta

Starkey's observations expressed a widely shared feeling in English public opinion. His book arrived while England was making rapid headway towards religious and political autonomy and felt the need to be autonomous also in the economy. Henry VII had already started to limit the freedom to export wool. The Tudor sovereigns that followed applied a broadly mercantilist system.

In the same year that Starkey's book was published, Henry VIII required landlords (many of whom were no longer feudal nobles, but rampant bourgeoisie) to reserve a part of their estates to the cultivation of flax or hemp, with the explicit aim of employing the poor in spinning and weaving, substituting importation of clothes with domestic products. In addition, the king brought in further limitations on the exportation of raw wool and textile raw materials in general.[14]

With a number of laws, Henry VIII and his successors, particularly Elizabeth I, provided instructions and norms for organisation of the poor. Parishes had the duty to gather them together so as to distinguish the unable from the able poor. The former were to receive hospitality and assistance through voluntary contributions by the members of the parish. Soon this contribution became a real tax, which the citizens had to pay.

As to the able poor, they were to be obliged to toil in the workhouses, which came somewhere between factories and prisons. The workhouses, especially those devoted to textile work, were to be financed with the same taxes. The work and management were to be supervised by specific overseers.[15]

Many authors of the time came up with plans for employment of the poor in some production sector. With a succession of norms, the Tudors built up a complex network that concurrently organised public assistance and investments to foster employment.

It was an impressive system, which combined solidarity with economic development. Only in the period of the welfare state, after World War II, do we find anything like the Tudors' policy for the poor in terms of support of the lower classes and boosting productivity. Thanks to its sixteenth and seventeenth century policy, England surpassed all the competitors in the race for development and became the leading national power in the world.

## The parasitic system of sixteenth- and seventeenth-century Spain

Spain, unfortunately, took the opposite line. The country had started developing very early. Its commercial and handicraft activities were flourishing, and the main cities became opulent and industrious under the direction of a dynamic bourgeoisie. However, there was a decisive difference from England. The English sovereigns had gradually increased their power in respect of the barons and nobles. In order to gain supremacy, they joined forces with the other enemies of the feudal nobles, namely the artisans and merchants. In Spain, not only did any such alliance between the sovereign and the modern classes fail to come about, but the king was in fact practically a hostage in the hands of the military caste. The feudal nobles had greatly increased their power and enlarged their estates thanks to the reconquest of Arabic Spain (*Reconquista*). This series of wars engaged the nobles from the ninth to the fifteenth century and forged the character of this class, based on honour, pride, aggressive attitudes and enrichment through plunder rather than commerce and production.

The last war was against the Arabic kingdom of Andalusia – rich, well organised and highly developed. The Spanish conquest (1492) destroyed that flourishing economy. It had a sort of continuation – in terms of culture and custom – in the conquest of the New World, discovered in the same year. Significantly, 1492 was also the year in which Arabs, Jews and Gypsies were expelled from Spain to safeguard the Spanish *limpieza de sangre* (purity of blood). The feudal landlords saw their power reinforced. Moreover, Charles V had run into enormous debt to buy his imperial title and was also dependent on the landowners in financial terms. Spain then underwent the lethal process of "re-feudalisation" (Viñas y Mey 1970).

Given the high demand for Spanish wool, the landowners extended their pastures and sheep farms to the detriment of the traditional crops. They took to seizing and illegally privatising public land and the common land of the medieval communities, without meeting with any resistance. They imposed their right to graze everywhere, even on cultivated land, where the herds trampled and devoured plants and buds.

Meanwhile, the nobles and their clients were harassing peasants illegally – with the complicity of administrative officials and judges – in order to force them to quit and undersell their properties to them. They managed to close the way to any enterprise in agriculture and any manufacture processing agricultural products, even against their own long-run interest (Lysón y Viedma 1622). In fact, they wanted to keep breeding and grain cultivation, which yielded them high prices both in export and in the domestic market, as dominant sectors. They also wanted to keep the poor unemployed in order to pay low wages during harvesting and for stock breeding.

The re-feudalisation also led to enormous disparities within the class of nobles. Land and riches went into the hands of relatively few families (thanks to the right of primogeniture), while Spain saw a proliferation of poor nobles, who were allowed to beg but not to work.

The other factor that impeded Spain's industrialisation was the arrival of huge quantities of gold and silver from America, imported year after year, resulting in unmanageable inflation. Nobles, soldiers, administrators, adventurers and clients of the nobles in possession of the gold, rather than using it in investments for production, found it easier to buy commodities from foreign producers – from the other European countries.

Together with "re-feudalisation", Spanish inflation dismantled production because of the excessively high prices, and inevitably the merchants, artisans, peasants and manufactures lost their clients. While the Spanish economy rapidly deteriorated, the neighbouring countries, including France, Holland and Great Britain, together with the Italian cities, prospered by selling the Spanish their products. The very same river of gold that was destroying Spain was also supporting the development of the other countries.

This shows just how wrong the economists are who point to this inflation as the only cause of Spain's economic ruin. They fail to see that inflation proved devastating because the landlords stood in the way of all modern activities, whether in agriculture or in manufacture. The landlords, together with their numerous servants and clients, the clergy, the multitudinous monks, friars and nuns and, finally, the enormous administrative and military apparatus formed an unsustainable parasitic burden on the residual production of Spain.

All this explains why the Spanish treated the issue of the poor in a very different way from the English, and so gave their economy the *coup de grace*. In 1526, Luis Vives, a great humanist, was the first European scholar to devote a (fairly voluminous) work to the poor. His approach is a mixture of patristic ideas – for example, the absolute right of the poor to enjoy the superfluities of the rich – and modern considerations, such as the severe criticism of arrogance in beggars, and the asserted duty for everyone to work, nobles included (Vives 1947–48 [1526], vol. 1, pp. 1368–98).

In 1547, there was a fierce dispute between the Benedictine Abbot Juan de Medina and the Dominican Domingo de Soto, a very influential professor in Salamanca. Medina had tried to follow on with the successful experience of Bruges and Ypres in Zamora, organising the poor and putting them to work, simply aiming to apply the 1540 Royal Decree (*Real Cédula*) on the organisation of the poor. This law was a solemn call on the local authorities to sort out this issue. It restrained the liberty of movement of vagrants and beggars and ordered that hospitals be built in which the unable poor could receive relief and the able poor should be put to work. These hospitals were to be financed through the alms collected by "pious persons" (see the *Real Cédula* in Campomanes 1775, pp. 250–67). It was precisely the same policy that was launched in England in the same period.

But Medina's initiative was scathingly attacked by Soto, effectively reviving all the medieval arguments: the poor, being the image of God, have the right to move everywhere (Soto held that moving was a basic natural right); their existence is part of the plan of divine providence to make the rich virtuous through alms; alms must be free and personal, to be morally appreciable; it is absurd to put bureaucratic obstacles to giving a piece of bread (Soto 1965 [1545]). Medina's weak answer suggests that the common feeling in Spain was sympathetic with Soto (Medina 1545, pp. 143–316). The public opinion, formed by the privileged and parasitic classes, reflected the desire of landlords to oppose manufactures.

The debate in Spain went on for more than a century, but the reform proposals became ever more tentative and uncertain, while positions similar to Soto's grew increasingly more arrogant. By refusing to treat the poor as unemployed and to see manufactures as necessary for development, Spain took a decisive turn on the way to decadence – decadence that had been feared and foreseen by the Spanish mercantilists, who were derided and despised like Cassandras (Sureda Carrion 1949), while their English colleagues were respected and listened to.

## Notes

I thank the participants in the Conference on Chinese and European Thought (Bad Homburg, Febr. 2019) for their useful comments.

1. Xenophon *Oeconomicus* Ch. 1. 1–23, Ch. 2. 1–9. Plato (1997) *Republic*, pp. 369–73, 416–17. Aristotle (1984) *Nicomachean Ethics*, 1096a.
2. Diogenes Laërtius *Lives*, b. VII. Seneca, *De Ira*, II.25, II.33. Marcus Aurelius, *Ricordi*, V.12.
3. Plato, *Laws*, 846d-850, 918b-920a. Xenophon, *Oeconomicus*, ch. IV.2–4. Aristotle, *Politics*, 1255b, 1256b, 1257, 1291a. Boethius *Consolation of Philosophy*, II.5.
4. Troeltsch (1911, pp. 118–20). Sassier (1990, pp. 28–36).
5. Cyprian *On Works and Alms*: 8. Ambrose *Letters*, "To Constantius"; "To Marcellina". Augustine, *Sermons*, vol. 2, sermon 39.6, p. 219.
6. St. Benedict, *Rule*, Introduction; Ch. 48, sections 1 and 8.
7. Troeltsch (1911, pp. 349–58). Little (1978, Chs 6–7). Baeck (1994, pp. 125–34).
8. Pascal R. (1935, pp. 136–38, 153–60). Manselli (1983, p. 838).
9. Olivi, *De usu paupere. Quaestio*, pp. 14–85. Vian (1989, pp. 12–13).
10. Mollat (1978, p. 140). Manselli (1983, p. 835). Burr (1992, pp. xxxii–xxxiii).
11. Thomas Aquinas, *Summa theologiae,* vol. 41, Quaestio 117.1. Vol. 34, 1975, Q.s 32,6 and 118.1, etc. Vol. 42, 1966, Q. 125, 4.
12. On Jean de Meun, see Ricci (1996, p. 30); Wood (2002, pp. 45–46).
13. Salutati (1399); Alberti (1969 [1432–41]), b. II, p. 180; b. III, pp. 199–200; 299–302); Valla (1953 [1431], pp. 80–164); Manetti (1452, pp. 427–87); Pontano (1520 [1500]), I, pp. 147, 159–60). On Ficino and others, see Garin (1941).
14. Henry VIII's law of 1531–32 is in Eden (1797, vol. I, pp. 122–27).
15. See in particular Elizabeth's law of 1601, in Eden (1797, vol. III, pp. clxvii–clxxiii).

## References

Alberti, Leon Battista: *Libri della famiglia*. Torino: Einaudi, 1969 [1432–41].
Ambrose: *Letters*. New York: Fathers of the Church, 1954 (fourth century CE).
Aquinas, Thomas *Summa theologiae*. London: Eyre & Spottiswoode, 1966.
Aristotle: *Nicomachean Ethics*. In: *Works, Vol. II*. Princeton, NJ: Princeton University Press, pp. 333–436, 1984.
Aristotle: *Politics*. In: *Works, Vol. II*. Princeton, NJ: Princeton University Press, pp. 437–548, 1984.
Augustine: *Sermons*. New York: New City Press, 1990–91 [fourth to fifth centuries CE].
Baeck, Louis: *The Mediterranean Tradition in Economic Thought*. London: Routledge, 1994.
Benedict of Nursia: *Rule*. Dublin: Four Courts, 1994 [fourth to fifth centuries CE].
Boethius, Severinus: *Consolation of Philosophy*. Harmondsworth: Penguin, 1969 [c. 524].
Bracciolini, Poggio: *L'avarizia*. In: Eugenio Garin (ed.): *Il Rinascimento italiano*. Anthology. Firenze: Il Portolano, 1941 [trans. from Latin (1428–29)], n.p., pp. 248–301, 1952.
Burr, David: *Introduction*. In: Peter Olivi (ed.): *De usu paupere …* Perth: University of Western Australia, 1992.

Campomanes, Pedro: *Apéndice a la Educación popular*, Vol. 2. Madrid: Sancha, 1775.
Cipolla, Carlo Maria: *Vele e cannoni* [trans. from English]. Bologna: Il Mulino 1965.
Cyprian: *On Works and Alms*. In: *Writings*, Vol. *II*. Edinburgh: Clark, 1869 [third century CE].
Diogenes Laërtius: *Lives of Eminent Philosophers*. Loeb Library. London: Heinemann – Cambridge, MA: Harvard University Press, 1966 [third century CE].
Eden, Frederic Morton: *The State of the Poor*, 3 vols. London: Davies, 1797.
Francis of Assisi: *Writings*. London: Burns & Oates, 1964.
Garin, Eugenio (ed.): *Il Rinascimento italiano*. Anthology. Firenze: Il Portolano; Bologna: Cappelli, 1941.
Kula, Witold: *Teoria economica del sistema feudale*. Torino: Einaudi [trans. from Polish], 1972 [1962].
Little, Lester: *Religious Poverty and the Profit Economy in Medieval Europe*. London: Elek, 1978.
Lysón y Viedma, Mateo: *Discursos y apuntamientos*. Madrid: Biblioteca Nacional, 1622.
Mandeville, Bernard: *The Fable of the Bees or Private Vices, Publik Benefits*, Vol. *1*. Oxford: Clarendon Press, 1988.
Manetti, Giannozzo: *Della dignità e dell'eccellenza dell'uomo*. Book IV. In: Eugenio Garin (ed.): *Il Rinascimento italiano*. Anthology, pp. 427–87. Firenze: Il Portolano, 1952 [1452].
Manselli, Raoul: Il pensiero economico del Medio Evo. In: Luigi Firpo (ed.): *Storia delle idee politiche, economiche e sociali*, vol. II.2, pp. 817–65. Torino: UTET, 1983.
Marcus Aurelius: *Ricordi*. Milano: Fabbri [Italian trans. from Latin], 1994 [second century CE].
Medina, Juan: *De la orden ... en la limosna ...* In: Domingo Soto: *Deliberación en la causa de los pobres*. Madrid: Instituto de Estudios políticos, pp. 143–316, 1965 [1545].
Mollat, Michel: *Les pauvres au Moyen Age*. Paris: Hachette, 1978.
Olivi, Peter: *De usus paupere ...* Perth: University of Western Australia, 1992 [thirteenth century CE].
Pascal, R.: Communism in the Middle Ages and Reformation. In: John Lewis, Karl Polanyi & Donald K. Kitchin (eds): *Christianity and the Social Revolution*. London: Gollancz, pp. 121–62, 1935.
Plato: *Laws*. In: *Works*, Vol. *II*, pp. 334–347. New York: Hackett, 1997.
Plato: *Republic*. In: *Works*, Vol. *I*, pp. 215–580. New York: Hackett, 1997.
Pontano, Giovanni: *De Prudentia ...* Florentiae: eredi di Iunta, 1520 [1500].
Ricci, Giovanni: *Povertà, vergogna, superbia*. Bologna: Il Mulino, 1996.
Salutati, Coluccio: *De Fato et Fortuna*. Firenze: Olschki, 1985 [1399].
Sassier, Philippe: *Du bon usage des pauvres*. Paris: Favard, 1990.
Seneca, Lucius Annaeus: *On Anger*. In: *Moral and Political Essays*. Cambridge: Cambridge University Press, 1995 [first century CE].
Soto, Domingo: *Deliberación en la causa de los pobres*. Madrid: Instituto de Estudios políticos, pp. 5–142, 1965 [1545].
Starkey, Thomas: *A Dialogue between Pole and Lupset*. T.F. Mayer (ed.) London: Royal Historical Society, 1989 [1529–32].
Sureda Carrion, José: *La Hacienda castellana y los economistas del siglo XVII*. Madrid: Instituto "Moncada", 1949.
Tolomei, Claudio: *Sette libri delle Lettere*. Vinegia (Venezia): Giolito de' Ferrari, 1565 [1547].

Troeltsch, Ernst: *The Social Teaching of the Christian Church*. New York: Macmillan [trans. from German], 1931 [1911].

Valla, Lorenzo: Del vero e del falso bene. In: *Scritti filosofici e religiosi* [trans. from Latin], 1953 [1431].

Vasoli, Cesare: Il pensiero politico della Scolastica. In: Luigi Firpo (ed.): *Storia delle idee politiche, economiche e sociali*. Torino: UTET, vol. II.2, pp. 367–462, 1983 [1982–89].

Vian, Paolo: Introduzione. In: Pietro di Giovanni Olivi, Scritti Scelti, Roma: Città Nuova, 1989.

Viñas y Mey, Carmelo: Notas sobre primeras materias, capitalismo industrial y inflación en Castilla durante el siglo XVI. In: *Anuario de Historia Económica y Social*. Madrid: Univ. de Madrid, 1970.

Viner, Jacob: Religious Thought and Economic Society. *History of Political Economy*, 10, 1978 [1957–62].

Vives, Juan Luis: *Del socorro de los pobres*. In: *Obras completes, Vol. 1*. Madrid: Aguilar, 1947–48 [1526].

Weber, Max: *Storia economica e sociale dell'antichità. I rapporti agrari*. Roma: Editori Riuniti, pp. 371–93 [trans. from German], 1981 [1909].

Weber, Max: *The Protestant Ethic and the Spirit of Capitalism*. London: Allen & Unwin [trans. from German], 1930 [1904].

Wood, Diana: *Medieval Economic Thought*. Cambridge: Cambridge University Press, 2002.

Xenophon: *Oeconomicus, Vol. IV*. London: Heinemann, pp. 363–525, 1968 [fifth to sixth centuries BCE].

# 12 After China, before Sweden and England: The circulation of paper money in Naples

*Lilia Costabile*

## Introduction

A book devoted to Chinese and European economic thought is an occasion to reflect on the history of monetary thought and its relationship with monetary history. In this chapter, I focus on the paper money introduced by the public banks of Naples in the 1570s, and its problematic relationship with two alternative theoretical approaches: metallism and cartalism, a version of nominalism depicting money as an artefact of the sovereign authority.

China introduced paper money many centuries ahead of Europe, and used it during the Song (960–1279), Yuan (1279–1368) and Ming (1368–1644) dynasties. In the fourteenth century, the country gradually began a transition from its paper money towards a system using uncoined silver, complemented by bronze coins for small payments (von Glahn 1996, p. 10). The monetary history of China thus provided examples of two extreme prototypes: fiat money on one side of the spectrum and commodity money on the other. Consequently, Chinese money began to appear as a trope in the European literature, with these two extremes sometimes used to support one or the other of the two approaches mentioned above. It may be interesting to note that the same theoretical division appears in the monetary thought of China itself, where the older cartalist approach describing "money as a magnanimous act on the part of the sage kings" (von Glahn 1996, p. 26) was criticised in the thirteenth and fourteenth centuries by metallist writers describing inconvertible paper as "orphans who had lost their mother in childbirth" (von Glahn 1996, pp. 61ff, esp. p. 63).

In what follows, I start with an illustration of the main tenets of the metallist and cartalist approaches and some of the problems they encountered when faced with actual facts. The European literature on money presents innumerable examples but, owing to reasons of space, I mostly concentrate on two Italian writers offering interesting versions of the two doctrines: Bernardo Davanzati (1529–1606) and Geminiano Montanari (1633–87) respectively. I then illustrate the origins and main features of the paper money introduced by the public banks of Naples and show why it presents an interesting counterexample that does not square well with either the metallist or the cartalist stories of the origins of money and the sources of its value. This example suggests that such

DOI: 10.4324/9780367434496-18

stereotyped representations may not capture well the complexity of the history of money.

## Metallism and cartalism

Paper money combines liquidity with cheapness. Liquidity means general acceptance. A successful paper money is liquid – that is, widely accepted as a medium of exchange and as a means of discharging obligations. At the same time, paper money is cheaper to produce than money "printed" on expensive supports such as gold and silver.

Ferdinando Galiani (1728–87), an acute eighteenth century monetary theorist, observed the disproportion between the purchasing power of paper money and the negligible value of its material substance, and raised the crucial question: What transformed into "precious money mere sheets of paper that are otherwise worthless"? (Galiani 1751, pp. 324–25; Galiani 1963 [1780], p. 269). We will discuss Galiani's answer at the end of this section.

This question posed a challenge to the traditional metallist approach, which focused exclusively on full-bodied money. Following D.H. Robertson (1928, p. 47), I define full-bodied money as money "whose value is not materially greater than the value of the stuff of which it is composed". With reference to metallic money, this definition implies that the value of coins is equal to the intrinsic value of their metal content. For instance, in a simple model with gold coins, the value of money would be equal to the relative price between goods and gold (units of goods per unit of gold, the latter being measured in weight units such as grams or ounces). David Ricardo expressed this point of view with admirable clarity:

> An ounce of gold coin cannot be of less value … than an ounce of gold bullion of the same standard; a purchaser of corn therefore is entitled to as much of that commodity for an ounce of gold coin (…) as can be obtained for an ounce of gold bullion.
>
> (Ricardo 1951 [1811], p. 239)

This is the essence of theoretical metallism. Practical metallism, the normative complement to theoretical metallism, stipulated that all coins *should* be full bodied (Schumpeter 1954, p. 288).

Theoretical metallism was problematic even before paper money made its appearance. First, in metallic systems few coins were full bodied, if only because the issuing authorities usually charged a seigniorage fee to cover minting costs and, often, also to secure for themselves some revenue from money creation. In other words, gratuitous coinage was not normally in place, although it had existed in England since 1666, and Ricardo assumed this rule as an assumption of his model (Costabile 2017; Feavearyear 1963, pp. 95–96).

Another wedge between the purchasing power of money and its intrinsic value was opened by the practice of debasements, by which sovereigns either reduced the metal weight of coins while keeping their face values constant or, in contrast, "cried them up" (raised their face values), leaving their metal weight unaltered.

Obsidional money posed still another challenge to metallism. *Obsidio* is the Latin word for siege, and this type of money was issued for commanders to pay besieged or sieging troops. When gold and silver were not available, these commanders used coins made of leather, lead or other base materials, including paper, and promised to redeem them with "the real thing" at the end of the siege. The literature reports several such episodes from antiquity to modern times. For instance, eighteenth-century erudite scholar Gian Rinaldo Carli (1720–95), in his treatise on money and minting, tells us about leather coins issued by Costantino Copronimo during the siege of Constantinople in 743, the Venetian Doge Michiel during the siege of Tyre in 1122 or 1124, and Frederick II during the siege of Faenza in 1240.[1] He also says obsidional coins made of copper were issued during the siege of Novara in 1495, in the context of Charles VIII's expedition in Italy; paper money was issued in 1574 during the siege of Leyden; pressed musket balls were used as money by the Spaniards when it was their turn to be besieged in Zursen in 1586;[2] and copper coins were issued in La Valletta in 1636 (Carli 1751, pp. 21–22). Although some of the older episodes may be apocryphal, episodes dating from the fifteenth century are historically true.[3]

Of interest here are the theoretical reactions to the three categories of facts demonstrating the disjuncture between the value of coins and the material elements of which they were made. In short, these facts led even the most adamant metallist authors to recognise trust and/or authority as being among the determinants of the value of money.

For instance, Bernardo Davanzati (1853 [1588], p. 443) defined money as "gold, silver, or copper coined by the public authority at pleasure, and by the people's consent made the price and measure of things, to contract them easily". He believed in the "commercial" – or, as it would later be called, "catallactic" – story about the origins of money. According to this perspective, money arose as the spontaneous product of market choices made by private individuals striving to remedy the inconvenience of barter (mainly the problem of the double coincidence of wants). In his view, gold, silver and copper were chosen because "they are the noblest and most portable metals, and contain much value in a small mass" (Davanzati 1853 [1581], p. 427).[4] He argued that if the prince used other materials, such as iron, lead, paper, wood and salt, these means of payment would not be accepted beyond the limits of the state – in other words, they would not be "universal money" (Davanzati 1853 [1588], pp. 443–44). With this statement, Davanzati (1853 [1588], pp. 443–44) unwittingly admitted that the prince's authority can make any money accepted by fiat within the territorial borders of his political jurisdiction. As for debasements, Davanzati (1853 [1588], p. 445) defined them as a betrayal of people's trust, implicitly recognising that people may accept coins at higher value than their intrinsic content, as long as they trust the issuing authority. In other words, he unwittingly admitted that there is normally a fiduciary element in the value of money. Finally, concerning minting costs, Davanzati (1853 [1588], p. 445) argued that, ideally, they should be financed by the community in order to eliminate any difference between the coins' face values and the intrinsic value of their material support. If this was impossible, then at least these minting costs should be reduced to a minimum. To achieve this end, he suggested going back to old, cheaper minting technologies. He even proposed using commodity money in the form of uncoined metals by weight "as they do in China" (Davanzati 1853 [1588], p. 436). In practice, faced with so many exceptions, Davanzati ended up adopting the principle of the intrinsic value of money as a normative precept rather than an explanatory variable.

Writing a century later, Geminiano Montanari was more consequential: he explicitly abandoned the metallist doctrine and adopted a state-centred version of the nominalist approach. He defined money as whatever – metal or anything – is "authenticated" by the public authority to serve as price and measure of other things (Montanari 1804, p. 52).[5] He further clarified his thought by saying:

> I for myself locate the essence of money and its formal reason (as they say) in its being destined to this purpose and authorised by the prince, so that, at least in the territory where he rules, it works as price and measure of all things that can be contracted.
>
> (Montanari 1804, p. 53)

Openly disputing Davanzati's distinctions, he said he saw no reason why monies made of tin, shells or cocoa beans should be denied the name "money" if the ruling authorities of their respective countries gave them that role. Consistently with this approach, Montanari dispensed with the usual metallist story about people's consent to using metals as money because of their intrinsic qualities (durability, portability, divisibility, etc.). Although he discussed the metallurgical properties of gold, silver and copper, he never ascribed their use as money to these physical characteristics (Montanari 1804, p. 92). Montanari's nominalist stance is also apparent in his analysis of small coins. He argued that while in open economies parities between the metal content of large coins must be roughly respected for the sake of international trade, lest foreign nations refuse the national currency, the value of small change depends uniquely on the sovereign's will, because it is only used in domestic transactions (Montanari 1804, pp. 107–09). Therefore, the sovereign can earn higher seigniorage on small coins than on large coins, but he must avoid over-issues of the former type because of their inflationary consequences. Finally, Montanari built on siege monies part of his argument in favour of nominalism. In his view, the experiences of Michiel in Tyre, Frederick II in Lombardy, and the Roman emperor in Vienna in 1529 clearly demonstrated "the prince's authority to be the only form that brings money into being, whatever the material substance due to receive it" (Montanari 1804, p. 55).[6] It is interesting to observe that

China's money makes its appearance in Montanari's treatise too, but exactly for the opposite reason than in Davanzati's work – to demonstrate that the value of money is nothing but the product of sovereign authority. Therefore, contrary to Davanzati, his model was China's paper money rather than uncoined metals (Montanari 1804, pp. 104–05).

While Davanzati and Montanari were telling their respective market- and state-based stories about the origins and nature of money, almost under their eyes a different type of money was emerging and establishing itself at the centre of the monetary system of the largest Italian state, the Kingdom of Naples – then a dominion of the Spanish empire.[7] The paper money invented in Naples did not square well with the metallist approach, nor did it sit completely at ease within the state theory of money, because it was not metallic money; it was not a temporary, emergency device like siege money; it did not emerge from repeated interactions between private trading partners; and it did not originate in an autonomous decision by the political authority. This money, called *fede di credito*, was a paper instrument that started to circulate as a means of payments in the early 1570s and performed this function for many centuries. It was the creation of the deposit branches of some charitable institutions, and it was not introduced by fiat. It was only in time that the ruling authorities chartered these "banks of the charities" (*banchi dei luoghi pii* in Italian) as "public banks" and authorised them to issue their *fedi*, and even then they did not do so without hesitation and second thoughts.

Why did this money establish itself as the mainstay of the Neapolitan monetary system and work so well for so many centuries, despite its "unlikely" nature, if judged by the canons of the two dominant theoretical approaches? Ferdinando Galiani offers us an invaluable clue: "it is a praiseworthy fruit of virtue that faith alone bestows value; it has transformed into precious money mere sheets of paper which are otherwise worthless" (Galiani 1751, pp. 324–25; Galiani 1963 [1780], p. 269).[8]

This sentence encapsulates the basic element of a theory of fiduciary money. Galiani explicitly referred to the public banks of Naples as his main source of inspiration for his formulation of this theory. To see what fiduciary money is, or at least what it was in the Kingdom of Naples, let us look into the nature of the banks of the charities and the monetary circulation that they initiated.

## The public banks and their fiduciary circulation[9]

Seven of the eight "public banks" originated as the auxiliary departments of some charitable institutions: four hospitals (Incurabili, Sant Eligio, S.Giacomo e Vittoria, Santissima Annunziata), two charitable pawnbrokers (Monte di Pietà and Monte dei Poveri) and one conservatory for indigent young women (Casa dello Spirito Santo).

The oldest were Sant'Eligio and Santissima Annunziata, founded in 1270 and 1318 respectively. Later on, in 1522, a pious lady, Maria Longo, founded the Incurabili hospital; and in 1571 Don John of Austria, returning from Lepanto, founded S.Giacomo e Vittoria. The two charitable pawnbrokers, Monte di

Pietà and Monte dei Poveri, were established in 1539 and 1563 respectively. All these charities were inspired by religious ideals, but had laical origins, and were administered by members of the local bourgeoisie. The Spirito Santo, a conservatory for indigent girls, was founded by Dominican friars in 1555. While the two pawnbrokers statutorily provided small loans to the poor, the other institutions provided shelter, accommodation and medical assistance to the poor, the ill and the disabled; assistance and education for abandoned children; dowries for indigent women; alms in the form of food, clothing and small money allowances for widows, orphans and "honest" inmates; and ransoms for captives held by the "Turks". The Incurabili hospital also engaged in medical research (Valerio 2010). On these foundations, they built a capital of trust and a system of social control extended over large swathes of society.

The charities developed their auxiliary branches in order to keep records of their accounts, pay for the goods and services needed by the people they assisted, accept donations by benefactors, and administer their own patrimonial assets. The deposit branch of Annunziata engaged in banking activities (loans and deposit acceptances) since 1462 (Di Meglio 2018; Vicinanza 2006). Between 1584 and 1600, all of them received formal charters as "public banks", meaning that they were entitled to receive deposits from the public and issue deposit certificates, and also that they were subject to some degree of government regulation.[10] While the pre-existing private banks failed, the seven public banks became the backbone of the kingdom's financial system. They were "no-profit" institutions because they used their profits to finance the philanthropic operations of their parent institutions that were their owners. Later on, in 1640, the flour tax-farmers founded the only for-profit public bank in the system.

The public banks of Naples issued *fedi di deposito* and *fedi di credito*. *Fedi di deposito* served as receipts, or to certify that money was kept in escrow for settling transactions between customers, such as property purchases. The first *fede di deposito* we know of was issued by the Annunziata on 20 September 1564 (Demarco & Nappi 1985, p. 25). If depositors needed to make a payment, they asked the bank for a *fede di credito*. In this case, the bank's governors issued a note acknowledging their debt, stating the amount owed and confirming the bank's obligation to honour the payment by giving back cash at any time, either to the original depositor or to any person she may be willing to indicate. The *fede* then circulated by endorsement (*girata*), with signatures by both the payer (the bank's depositor) and the payee.[11] They also normally contained detailed descriptions of the reason for the payment by *girata*. The oldest *fede di credito* we know of was issued in 1573 by the Monte di Pietà. *Fedi di credito* were negotiable instruments that were universally accepted as means of payment. They were divisible. For smaller payments, depositors used *polizze* drawn on the original *fedi*, thus remaining in credit with the bank for the excess value.[12]

*Fedi di credito* and *polizze* were collectively called *bancali*. On receiving a *bancale*, the endorsees would simply go to the issuing bank, or to any other bank in the system, and had them converted into cash or credited to their own accounts; alternatively, they could make another *girata*. The last endorsee would then go to the bank either to redeem the amount in cash or to have it credited to their account. These chains of payments were sometimes quite long, acting as a money multiplier.[13] The circulation of the *fede di credito* thus increased the velocity of circulation of money because it facilitated transactions. In addition, the interbank clearing system reduced costs for customers, thus helping to enhance the liquidity and viability of the system as a whole.

Three points should be emphasised. First, generalised trust in the public banks is what conferred the *fede* its "moneyness" – that is, its *liquidity* (general acceptability) – because the *fede* was a liability of the bank, not of the individual payer. It stated that the original depositor had deposited X ducats and that they were trustworthy just because they were in credit with the bank for that amount of money. *Fede* in Italian means both statement and trust. Thus, the *fede* was a "statement of trustworthiness" used to transfer the depositor's credit towards the bank to the payee. It was universally accepted because it was the bank's promissory note. Trust in the banks had two main roots: one was the prestige of the charities as powerful benefactors; the other the patrimonial assets they gave as guarantees for their banks (Tortora 1882, pp. 134–35). These assets were used to compensate the banks' depositors and creditors in difficult times. In 1702, for example, when the Annunziata bank failed, the Holy House of the Annunziata (the hospital) paid for its debts, if only reluctantly and under judicial ordinance.

For its characteristic features, the *fede di credito* was different from other paper instruments already existing in the Western world. For instance, bills of exchange lacked liquidity because they were the liabilities of private individuals, and consequently were not accepted universally as a means of payment. The *fede di credito* was also different from the book-entry (or "ledger") money used by banks in various parts of Europe. Ledger money consisted in payment by transfer on the banks' books. It required the simultaneous presence of both the payer and the payee at the bank, and did not circulate from hand to hand. In short, the Neapolitan public banks initiated the *circulation* of paper money in the Western world, thus marking the beginning of a new era in banking practices ahead of similar developments in other parts of Europe, such as Genoa, Sweden and England.

Second, in order to protect the depositor, the regulatory system prohibited all active operations including loans to individuals and even to the banks' own parent institutions, although an exception was made for lending to the authorities, namely the Viceroy's Court and the City council. According to the regulatory system, note issuing should only originate in, and document, a passive operation by the bank. This regulation meant that the depositor was the only person entitled to receive a *fede di credito*, and for a value not exceeding the value of her deposit. The implication was that not a single *fede* should come into existence unless the same value in coins was withdrawn from the circulation. In other words, circulating notes were to be mere substitutes for metallic money, and banks were due to keep 100 per cent metal reserves (with the exception of loans to governmental institutions). But only in the edicts and in the perception of some of the banks' customers were the *fedi* mere substitutes for metallic money. In reality, the public banks, as most financial innovators, were very good at eluding the prohibitions and circumventing the rules. Consequently, their first revolutionary step – the invention of the *fede* – produced another epochal innovation: the banks became *creators* – as opposed to mere intermediaries – of money. In other words, they did not merely transfer purchasing power between their depositors' and their borrowers' accounts; rather, they expanded the money supply by writing or accepting *fedi di credito* not "covered" by cash deposits. Money was created "by a stroke of the pen" through multiple techniques. One of the public banks' most innovative techniques of money creation consisted of granting overdraft facilities in the form of standing orders, which may be used by their customers "whenever the need may arise" (*nell'occorrenze*). These facilities were the predecessors of modern cash credits. Pietà was granting cash credits in 1612, more than a century in advance of the Royal Bank of Scotland, which some modern sources credit with the invention of this innovative instrument (Checkland 1975). The public banks were innovators because their loans and overdrafts were based on a paper circulation. Thus, while an overdraft granted in systems of ledger-money (by, say, the Taula de Canvis in Barcelona or Banco di Rialto in Venice) settled payments in the bank's books without bringing any circulating note into existence, the Neapolitan banks, in contrast, made loans by creating new *fedi di credito*, thereby expanding their monetary circulation (Costabile & Nappi 2018). This system brought great benefits to commerce, as contemporary writers were quick to observe.[14]

Third, the Neapolitan circulating note was not introduced by fiat. It was an autonomous innovation of the bank of the charities. As hinted at above, the Spanish authorities were ambivalent towards both these banks and their money. They encouraged them on some occasions. For instance, in 1549 the Viceroy Pedro de Toledo established a "privilege" by which the population should prefer the Monte di Pietà over any other lender for loans upon pledge up to four ducats (raised to 10 ducats by Viceroy Granvela in the 1570s). In 1553, a more comprehensive edict ordered that the population should always prefer the not-for-profit banks (*banchi senza lucro*) over those for-profit (*banchi con lucro*) (*Prammatica III De Nummulariis*, 17 July 1553; Giustiniani 1804, 8, p. 130). But at other times they seemed to prefer alternative arrangements. This happened in 1580, when a pool of foreign private banks offered the Viceroy a multi-year loan at very good conditions in exchange for a 20-year bank monopoly. This project amounted to suppressing all other banks. All banks resisted and the King eventually renounced the project. But a similar plan surfaced in 1598. At this stage, almost all the banks of the charities had been chartered as public banks and authorised to receive deposits and issue their *fedi di credito*. They vigorously opposed the new project. The whole population went to the streets in order to back their protests, in a rare display of unity in a society where social conflict was endemic. Thus, popular pressure led the court to fully recognise the banks of the charities. Similarly, official recognition of the banks' notes as money occurred as a ratification of a function they were already playing. The official

166  *Lilia Costabile*

charters of the public banks ordered all the courts of the kingdom to "hold for real and good" the *fedi di credito*.[15] In other words, they legitimised them as an official means of payments.

## Conclusion

In Naples, the circulation of paper money emerged from the system of trust created by the bank of the charities. Even in 1681, after the system had undergone several banking crises, the feelings of the Neapolitan population were captured by the words of a foreign observer: "each bank constitutes a potentate, and the more so as it rules over the hearts, the arms, and the religious devotion of the aristocracy and the lower ranks of the population alike" (de Fonseca 1681, p. 13).

The paper money of the public banks was originally fiduciary, but not fiat money, because it was not imposed by the will of a sovereign authority. State support was of paramount importance as a pillar in the banks' system of trust, but it was not the originating factor.

Fiduciary money coexisted with metallic money, which in theory constituted the "base" constraining the banks' emissions and conferring its value to the "worthless paper" of which the bank notes were made. In practice, however, the *fede di credito* derived its value from generalised trust in the holiness of the charities and their banks, rather than from the value of the precious metals, because its emissions were to a large extent independent from the metallic base (Costabile & Nappi 2018).

It is also worth noting that we are not referring to a minor episode in monetary history. The monetary circulation of the Neapolitan banking system was one of the largest in Europe in the sixteenth, seventeenth and eighteenth centuries (Velde 2018); the Kingdom of Naples was the largest in Italy, and Naples itself was one of the largest cities in Europe in the sixteenth and seventeenth centuries. The Neapolitan banking system was long lived and resilient in the face of frequent shocks. The bank of the Annunziata failed in 1702, but the others went on with their activities until they merged into Banco Nazionale di Napoli (1794), later called Banco delle Due Sicilie (Bank of the Two Sicilies) and, finally, Banco di Napoli at the time of Italy's unification in 1861. In the new nation, the Banco di Napoli was one of the three banks of issue until 1926 (when the Bank of Italy took this function over), and then continued as one of the main Italian commercial banks until the consolidation process in banking and other events led to its extinction in 2019.

Thus, the historical example of the Neapolitan fiduciary money disproves to some extent both the metallist and the cartalist theory of money, opening the way to more complex and circumstantial interpretative models.

## Notes

1 Medieval sources narrated Frederick II's coinage in 1140. These sources are Ricordano Malaspini (c. 1220–90), *Istoria antica,* Ch. CXXX, p. 9; Giovanni Villani

(about 1280–1348), *Nuova Cronica*, VI, 21, 1823, p. 32–33. See also Martinori (1915, p. 302) under the heading "moneta di cuoio" (leather money). For a list of Italian towns that minted siege coins from the sixteenth to nineteenth centuries, see Martinori (1915, p. 358, under the heading "ossidionali".)

2 Carli (1751, p. 22) says these coins were issued by Gian Battista Tassis with the inscription *Mon. st. obsidio Zutsaniae anno 1576*, and one of them was in the collection of the Count Leopoldo Tassis. Carli declared himself happy to be able to refer to this money because not even the most informed writers knew about it (Carli 1751, p. 22). He referred to van Loon (1723–37) as one of the authorities in this field.

3 Some authors argue that obsidional coins may have had the nature of jettons, or promises to pay, rather than money, but this interpretation seems to reflect old metallist prejudices and is in fact derived from the old metallist literature. In fact, these coins were issued and accepted as means of payments, meaning that they performed one of the functions of money.

4 Davanzati (1853 [1588], pp. 445–48) also explained that these metals were not chosen by virtue of their direct utility – that is, their ability to satisfy human needs. To explain the value of the precious metals, he introduced his version of what would later be called the paradox of water and diamonds, one of the *loci classici* of metallist thought.

5 I refer to the 1804 edition of his *La Zecca in consulta di Stato*, renamed on the occasion *Della Moneta trattato mercantile*.

6 Given Montanari's repeated statements of his nominalist position, it is paradoxical that he is defined a metallist by many interpreters. An exception is Bianchini (2012).

7 The Spaniards conquered the Kingdom of Naples in 1503 and ruled over it until 1707.

8 For more details on Galiani's theory of money, see Costabile (2016a).

9 In this section, I draw freely on Costabile & Nappi (2018).

10 Deposits were "irregular", meaning that the bank was not due to give back the same coins, but coins of the same value.

11 In addition to these circulating notes, sometimes referred to as *free fedi di credito* (*libere*), there were other categories: "conditioned *fedi di credito*" (*fedi conditionate*) could only be cashed on the occurrence of some specified conditions or after a certain date; *judicial fedi* were issued by the bank on receiving sums deposited on judicial order. The banks profited from the long delays before the judges eventually ordered the conversion of this last category of *fedi* into cash.

12 *Polizze* were usually written on pieces of paper of uniform quality and size, suggesting that they were issued by the banks and delivered to their customers at their request.

13 The banks' acceptance of each other's notes and their interbank clearing system (*riscontri*) reduced costs for their customers, as they were free to choose their bank according to convenience and location, which helped them to create a demand for their notes.

14 In Naples there was a lively debate on the role of bank money. For more details, see Costabile (2015, 2016b).

15 This provision was included in the charter of the bank of the hospital of the Incurabili, which was called Santa Maria del Popolo. This charter, issued in 1590, referred to the banks of the Annunziata and San Giacomo as holding similar licences (Tortora 1882, pp. 69–71).

## References

Bianchini, Marco & Montanari, Geminiano: Il contributo italiano alla storia del pensiero – Economia, *Treccani*, www.treccani.it/enciclopedia/geminiano-montanari_%28Il-Contributo-italiano-alla-storia-del-Pensiero:-Economia%29, 2012.

Carli, Gian Rinaldo: *Dell'origine e del commercio delle monete e dell'istituzione delle zecche d'Italia*. Venice: L'Haya, 1751.

Checkland, S.G.: *Scottish Banking: A History*. Glasgow: Collins, 1975.

Costabile, Lilia: Monetary Analysis, Financial Innovation, and Institutions before the Industrial Revolution: A Paradigm Case. In: Mauro Baranzini, Claudia Rotondi & Roberto Scazzieri (eds): *Resources, Production and Structural Dynamics*. Cambridge: Cambridge University Press, pp. 213–31, 2015.

Costabile, Lilia: The Value and Security of Money: Metallic and Fiduciary Media in Ferdinando Galiani's Della Moneta. *European Journal of the History of Economic Thought*, 23(3), pp. 400–24, 2016a.

Costabile, Lilia: External Imbalances and the Money Supply: Two Controversies in the English "Realme" and in the Kingdom of Naples. In: Sophus Patalano & Rosario Reinert (eds): *Antonio Serra and the Economics of Good Government*. Basingstoke: Palgrave Macmillan, pp. 166–90, 2016b.

Costabile, Lilia: Ricardo's Monetary Theory and the Minimalist Approach to Central Banking, mimeo, 2017.

Costabile, Lilia & Nappi, Eduardo: The Public Banks of Naples Between Financial Innovation and Crisis. In: Lilia Costabile & Larry Neal (eds), *Financial Innovation and Resilience: A Comparative Perspective on the Public Banks of Naples (1462–1808)*. London: Palgrave Macmillan, pp. 17–53, 2018.

Davanzati, Bernardo: Notizia dei cambi. In: Enrico Bindi (ed.): *Le opere di Bernardo Davanzati*, Vol. 2, a cura di, 2 vols. Firenze: Le Monnier, pp. 425–36, 1853 [1581].

Davanzati, Bernardo: Lezione delle monete. In: Enrico Bindi (ed.): *Le opere di Bernardo Davanzati*, Vol. 2, a cura di, 2 vols. Firenze: Le Monnier, pp. 438–57, 1853 [1588].

de Fonseca, Luis Enriques: *Tratado Y Discurso sobre la Moneda De El Reyno de Napoles. Su Estado, el origen de sus danos. El remedio para su consummo*. Napoles: Salvador Castaldo, 1681.

Demarco, Domenico & Nappi, Eduardo: Nuovi documenti sulle origini e sui titoli del Banco di Napoli. *Revue internationale d'histoire de la banque*, 30–31, pp. 1–78, 1985.

Di Meglio, Rosanna: Before the Public Banks. Innovation and Resilience by Charities in Fifteenth Century Naples. In: Lilia Costabile & Larry Neal (eds), *Financial Innovation and Resilience: A Comparative Perspective on the Public Banks of Naples (1462–1808)*. London: Palgrave Macmillan, pp. 55–70, 2018.

Feavearyear, Albert: *The Pound Sterling: A History of English Money*, 2nd ed. Oxford: Clarendon Press, 1963.

Galiani, Ferdinando: *Della moneta. Libri Cinque*. Napoli: Giuseppe Raimondi, 1750 [1751].

Galiani, Ferdinando: *Della Moneta. Libri Cinque*. 2nd ed. Napoli: Stamperia Simoniana, as reprinted in: A. Caracciola (ed.), Della moneta e scritti inediti. Milano: Feltrinelli, 1963 [1780].

Giustiniani, Lorenzo: *Nuova Collezione delle Prammatiche del Regno di Napoli*, t. 8. Napoli: Stamperia Simoniana, 1804.

Martinori, Edoardo: *La Moneta. Vocabolario Generale*. Roma: Istituto Italiano di Numismatica, 1915.

Montanari, Geminiano: *Della moneta trattato mercantile*. Milano: De Stefanis, 1804.

Ricardo, David: *Reply to Mr Bosanquet*. Reprinted in: Pierro Sraffe (ed.) *The Works and Correspondence of David Ricardo, Vol. III*. Cambridge: Cambridge University Press for the Royal Economic Society, pp. 155–256, 1951 [1811].

Robertson, Dennis Holme: *Money*. Cambridge: Nisbet & Co., 1928.

Schumpeter J.A.: *History of Economic Analysis*. London: George Allen & Unwin, 1954.

Tortora, Eugenio: *Raccolta di documenti storici edelle leggi e regole concernenti il Banco di Napoli*. Napoli: F.Giannini, 1882.

Valerio, A. (ed.): *L'ospedale del Reame. Gli Incurabili a Napoli. Storia e arte*. Napoli: Il Torchio della Regina Editore, 2010.

van Loon, Gerard: *Histoire métallique des XVII provinces de Pys-Bas, depuis l'abdication de Charles Quint, jusq'a la paix de Bade en 1716*. Le Haye: P. Gosse, 1723–37.

Velde, François R.: The Neapolitan Banks in the Context of Early Modern Public Banks. In: Lilia Costabile & Larry Neal (eds), *Financial Innovation and Resilience: A Comparative Perspective on the Public Banks of Naples (1462–1808)*. London: Palgrave Macmillan, pp. 201–41, 2018.

Vicinanza, Monica (ed.): *Napoli: Petruccio Pisano 1462–1466*. Acerra: Athena, 2006.

von Glahn, Richard: *Fountain of Fortune: Money and Monetary Policy in China, 1000–1700*. Berkeley, CA: University of California Press, 1996.

# 13 European models and transformations of the welfare state

*Hans-Michael Trautwein*

There are basically two different economic discourses about social policy in market economies. The first is about poverty relief; the second is about the welfare state, often described as a "social market economy". In the "poverty relief" perspective, social policy is a repair shop at the fringes of the market economy, confined to providing basic social security with regard to invalidity, unemployment and old age. The perspective taken in economic research is essentially microeconomic, focusing on cost efficiency, incentive compatibility and moral hazard problems. The "welfare state" perspective, by contrast, is essentially macroeconomic. The objective is a comprehensive "design" of institutions that foster economic growth and reduce systemic risks by strengthening social cohesion and political participation. In this wider notion of social policy, the core field of providing social security is flanked by fiscal redistribution, public provision of education at all levels, labour market activation and other programmatic measures.

The People's Republic of China (PRC) is officially described as a "socialist market economy with Chinese characteristics". Yet few people would call it a social market economy. It is only recently, after some 30 years of economic reforms, that the governing bodies have begun to set comprehensive concepts of social policy on their agenda. Their deliberations reflect to some extent ideas and institutional settings of social policy that were developed in various European countries in the nineteenth and twentieth centuries, when they underwent their "Great Transformation" (Polanyi 1944) to industrialised and urbanised market societies. Some of the European economies co-evolved with welfare state systems that, beyond providing basic social security, began to aim at supporting economic growth by social policies in the wider sense. Their welfare state policies are based on different national views on subsidiarity and solidarity, two basic principles for burden-sharing. While subsidiarity is more market oriented, assuming a close correspondence between insurable risks and returns, solidarity is more community oriented, to deal with systemic risks and large-scale inefficiencies that smaller units cannot handle.

This chapter presents two socio-economic "model cases" of welfare state societies that have put contrary emphasis on subsidiarity and solidarity. The selected cases are Germany and Sweden between the 1950s and the 1980s. At

DOI: 10.4324/9780367434496-19

the time, these two countries were considered as small open economies that successfully coped with the social challenges of opening up to international trade and pervasive technical change. They were (and still are) running comprehensive social policies embedded in export-led growth strategies. While the politics in the business and financial spheres of both countries can be characterised as pragmatic neo-mercantilism, their ideological superstructures differed substantially, thus contributing to differing economic styles (or self-stylisations). The dominant ideology was ordoliberalism in Germany, stressing subsidiarity, and welfare socialism in Sweden, emphasising solidarity.

The next section defines the notions of subsidiarity and solidarity as basic principles of welfare state policies. It points to older European traditions of economic and social thought that also have had an influence on the shaping of the European Union. The latter is, however, an entity that comprises many varieties of capitalism. Germany and Sweden have long been considered as representative models for the two major welfare state systems in the range of varieties. Hence, the following sections briefly outline the German and Swedish concepts of the welfare state, respectively, describing both as specific policy mixes that are unconventional by Anglo-Saxon textbook standards. Socio-economic success in Germany and Sweden bred failure after the 1980s, inter alia by making systemically important firms grow out of the national constraints of welfare state policies. Yet failure is relative; in many aspects it is rather a loss of model specificity that followed from integration and convergence in the European Union. Current global trends of de- and re-globalisation as well as digitalisation might nevertheless prompt economists and policy-makers, in both Europe and China, to reconsider mixes of subsidiarity and solidarity that help market societies to cope with these challenges.

## Principles of welfare state policies

Subsidiarity and solidarity are two principles of community-building and governance that have a long history in European social thought. "Subsidiarity" means to assign responsibility for the fulfilment of social and economic tasks to the smallest possible unit, such as a family in a local community, a local community in a region, a region in a state, and a state in a union. The intention is to delegate decision-making to the level of society that is directly involved and hence considered most effective in accomplishing the tasks. The unit at that level is also liable for the outcome, so as to minimise losses from risk-taking and risk-sharing and, in particular, to avoid moral hazard. Only in cases in which the responsible unit is unable to perform its tasks for no fault of its own should institutions at the next higher level come to assistance. As "a principle of structured power allocation in systems of plural governance" (Hueglin 1999, p. 153), subsidiarity is thus a category of vertical relations.

"Solidarity" means to create social, economic and political cohesion of a group by reciprocity in terms of mutual support and mutual liability. It is a shared value that recognises interdependence and "kinship" ties at various levels, be they the primary ties between family members or wider associations with other individuals who have similar economic interests, cultural beliefs, political views or simply a basic right to be treated as fellow humans. The intention of appealing to solidarity is to reduce existential risks and provide social opportunities for each individual member by creating mutual obligations of support. In terms of governance, solidarity is thus a category of horizontal relations.

While subsidiarity deals with relations *between* units of different levels, solidarity deals primarily with relations *within* and *between* units of the same level. The two principles can be envisaged as complementary elements in constructing modern systems of governance, but they are often seen as conflicting with each other. In a wider sense, subsidiarity is a top-down modality of solidarity if the higher level comes to the rescue of the lower level without adverse restraints; the conditionality, however, is a recurrent matter of dispute (as we will see below). The main reason for this ambiguity is the use of "solidarity" and "subsidiarity" as weasel words, as strategic catchwords for shaping political consensus as well as for staging controversies. Their versality is explained partly by the variety of their origins in the history of thought.

The notion of "subsidiarity" can be traced back to Johannes Althusius, a Calvinist political philosopher of the early seventeenth century, who argued for leaving decision-making to the lowest possible level of (self-)governing bodies.[1] This principle has appealed to various strands within liberalism and socialism alike: to advocates of liberalism because it helps to provide protection of individuals and their voluntary associations from state intervention; and to advocates of cooperative socialism because it would strengthen collective responsibility at the ground level while ensuring solidarity from the greater collective.

The notion of "solidarity" began to circulate in the wake of the French Revolution, in the mid-nineteenth century, when the triad of "liberty, equality, fraternity" became the official national motto. Solidarity was frequently used to replace either equality or fraternity, because it was considered to be more inclusive (Wildt 1999). The revolution had started a secularisation process to free public institutions from religious indoctrination and the political influence of the Catholic Church. Yet the notion of solidarity came also to play a key role in the Catholic social doctrines that emerged in Germany, Italy and France at about the same time. They were developed in reaction to the "social question", the misery of workers in early industrialisation, and they combined subsidiarity and solidarity as principles for transforming and expanding the church's pre-capitalist charities into regular welfare institutions in market economies. Still today, Catholic social teaching propagates "personality, solidarity, subsidiarity" as a triad of basic principles to form an alternative, more conservative view to the worldly ideologies of liberalism and socialism.[2]

Thus there was a common legacy in the use of the terms "solidarity" and "subsidiarity" when the process of European integration started after World War II, even if the specific content and context varied and shifted between the countries and the political camps. The two principles were valuable rhetoric devices for Christian Democrats, Socialists and Liberals, the three camps that dominated the political systems in the founding states of the European Economic Community (EEC). Appeals to them facilitated compromise and consensus.[3] Over time the EEC grew into the European Union (EU), with many more members, developing a comprehensive common set of regulations, the *acquis communautaire*. This achievement is remarkable in view of the present diversity of governance systems and related socio-economic philosophies across the member states. Fundamental differences between them persist even many years after opening up to the European common market.

Some of these differences have been categorised in four typical "varieties of capitalism": the Anglo-Saxon, the Continental, the Nordic and the Mediterranean market economies (Hall & Soskice 2001).[4] Even if this typology is contestable for its static view and neglect of heterogeneity within each "region", I will use it here to highlight differences with regard to the status of social policy in the perspectives on economic growth:

- The *Anglo-Saxon* variety of capitalism is characterised as a liberal market economy; social services are in principle "commodified" – that is, left to providers in the market; social policy is essentially reduced to basic poverty relief; any further redistribution of market incomes is considered to be *obstructive* to economic growth.
- The *Continental* variety is characterised as a sectorally coordinated market economy, in which major interest groups negotiate with each other through their organisations; social policy is defined as a comprehensive network of institutions in the social and economic order; the redistribution of market incomes is to *safeguard* economic growth by producing social harmony and political stability.
- The *Nordic* variety is characterised as a nationally coordinated market economy, in which the cooperation of the public authorities with private sector organisations is even more intense; social policy is defined as comprehensive framework to provide for equality; the redistribution of market incomes is to *promote* economic growth by activating human resources and creating high social acceptance of structural change.
- The *Mediterranean* variety is characterised as a hybrid market economy, in which some markets are highly organised in a coordinated fashion while most others are not; social policy is largely confined to basic poor relief and some support for families as the primary providers of social care; the redistribution of market incomes is partly seen as rent-seeking that *hampers* economic growth, and partly as incidental expenses necessary for social acceptance.

These definitions of European varieties of capitalism are "ideal types" in Max Weber's terms, pinpointing certain characteristic aspects rather than attempting fully representative descriptions of reality in different EU countries. They serve to argue that the comprehensive welfare-state perspective on social policy is taken only in those EU countries that can be subsumed under the Continental and Nordic varieties.[5] Within these groups, two countries stick out as emblematic "model cases" that differ in their emphasis on subsidiarity and solidarity: Germany and Sweden. Their socio-economic systems are frequently described as models because they are seen as successfully coping with social challenges of international trade and technical progress. Both countries have embedded comprehensive social policies in their export-led growth strategies, with a conservative-liberal "touch" in Germany, and with a social democratic "touch" in Sweden.

It should be noted, though, that much of the economic development in the two countries has been achieved by pragmatic adjustment of policy-makers to pressures; it was a "muddling through" rather than the result of "modelling" the economy via a well-designed strategy. There is nevertheless a hard core in their stylisation as models, which is perceptible from the ordinary interaction of political vision, business practice and public discourse to shape social acceptance for structural change in the economy. That "hard core" is aptly captured by the soft notion of "economic styles" *(Wirtschaftsstile)*, a concept developed in the (Younger) German Historical School. It was later adapted by Alfred Müller-Armack, one of the leading ordoliberals, to describe the vision of a "social market economy" in Germany[6] – to which we now turn.

## Germany's social market economy

Post-war economic thinking in Germany has been strongly influenced by ordoliberal ideas, which originated from the works of Walter Eucken and the Freiburg School.[7] Other patron saints are Wilhelm Röpke, the aforementioned Müller-Armack and Ludwig Erhard, the second chancellor of the Federal Republic of Germany in the 1960s and widely famed for his leading role in the post-war economic reforms that contributed to the so-called German economic miracle. Ordoliberalism is based on the proposition that the best mode of governance to foster economic growth and social welfare is to regulate the economy so that it closely approximates the theoretical norm of perfectly competitive markets. The creation of a market order that prevents private enterprises from attaining and abusing market power requires a strong state – a position by which ordoliberals distinguish themselves from neoliberals while opposing Keynesian strategies of macroeconomic stabilisation and other concepts of state intervention in the markets. The emphasis is on *Ordnungspolitik,* confining state governance to setting and enforcing *rules* for competition *and* cooperation in the market and civil society.

A related tenet of ordoliberalism, which follows from its rule-based approach, is the "interdependence of orders", which requires the social, legal and political subsystems of society to be compatible with the economic order. To avoid abusive concentration of power, the legal and political orders need to ensure the functioning of democracy with proper checks and balances. The social order is to be based on the principle of subsidiarity in terms of "self-responsibility" *(Eigenverantwortung)*, while providing for equal opportunity *(Chancengleichheit)*.

This is, in a nutshell, the political self-image of Germany as a "social market economy", a concept propagated by Müller-Armack and Erhard in the founding years of the Federal Republic. It stresses the importance of stable money, fiscal solidity, consensus-oriented industrial relations and social insurance as interdependent counterparts of competition policy.

Under the defining norm of equal opportunity, the basic element of social policy in the German model is statutory social insurance, with roots in the Bismarckian social legislation of the 1880s, a top-down initiative to detract support for the labour movement.[8] The provision of healthcare, pensions and unemployment benefits in the system of statutory social insurance is based on joint contributions from employees and employers, and on pay-as-you-go schemes, in which current collective expenditures are financed by current contributions. The principle of solidarity applies within the generations and in the pension part of the system between them. The principle of subsidiarity applies insofar as the central government finances deficits in the social insurance systems whenever contributions fall short of statutory rights to transfers. However, statutory social insurance covers only those who are or have been in regular employment, and only up to some limits. Basic social assistance to all those who fall outside the criteria is means-tested and makes family members liable in reciprocity. Here, the subsidiarity principle kicks in from the other end, defining the family as the basic unit responsible for social welfare. This is a traditional element in the German model, for a long time backed by conservative family policy in terms of fiscal relief and legal protection of kinship ties and traditional gender roles.

A core field of providing for equal opportunity is the education system. The German welfare state provides free (i.e. essentially de-commodified) and comprehensive education at all levels. A specialty is dual education, which combines apprenticeships in private companies and other workplaces with public vocational schooling. From a growth perspective, it helps to produce a large class of qualified workers with special skills from parts of the population that would otherwise enter the labour market with few or no skills. It also contributes to fostering self-responsibility under the subsidiarity principle.

In ordoliberal thinking, even macroeconomic policies are intended to combine equal opportunity and subsidiarity. The insistence on "stable money" – that is, the task of the central bank to minimise changes in the value of money – takes recourse to the argument that inflation is unfair. It tends to redistribute purchasing power and real incomes to the disadvantage of those who do not have the bargaining power to adjust their incomes. Furthermore, inflation tends to undermine the reliability of contracts that are conventionally and most conveniently concluded in nominal terms. As ordoliberals typically refer to fiscal profligacy as the main cause of inflation, they plead for fiscal solidity. Since they see expenditures for comprehensive measures of social policy as a major cause of excessive fiscal spending, they plead for subsidiarity. In their view, there is no substantial difference between private households and the public household when it comes to the need to practise the virtue of frugality.

The ordoliberal concept of the social market economy has framed the political rhetoric as well as the economic policy discourse in academia and the media in Germany for most of the time since the end of World War II. It coexists with a neo-mercantilist focus on the competitiveness of the nation, a more pragmatic mindset for policy-making and industrial business (Körner & Trautwein 2017). In that context, the ideal of perfect competition is translated into demands for state support, to level the playing field for small and medium-sized enterprises and to open export markets for German business. While state intervention by Keynesian demand-management is anathema (except, perhaps, when crises bite deeply), the neo-mercantilists welcome selective supply-side interventions in frameworks of strategic industrial policy. They see the combination of industrial co-determination by work councils and sectoral wage-bargaining between trade unions and employers' federations as a competitive advantage – at least as long as (a) the major export industries take the lead, and (b) the system produces a high degree of "social harmony". They consider the anti-inflationary stance of monetary policy as a further competitive advantage, since it tends to produce an undervaluation of the domestic currency (originally the Deutsche mark, now the euro). This favours German exports and tends to make Germany a strong international lender over time. All in all, official ordoliberalism and pragmatic neo-mercantilism have complemented each other in framing support for the strategy of export-led growth that made Germany the economic powerhouse of the European Union (Körner & Trautwein 2017).

## Swedish welfare socialism

The term "Swedish model", which came into use in the 1960s, denotes a variety of social-democratic policy concepts that describe a welfare state, in which solidarity is given priority to subsidiarity because of a particular emphasis on the importance of social security and equality for economic efficiency. Since Sweden experienced strong economic development in the post-war era, the country acquired international fame as a society in which social engineering managed to produce a high degree of welfare. The extent to which the rise of living standards was caused by specific policy strategies, or just by favourable external conditions, has been debated (Erixon 2010; Lundberg 1985). Yet it is generally accepted that the strategy devised by the trade union economists Gösta Rehn and Rudolf Meidner in the late 1940s strongly influenced (or at least anticipated) the macroeconomic policy regime that transformed Sweden between the 1950s and the early 1970s. The Rehn-Meidner model is firmly embedded in a comprehensive understanding of social policy in traditions of thought that were inspired, for example, by Knut Wicksell, (the early) Gustav Cassel, and Alva and Gunnar Myrdal (Trautwein 2011).

The peculiar construction of the Rehn-Meidner model emerged against the background of the post-war boom that resulted from strong demand for Swedish exports in the course of European reconstruction. The boom created a situation of "overfull employment" and presented a trilemma for the Swedish trade unions. They were facing bad choices between:

- wage drift in the export industries that tends to undermine solidarity among the trade unions if other sectors in the economy would be unable to follow
- losses of jobs if the unions succeed in achieving an increase in the general wage level that would increase inflation and make the export industries less competitive
- a deficit in legitimising union membership if the trade unions manage to exert wage restraint to safeguard jobs and avoid inflation, but thereby contribute to profit inflation in the export industries and an "unfair redistribution" of incomes and wealth.

In view of this trilemma, Rehn and Meidner fervently rejected the idea of a tradeoff between full employment and price-level stability – almost two decades before the famous Phillips curve debates began to engage mainstream economists. In their 1951 memorandum for the Swedish trade union federation, they devised an unconventional strategy to deal with the trilemma. With hindsight, the Rehn–Meidner model can be described as a comprehensive concept that aimed to eliminate the tradeoffs in the "magic pentangle" of high GDP growth, full employment, internal and external monetary stability and a fair income distribution. It is formally in line with the Tinbergen rule, by which the number of instruments must correspond to the number of targets, and each instrument must be clearly assigned to one target. Yet it is unconventional in that the instruments are intricately linked with each other so as to create a virtuous circle of economic growth and stability. Each instrument is supported by at least two other instruments, even if the latter primarily serve their own targets (see Figure 13.1).

Three instruments are at the core of Rehn–Meidner model: solidaristic wage policy, restrictive fiscal policy and active labour market policies; the policies of collective funding and structural adjustments follow from them as corollaries. Solidaristic wage policy is characterised by the slogan "equal pay for equal work". The intention is to close wage gaps between comparable jobs in highly profitable and less profitable firms, where comparability is expressed in terms of skill requirements, occupational hazards and observable effort. The compression of wage differentials that are not justified by such factors requires the coordination of wage negotiations in a centralised bargaining system (which came into force in the 1950s). The macroeconomic guideline for the consequential redistribution of wage gains is a nominal wage increase that on average corresponds to average productivity growth, and hence gives no inflationary impulse. However, this policy implies wage restraint in highly profitable companies, where subsequent excess profits could create legitimatory problems for the solidaristic wage policy. Hence, Rehn and Meidner pleaded for restrictive

| Target | Instrument | supported by: |
|---|---|---|
| Full employment | ← Active labour market policy | ← Restrictive fiscal policy<br>← Collective funding |
| Fair distribution of income | ← Solidaristic wage policy | ← Active labour market policy<br>← Restrictive fiscal policy |
| Price-level stability | ← Restrictive fiscal policy | ← Solidaristic wage policy<br>← Active labour market policy |
| Growth | ← Collective funding | ← Structural adjustments<br>← Restrictive fiscal policy |
| External stability | ← Structural adjustments | ← Solidaristic wage policy<br>← Collective funding |

*Figure 13.1* Targets and instruments in the Rehn-Meidner model

Source: Trautwein (2011, p. 77).

fiscal policy that contributes to a fair income distribution by progressive taxation and helps to control inflation by a sales-tax policy. The public savings that accrue from high taxation are intended to create budget surpluses over the cycles. In combination with tax-subsidised investment funds and pension funds under trilateral governance (trade unions, employers' federations and the government), these surpluses allow for the "formation of collective capital". This is used to fund improvements in the infrastructure and to finance other measures of structural adjustments that are required to make fast productivity growth consistent with full employment.

The key instrument for mitigating the consequences of fast structural change and ensuring full employment is "active" labour market policy. Solidaristic wage policy favours employment in firms that generate high profits by means of technological progress and other innovation. On the downside of wage equalisation, less-productive firms will not have their profits subsidised by local wage restraint. They are instead allowed to exit from their markets, thus indirectly contributing to an increase in productivity levels, but at the cost of displacing labour, mainly in peripheral regions. Active labour market policy takes comprehensive care of displaced workers by measures of retraining, matching and mobility support instead of being limited to "passive" policies of unemployment benefits and wage subsidies. Such policies may now look fairly conventional in international comparison, frequently described as "workfare" or "flexicurity", but they were a novel feature that distinguished the Swedish model from practices in other countries at the time of invention.

In the Swedish model, social acceptance of fast structural change in the economy, which required strong internal migration over a long period, has further been supported by comprehensive social policy with an egalitarian touch. Unlike the German practice of subsidiary basic assistance, it is not means tested and family related in Sweden, but rather based on taxpayers' solidarity and a strong work ethic (which in turn is fostered by an active labour market policy). Healthcare is likewise tax-funded and provided by the public sector, as is the basic "general pension".[9] Unemployment funding is tied to economic associations within trade unions *(a-kassor)*, a traditional instrument to increase union membership and thereby foster solidarity among workers. Another distinctive element of social policy in Sweden is family policy, which does not provide tax incentives for housewives (as in the German system) but has traditionally been oriented towards a high participation rate of women in the labour market. Sweden has taken a pioneering role in developing gender equality programmes in comprehensive day care, parental leave and other fields.

In the context of this chapter, three things are notable about the Swedish model. The first feature is the confinement of "welfare socialism" to the sphere of distribution. It is not about the socialisation of means of production or other state control of industries, but about a redistribution of incomes that makes all citizens participate in the results of growth in the economy's productivity. The second feature is the focus on "supply-side policies". In political economy debates, redistributive policies in welfare states are frequently associated with Keynesian management of aggregate demand. By contrast, the Swedish model-builders favoured a mix of restrictive demand management with selective supply-side measures, especially in the labour market and in subsidising export industries, in order to keep inflation consistent with full employment. Both these features amounted to a strategy to secure equitable growth, by which trade unions would support rather than resist labour-saving technical progress. The third feature is shared with the German model: an export-led growth strategy and pragmatic neo-mercantilism, as solidaristic wage policy and strategic industrial policy tended to support big companies in the export industries.

## Dynamic instability and transformation

The description of the German and Swedish models of the welfare state in the preceding sections is highly stylised. Characterising the economic styles in the two countries in the narrow space of this chapter is hardly possible without blending elements of ideal-type and real-type reasoning. The functional rationality of social policy in the model thinking corresponded most closely to reality between the 1950s and the early 1970s, and partly until the late 1980s. From the mid-1970s onwards, both economies experienced macroeconomic instability, as external preconditions for the success of export-led growth strategies began

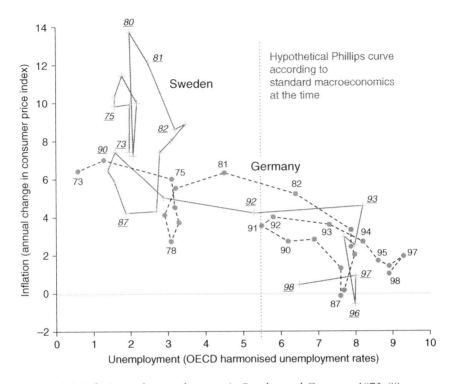

*Figure 13.2* Inflation and unemployment in Sweden and Germany, 1973–98

to vanish, most notably the Bretton Woods regime of fixed exchange-rates and national compartmentalisation of labour and financial markets. When the Bretton Woods regime had collapsed, Germany and Sweden became autonomous in their monetary policies, as they were no longer obliged to follow dollar exchange-rate targets. The era of floating national currencies (between 1973 and 1998, just before the European Monetary Union was established) revealed an important difference in the prioritisation of targets for macroeconomic policy in Germany and Sweden (see Figure 13.2).

Contrary to the conventional wisdom at the time, and contrary to the intentions of the German ordoliberals and the Swedish welfare socialists, Figure 13.2 indicates that a Philipps curve tradeoff between high employment and a stable value of money existed, at least for a time. In the 1970s and 1980s, Sweden apparently chose to safeguard jobs at the cost of accelerating inflation, while Germany chose to keep inflation (relatively) low by incurring the costs of increasing unemployment. However, from the early 1990s onwards, the Swedish model appears to have failed by giving up on full employment in order to bring down inflation and to keep Swedish industries competitive at a time when many new low-wage countries entered the world markets. Solidaristic wage policy was given up, as the employers' federations refused to continue centralised wage bargaining, and active labour-market policy quickly reached its limits. However, the German model failed too, at least in terms of the promises of "social harmony", since unemployment had become chronically high by the early 1980s, creating a divide between insiders and outsiders in the labour market – a divide that was deepened by the economic consequences of German reunification in the 1990s.

Yet it was not simply external change that undermined the two welfare state models. In both cases, success bred failure, since the export-led growth strategies had helped many German and Swedish companies to expand large parts of their business across borders, particularly into the common market of the European Union. This created exit options for avoiding tax payments and other contributions to the welfare states in the old national containers. Both countries saw attempts of adaptation and transformation – for example, by hybrid commodification of education and health services in Sweden, and by austere labour-market reforms in Germany. Many observers have interpreted such changes in the earlier representatives of the Continental and Nordic welfare states as shifts towards more limited settings of social policy in the Anglo-Saxon variety, the dominant model for globalisation of trade and finance.

## Conclusion

The German and Swedish welfare state models may have lost some of their once-distinctive characteristics, but have they really failed? The ordoliberal norms of competitiveness, subsidiarity and equal opportunity have retained a strong influence on the mindsets of policy discourse in Germany, even though the German economy has undergone massive structural change since the heyday of the post-war economic miracle (Körner & Trautwein 2017). The same can be said for Sweden, where many of the institutional pillars of the classical model have been abandoned, while equity and solidarity norms have survived in debates about the effects of globalisation. The public persistence of norms from earlier economic thinking is a valuable reason to study the underlying theories, especially at times when perceptions of inequality generate discontent with the course of globalisation and the current state of economics. Despite some erosion of their welfare systems, Germany and Sweden are countries where relatively low income inequality appears to remain compatible with strong economic performance and openness to trade.

Furthermore, what were once specificities of national welfare systems have been adopted in other countries and systems as best practice; the Swedish approach to labour-market policy is an example that has found followers outside Germany. On a more general plane, there is a clear need to re-evaluate national systems of social policy under the principles of subsidiarity and solidarity across the whole European Union. The challenge is to find a balance between these principles in view of the transnational regimes of trade and production, and in the interest of social cohesion and political order beyond the national confines. The greater interconnectedness in the economic sphere creates more systemic risks in the social sphere. Hence, elements of solidarity within *and* between national systems ought to gain greater weight. Self-responsibility is clearly a basic precondition for a good functioning of market economies, but it needs to be recognised that subsidiarity is a modality of solidarity. The general challenge to foster economic development by comprehensive welfare systems is not applicable to Europe alone; it is also relevant to other large economies, such as China.

## Notes

1 "What emerges from Althusius' federalism as the meaning of subsidiarity ... is an expression of a complex relationship and tension between autonomy *and* solidarity in a multilevel system of governance that can claim universal validity. It is as much applicable in the family and kinship relationships as in a commonwealth or, indeed, in an international political order." (Hueglin 1999, p. 153).
2 Two influential figures in the development of Catholic social teaching and its combination of subsidiarity and solidarity principles were the German theologians Wilhelm Emmanuel von Ketterer (1811–77) and Oswald von Nell-Breuning (1890–1991).
3 The founding Act was the Treaty of Rome in 1957, and the founding states were Belgium, France, Germany, Italy, Luxemburg and the Netherlands.
4 To the best of my knowledge, the EU accession countries in Central and Eastern Europe have not acquired the status of a specific variety in the literature; some of them (such as the Baltic states) range under "Anglo-Saxon", others under "Continental" or "Mediterranean". The regional attributes of the four listed varieties should not, at any rate, be seen as strictly geographical divisions; see also Arts & Gelissen (2010).
5 In line with Esping-Andersen (1990), it could be criticised that the characterisation of the Anglo-Saxon variety ignores the British welfare state, the classical example of decommodified public care "from the cradle to the grave". In the Hall-Soskice tradition, however, the Anglo-Saxon variety is the neoliberal world of Margaret Thatcher rather than the Fabian world of Lord Beveridge.
6 See Schefold (2017) for Müller-Armack's approach to "economic styles".
7 For an English-language collection of standard texts on ordoliberalism and the social market economy, see Goldschmidt and Wohlgemuth (2008).
8 At the time, these reforms were dubbed "state socialism", inspired by "socialists of the chair" *(Kathedersozialisten)* – that is, influential professors who were associated with the *Verein für Socialpolitik*, which is still the leading professional organisation of German-speaking economists. Most of the "socialists of the chair", such as Adolph Wagner, were anti-socialist conservatives who intended to conserve the political and economic order.
9 In addition, mandatory occupational pension schemes cover employees in industries under nationwide collective bargaining agreements. Nowadays, a share of the statutory social security contribution is paid into individual investment accounts and a funded pension is built up with independent fund management companies responsible for the asset management.

## References

Arts, Wil A. & Gelissen, John: Models of the Welfare State. In: Francis Castles, Stephan Leibfried, Jane Lewis, Herbert Obinger & Christopher Pierson (eds): *The Oxford Handbook of the Welfare State*. Oxford: Oxford University Press, pp. 569–83, 2010.

Erixon, Lennart: The Rehn–Meidner Model in Sweden: Its Rise, Challenges and Survival. *Journal of Economic Issues,* 44(3), pp. 677–715, 2010.

Esping-Andersen, Gøsta: *The Three Worlds of Welfare Capitalism.* Cambridge: Polity Press, 1990.

Goldschmidt, Nils & Wohlgemuth, Michael: Social Market Economy: Origins, Meanings, and Interpretations. *Constitutional Political Economy,* 19(3), pp. 261–76, 2008.

Hall, Peter & Soskice, David (eds): *Varieties of Capitalism: The Institutional Foundations of Comparative Advantage.* Oxford: Oxford University Press, 2001.

Hueglin, Thomas O.: *Early Modern Concepts for a Late Modern World: Althusius on Community and Federalism.* Waterloo, ON.: Wilfried Laurier University Press, 1999.

Körner, Finn Marten & Trautwein, Hans-Michael: German Economic Models, Transnationalization and European Imbalances. In: Ivano Cardinale, D'Maris Coffman & Roberto Scazzieri (eds): *The Political Economy of the Eurozone,* Cambridge: Cambridge University Press, pp. 241–83, 2017.

Lundberg, Erik: The Rise and Fall of the Swedish Model. *Journal of Economic Literature,* 23(1), pp. 1–36, 1985.

Polanyi, Karl: *Origins of Our Time: The Great Transformation.* New York: Farrar & Rinehart, 1944.

Schefold, Bertram: Moderns – Alfred Müller-Armack's Path: From Interventionary State to the Social Market Economy. In: Bertram Schefold (ed.), *Great Economic Thinkers from the Classicals to the Moderns: Translations from the series Klassiker der Nationalökonomie.* Abingdon: Routledge, pp. 353–71, 2017.

Stützel, Wolfgang, Watrin, Christian, Willgerodt, Hans & Hohmann, Karl (eds): *Standard Texts on the Social Market Economy: Two Centuries of Discussion.* New York: Gustav Fischer, 1982.

Trautwein, Hans-Michael: From Austrian Economics to the Swedish Welfare State: Wicksellian Views on Money and Income Distribution. *Cahiers d'Économie Politique/ Papers in Political Economy,* 61, pp. 51–90, 2011.

Wildt, Andreas: Solidarity: Its History and Contemporary Definition. In: Kurt Bayertz (ed.): *Solidarity.* Dordrecht: Springer, pp. 209–20, 1999.

# Part III
# Contact, comparison and interaction

# Section 1
# Before the revolutions

# 14 Xunzi and Plato on the economics of totalitarianism

A meeting of distant minds

*Terry Peach*

Xunzi 荀子 ("Master Xun") lived in the latter part of the aptly named Warring States period (c. 312–221 BCE), at a time when the 15 constituent states of the Western Zhou (1122–771 BCE) had been whittled down to single figures, on a trajectory of conflict that was to pause in 221 BCE with the conquest of "all under Heaven" by Qin, in turn replaced by the Han dynasty in 206 BCE. While the details of Xunzi's life are hazy, it has been suggested that he followed the example of Confucius (Kongzi 孔子), whose teachings he professed to endorse, in travelling between states in the hope of securing high office and implementing his plans for the restoration of "order", as set out in the book that bears his name.[1] Although his own lifetime achievements seem to have been modest,[2] he achieved vicarious success of sorts through two of his reputed students: Han Fei 韓非 (280–233 BCE), whose "Legalist" writings found a receptive audience in the Qin; and Li Si 李斯 (c. 280–208 BCE), who was to become chancellor in the new Qin empire and, according to some accounts, Han Fei's nemesis.[3]

By the time of the Southern Song dynasty (1127–1279 CE), Xunzi's association with Han Fei's "Legalism" and Qin authoritarianism, his criticisms of Mencius (Mengzi 孟子), and his doctrine that human nature is bad (or "evil"), resulted in his eviction from the "Confucian pantheon" (Chin 2007, p. 218) and, into the twentieth century, he was criticised for having "derailed the original Confucian mission and plunged China into a cycle of authoritarianism and corruption that lasted for more than two thousand years" (Goldin 2011, p. 68). But then came his reappraisal, with scholars seeming almost to compete to bestow the most lavish praise: "Truly, Xunzi was one of the greatest of Chinese thinkers, one of the great philosophers of the world" (Dubs 1927, p. xxx); "Xunzi contributed theories of philosophy and argumentation with perhaps more impact on Chinese culture and history than any other historical figure (Lu 1988, p. 182).[4] Not surprisingly, given his newly recovered credentials as a leading figure in China's "Period of the Philosophers" (Fung 1937), Xunzi was awarded a starring role in comparisons between ancient Chinese philosophy and "the classical period of Greek thought with which it coincided in time" (Dubs 1927, p. xviii), and such comparative studies have continued to the

DOI: 10.4324/9780367434496-22

present. But whereas these efforts have focused on "philosophy",[5] comparisons involving "political economy" or "economic" thought have been less forthcoming. As for the studies that have been undertaken,[6] it *could* be inferred that Xunzi's contributions are to be praised on the curious grounds that they are no less fragmentary and insubstantial than those of his "classic" Greek counterparts, which hardly inspires further scholarly investigation.

Of course, everything depends on what we mean by "political economy" and "economic" thought. If we have in mind the varieties that developed in Europe towards the end of the eighteenth century – particularly with the investigation of the workings of a market economic system – or "machine", to use Adam Smith's (1776) analogy – then it will be, and has been, the case that "later excavators [of "classical' writings], in search of the origins of economic theory, can only dig out disconnected fragments and mangled remains" (Gray 1931, p. 4), examples from Xunzi being *obiter dicta* on "division of labour", "scarcity" and "human wants". However, I suggest that the reason why these "fragments" and "remains" appear "disconnected" and "mangled" is that they have been prised from the "systems" of which they *were* a part, then compared with their namesakes in systems of a radically different provenance and purpose.

I will argue in this chapter that we *do* find a coherent and connected body of "economic" thought and analysis in Xunzi's writings, notably an analysis of the pathology of unrestrained economic (gain-seeking) behaviour, and a detailed model of economic planning, that together constitute what I term the "economics of totalitarianism". I will also suggest that there are striking similarities with the "economics" in Plato's *Republic*, notwithstanding certain differences that reflect intellectual and cultural legacies. Xunzi and Plato bequeathed remarkably similar "economic" systems that addressed similar problems and were informed by similar values. To that extent, there was indeed a "meeting of distant minds".

## Xunzi's "economics of totalitarianism": Overview

Xunzi painted a bleak picture of an external reality that was beset by "disorder" and "vile teachings" (6.40),[7] a society that, with the "sage kings" having passed away (22.237), was led by those who were motivated by "greed" and "an unquenchable thirst for profit" (6.44–45). Such behaviour was taken as symptomatic of a fundamental problem in human nature, insatiable desires:

> The natural disposition of people is that for food they want meats, for clothes they want embroidered garments, for travel they want chariots and horses, and moreover they want the riches of surplus wealth and accumulated goods. Even if provided with these things, to the end of their years they would never be satisfied; this is also the natural disposition of people.
>
> (4.29)

Insatiable desires are "natural" in the sense that people are "*born* with a fondness for profit [gain]" (23.248, my emphasis), and there is no point in hoping that this aspect of human nature can change: "Having desires and lacking desires fall under two different kinds, namely being alive and being dead" (22.243). But if measures are not taken to control desires, disaster will ensue: people will "commit brutality from ferocious greed, ravenously seeking only benefit" (4.24–25), and "the strong would harm the weak and take from them … [the] many would tyrannise the few … [and] all under Heaven [would] arrive at unruliness and chaos and perish" (23.252).

To cap it all off, "ravenously seeking only benefit" does not make people happier:

> Anyone who greatly values material goods on the outside will be worried on the inside … If one's heart is worried and fearful, then even if one's mouth is stuffed with grass-fed and grain-fed meats, one will not know their flavour … Thus one can be confronted with the finest of the myriad things and yet not be able to feel satisfaction.
>
> (22.246)

In short, he "who forgets the Way in the pursuit of desire will fall into delusion and joylessness". (20.221, Watson's translation)

Xunzi had given an analysis of the pathology of unrestrained economic behaviour: the (futile) attempt by individuals to satisfy their insatiable desires will result in widespread disorder, leading ultimately to social annihilation; even abstracting from that cataclysmic outcome, it is not as if the desire-fulfilment seekers will be made anything other than miserable by their unrelenting efforts. What, then, can and should be done?

As with most other ancient Chinese thinkers, Xunzi's formal answer was to seek inspiration from the "sage kings" of antiquity (Yao, Shun and Yu). But these were kings who supposedly reigned almost two millennia earlier, so how was it possible to obtain reliable information about their systems of governance? Having anticipated the question, Xunzi had prepared the answer:

> [If] you wish to observe the tracks of the sage kings, then look to the most clear among them. Such are the later kings[8] … If you wish to understand the ancient ages, then examine the way of the Zhou …Use the near to know the far.
>
> (5.35–36)

Having taken his own advice, ostensibly, Xunzi set forth his understanding of the predicament that had confronted the kings:

> People all desire the same things and all hate the same things. But while their desires are many, the things to satisfy them are few, and since they are few, people are sure to struggle over them … If they [the people] live

apart and do not help each other, then they will be impoverished. If they live together but have no social divisions, then they will struggle with each other. Poverty is a catastrophe, and struggle is a disaster.

(10.83)

People cannot live outside society, but society is not viable if they attempt to satisfy their unlimited desires from the limited means available. Realising the problem, the kings came up with a solution based on the assignment of people to particular ranks within a hierarchical social structure. But what criteria were used, and by whom were they applied to determine the ranking of individuals? Were assigned ranks and specific functions a reflection of natural ability or something else? What were the supposed benefits from the system? And how was ranking to be enforced?

The ancient kings were intertemporally omniscient; they comprehended "the Way":

> One who knows the Way and observes things by it … and puts it into practice, is one who embodies the Way … For such a one, none of the myriad things takes form and is not seen. None is seen and not judged. None is judged and loses its proper position. He sits in his chamber yet sees all within the four seas. He dwells in today yet judges what is long ago and far away in time. He comprehensively observes the myriad things and knows their true dispositions. He inspects and examines order and disorder and discerns their measures. He sets straight Heaven and Earth, and arranges and makes useful the myriad things. He institutes great order.

(21.229)

The sage king "assigns rank by reckoning virtue, awards official positions by assessing ability, and in each case makes it so that the people undertake the right tasks" (18.191).

Assigned rank depends on the degree of approximation to the virtue "of the hundred kings" (8.59). The "common people" do least well on that account. In general, they are "extremely foolish, ignorant, stupid and dense" (8.66) and, in their vulgarity, take "material goods and money as treasures" (8.59). Hence their position at the base of the social hierarchy. Above them come "officials and functionaries", the "officers and grand ministers", the feudal lords and, in an ideal world, the sage king himself (4.26).

Whatever may have been the case with the rankings at the dawn of history, it seems inevitable, given Xunzi's view of human nature,[9] that the ranking procedure is more akin to an evaluation of people's *acquired* capabilities and performance in societies in which a hierarchical structure already exists. The assignment of rank is more accurately a process of *reassignment*, with demotion of those who have failed to meet the expected standards and, if only in principle, promotion of those who have displayed ability that exceeds expectations.

It also becomes clear that the task of evaluating the performance *of the masses* is devolved by the sage-king to his officials, referred to as "gentlemen" (*junzi*).

The (true) gentleman displays "scrupulousness, honesty, integrity, trustworthiness, self-control, and meticulousness" (2.12). Having "overcome capricious personal desires" (2.15), he is one for whom "external goods carry little weight" (2.12). Although he "is not as good as" – that is, not as good at *being* – a farmer, a merchant or a craftsman, he possesses an ability that the toiling masses do not: "the gentleman pursues the Way single-mindedly and uses it to guide and oversee things" (21.230), where this guidance and oversight extends to assigning ranks, ensuring that people's work "is always directed to appropriate tasks" and making sure that "every kind of work and practice … is to the benefit of good order" (8.56). As for "efficiency", the gentleman applies the principle that "diversity is impractical"; history has taught him that "there has never been a man who attained mastery by trying to attend to a diversity of things at one time" (21.30, Watson's translation). Thus he will see to it that "the farmers devote all their strength to their fields, the merchants devote all their cleverness to their earnings, and the hundred craftsmen devote all their skilfulness to their products" (4.30). Put another way, the gentleman is aware that efficiency is promoted *by enforcing division of labour*. In consequence:

> People will each practice their tasks and become firmly settled in them, and people's performance of the hundred tasks will be just like the way that the ears, eyes, nose, and mouth cannot be borrowed to perform one another's office.
>
> (11.125)

Xunzi's ideal society is one in which every single task is performed by those who are the most competent and skilful at performing it (subject to an important constraint, discussed below).

But why, for example, does one person finds himself confined to a lifetime of craftwork, and another to the socially elevated life of a gentleman? One answer that Xunzi firmly rejects is the influence of inborn, natural characteristics: "Anyone on the streets can become a Yu [the sage king]" (23.254); "With regard to endowment, nature, intelligence, and capabilities, the gentleman and the petty man are one and the same" (4.26). However, in the case of *some* people, their natures and fortunes are transformed "by teachers and proper models" (23.249); through "practice and habituation" (8.65), they "accumulate culture and learning" (23.249), thereby clearing the path to their anointment as gentlemen and sages (depending on the point they reach through their "deliberative efforts" (23.250).

But why is it that only a small minority of people are blessed with a "good education" and the advantages it may bring? The answer is "environment", the behaviour and values of those "you live alongside": "Everything depends on what you rub up against!" (23.257).

For the masses, those against whom they "rub up" take "wealth and profit" as their "exalted standards" and do not "study or question" (8.63); they are "petty people" who "seek only benefit" (4.28). Hence, the "masses of people are fit" – they are *only* fit – "to be craftsmen, farmers, and merchants" (8.67). And, it seems, their occupation may well be determined by paternal example: "If people accumulate experience in weeding and ploughing, they become farmers. If they accumulate experience in chopping and carving, they become craftsmen. If they accumulate experience in selling and vending, they become merchants … *The sons of craftsmen all continue their fathers' work*" (8.66, my emphasis).

Returning to the benefits of division of labour, it emerges that tasks will be undertaken by the most competent and skilful, *but only from eligible subsets of the population* as determined primarily by parental circumstances: children from the masses are likely to remain within the masses, and may be expected to follow their father's occupation, while children of "well-bred" individuals are far more like to "rub up against" good teachers and "proper models" because they have been born into a milieu that is populated by these "treasures for mankind" (8.65). As for mobility between social ranks, although *demotion* may be relatively unproblematic, *promotion* of the "sons and grandsons of commoners … [even] to the status of prime minister, gentry, or grand ministers" seems vanishingly improbable. On Xunzi's own account, promotion is possible only if the children of commoners "accumulate culture and learning" (9.68), which would be a tall order in an immediate environment that places no value on cerebral and cultural pursuits.

In addition to "efficiency", albeit in its constrained form, arguably the most important benefit of the ranking system is its deployment as a means of addressing the "scarcity" problem, itself a manifestation of unrestrained and insatiable desires. According to Xunzi, this had been a principal concern of the former kings:

> if you followed along with people's desires, then their power could not be accommodated, and the goods could not be made sufficient. Accordingly, for their sake the former kings … divide[d] the people up and cause[d] there to be the rankings of noble and base, the distinction between old and young, and the divisions between wise and stupid and capable and incapable. All these cause each person to carry out his proper task and each to attain his proper place. After that, they cause the amount and abundance of their salaries to reach the proper balance. This is the way to achieve community life and harmonious unity.
>
> (4.30)

The "proper place" in the ranking system is associated with a specific *real* "income" that increases with rank and, critically, fully satisfies (and in some cases more than satisfies) the desires of the individual. As for the "proper balance" (or "balanced arrangement", 10.85), this requires the adjustment of the specified real incomes so that the social aggregates of all goods required to satisfy all ranked individuals (the aggregate consumption demand) is precisely equal to the aggregate quantities of the same goods that the economy is *capable* of producing. Thus, when the "balanced arrangement" is met, there is neither excess aggregate demand nor excess aggregate supply of consumption goods, desires are satisfied and the "scarcity" problem is resolved.

The practicalities of achieving the "proper balance" are discussed in the next section. The question addressed here is how Xunzi has managed to subdue "insatiable desires" so that individuals are satisfied with the centrally determined real income corresponding to their rank.

The question has a threefold answer: rites (or "ritual"); the provision of "welfare"; and law and punishment, the combined force of which is to habituate and tranquillise people to acceptance of their rank and the level of real income that comes with it.

Rites are described as "the height of good order and proper distinction ... the fundamental point for making the state strong ... the way to inspire awe pervasively ... the crucial element for gaining accomplishment and fame" (15.157). Encompassing virtually all aspects of family and social behaviour, rites serve the purpose of cementing people in their social "place".

Ideally, rites will resign people to their ranking, and to the associated level of real income, and desires will be "trained" to extend no further than the real incomes to which people become habituated (19.201). But what may seem strange is that higher levels of real income are allocated to gentlemen and other "worthies" who are virtuously indifferent to material rewards. The solution to this apparent paradox is that the more generous allocations in these cases are made *not* to satisfy desires, but to reinforce the hierarchical system by inspiring awe and deference among the masses.

Regarding the masses, Xunzi evidently believed that rites alone were unlikely to mollify them completely. Hence the state provision of "welfare": a "safety net" that could not be financed from their or their relatives' limited resources:

> The five types of handicapped people [mute, deaf, crippled, missing an arm or leg, or dwarfed] should be received by their superiors and nurtured, put to work according to their talents. Employ and feed and clothe them.
> (9.68)

The government is further enjoined to take in "those who are orphaned or widowed" and to assist "those who are poor and in dire straits" (9.70). As a result, "the common people will feel at ease with the government" and the gentleman will "feel at ease in holding his position" (9.70).[10]

Just in case "the common people" did *not* "feel at ease with the government", they "must be controlled by legal arrangements" (9.85) or, less euphemistically, by "punishment and execution" (4.26). One way or another, they *will* accept their social position and income and, as the "former kings" had beneficently intended, the "scarcity" problem is dealt with accordingly.

## Xunzi's political economy: further considerations

The degree of *direct* control over "economic" activities that Xunzi envisaged, and the level of detail he provided in the specification of the state's managerial activities, are without parallel in ancient Chinese literature.[11] Not only will officials determine "macroeconomic" objectives such as the allocation of resources between different sectors of the economy; they will also plan output targets in every sector, oversee the "efficient" execution of their plan, and ensure that *everything* of "economic" importance is controlled by them, leaving no scope for individual initiative on the part of those who undertake the "economic" activities.[12]

The principal "macroeconomic" objective was to prioritise "the fundamental tasks" of agriculture and textiles. By so doing, "the state will naturally become rich" (in terms of "essentials"), and it will be possible "to keep people alive and nurture them" (9.80, 12.123). Alternatively, "If there are great numbers of craftsmen and merchants, then the state will be poor" (10.95), the implication being that craftsmen and merchants are types of "unproductive labour" who merely consume essential products at the expense of everyone else. But they are not the only culprits: "If there are a great number of nobles and grand ministers, then the state will be poor" (10.95), suggesting that their numbers must also be subject to critical scrutiny.

Xunzi recognised that some material products – such as implements (9.77) – were necessary to the performance of "fundamental tasks", and that some non-essential material products – luxury goods – were necessary to the stability of the political system. As explained above, the social ranking system *requires* the production of a range of luxury goods, not because the "higher ups" have a burning desire for these things, but because their ostentatious display may inspire awe and deference among the masses.

Having decided the main priorities, the next task for the "gentlemen planners" – and by far the most stupendously challenging – is to draw up the requirements for the "balanced system": a specification of *all* outputs, including the outputs of necessary inputs, for an aggregate equality with the real incomes of *all* consumers from *all* social ranks. In addition, allowance must be made for the provision of "public works", including "building city walls", repairing "dykes and weirs", and constructing "canals and irrigation ditches" (9.77).

Implementation of the plan involves the oversight of a small army of specialist officials. Among them, the "Director of Workers" oversees the "provision of implements"; the "Administrator of the Fields" decides "what type of grain should be planted" and makes sure that "the farmers are dedicated in their work and restrict their efforts in other areas"; and the "Master of Craftsmen" is tasked with "judging the hundred craftsmen", keeping "watch over the seasonal tasks", distinguishing between "success and failure", honouring "perfection and usefulness", preparing "equipment and materials so that the people do not dare to make up ways of carving, polishing and patterning by themselves" and honing the workers' "skilful performance of their jobs" (9.77–78, 11.115).

Officials must also ensure that goods and grain "circulate without delays … so that the region within the four seas becomes like a single family" (9.74). But this poses a problem because those who circulate goods – merchants – are viewed by Xunzi as no better than common thieves: they "strive for benefit in all affairs … struggle over goods and wealth … act from brazen daring … [and] commit brutality from ferocious greed" (4.24). In Xunzi's ideal state, however, merchants have been reduced in number, and those who remain are "earnest, honest, and without deception" (11.115), all fearing the law and taking heed of the state's warning that "those who in their talents and conduct go against the times should die without pardon" (9.68) Their erstwhile selves have been eviscerated from the social landscape.

## Xunzi and Plato: A comparison

There are obvious similarities between Xunzi's ideal state and the one promoted in Plato's *Republic*. Both are totalitarian, with pervasive control exercised over the masses of "vile common people" (Xunzi), or the "many inferior people" (Plato),[13] by a ruling class of superior beings (*junzi* and the sage-king for Xunzi, guardians and the philosopher-king for Plato), whose existence as a separate class of "specialists", freed from the necessity of performing any "economic" task, is justified by analogy with the advantages of specialisation (division of labour or "effort") in those very same occupations. For both ruling classes, position is determined meritoriously following decades of education. While their curricula differ, along with the descriptions of the ultimate goal – knowledge of "the Good" for Plato, and "the Way" for Xunzi – the end result is the same: the most elevated within both ruling classes come to an understanding of the "ideal" society, which they then seek to implement with the assistance of lower-ranking members of their class (Plato's auxiliaries and Xunzi's "lesser *ru*").

One possible difference concerns the basis for the rulers' superiority. For Xunzi, this comes *not* from innate or "natural" ability, but from the environment into which children are born. For Plato, guardians are *by inborn nature* a superior class, and must be kept that way through careful oversight of breeding arrangements. Yet, despite these apparently radical differences, the outcome is similar: future rulers will come overwhelmingly from the existing ruling class, and children of the masses will overwhelming remain among the masses, warm words about the possibilities for promotion notwithstanding.[14]

Xunzi and Plato also broadly agreed in their analysis of the pathology of unrestrained "economic" life. For both, the root of social and political problems was to be found in human nature, specifically from *insatiable desires* (insatiable "appetite", for Plato).[15] Thus, in the absence of the control of desire, either by individuals themselves or by an external authority, they agreed that the consequences would include inequality, crime, revolution and war,[16] and misery from the deluded association of wealth with happiness.[17]

It is at this point that differences emerge, not over the general objective, but rather the means for its achievement. While Plato and Xunzi were united in believing that a solution to "desires" must come from the *imposition* of order by an enlightened ruling class, they differed over the circumstances of rulers, policies for achieving order and proposals for "economic" control.

Plato was emphatic that *his* rulers "shall have no private property beyond the barest essentials", where "private property" includes land, houses, money, spouses and children. The consequences of allowing rulers to acquire private property are described in florid terms: "they will be householders and farmers instead of guardians, they will become hostile masters instead of allies of the rest of the citizens … they will lead the whole of their lives hating and hated, plotting and plotted against, fearing those within the state far more than the enemy outside [and] they and the rest of the state will be running a course very near destruction". Indeed, so worried was Plato about the corrosive effect of private wealth on his rulers' values that he urged the following restriction: "For them alone … it is not lawful to deal with and touch the gold and silver belonging to those in the state, nor to come under the same roof where it is to be found, nor adorn themselves with it, nor drink from silver or gold vessels" (*Rep* 417a–b).

The contrast with Xunzi's rulers is stark. His *junzi* and other "worthies" are not so much allowed as *required* to have, and to flaunt, their privately owned material wealth. Moreover, for ingrained cultural reasons, it is hard to imagine a response from Xunzi (or most other "Confucians") of anything other than shock and bemusement to the proposal for the dissolution of family among the ruling class (or any class). Abolition of private property, either in things or people, played no part in *his* system, while the emphasis on rites, private property and the conspicuous consumption of rulers, were equally foreign to Plato's system.

Something else without parallel is Xunzi's use of "welfare" measures to placate the labouring masses. For one thing, the population of the "five incapacitated groups" will have been reduced dramatically in Plato's state, with "defective offspring … quietly got rid of" at birth (*Rep* 460c), unhealthy adults "left to die" and "those whose psychological constitution is incurably warped … put to death" (*Rep* 410a). As for the desperately poor, Plato provides the assurance that guardians will "at all costs" prevent the scourge of poverty "from slipping unobserved into our state" (*Rep* 421e), although exactly how this feat is accomplished is not revealed.[18] It could therefore be said that he deals with "welfare" by disposing of its likely recipients. Where there is undoubted agreement, however, is in the threat and use of force to keep people in their assigned positions.[19]

The prevention of poverty among the bronze and iron class, supported by the argument that destitution causes "meanness and bad workmanship and revolution into the bargain" (*Rep* 422a), is one of the few specific "economic" policies that Plato unveils in *Republic*. Guardians will also prevent the appearance of wealth among the masses, the aim being to eradicate "luxury and idleness and a passion for novelty" and, when combined with poverty, a disunited state in which rich and poor are "at enmity with each other" (*Rep* 423a). Unlike the ruling class, however, the masses are not restricted to the consumption of "necessaries"; they are allowed private property in spouses, children and things, and there is no suggestion of enforcing an equality of income and wealth among their ranks. On the contrary, the idea seems to be that if each class is indeed allowed to "enjoy the happiness that its nature permits",[20] the "less reputable majority", who are dazzled by the chimerical association of happiness with wealth, must be permitted *some* latitude to pursue their delusive quest. But the extent of that latitude will be determined by guardians, who will ensure that it never reaches the point of endangering the state.

Otherwise, guardians must keep a watchful eye on the population and, in general, they will ensure that individuals work diligently at the (single) task for which they are "naturally suited". But that is where the instruction manual concludes. Compared with Xunzi, there is a dearth of detail on the micro-management of the "economic" plan, and there is certainly nothing approaching the depth of analysis that is found in Xunzi's treatment of the "scarcity" problem. Plato, it seems, was content with a "broad brush" portrayal of the planned economy in his ideal totalitarian state. For a more rigorous version, we should look to Xunzi.

## Conclusion

Xunzi and Plato both lived in turbulent times, and both sought to provide an analysis of the causes of "disorder" together with a vision for its elimination, the latter taking the form of authoritarian states ruled by "superior" people not unlike themselves. In the absence of enforced regulation, it was a shared belief, rationalised by a shared view of human nature, that the undisciplined masses would wreak havoc in their futile attempts to satisfy insatiable desires. In this regard, Xunzi and Plato concurred in their analysis of the pathology of unrestrained economic life. They also concurred in their belief that remedial action necessitated central control over *all* aspects of "economic" life, although here there are differences in (the reasons for) specific proposals, such as levels of wealth and property ownership for the ruling class, reflecting differences in cultural heritage (a key example being Xunzi's incorporation of rites into his control system). Finally, while it is undoubtedly true that both Xunzi and Plato made use of ideas and concepts – such as division of labour or effort, scarcity, and human wants and desires – that were to resurface in "modern" economic analysis, these were not so much "disconnected fragments and mangled remains" as *integral parts of their systems*: systems that developed an "economics of totalitarianism" that was evidently not the unique bequest, glorious or inglorious, of either ancient civilisation.

## Notes

1 *Xunzi*, the book, was compiled by Liu Xiang in 77–76 BCE. Dating and authorship of individual chapters is uncertain, although the overwhelming majority of them

are "more likely to contain material that comes directly from Xunzi" (Hutton 2014, p. xxi; see also Goldin 2011, p. 68; Lu 1998, p. 183).
2   It has been suggested that he obtained positions in Qi, Chu (where he was magistrate of Lanling) and (what remained of) his native state of Zhou (Hutton 2014, p. xx).
3   According to Sima Qian, Han Fei visited Qin as an envoy in 233 BCE. On the advice of Li Si, he was imprisoned then took his own life. (Watson 1993, pp. 39–40).
4   See also Goldin (2011, p. 68); Watson (2003, p. 4).
5   Albeit with reservations over the applicability to Chinese thought of "philosophy" in the classical Greek sense. See Tanner (2009).
6   For example, Hu (1998, pp. 162–76).
7   References of this type are to the translation of *Xunzi* by Hutton (2014) and give the chapter number followed by page number.
8   These being Kings Wen and Wu and, although not a king, the Duke of Zhou. Also, "Confucius was *ren* 仁 [humane], was wise, and was not fixated, and so through his study of various methods, he was worthy of being one of the former kings" (21.227).
9   See below. If people's inborn natures *are* the same, as Xunzi maintains, their selection at birth for some particular position would have nothing to do with *them*.
10  The "sage ruler" is also counselled not to be too soft in dealing with the "vile common people": "If one neglects important tasks to nurture the common people, coddling and babying them, making gruel for them in the winter and giving them melons and porridge in the summer, in order to steal a brief moment's praise from them, this is a thieving way. In this manner, one can briefly obtain the vile common people's praise, but it is not a way one can persist in for a long time. Important tasks are sure not to be completed, and accomplishments are sure not to hold up" (10.91).
11  Perhaps the strongest contender for a "runner up" prize would be Mozi 墨子 (c. 479–372 BCE).
12  Standard "Confucian" policies endorsed by Xunzi include a tax rate of 10 per cent, restriction of corvée labour to times that do not interfere with agricultural work, and measures to control the exploitation of natural resources (9.74, 77, 11.85). However, it is the nature and extent of his economic planning that distinguishes him from his predecessors, and it is these distinctive characteristics that are the focus of my discussion.
13  *Republic* (hereafter *Rep*) 431c.
14  For Xunzi on "promotion", see above, p. 194. As part of Plato's "noble lie", people are told that offspring of "bronze" or "iron" parents (metals that identify the lower classes) who are born with "a proportion of gold or silver" will be elevated to the higher classes that the more precious metals are taken to signify (415c). But, as pointed out by Popper (2003, p. 149), Plato subsequently warns that when "iron is mixed with silver and bronze with gold", the result will be "war and hostility" (547a). "Impure" specimens are therefore more likely to face extinction than promotion.
15  *Rep* 442a.
16  For Plato, see for example, *Rep* 373e, 422a, 551d, 552d.
17  *Rep* 586a–c.
18  In *Laws*, he suggests that the desperately poor must have brought that fate upon themselves, because a person of any virtue would surely find support from *somewhere*. Hence, "if anybody begs ... let the wardens of the country send him out [i.e. into exile] ... in order that the land may be cleared of this sort of animal." (936b–c)

19 Legislation "uses persuasion *or force* [or "compulsion"] to unite all citizens and make them share together the benefits that each individually can confer on the community" (*Rep* 520a).
20 *Rep* 421c.

# References

Chin, A.: *Confucius: A Life of Thought and Politics*. New Haven, CT: Yale University Press, 2007.
Dubs, H.H.: *Hsüntze: The Moulder of Ancient Confucianism*. London: Arthur Probsthain, 1927.
Fung, Y.-L.: *A History of Chinese Philosophy,* vol. 1. Trans. D. Bodde. Princeton, NJ: Princeton University Press, 1937.
Goldin, P.R.: *Confucianism*. Durham, NC: Acumen, 2011.
Gray, A.: *The Development of Economic Doctrine*. London: Longman, 1931.
Hu, J.: *A Concise History of Chinese Economic Thought*. Beijing: Foreign Languages Press, 1998.
Hutton, E.L. (ed.): *Xunzi: The Complete Text*. Princeton, NJ: Princeton University Press, 2014.
Lu, X.: *Rhetoric in Ancient China, Fifth to Third Century B.C.E.* Columbia, SC: University of South Carolina Press, 1998.
Popper, K.: *The Open Society and Its Enemies*. Abingdon: Routledge, 2003 [1950].
Smith, A.: *The Wealth of Nations*. London: W. Strahan & T. Cadell, 1776.
Tanner, J.: Ancient Greece, Early China: Sino Hellenic Studies and Comparative Approaches to the Classical World. A Review Article. *Journal of Hellenic Studies*, 129, pp. 89–109, 2009.
Watson, B. (ed.): *Records of the Grand Historian: Qin Dynasty*. New York: Columbia University Press, 1993.
Watson, B. (ed.): *Xunzi: Basic Writings*. New York: Columbia University Press, 2003.

# 15 *Yantie lun* in the Pro-Legalist and Anti-Confucian Campaign

*Qunyi Liu*

In 81 BCE, the government of West Han (202 BCE — 8) invited more than 60 literati to a debate with civilian officials in Jingshi 京師 (the former name of Xi'an 西安, Shanxi 陝西 province). The first recorded hearing in China's history was called the "*Yantie* meeting" (the Meeting of Salt and Iron). Approximately 10 years later, Huan Kuan 桓寬 edited the meeting record and transformed it into the *Yantie lun* 鹽鐵論 (On Salt and Iron) (Huan, Kuan 1931), which was selected as a must-read classic in the *Pingfa piru* 評法批儒 Campaign (the Pro-Legalist and Anti-Confucian Campaign) in the 1970s. Hundreds of translations and thousands of related articles appeared in less than five years. Even the end of the Cultural Revolution did not bring an end to the enthusiasm for the book. Since 2013, the new government has included the *Yantie lun* as part of a "reading history" series, along with six other Chinese classics, such as *Lunyu* 論語 (Analects of Confucius) and *Zizhi tongjian* 資治通鑑 (General Mirror for the Aid of Government).

This chapter focuses on the role of the *Yantie lun* in the *Pingfa piru* Campaign. First, I introduce the *Yantie* meeting and the *Yantie lun* to provide background information and then hermeneutically examine the role of the book in the campaign. In the conclusion, I attempt to summarise the book's role within a reduced framework of China's new political economy, which is conducive to understanding the influences of traditional culture on China's economic policies.

## Rhetoric and the origin of Confucian–legalist conflict

We lack any direct records of the Yantie meeting except for the *Yantie lun*. The *Hanshu* 漢書 (Book of Han) offers several clues about the background of the meeting, but only one sentence describing it.

According to *Duzhou zhuan* 杜周傳 (biography of Duzhou), Du Yannian 杜延年(?–52 BCE) suggested holding the meeting. He observed the rise in depression among citizens after years of military aggression by Emperor Wu 漢武帝 (156–87 BCE) and suggested to Huo Guang 霍光 (?–68 BCE) that developing a recovery process was necessary for the desperate people. Huo Guang had been a king-maker along with four other high officials, including Sang Hongyang

桑弘羊 (155–80 BCE), the main figure at the *Yantie* meeting. All of them were assistants to Emperor Zhao 漢昭帝 (94–74 BCE), the emperor who held the meeting. Huo adopted Du's suggestion that the government abandon the state monopoly on wine, salt and iron following the *Yantie* meeting. Huo attempted to cautiously achieve the goal of eliminating the state's monopoly, even though that monopoly contributed greatly to the state's revenue.

In 81 BCE, the king-makers invited literati from all over the country to the capital on behalf of the 13-year-old emperor. In the Han dynasty, the government held hearings from time to time to discuss important policies and recruit officials. Such a meeting was called a *cewen* 策問 (policy inquiry), and the literati were usually assigned different positions according to the quality of their suggestions (Qian, Mu 2001, p. 14). The aim of the *Yantie* meeting in 81 BCE was well known: to determine whether the government should abandon its monopoly and other significant policies – for example, of attacking Huns. After the meeting, some mechanisms of the monopoly were stopped, which meant that the literati had effectively persuaded officials to keep their hands out of the market. Unfortunately, there was no formal record of the meeting to help us understand the procedure, and the only detailed description was the *Yantie lun*, written by Huan Kuan (1931) during the reign of the succeeding emperor 漢宣帝 (Han Xuandi 91–48 BCE). Huan Kuan did not attend the meeting. His book was written from the perspective of only one participant, but was not limited by this, as he used his imagination to embellish the record. It was thus reasonable that modern scholars such as Guo Moruo 郭沫若 (1892–1978) classified the *Yantie lun* as a historical novel in the form of a dialogue (Guo, Moruo 1957, p. 4).

The *Yantie lun* does not belong to the classical genre of dialogue because the author demonstrated his Confucian beliefs directly. Huan Kuan was a *wenxue* 文學 (a type of literati), who studied Confucian books and was promoted to a middle-level local official position, possibly through the same procedure that applied to the *cewen*. He praised his peers in the meeting rhetorically and introduced several fabricated generic speakers with the titles of *xianliang* 賢良 (another type of literati) and *wenxue*. He named only two persons (Liu Ziyong 劉子雍 and Mr Zhu 祝生) in his comments in the last chapter, and he distinguished Sang Hongyang and Tian Qianqiu 田千秋 as representative officials in the same chapter. All the other characters held the generic titles of "literati" or "official". Huan seemed to mix his own comments into the proclamations made by his characters. The *Yantie lun* was not a novel, and it functioned more like a dialogue of first-person narrators (Wang, Yong 2009, introduction 9) than an objective record.

Huan Kuan emphasised the controversy between the literati and officials. In line with his own Confucian viewpoint, he over-praised the literati and concluded that the officials had been defeated by the Confucian adherents. In fact, the literati stood against the officials and put forward bold suggestions partly to gain attention and obtain promotions. However, the opposition of the two sides has been exaggerated by modern Chinese (Huang, Yanan 2018) and foreign scholars (Schefold 2002). The officials have been dubbed *fajia* 法家 (Legalists), and the meeting has become a debate between Confucians and Legalists, regardless of the fact that Legalism disappeared after the early Han period (Li, Ling 2011, p. 100). So how did the argument of the *Rufa* 儒法 conflict (conflict between Confucians and Legalists) originate?

The original *Yantie lun* by Huan Kuan was lost, and a new version did not appear until a reprint appeared in the Jiatai period (1201–04) during the Southern Song dynasty. The first-known annotator was Zhang Zhixiang 張之象 (1496–1577). Neither Zhang Zhixiang nor earlier commentators such as Jia Sixie 賈思勰 (?–?), Liu Yan 劉晏 (716–80), Wang Anshi 王安石 (1021–86), Fang Xiaoru 方孝孺 (1357–1402) or Qiu Jun 丘濬 (1421–95) had ever labelled the officials in the meeting as Legalists. However, the commentators and annotators can be divided into two groups according to their attitudes towards the state monopoly and the government's intervention in economic affairs. Since the middle of the Ming dynasty, an increasing amount of literature supported the government in engaging in business and monopolising the salt and iron trades (Nie, Jidong 2017), which was in accordance with the pragmatic inclinations of the Ming and Qing dynasties. Qing scholars noticed the fictional elements mixed into the *Yantie lun* and classified the book as Confucian literature instead of history in the *Siku quanshu* 四庫全書 (Complete Library in the Four Branches of Literature). In other words, the book was considered a Confucian classic and an objective evaluation until the end of the Qing dynasty and the beginning of Republican China.

It was probably Yang Shuda 楊樹達 (1885–1956) who first argued about the *Rufa* conflict in his annotation of the book. In the preface to his annotation of the *Yantie Lun* (Yang, Shuda 1924), he wrote:

> I have referred to the event in the Han dynasty. The emperor ordered several officials to debate with literati about the policies. It was indeed the origin of the democracy that encourages ordinary people to become involved in the policy process. Concerning the context of the tyranny, it was especially unique in China's history that the government agreed with the literati and quit its exploitation after the debate … According to the author, the officials and literati discussed the topics again and again. I have found no classics to be comparable. Sang Hongyang, as a student of the Legalism school, thought highly of Guanzi 管子 and Shang Yang 商鞅, and the literati, the students of the Confucianism school, abided by the learning of the Zhou dynasty. In the end, the Confucians defeated the Legalists, which could be regarded as the advantage held by the former.
>
> (Translated by the author)

Yang Shuda focused his research on classical Chinese texts, but his comments went beyond the borders of the field and stepped into political science. Through his diaries, we can relate Yang's bold hypothesis to the work of Liang Qichao 梁啟超 (1873–1929), one of his admirable mentors. However, Liang did not assume a conflict between the two schools. It was Yang who integrated Liang's classification of Legalism into his interpretation of the *Yantie lun*. On 3 February 1923, Yang first encountered the *Yantie lun* (Bai, Jian 1987). On 1 January 1924, he finished his annotation. During that period, he worked on the text intermittently while reading *Hanshu*. He recorded that Liang had given his own book, titled *Xianqin zhengzhi sixiangshi* 先秦政治思想史 (History of Political Thought in the Pre-Qin Dynasty) (Liang, Qichao 2014), to him, and Yang browsed the book the next morning. On 11 November 1923, Yang went to Beijing Normal University with Li Liuru 李六如 (1887–1973) to attend a lecture on "the relation between academia and politics in Qing dynasty" by Liang. In the afternoon, Yang annotated the 10th volume of the *Yantie lun*. Around the same time, he attended two other lectures by Liang on the same topic. The abovementioned book by Liang and another, the *Zhongguo jinsanbainian xueshushi* 中國近三百年學術史 (Academic History of China in the Last 300 Years), offered Yang a possible explanation of the origin of the *Rufa* conflict, for Liang summarised his arguments on traditional schools of philosophy in political terms, describing Confucians as neutral officials with morals and ethics and Legalists as extreme rightists (Liang, Qichao 2014, pp. 77–78).

Even if Yang Shuda was not the first to promulgate such comments, his interdisciplinary endeavour involving philology and philosophy contributed to the sudden appearance of the assumption of the *Rufa* conflict in the New Culture Movement (around the time of the May Fourth Movement in 1919) (Chang, Naide 1922, pp. 186–88). It was something of a turning point, and after that Sang Hongyang received increasingly positive evaluations. With the arrival of Western economics, Confucianism was related to *laissez-faire* economics and, in contrast, Legalism was associated with economic intervention (Lin, Zhenhan 1934; Tang, Qingzheng 1929). The relationship between the book and the celebrated political movement proved coincidental. The list of notable figures who read the *Yantie lun* includes Sun Yat-sen 孫逸仙 (1866–1925) (Sun, Zhongshan 1985, p. 176), Mao Zedong 毛澤東 (1893–1976) and even theatrical figures.

Therefore, contrary to common opinion, Chinese scholars only recently transformed the *Yantie lun* into a work on the *Rufa* conflict. The first-person narration style was conducive to the hermeneutics of the book, and the politicisation of academia supplies another essential explanation for this transformation. It is obvious that the latter induced a transformation of the different opinions on the book into two opposing schools.

## Innuendo during the Cultural Revolution

Yang Shuda kept intimate contact with Mao Zedong, as he was one of Mao's mentors. After the liberation in 1949, Mao visited Yang at least once and accepted Yang's book as a gift (Sun, Qin'an 1993). Their relationship presaged the formation of historical hermeneutics during the Cultural Revolution (1966–76). Some top-level advisors presented a special topic and main theme for the book, and subsequent scholars endeavoured to prove the book's reasonability on the basis of historical materials and necessary theories, even using innuendo if needed. Some academic bureaucrats moved between the top levels of government and the masses because the top always distributed orders indirectly, such as through poems or descriptions of a rumoured encounter, to avoid direct conflict with political opponents. Intermediates were in charge of supervising the literati and simplifying their tasks. Therefore, the process was composed of an emperor, several Legalists and even more Confucians. The system had worked continually until the top leader felt that his reign was threatened by followers who might destroy the balance – that is, he felt threatened by the Pro-legalist and Anti-Confucian Campaign.

Guo Moruo and Wang Liqi 王利器 (1911–98) contributed greatly to the argument of the *Rufa* conflict with their annotation of the *Yantie lun*. Guo collated the book with an edition of the work of Hu Weixin 胡维新 (1534–?) that he owned (Wang, Liqi 1958, p. 9). In Guo's preface, he adopted Yang Shuda's argument that the Yantie meeting was actually a struggle between Confucians and Legalists. He related the debate with political struggles between Huo Guang and Sang Hongyang, which reinforced the positive image of the latter (Guo, Moruo 1985, pp. 471–83). When he learned that Wang Liqi was annotating the *Yantie lun*, Guo wrote a letter to Wang:

> Comrade Wang Liqi: I hear that you are annotating the *Yantie lun*. It is fine. There are quite a few errors in the book. What you pointed out was almost right… The Yantie meeting was in fact the struggle between Huo Guang and Sang Hongyang. Huo Guang represented the landowners and the small business traders. *Wenxue* and *xianliang* had been recruited, and they were not the ordinary people at all. I feel deep sympathy for Sang Hongyang, who was a great figure. Emperor Wu based most of his achievements on the financial and economic policies suggested by Sang Hongyang. Sang should be reappraised at present, like other great politicians, such as Li Kui 李悝, Wu Qi 吴起, Shang Yang and Wang Anshi. Most of them died tragically, except Li Kui. Please calculate how many times the literati and officials are described as speaking in the book. Other non-dialogues should also be recorded. I want to do the work by myself, but I am too busy to do it, even if it is actually simple. Please send a copy to me if you finish the work. I could write the introduction. Huan Kuan took the standpoint of Confucianism and represented the class of landowners as well. I did not agree with him except for his description about Sang Hongyang. He persevered in presenting an objective image of Sang and contributed to history by doing so. Were there other sources for Huan Kuan's biography, including the *Tian Qianqiu Zhuan* 田千秋傳 (Biography of Tian Qianqiu)? I hope we can meet and discuss this with each other.
>
> Sincerely,
> Guo Moruo
> December 23
> (Translated by the author)

In 1954, Guo Moruo reiterated his arguments as the chairperson and keynote speaker of the Allied Conference of Litterateurs and Artists. The speech was later published in an official newsletter, the *Kexue tongbao* 科學通報 (Science Newsletter) (Guo, Moruo 1955). Wang Liqi adopted Guo's suggestion in his first annotation in 1958 (Wang, Liqi 1958, p. 6). However, he revised his argument in two later editions in 1978 and 1989. He changed his conclusion that the *Rufa* conflict occurred (Wang, Liqi 1958, p. 3) to the opposing opinion that the debate was between pure Confucian ideas and more integrated ones (Wang, Liqi 1983, p. 2; Wang, Liqi 1992, p. 2). Apparently, he doubted the existence of the *Rufa* conflict. He did not calculate the proportion of dialogue attributed to different figures, as Guo had requested; interestingly, however, other scholars fulfilled the task (Ma, Feibai 1981, p. 1; Lai, Jiancheng 2011, pp. 234–35).

Guo Moruo similarly interfered with He Changqun's 賀昌群 *Lun Xi han de tudi zhanyou xingtai* 論西漢的土地占有型態 (On the Form of Land Ownership in the West Han Dynasty) (Huang, Chunhao 1992, pp. 177–80). Guo emphasised the class struggle during Emperor Wu's reign, which has helped to orient contemporary studies on the *Yantie lun*.

Mao Zedong had written at least three poems for Guo Moruo, the first two of which, written in 1961 and 1963, were responsories to Guo. The third, written in 1973 (a verse with eight seven-character lines titled *Qilü: du fengjianlun cheng guo lao* 七律・讀<封建論>呈郭老 (A Qilü poem 'On Feudalism' presented to the Venerable Guo), essentially criticised Guo and declared Mao's alignment with Legalism and various Legalists, such as Qin Shihuang, Emperor Wu and Sang Hongyang, which symbolised the beginning of the Pro-Legalist and Anti-Confucian Campaign. At almost the same time, Mao borrowed Guo's book, *Du suiyuanshihua zhaji* 讀<隨園詩話>札記 (Notes and Comments on Poetry at Suiyuan), to confirm his continued confidence in Guo and alleviate the latter's concerns (Chen, Chuang 2019, pp. 38–39) regarding the campaign.

Mao's reorientation proved so effective that enthusiasm for Legalist classics, including the *Yantie lun*, rose almost immediately. During the last phase of the Cultural Revolution from 1973 to 1976, hundreds of annotations and research works about the *Yantie lun* were published in China. Labourers constituted 20 per cent of the authors, and the other 80 per cent came from academia (Fang, Houshu 2005). Two typical official sources, the *Renmin ribao* 人民日報 (People's Daily) and *Hongqi* 紅旗 (Red Flag), published more than 40 relevant articles, offering a baseline understanding of the *Yantie lun* and other classics. Some of the most important articles were written by Liangxiao 梁效 (a penname pronounced similarly to the names of two schools, thus indicating that the authors came from Peking University and Tsinghua University) and Luosiding 羅思鼎 (a penname pronounced similarly to the word "screw", indicating that the authors, who came from Fudan University, behaved like screws in a machine). The Gang of Four overtook Guo Moruo as the main intermediates. One of the four, Yao Wenyuan 姚文元 (1931–2005), asked Luosideng to write an article titled "Handai de yichang rufa da lunzhan: du yantielun zhaji" 漢代的一場儒法大論戰讀鹽鐵論札記 (A Great *Rufa* Conflict in the Han Dynasty: on the *Yantie lun*, 1973), and another famous member, Jiang Qing

江青 (1914–1991), guided Liangxiao in presenting the most important column, titled *Du yantie lun: xi han zhongqi rufa liangjia de yichang da lunzhan* 讀<鹽鐵論>——西漢中期儒法兩家的一場大論戰 (Reading *Yantie lun*: A Great Debate Between Confucians and Legalists in the Middle of West Han dynasty, 1974) (Fang, Houshu 2005; Fan, Daren 2014).

Fan Daren 范達人 (2014) was one Liangxiao author. He was a faculty member in the history department at Peking University, but his research field was world history. He reminded readers that his familiarity with Marxism was a major reason why he was qualified to write an article on historical Chinese works like the *Yantie lun*. The editors required the authors to stress the country's central authority and attack the former Soviet Union by allusions to the Huns. Fan raised a question about how to deal with Huo Guang, for it was difficult to consider him either a Confucian or a Legalist. The response was that he should not be included, though in the published article, the editor added one sentence noting that Huo Guang had not shown up in the meeting but had instead dispatched the literati, the Confucian followers, to be his scapegoats. The article also concluded, as required by the editor, that the debate revealed the marked conflict between Confucians and Legalists, representing two opposite historical views: conservatism and reformism.

Based on the abovementioned articles, the governments of metropolises such as Shanghai and Beijing received guidelines for annotating selected Legalist classics. The basic level of the theoretical system had been extended to *Xiao sanjiehe* 小三結合 (small groups of students, teachers and other university employees) and *Da sanjiehe* 大三結合 (larger groups of workers, farmers and soldiers). Government offices distributed the classic works according to their own purview. For example, the Grain Bureau in Beijing was in charge of annotating the *Lun guishu shu* 論貴粟疏 (On the High Price of Grain) by Chao Cuo 晁錯 (200–154 BCE) (Chen, Tushou 2020), while the *Yantie lun* was assigned to the Beijing Foreign Language College and Peking University.

## *Zhua geming cu shengchan* 抓革命、促生產 (Engaging in revolution, promoting productivity), enlightenment and reform

The various annotations revealed China's recent pan-economisation tendency. As mentioned above, the early twentieth century witnessed the politicisation of academia with the aim of introducing democratic ideology into the new republic after the collapse of the Qing dynasty. Liang Qichao and his contemporary intellectuals dominated the social mainstream. In contrast, the policy of opening up in place since 1978 went to another extreme – that is, it took economic development as its central goal. Generally, the change in policy was due to Deng Xiaoping 鄧小平 (1904–97), the celebrated designer of the economic reform. As he was a representative of Confucian civil servants, Deng's contributions should not be neglected; nonetheless, his peers, such as Liu Shaoqi 劉少奇 (1898–1969) and Zhou Enlai 周恩來 (1898–1976), also played important roles in different periods and strengthened the economic pragmatism derived from the Ming dynasty.

A popular poster (1975) from the Pro-legalist and Anti-Confucian Campaign includes the slogan "*Shen ru pi Lin pi Kong, mengzu gongye shengchan* 深入批林批孔，猛促工業生產" ("Criticising Lin Biao and Confucius fiercely, improving industrial production effectively"), which was familiar to the public at that time. This poster and other propaganda echoed the famous slogan "*Zhua geming cu shengchan*" ("Engaging in revolution, promoting productivity") as early as 1966, when it first appeared in an editorial in the *People's Daily*, and appeared repeatedly throughout the Cultural Revolution in various forms, such as news articles, research articles and administrative instructions. As with the slogan, creative authors from various fields, such as scientific research, medicine, astronomy, hydraulic work, agriculture and industry, referenced the *Yantie lun*.

There are two possible explanations for the convoluted hermeneutics described above. First, historical materialism proclaims that productive forces transform the social system by overcoming lagging production relationships, and this is the essence of class struggle. Second, pan-economisation is conducive to the promotion of mass movements, as the upper echelons were severely in need of labourer support to fight against its imaginary political enemies, the Confucian technocrats involved in the campaign.

China's pan-economisation reminded both the Confucian technocrats and the ordinary people of the basic need of subsistence. According to the estimation (Figure 15.1), China's economy had lagged in total output and productivity since the beginning of the Revolution, which benefited the resurgence of Zhou Enlai, Deng Xiaoping and Hua Guofeng 華國鋒 (1921–2008) in the early 1970s. These men promoted the initial plan of opening up to the West, established foreign relations with Japan, and established Sino-US communication

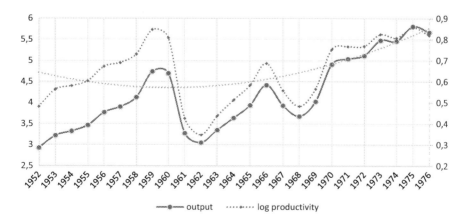

*Figure 15.1* Estimated output and productivity, 1952–76

Sources: Kwan, Yum K. & Gregory Chow (1996).

channels. However, Lin Biao's (林彪 1907–71) attempted flight from China caused Mao to draw back and arrange for Legalists such as the Gang of Four to check the opposition, launching the Pro-Legalist and Anti-Confucian campaign. The growth slowed down, and light industries grew more slowly than the heavy ones, which affected the daily life of ordinary people.

An increasing number of youths participated in the campaign and learned about traditional Chinese culture through annotations or other readings. From 1970 to 1976, 940,000 *gongnongbing xueyuan* 工農兵學員 (worker-peasant-soldier students) entered university (Dong, Baoliang 2007, p. 367) and joined the small groups mentioned above to annotate Legalist classics (Zhou, Quanhua 1999, pp. 251–52). During the initial opening-up period, dozens of students studied abroad and helped to encourage the import of foreign machines. These special students are currently in their sixties, and occupy many important positions. Even others who did not have the opportunity to attend college were enlightened through the campaign. Sociologist Zhao Dingxin 趙鼎新 was one of them. In one of his books, he wrote the following:

> It was more than forty years ago, in 1974, that I first became interested in the topics I write about in this book, when I was a member of a writing group organised by the propaganda cadre of my factory in Yinchuan 銀川, Ningxia. The writing group had assembled in a grassroots affirmation of the government-initiated "Criticise Lin [Biao], Criticise Confucius" campaign, which was gaining momentum in early 1974 … The Chinese in my generation grew up in an intellectually unhealthy environment. Before joining the writing group, I had never read any ancient Chinese philosophical text in its original form or any serious writing by historians. Joining the writing group gave me a chance to read some of the ancient Chinese texts written by or credited to Confucius, Mencius, Laozi, Zhuangzi, Mozi, Xunzi, Guanzi, and Hanfeizi and to read famous essays such as "On Salt and Iron," compiled by a Western Han dynasty scholar, and "On Feudalism" (*Fengjian lun* 封建論) by Liu Zongyuan 柳宗元 … Still, I could see that ancient Chinese philosophies were highly eclectic and that dividing premodern Chinese thinkers and politicians into Legalists and Confucians was absurd. It was also not hard for me to see that the history of ancient China was not about the struggles between Legalists and Confucians … My doubts scared me. Independent thinking was dangerous in Maoist China … Nevertheless, my experience in the writing group was invaluable. It not only gave me a chance to read those Chinese classics that I would otherwise never have had the chance to see but also greatly deepened my interest in Chinese history …
> 
> (Zhao, Dingxin 2006, pp. 1–2; Zhao, Dingxin 2015a Preface, pp. ix–xi)

Zhao was fortunate in that he was young enough to take advantage of the opportunities following the opening up in 1978, while some Confucian technocrats, as noted by the campaign, were not fortunate enough to survive the severe persecution. The enlightenment effect of the campaign should not be exaggerated, even though it offered sparks of intellectual fire during a very long night.

## A balance of Confucians and Legalists: A tentative framework of the new political economy in China

Bertram Schefold (2019) compares the *Yantie lun* with Aristotle's *Oeconomica*: "The *Yantie lun* is still a focus of debates on how to govern China and Aristotle's *Ethics* and *Politics* continue to inspire Western political and economic thought." This comment reveals the essence of the book – that is, state governance. Zhao Dingxin puts forward a similar argument and defines a Confucian-Legalist state: "It has been a form of state governance since the West Han dynasty that integrates imperial Confucianism and legalist measures, the former as an ideology and the base of legalisation, the latter as the essential form of state governance" (Zhao, Dingxin 2006, p. 7, translated by the author). According to Roy Bin Wong, state governance includes the ideology, material benefits and enforcement through which officials cooperate with social elites to stabilise the social order (Wong, Roy Bin 1998, p. 103). All the above scholars and Jurij Kroll have been wary of the unity in China, describing it using different terms, such as "universalism" (Jurij Kroll 1978–79), "cosmological order" (Schefold 2019, p. 154) and "unitary" (Wong, Roy Bin 1997, p. 169). Zhao Dingxin understands unity as imperial Confucianism (Zhao, Dingxin 2015b, p. 100), while Zhou Xueguang 周雪光 pays more attention to the relationship between central and local governments and proposes the idea of "imperial logic" (Zhou, Xueguang 2014), which is similar to the positive effect of the Wallis-North paradox. Zhou argues that the enormous Chinese empire had created a number of effective and principled government agents. Zhou Haiwen 周海文 notices the functional division among different departments in governments and concludes that the ruler tends to provide more incentives to the military sector than to the civilian sector because the former can perform tasks more efficiently (Zhou, Haiwen 2011).

From the beginning of the campaign, some research focused on the conflict between the so-called Legalists and Confucians (Peter Moody 1974; Merle Goldman 1975), which points to the lack of concordance on these divisions at the central level. Referring to Michael Mann's Power Network (Mann 1993, p. 62) and the foregoing analysis, we intend to summarise the chapter by presenting a simplified governance framework in China (Figure 15.2). The supposed schools of Confucianism, Legalism and other theories in the *Yantie lun* have been mapped to different political parties. Despite the principle of "oneness", the central government has not been unified throughout history. Emperors deliberately divided officials into at least two opposing sects simply to control ideology and the economy separately. The Legalists had superficial supervision over the Confucians. In fact, both parties were puppets controlled by the head of government. The state's monopolies and state-owned economy

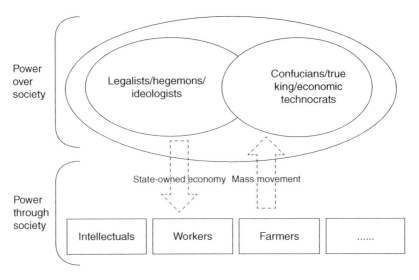

*Figure 15.2* A simplified governance framework of the new political economy in China
Source: created by the author.

act as channels to direct power into the social base. Mass movement is a method of intensifying power and supervising lower levels of government if necessary. Government leaders allow a free economy so long as the country's oneness is not threatened. Thus, the stability of this state has remained strong longer than that of any other states.

## Acknowledgements

The author appreciates the valuable comments and suggestions made by Ma Keyao 馬克垚, the German version of *Yantie lun* offered by Bertram Schefold and the introduction of the Russian version offered by Jurij Kroll. The project is supported by the Major Research plan of the National Social Science Foundation of China (Grant no. 18BJL011).

## References

Bai, Jian 白吉庵: Yang Shuda jiweiju riji jielu 楊樹達積微居日記節錄. *Wenxian*, 3, pp. 242–57, 1987.

Chang, Naide 常乃悳: *Zhongguo sixiang xiaoshi* 中國思想小史. Shanghai: Zhonghua Shuju, 1922.

Chen, Chuang 陳闖: Pingfa piru yundong zhong de gudian xueshu yanjiu 評法批儒運動中的古典學術研究. PhD dissertation, Shandong University, 2019.

Chen, Tushou 陳徒手: Fajia zhuzuo zhushi chuban de qianyinhouguo 法家著作注釋出版的前因後果. *Suibian*, 1, 2020.

Dong, Baoling (ed.) 董寶良: *Zhongguo jinxiandai gaodeng jiaoyushi* 中國近現代高等教育史. Wuhan: Huazhong keji daxue chubanshe, 2007.

Fan, Daren 范達人: Liangxiao ji pian zhongdian wenzhang de xiezuo jingguo 梁效幾篇重點文章的寫作經過. *Yanhuang Chunqiu*, 3, pp. 16–24, 2014.

Fang, Houshu 方厚樞:Wenge Houqi Chuban Gongzuo Jishi 文革後期出版工作紀事. *Chuban kexue*, 1, pp. 61–66, 2005.

Goldman, Merle: China's Anti-Confucian Campaign, 1973–74. *The China Quarterly*, 63, pp. 435–62, 1975.

Guo, Moruo 郭沫若: Sandian jianyi 三點建議. *Kexue Tongbao*, 1, pp. 1–6, 1955.

Guo, Moruo 郭沫若: *Yantielun duben* 鹽鐵論讀本. Beijing: Kexue chubanshe, 1957.

Guo, Moruo 郭沫若: *Guo Moruo quanji (Lishi bian dibajuan)* 郭沫若全集（歷史編第八卷）. Beijing: Renmin Chubanshe, 1985.

Huan, Kuan: *Discourses on Salt and Iron: A Debate on State Control of Commerce and Industry in Ancient China*, trans. Esson McDowell Gale. Leyden: E.J. Brill, www2.iath.virginia.edu/saxon/servlet/SaxonServlet?source=xwomen/texts/yantie.xml&style=xwomen/xsl/dynaxml.xsl&doc.view=tocc&chunk.id=tpage&toc.depth=1&toc.id=d2.24&doc.lang=bilingual, 1931.

Huang, Chunhao (ed.) 黃淳浩: *Guo Moruo shuxinji* 郭沫若書信集. Beijing: Zhongguo Shehui Kexue Chubanhe, 1992.

Huang, Yanan 黃亞楠: Ershi shiji 50 niandai yilai yantielun zongshu 20世紀50年代以來鹽鐵論綜述，MA thesis, North-East Normal University, 2018.

Kroll, Jurij: Toward a Study of the Economic Views of Sang Hung-yang. *Early China*, 4, pp. 11–18, 1978–79.

Kwan, Yum K. & Chow, Gregory C.: Estimating Economic Effects of Political Movements in China. *Journal of Comparative Economics*, 23(2), pp. 192–208, 1996.

Lai, Jiancheng 賴建誠: *Jingjishi de quwei* 經濟史的趣味. Huangzhou: Zhejiang Daxue Chubanshe, 2011.

Li, Ling 李零: *Lantai wanjuan: Du Hanshu yiwenzhi* 蘭台萬卷：讀漢書・藝文志. Beijing: Shenghuo Dushu Xinzhi Sanlian Shudian, 2011.

Liang, Qichao 梁啟超: *Xianqin zhengzhi sixiangshi* 先秦政治思想史. Beijing: Shangwu Yinshuguan, 2014.

Liang, Xiao 梁效, Du Yantie lun - Xi Han zhongqi rufa liang jia de yi chang da lunzhan 讀《鹽鐵論》——西漢中期儒法兩家的一場大論戰, *Beijing daxue xuebao (Zhexue shehui kexue ban)* 5, pp. 16–22, 1974.

Lin, Zhenhan 林振翰: *Yantielun Zaiban (Yantielun Shiyi)* 鹽鐵論再版（鹽鐵論釋義）. Beijing: Shangwu Yinshuguan, 1934.

Ma, Yuancai (Feibai) 馬元材 (非百): *Sang Hongyang zhuan* 桑弘羊傳. Zhengzhou: Zhongzhou Shuhuashe, 1981.

Mann, Michael: *The Sources of Social Power (Volume II), The Rise of Classes and Nation-states, 1760–1914*. Cambridge: Cambridge University Press, 1993.

Moody, Peter: The New Anti-Confucian Campaign in China: The First Round. *Asian Survey*, 14(4), pp. 307–24, 1974.

Nie, Jidong 聶濟冬: Ming zhouhouqi yantielun de jieshou ji sichao yingxiang 明中後期鹽鐵論的接受及思潮影響, In: Zhu, Jieren (ed.) 朱傑人: *Lishi wenxian yanjiu* 歷史文獻研究, 39. Shanghai: Huadong Shifan Daxue Chubanshe, pp. 238–50, 2017.

Qian, Mu 錢穆: *Zhongguo lidai zhengzhi deshi* 中國歷代政治得失. Beijing: Shenghuo dushu xinzhi sanlian shudian, 2001.

Schefold, Bertram (ed.): *Vademecum zu dem Klassiker der chinesischen Wirtschaftsdebatten. Kommentarband zum Faksimile des 1501 erschienenen Drucks (Hongzhi 14) von Huan Kuan:* Yantie lun. Düsseldorf: Verlag Wirtschaft und Finanzen, 2002.

Schefold, Bertram: A Western perspective on the *Yantie lun*. In: Lin Cheng, Terry Peach & Fang Wang (eds): *The Political Economy of the Han Dynasty and Its Legacy*. London: Routledge, pp. 153–74, 2019.

Sun, Qinan 孫琴安: Mao Zedong yu Yang Shuda 毛澤東與楊樹達. *Renwen zazhi*, 5, pp. 1–3, 1993.

Sun, Zhongshan 孫中山: *Sun Zhongshan quanji 6 (1919.12–1922.12)* 孫中山全集 (1919.12–1922.12). Beijing: Zhonghua Shuju, 1985.

Tang, Qingzeng 唐慶增: Huan Kuan yantielun jingji xueshuo jinjie 桓寬鹽鐵論經濟學說今解. *Dongfang Zazhi*, 17, pp. 79–89, 1929.

Wang, Liqi 王利器: *Yantielun jiaozhu* 鹽鐵論校注. Shanghai: Gudian wenxue chubanshe, 1958.

Wang, Liqi 王利器: *Yantielun jiaozhu* 鹽鐵論校注. Tianjin: Tianjin guji chubanshe, 1983.

Wang, Liqi 王利器: *Yantielun jiaozhu* 鹽鐵論校注. Beijing: Zhonghua shuju, 1992.

Wang, Yong 王永: *Yantielun Yanjiu* 鹽鐵論研究. Yinchuan: Ningxia renmin chubanshe, 2009.

Wong, Roy Bin: *China Transformed: Historical Change and the Limits of European Experience*. Ithaca, NY: Cornell University Press, 1997.

Wong, Roy Bin 王國斌: *Zhuanbian de Zhongguo: Lishi bianqian yu Ouzhou jingyan de juxian*, trans. Li Bozhong & Lian Lingling) 轉變的中國——歷史變遷與歐洲經驗的局限(李伯重、連玲玲譯). Nanjing: Jiangsu Renmin Chubanshe, 1998.

Yang, Shuda 楊樹達: Yantielun jiaozhu zixu 鹽鐵論校注自序. *Guowen Xuehui Congkan*, 2, pp. 3–4, 1924.

Zhao, Dingxin 趙鼎新: *Dong Zhou zhanzheng yu rufa guojia de dansheng* 東周戰爭與儒法國家的誕生. Shanghai: Huadong Shifan Daxue Chubanshe, 2006.

Zhao, Dingxin 趙鼎新: *Guojia zhanzheng yu lishi fazhan: Qian xiandai Zhong Xi moshi de bijiao* 國家、戰爭與歷史發展：前現代中西模式的比較. Hangzhou: Zhejiang Daxue Chubanshe, 2015a.

Zhao, Dingxin 趙鼎新: *The Confucian-Legalist State: A New Theory of Chinese History*. New York: Oxford University Press, 2015b.

Zhou, Haiwen: Confucianism and the Legalism: A Model of the National Strategy of Governance in Ancient China. *Frontiers of Economics in China*, 6(4), pp. 616–637, 2011.

Zhou, Quanhua 周全華: *Wenhua da geming zhong de jiaoyu geming* 文化大革命中的教育革命. Guangzhou: Guangdong Jiaoyu Chubanshe, 1999.

Zhou, Xueguang 周雪光: *Xingzheng fabaozhi yu diguo luoji. Zhou Li'an xingzheng fabaozhi duhougan* 行政發包制與帝國邏輯-周黎安行政發包制讀後感. *Shehui*, 2, 2014.

# 16 A critical examination of Chinese influences on Quesnay

*Richard van den Berg*

## Brief history of an interpretation

The thesis that François Quesnay's social and economic thought was substantially influenced by conceptions and insights imported from China has been reiterated in various forms for nearly a century. In the 1920s, the German scholar Adolph Reichwein (1898–1944) devoted a separate chapter to the influence of Chinese examples on the physiocrats in his *China und Europa*, a work that was most widely read in its English translation of 1925 (Reichwein 1925). At about the same time the Polish socialist politician and economics professor Zofia Daszyńska-Golińska (1866–1934) published the short work *La Chine et le système physiocratique en France* (Daszyńska-Golińska 1922), in which she developed – probably independently – a somewhat similar thesis to that of Reichwein.

Afterwards, during the 1930s, the thesis was taken up by an increasing number of scholars. Perhaps best known in the West was a study by the Oxford orientalist Geoffrey Hudson (1903–74), who knew Reichwein's book, but who in his *Europe & China* (Hudson 1931) provided some additional arguments for essentially the same thesis. Less known are two doctoral theses that defended similar views: part of the thesis of the Chinese student Ly Siou Y (1936, university of Dijon, France) and all of the thesis of Edgar Schorer (1938, university of Fribourg, Switzerland) were devoted to the topic.

During the 1920s and 1930s, a number of scholars of the Republican period also developed an interest in the history of Chinese and Western economic thought (see Ye, Tan 2014). In his landmark *History of Chinese Economic Thought* (1936), Tang Qingzeng (1902–72) was possibly the first Chinese scholar to develop in some detail the view that "ancient Chinese economic thought actually exercised a significant influence on the countries of the West; the most noticeable was the [influence] on the French physiocrats" (Ye, Tan 1936, p. 366 quoted in Borokh 2013, p. 147).

Meanwhile, in the United States, in a number of contributions culminating in the publication of the first English translation of Quesnay's (1767) *Despotisme de la Chine*, Lewis A. Maverick (1946) documented a large number of eighteenth-century French publications that demonstrated the frequency with which Chinese examples had figured in political and economic writings.

DOI: 10.4324/9780367434496-24

Maverick's work constituted the most detailed exposition of the interwar period and thereafter became a standard reference for this line of argument that proliferated in various publications (see e.g. Clarke 1997, p. 50; Jacobsen 2013; McCabe 2008, pp. 271–72; Millar 2017; Pak 1974, pp. 56–57; Shrecker 2004; Tan, Min 2014; Witzel 2012, p. 19).

This extremely brief review shows, first, that from the start proponents of the thesis that Quesnay had been "influenced by China" already came from a range of countries and were drawn to it for different reasons. For example, Reichwein (1925, chapter 1) was fascinated by what he perceived as fundamental communalities in the ethical principles of the East and West, and more specifically he believed that the mystical and pacifist beliefs shared by Leo Tolstoy and Laozi offered hope against the widespread spiritual disillusionment experienced after WWI. Very differently, for Tang Qingzeng the thesis was part of a larger effort of intellectual emancipation from Western economic theories, motivated by a general desire during the Republican period "for a strong country [which] provided the impetus for economic development and theoretical construction" (Ye, Tan 2014, p. 177).

Second, the focus on Quesnay's thinking was due, at least in part, to the belief that his case showed that the interest in China had not just been an isolated preoccupation of minor economic thinkers. The supposed influence on the founder of physiocracy signified something more momentous: Quesnay's work was seen as the principal conduit through which, at a crucial juncture, Chinese civilisation had influenced Western economic and social thinking more generally. Maverick (1938, p. 66) summed up this view most confidently:

> The physiocrats occupy a basic position in the history of economic thought. It seems clear that they were definitely influenced by the Chinese. Very likely, furthermore, our twentieth-century heritage from them has retained deposits from the Orient. Western economists who study the economic and social thought of the Chinese may well regard it not as something alien and irrelevant to Western civilization, but as having contributed directly to the development of Western thought.

While even some recent commentators have made similarly bold claims (see Tan, Min 2014, p. 97), not all students of Quesnay's interest in China were prepared to go this far. Daszyńska-Golińska (1922), for example, had already distinguished clearly between Quesnay's political and social theories on the one hand, which she felt did show influences from Chinese examples, and his economic theories on the other, which she felt did not. She also did not imply that beyond Quesnay's writings a more general and lasting influence on Western social and economic thought was at stake.

## What do we mean by "influence"?

Another significant aspect of most of the literature mentioned in the previous section is that the term "influence" tends to be used in a loose and uncritical manner. For an assessment of the nature and extent of "influence" in the case in question, it is perhaps useful to make two general distinctions: first, between *formative* and *confirmative* impact; and second, between *exact* and *transformed* adoption. The first distinction revolves around the question of whether or not a reader already held particular views prior to the exposure to related ideas or information – or indeed whether they would have arrived at those views had they not read specific texts at all. The second distinction is about the question of whether ideas or information adopted in a later text were interpreted in line with their intended meaning (or, probably better, the understanding(s) of the time and culture in which they were originally conceived), or whether they were reshaped within the cultural or intellectual frameworks of the adopter. Clearly, with regard to both distinctions, it should be acknowledged first that they are not absolute opposites, but can be seen as shades on a spectrum, and second that where on the spectrums one places particular cases is, at least to some extent, a matter of judgement that is not subject to rigorous "proof".

In the remainder of this chapter, I will argue that whatever influences the literature from and about China may have exercised on Quesnay's thinking, they were firmly on the *confirmative* and *transformative* ends of the spectrums. In the next section, I support this argument by considering the evidence of Quesnay's study of sources about China. I then examine some of the themes in his writings for which a Chinese inspiration has been claimed.

## Quesnay's sources

There is little concrete evidence to support the view, found in the literature mentioned earlier, that the founder of physiocracy made a profound and prolonged study of a range of sources from and about China. Instead, Quesnay may have been intensely interested in the oriental empire for only a short period late in his writing career, and even then his studies appear to have lacked scholarly depth (cf. Maverick 1946, p. 114). With regard to the first point, it is striking that, prior to *Despotisme*, which was most probably composed in 1766, China figured only sporadically in his writings. To be precise, there are some short passages that mention China in *Hommes* (2005 [1757]), the *Traité de la Monarchie* (Mirabeau and Quesnay 1999 [1757–1759], p. 58) and *Philosophie rurale* (Mirabeau 1763). These passages deal with the theory of population stating generally that a nation's population may expand to a point where "excessive" overpopulation "reduces consumption to the strictly necessary":

> Such a nation will be forced to limit any produce of the land to the substances of first necessity, and also to reduce their consumption [per head], like that numerous population of China whose vast and fertile territory is scarcely enough to provide it with rice and other cereals for its subsistence. This nation which is well governed, which is not exposed to wars, and which does not spread into other countries, has multiplied to such a degree that it surpasses the subsistence provided by a country that is well cultivated and plentiful.
>
> (Quesnay 2005 [1757], p. 316)

Rather than seeing evidence in this early passage that Quesnay must by this time have made a sustained study of China, inspired by the fashion of *chinoiserie* at the royal court (Jacobsen 2013, p. 16; cf. Reichwein 1925, p. 102), one may explain it as a reflection on the works of Cantillon and Melon.[1] The first sentence, with its emphasis on the idea that in China all arable land is devoted to the cultivation of foodstuffs, and that the consumption of the many is reduced to the strictest necessary level, is reminiscent of Cantillon's discussion of population in China (see Cantillon 2015, pp. 140–41). The second sentence appears to respond to Melon, especially since in *Philosophie rurale* (1763, II, viii, pp. 5–6) and *Despotisme*, Quesnay would add more extended reflections on precisely the same points that were doubtlessly written in response to the author of the *Essai politique* (see Melon 1736, pp. 382–89). These few passages, plus the picture at the beginning of the first chapter of *Philosophie rurale* of the plowing ceremony of the Chinese emperor, hardly amount to a solid basis for the claim that Quesnay made a decade-long study of the ample literature on China available in his day.

When it comes to the first print edition of *Despotisme de la Chine*, which appeared in the physiocratic journal *Ephémérides du citoyen* in 1767, there is of course the appearance of his wide reading of that literature. That this appearance is misleading was pointed out long ago by Pinot (1906), acknowledged in an awkward manner by Maverick (1946) and forcefully reiterated by Maffei (1973). The most recent edition of Quesnay's economic writings confirms their point in great detail, namely that large parts of *Despotisme* are near verbatim excerpts from volumes 4 and 5 of the work *Mélanges intéressans et curieux* by the administrator Jacques-Philibert Rousselot de Surgy (1737–91).[2] The extent to which Quesnay had relied on this one source was less apparent in the original *print* edition,[3] and subsequent versions that derived from it.[4] What is the significance of this? The *Mélanges*, as well as another work from which Quesnay borrowed to a far lesser extent,[5] were derivative multi-volume compilations of travel accounts and histories from around the world. The composer of Quesnay's main source, Rousselot, was not a sinologist or orientalist, but a prolific non-specialist editor of travel accounts and descriptions of exotic places. Quesnay's decision to rely largely on Rousselot's popularising compilation and not to go back to sources like Du Halde's standard work, or indeed the sources of that author including the famous *Lettres édifiantes et curieuses*, does *not* suggest a deep scholarly attitude to his study of China.

The only chapter of *Despotisme de la Chine* that was written entirely by Quesnay was placed at the end of that work, and numbered Chapter VIII in the version published in the *Ephémérides du citoyen*. An introductory paragraph was inserted, which finishes with the statement that:

> These clear facts [contained in the preceding compilation of accounts of statesmen, travellers and historians] serve as a basis for the summary that may be read in this last part, which is but a systematic digest of the Chinese doctrine, worthy to be used as a model for all states.
>
> (Quesnay 1767, vi, p. 6; translation in Maverick 1946; emphases added)

*Chinese influences on Quesnay* 219

However, this passage – which appears to confirm that Chinese doctrines formed "*un modèle*" for Quesnay, that is, a readily available set of conceptions that formed a basis for imitation in his own writings, and which has often been cited in this vein (e.g. Reichwein 1925, p. 108; the title of Maverick 1946; Jacobsen 2013, p. 20) – is not found in the manuscript versions. More importantly, in those manuscript versions of *Despotisme*, the "final" chapter actually occurs at the beginning of the work. From this and some other aspects of the manuscript, the editors of Quesnay's *Œuvres Économiques* infer that he wrote "Chapter VIII" "as a generic text about the theory of good government", *independently from and before* he collated the many fragments from Rousselot de Surgy (Quesnay 2005, p. 1008).

One *could* conclude from this that any facts and opinions about China played no role whatsoever in the original formation of Quesnay's views about such notions as natural order and legal despotism, and were only added later to confirm and dress up the argument by means of oriental illustrations. However, that is merely one interpretation of the significance of the differences in the arrangement of the manuscript vis-à-vis the printed text. An opposite interpretation might be that the changes that occurred in the print edition were simply more explicit acknowledgements of what had been Quesnay's intellectual indebtedness all along. Thus, in order to arrive at a balanced assessment of the kinds of influence "China" may have exercised on Quesnay's mind, we need to look at some of the substantive issues in his writings.

## Aspects of alleged influence

The various Chinese inspirations of aspects of Quesnay's writings, as discerned in the literature indicated previously, can be grouped into three main themes.

### *The* Tableau économique *and circular flow*

The first theme concerns the economic analytical content of Quesnay's writings. In particular, some students have alleged a Chinese inspiration for the depiction of the economic process as a circular flow in Quesnay's famous *Tableaux économiques*. This interpretation leans heavily on the "mysterious" and "auspicious" nature (Reichwein 1925, p. 103) that the *Tableaux* and the ancient hexagrams of the I Ching (or Yijing, Book of Changes) are presumed to have had in common. The original association was due to Nicolas Baudeau, who wrote in an editorial piece in *Ephémérides*:

> A single formula, less mysterious but not less fruitful than those of the Founder of the Chinese Empire, paints to the astonished eye all the principles of the social order, or of political philosophy, contained in an arithmetical demonstration that can be seen and verified at a single glance. It would doubtlessly require several volumes to develop the original truths that the *Tableau Economique* contains in four lines, just as it took many to

explain the 64 figures of Fohi, but the Conficius [sic] of Europe has already found zealous disciples among the first order of the French Nation.

(Baudeau 1767a, i, pp. 22–3; cf. ibid. pp.13–14)

Presumably, Baudeau's reason for this florid comparison was that he wanted to impress upon his readers, ahead of the publication of *Despotisme*, the auspicious potential of the *Tableau* for the French nation. But such a pretentious association offered an acerbic critic like Linguet too good an opportunity to miss. Baudeau was quite right, as Linguet (1771, p. 14) would mock: both constructions were equally unintelligible mumbo jumbo. Presenting reproductions of the divinatory hexagrams and the *Tableau* side by side (Figure 16.1)[6] with *faux* serious commentary, he asked:

> but what century do we live in, if a same absurdity, ventured at a thousand years and a thousand leagues distance could give consistency and justification to a dizzying impression [vertige] painted in front of our eyes? What!, an ancient Chinese extravagance could render a modern European extravagance respectable, simply by virtue of similarity?
>
> (Linguet 1771, p. 31)

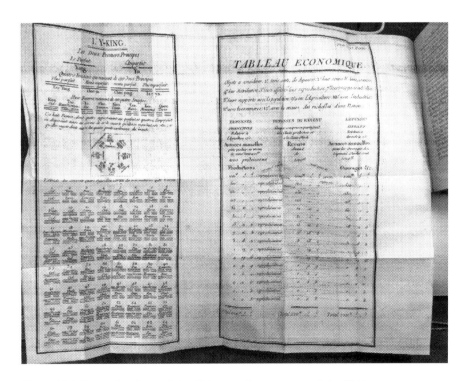

*Figure 16.1* Reproductions of the divinatory hexagrams and the *Tableau*

What should be noticed is that Linguet did not actually suggest that the divinatory pictures in the Book of Changes somehow *inspired* Quesnay's *Tableau*. His main reason for focusing on Baudeau's association of the *Tableau* with the Chinese hexagrams was to ridicule the supposed esoteric nature of Quesnay's artefact. Stressing the mysterious and unintelligible nature of the *Tableau* was a common tactic of the physiocrats' critics (see Orain 2015, pp. 406–14; van den Berg 2002, pp. 297–98). Nevertheless, more recently both Jacobsen (2013, p. 23) and especially Tan Min (2014, pp. 86–87) have given credence to the possibility of an actual correspondence.

It has to be said that the positive evidence for this is very slender. It is true that Quesnay copied from Rousselot the observations that Fohi had been known as an "able legislator" and a "profound mathematician" and that he "invented symbolical figures to publicize the laws that he had made" (Quesnay 2005, p. 1034). However, unlike Baudeau, Quesnay nowhere suggested any connection with the *Tableaux*, which he had devised in the late 1750s. The mere fact that the *Tableaux* are pictorial, just like "Fohi's" hexagrams, can hardly be taken as proof that the latter were an actual inspiration for Quesnay. What this interpretation ignores is that the *Tableaux* were actually much more than just mystifying line patterns. The substantive economic content of the *Tableaux* and the logic of their operations is the subject of a substantial literature that interprets Quesnay's schemes in the light of later developments in input–output theory and dynamic analysis.[7] The good deal of sense that this literature makes of Quesnay's assumptions and calculations renders it highly dubious that the doctor drew any substantial inspiration from ancient Chinese divinatory symbols, however open these were over the centuries to a wide range of interpretations (see Smith 2012).

## *The "natural order" and* **laissez-faire**

A more general and more frequently alleged Chinese influence on the founder of physiocracy concerns ancient conceptions of orderly, just and "natural" social arrangements, and especially Confucian philosophy (see e.g. Reichwein 1925, p. 107; Hudson 1931, p. 322; Jacobsen 2013, pp. 21–22; Tan, Min 2014, pp. 82–86). Related to this is the view that the restricted role of government in the economic sphere advocated by Quesnay was also adopted from Chinese sources. Specifically, a succession of commentators, starting with Hudson (1931, p. 322) and more recently Priddat (2001), Gerlach (2005) and Citton (2007), have argued that Quesnay's notion of *laissez-faire* was inspired by the ancient Daoist doctrine of *wu-wei*, or "non-action".

With regard to the first view, *Despotisme* does, of course, suggest that Quesnay approved of many aspects of the account in Rousselot's *Mélanges* of Chinese moral philosophy and various descriptions of society. For example, he copied the whole section Loi naturelle", which sketched what was essentially a Christianised version, going back on Jesuit writings, of the providential basis of ancient Chinese legal and political principles. In his manuscript, he also copied the positive account about the life of Confucius.[8] Above all, it is hard to deny that Quesnay idealised the ancient Chinese nation as an exemplary "agricultural empire". He noted, among other things, the great regard in which farmers had long been held, the laws that had been passed in ancient China to favour agriculture and the flourishing internal trade (Quesnay 2005, pp. 1078–83).

However, it is not at all evident that the distinctive characteristics of Quesnay's conception of natural order were due to Chinese influences. For a start, his distinction in *Despotisme* (2005, p. 1013) between *natural* laws – the salutary principles presumably universally applicable in any established society – and *positive* laws – the actual bodies of law enacted in specific political states – was commonplace among European natural law philosophers. Also, the "teleological or providential naturalism" of Quesnay's conception of natural law was hardly unique, but instead "formed the mainstream of Enlightenment moral philosophy and was the basis for its 'scientific' approach to morals and institutions" (Haakonssen 1996, p. 61).

What did distinguish Quesnay's conception of natural law was, first, his belief about the way one accesses knowledge about the intended natural order and, second, the substantive content of the natural principles and their implications for positive laws and policy. With regard to the first aspect, Quesnay distinguished himself from (other) natural law philosophers by insisting that a deep contemplation of the *physical* nature of man and society would yield certain knowledge (*evidence*) about the social organisation that Providence had intended for the human race. In *Despotisme* he wrote that "the natural laws of the order of societies are the very physical laws of the perpetual reproduction of goods necessary to subsistence, to conservation and to the convenience of men" (Quesnay 2005, p. 1015). This strikingly straightforward identification of natural order with the "material purpose" of society was distinctive for the writings of other physiocrats too.[9]

Regarding the second aspect, for Quesnay the crucial condition for the establishment of the "natural moral order" was the strict observance of exclusive and perfect private property rights. This focus on property rights (as opposed to, say, "virtue" or "beneficence") as the necessary and sufficient guarantee for the establishment of a moral social order had been part of the natural law tradition in Europe at least since Grotius (see Hont 1987, p. 255) but the physiocrats' position was a radical and outspoken version (see e.g. Le Trosne 1777, p. 25).

There is no compelling argument for a Chinese origin of these two principal distinguishing features – that is, the straightforward, even crude, identification of agricultural prosperity as the basis for social morality and the narrow conflation of the latter with little more than the absolute respect for private property. The way *Despotisme* is composed suggests that Quesnay saw at most a loose and imperfect correspondence. If his conception of natural moral order, with its strong emphasis on the strict observance of exclusive private property rights, had been *derived from* ancient Chinese moral codes, one would expect to find in *Despotisme* a serious attempt to demonstrate how the content of the teachings of Confucius or Mencius were identical to physiocratic notions of natural order. No such attempt can be found.

The view that Quesnay's notion of *laissez-faire* was inspired by the ancient Daoist doctrine of *wu-wei*, or "non-action" is even more questionable. The difficulty here is chiefly twofold. First, it entails the view that *wu-wei* and subsequent related ancient Chinese doctrines resemble modern free market principles. Whether this is a credible interpretation is a long-standing question.[10] However, it might be argued that the question of whether the doctrine of *wu-wei*, in the context of the history of Chinese social thought, had connotations that suggest economic policies of *laissez-faire* is not essential for the topic of this chapter. That is to say, even if it did not, it might be argued that Quesnay gave his own "transformed" interpretation of the doctrine of *wu-wei*. Even then, however, it is at least required that he was aware of it. This is not at all obvious.

For instance, we can safely discard the statement that Quesnay borrowed the term *laissez-faire* from the translation of *wu-wei* by a Jesuit translator (Witzel 2012, p. 19). The simple reason for this is that Quesnay nowhere used the actual term *laissez-faire*. The formulation he uses in *Despotisme* that comes close to that notion is that the "natural administration of commerce consists in … free and immune competition" both in internal and external trade (Quesnay 2005, p. 1027). This formulation, however, only occurs in the chapter Quesnay wrote himself, and nothing close to it is found in the seven other chapters with borrowed excerpts that specifically discuss China. Nowhere does Quesnay state that Chinese philosophers had advocated the kind of radical freedom of trade he favoured, or that such economic policies were in practice observed in China. Neither does he mention any of the ancient maxims that some modern commentators have interpreted as being akin to liberal economic attitudes. References that *can* be found to the presumed stable and orderly government of China, its care for agriculture and the prosperity of the people are too general in this context, since they do not imply economic policies of *laissez-faire* per se. On this particular point, we can agree with Jacobsen (2013, p. 28), who concludes that, "As long as there is no direct indication in the oeuvre of any physiocrats, one must regard the direct coupling of *wu-wei* and the economic concept of laissez-faire as a myth."

What makes any substantial influence of Chinese moral philosophy or governmental traditions on the physiocrats' advocacy of *laissez-faire* unlikely is that their economic liberalism is underpinned by very reductive views on the relationships between citizens and the state, between common and private interests. Society is viewed as essentially a vehicle for the peaceful pursuit of material self-interest. Quesnay's largely negative comments on the paternalistic role of the Chinese emperor as a provider for the poor (Quesnay 2005, pp. 1049, 1113) can best be understood against the background of French political debates on poor relief and freedom in the grain trade. In these debates, the physiocrats advocated a strict enforcement of the private property rights of farmers and grain merchants.

## Legal despotism

The doctrine of "legal despotism", which Quesnay did indeed first spell out in *Despotisme de la Chine*, attempted to answer the question of what form a government should take that respects and enforces the precepts of natural laws. For Quesnay, the question of political legitimacy was not about the classical mixture of monarchical, aristocratic and democratic elements because any such system would be "troubled by the exclusive particular interests of the different orders of citizens". Instead, "[political] authority must be single and impartial in its decisions and its operations" (Quesnay 2005, pp. 1011–12). Yes, he stated provocatively, one may call such an authority *despotic*, but one should recognise that "there are legitimate despots and arbitrary and illegitimate despots" (Quesnay 2005, p. 1009). The distinction was eminently clear, at least to Quesnay: legitimate despots take sole charge of instituting and enforcing a body of positive laws that is in accordance with natural law (Quesnay 2005, pp. 1015–16). A sovereign who reigned according to providential rules, "demonstrated geometrically and arithmetically" (Quesnay 2005, p. 1019), would obviously be the opposite of an arbitrary ruler.

For all its political and epistemological absolutism, Quesnay's conception of the "legal despot" implied at the same time a limited and precisely circumscribed, indeed anti-paternalistic, remit for the exercise of political power in the economic sphere. The idea was that the single ruler exercised his power above all as *une autorité tutélaire*, an authority who protected the private property rights of his subjects (Quesnay 2005, p. 1022). In this view, *any* government policy that violated private property rights was at odds with the natural order, and hence "arbitrary".

Given this doctrine of "legal despotism", one should consider whether Quesnay was inspired by accounts about the Chinese state. There may be some truth in this since, especially where the despotic nature of the Chinese state is dealt with in *Despotisme*, his own reflections do more frequently supplement the excerpts from Rousselot.[11] These added passages show Quesnay's keen interest in correcting the view of European commentators, and in particular Montesquieu, that the Chinese emperor was an *arbitrary* despot (Quesnay 2005, p. 1091). He also rejected various negative views about the Chinese government expressed by the author of the *Esprit des Lois*: the excessive severity in penal law and lack of enforcement of commercial law, the religious and political intolerance are all denied (Quesnay 2005, pp. 1100–03).

However, Quesnay's criticism of Montesquieu is less a disagreement about empirical facts about China, and more taking a position within a wider French debate about the legitimacy and ideal design of systems of government (see e.g. Jacobsen 2019; Volpilhac-Auger 2003, p. 27). In other words, Quesnay projected *onto* accounts about the Chinese state aspects of his ideal system of government. Here, one should think in particular of (1) the designation of the Chinese emperors as the "sons of heaven and holy emperors" (Quesnay 2005, p. 1091), and the implied providential basis for political legitimacy in that nation; (2) the regular administration of the empire by professionally trained officials (Quesnay 2005, p. 27; pp. 1031, 1097–99); and (3) the organisation of universal education by the state (Quesnay 2005, pp. 1014, 1098–99). Quesnay was less interested in the accurate understanding of these aspects of Chinese political and administrative culture than in the opportunity to paint a picture of his ideal political system in more abstract terms.

Understood in this way, one may perhaps say that the Chinese political system was an inspiration for him. Quesnay's interpretation of the rule of the Chinese emperor was a convenient fiction to be contemplated and, when understood in that way, one may also say that it "influenced" him. In a modern context, this use of the "Chinese example" is, of course, salient precisely since Quesnay used it as part of a defence of the possibility of economic liberalism under an authoritarian political regime. This difficulty has, in various forms, occupied Western liberal thinkers ever since. At the same time, his insistence on the strict enforcement of private property rights as the principal duty of the state implies that it could not be seen as an endorsement of anything close to the modern Chinese model of state capitalism.

## Conclusion

*Despotisme de la Chine* is an interesting example of how, during the eighteenth century, the growing body of descriptions of all aspects of the ancient Asian civilisation fed into specific European religious, moral, aesthetic and political debates. Later European historians were often guilty of judging China with an attitude of Western cultural superiority. For instance, to the famous French historian Alexis de Tocqueville (1856, pp. 198–99), writing after the first Opium War, it seemed inconceivable that someone like Quesnay would have taken an oriental "barbarous and imbecile government" as his model. Therefore, according to de Tocqueville, as a reflection of historical reality, Quesnay's image of China must have been "pure nonsense". Since the aftermath of World War I, however, historians from a variety of backgrounds have offered a corrective, and have seriously considered the possibility that accounts about the Middle Kingdom and translations of ancient Chinese texts exercised a substantial influence on François Quesnay and, through him, on the emerging European discipline of political economy.

This chapter has been critical of such views, but it is hoped that this assessment is not dismissed as another example of "the prejudice of euro-centrism" (Tan 2014, p. 95). Some – admittedly limited points were made. First, the textual evidence suggests that the 'Chinese example' was attractive to Quesnay because he felt he could use it to *confirm* his conceptions about an ideal agricultural kingdom. The opposite interpretation that the Chinese "model" actually inspired this conception in the first place, while not impossible, lacks sound textual support. Second, when examining the content of Quesnay's doctrines in more detail, the affinity with Chinese thought and practices appears limited. In the case of Quesnay's most famous creation, the *Tableau économique*, the relevance of Chinese precedents should simply be discounted altogether. In other cases, matters are perhaps less clear-cut. For example, Quesnay's belief that there is a natural moral code (essentially consisting in the strict observance of private property rights) appears to be rooted in an original mixture of earlier European natural law philosophy and his own understanding of the "physical" principles dictated by the economic system of agricultural reproduction. If Quesnay's understanding of Chinese political and moral principles and practices had anything to do with these notions, then this was a much "transformed" understanding by a creative European social thinker. The same is largely true for Quesnay's peculiar theory of legal despotism, although here the argument in favour of "Chinese influences" is strongest. Given the fact that it was only in *Despotisme* that Quesnay formulated detailed views on the political legitimacy of a single ruler, the nature of government in China may indeed have been an inspiration. But, of course, it was his own, idealised vision of the Chinese state.

## Notes

1 At least this interpretation has the merit that there is evidence that Quesnay knew their works; for the first, see Cantillon (2015, p. 71); for the second, see Quesnay (2005, p. 758). Both authors discussed China primarily in the context of population theory.
2 The manuscript on which Quesnay (2005, pp. 1009–1114) is based is preserved in the papers of Du Pont at the Hagley Museum and Library, Wilmington, Delaware (item W2–5678). Another extant manuscript of *Despotisme* is in private hands. Sabbagh (2019) discusses some of the variations found in that manuscript.
3 To be sure, a number of references to *Mélanges intéressans* could still be found in the *Ephémérides* version, but mostly as the source of specific short passages. Sabbagh (2019, 5, n. 25) gives the full list of these references: Quesnay (1767, iii, p. 26; 55; iv, p. 22; 28; 34; 44; 54; v, p. 19). At the same time, the print version omitted a number of marginal notes that in the manuscript referenced Rousselot's work, while integrating in the body of the text a further number of manuscript footnotes referring to prior sources without indicating that they were quoted *through* Rousselot. This would have led any reader to mistake further second-hand references for first-hand references. The question of whether this makes Quesnay a plagiarist, as forcefully argued by Maffei (1973), is not easy to answer and, due to limited space, cannot be addressed here.
4 Sabbagh (2019) and (2022) reports a number of eighteenth-century republications and German translations of *Despotisme*, which all ultimately derived from the version that had appeared in *Ephémérides*. The same was true for the first modern edition of the text in August Oncken's *Oeuvres de Quesnay* (1888, pp. 563–60), and the later translation in English by Maverick (1946) and in Chinese by Tan Min (1992).
5 Sabbagh (2019, pp. 4–5) shows that Quesnay used a fragment from volume 6 (pp. 398–402) of a popular *Histoire générale des voyages* (1748) in Chapter VII of *Despotisme* after his borrowings from Rousselot came to an end (Quesnay 1767, v, pp. 38–43; Quesnay 2005, pp. 1106–07).

6   Note that Linguet used the early 'zig-zag' version of the *Tableau* for his tongue-in-cheek comparison. Baudeau, on the other hand, by describing the *Tableau* as consisting of "four lines" (see the quotation on p. 219), apparently had the later "Analyse" form in mind. None of the modern commentators that allege similarities between the *Tableaux* and Chinese conceptions specify which version of the former (that is the "zig-zag", the "précis" or the final "Analysis" form) they mean.
7   See Steenge & van den Berg (2007) for references to this literature and an interpretation of the differences between the principles informing the *Tableaux* and standard I-O theory.
8   This account was omitted in the printed version. It seems that physiocrats started using the sobriquet "Confucius of Europe" for Quesnay from 1767. Baudeau's use in the quotation on p. 220 is one of the earliest. However, later commentators have surely made too much of this identification of Quesnay with Confucius. Fox-Genovese's argument (1976, pp. 74–75) about Quesnay's projection of himself onto the figure of Confucius is fatally undermined by the fact that this manuscript section was actually taken verbatim from Rousselot. The interpretation of Jacobsen (2013, p. 18) suffers from the same drawback, while his opinion that Quesnay "actually attributed to Confucian thought" an important role "throughout his oeuvre in the 1760s" (Jacobsen 2013, p. 31, n. 2) simply lacks textual evidence.
9   Especially instructive is Baudeau's (1767b) review of the various attempts since Grotius to find a foundation for the natural principles of societies and his conclusion that none had discovered their *physical* basis (pp. 119–20).
10  In 1936, Tang Qingzeng already rejected the view that the teachings of Lao Zi bear anything more than superficial similarity to the notion of *laissez-faire* (see Borokh 2013, p. 148), but the rich and varied moral and political traditions of ancient China and the substantial and growing scholarship on aspects relevant to the history of Chinese economic thought make it perilous for a non-specialist to conclude anything definitive about the presence and importance of liberal economic ideas for the management of the Chinese economy. The carefully considered introductory chapter by Lin, Peach and Fang (2014) gives an indication of the intricacies of this topic, which, it must be stressed, are *not* the topic of this chapter.
11  In addition to the '*Avant-Propos*', which is entirely of his hand and is placed at the beginning of both the manuscript and printed text (Quesnay 2005, p. 1009), the most relevant sections are the ones entitled '*Autorité*' (pp. 1091–92) and the beginning of '*Défauts attribués au gouvernement de la Chine*' (pp. 1099–1106). For Quesnay's more original contribution to the latter section, see the editors' note on p. 1099.

## References

Baudeau, Nicolas: Avertissement de l'Auteur', *Ephémérides du citoyen*, vol.1, part 1, pp. 3–25, 1767a.
Baudeau, Nicolas: Essai sur l'Histoire du Droit Naturel, *Ephémérides du citoyen*, vol. 1, pp. 97–160; vol. 2, pp. 113–92, 1767b.
Borokh, Olga: Chinese Tradition Meets Western Economics. Tan Qingzeng and His Legacy. In: Ying Ma & Hans-Michael Trautwein (eds): *Thoughts on Economic Development in China*. London: Routledge, pp. 136–57, 2013.
Cantillon, Richard: *Richard Cantillon's Essay on the Nature of Trade in General: A Variorum Edition*. Richard van den Berg (ed.). London: Routledge, 2015.

Citton, Yves: Concate Nations: Globalization in a Spinozist Context. In: D. Morgan & G. Bantham (eds): *Cosmopolitics and the Emergence of a Future*, pp. 91–117. London: Palgrave Macmillan, 2007.

Clarke, J.J.: *Oriental Enlightenment: The Encounter Between Asian and Western Thought*. London: Routledge, 1997.

Daszyńska-Golińska, Zofia: *La Chine et le système physiocratique en France*. Warsaw: Bibliotheca Universitatis Liberae Polonae, 1922.

de Tocqueville, Alexis: *The Old Regime and the Revolution*. New York: Harper, 1856.

Fox-Genovese, Elizabeth: *The Origins of Physiocracy: Economic Revolution and Social Order in Eighteenth Century France*. Ithaca, NY: Cornell University Press, 1976.

Gerlach, Christian: Wu-wei in Europe: A Study of Eurasian Economic Thought. London: London School of Economics and Political Science, 2005.

Haakonssen, Knud: *Natural Law and Moral Philosophy. From Grotius to the Scottish Enlightenment*. Cambridge: Cambridge University Press, 1996.

Hont, I.: The Language of Sociability and Commerce: Samuel Pufendorf and the Theoretical Foundations of the "Four-Stages" Theory. In: A. Pagden (ed.): The Language of Political Theory in Early-Modern Europe, pp. 253–76. Cambridge: Cambridge University Press, 1987.

Hudson, Geoffrey Francis: *Europe and China. A Survey of Their Relations from the Earliest Times to 1800*. London: Edward Arnold, 1931.

Jacobsen, Stefan Gaarsmand: Physiocracy and the Chinese Model: Enlightened Lessons from China's Political Economy? In: Ying Ma & Hans-Michael Trautwein (eds.): *Thoughts on Economic Development in China*. London: Routledge, pp. 12–34, 2013.

Jacobsen, Stefan Gaarsmand: Against the Chinese Model: The Debate on Cultural Facts and Physiocratic Epistemology. In: S. Reinert & S. Kaplan (eds): *The Economic Turn: Recasting Political Economy in Enlightenment Europe*. London: Anthem Press, pp. 89–116, 2019.

Le Trosne, Guillaume François: *De order social*. Paris: Chez les Freres Debure, 1777.

Lin Cheng, Peach, Terry & Fang Wang (eds): Introduction. In: *The History of Ancient Chinese Economic Thought*. London: Routledge, pp. 1–31, 2014.

Linguet, Simon Nicolas Henri: *Réponse aux Docteurs Modernes, Ou Apologie Pour L'Auteur De La Théorie Des Loix, Et Des Lettres Sur Cette Théorie*, Vol. 3, n.p., 1771.

Ly, Siou Y.: *Les Grands Courants de la Pensée économique chinoise dans l'Antiquité (du VI$^e$ au III$^e$ siècle avant J.-C.) et leur Influence sur la Formation de la Doctrine physiocratique*. Paris: Jouve, 1936.

Maffei, Aldo: Un plagio di F. Quesnay: Il Despotisme de la Chine. *Il Pensiero Politico*, 6(1), pp. 37–56, 1973.

Maverick, Lewis Adams: Chinese Influences upon the Physiocrats. *Economic History*, 3(13), pp. 54–67, 1938.

Maverick, Lewis Adams: *China A Model for Europe*. San Antonio, TX: Paul Anderson, 1946.

McCabe, I.B.: *Orientalism in Early Modern France: Eurasian Trade, Exoticism and the Ancien Regime*. London: Bloomsbury, 2008.

Melon, Jean-François: *Essai politique sur le commerce. Nouvelle Edition*. n.p., 1736.

Millar, Ashley Eva: *Singular Case: Debating China's Political Economy in the European Enlightenment*. Montreal: McGill-Queen's University Press, 2017.

Mirabeau, Victor Riquetti, Marquis de and Quesnay, François: *Traité de la monarchie*. Ed. Gino Longhitano. Paris: L'Harmattan 1999. [1757–1759].

Mirabeau, V. Riquetti Marquis de: Philosophie rurale ou economie generale et politique de l'agriculture. Amsterdam: Les Libraires associes. 1763.

Oncken, Auguste: *Œuvres Économiques et Philosophiques de François Quesnay*. Paris: Rozier, 1888.

Orain, Arnaud: Figures of Mockery: The Cultural Disqualification of Physiocracy (1760–1790). *European Journal of the History of Economic Thought*, 22(3), pp. 383–419, 2015.

Pak, Hyobom: *China and the West: Myths and Realities in History*. Leiden: Brill, 1974.

Pinot, Virgile: Les Physiocrates et la Chine au 18ᵉ siècle. *Revue d'Histoire Moderne et Contemporaine*, 8, pp. 200–14, 1906.

Priddat, Birger P.: *Le concert universel. Die Physiocratie. Eine Transformationsphilosophie des 18. Jahrhunderts*. Marburg: Metropolis, 2001.

Quesnay, François: Despotisme de la Chine. In: *Ephémérides du citoyen, Vol. 3*, March, pp. 7–88; *Vol. 4*, April, pp. 5–72; *Vol. 5*, May, pp. 5–61; *Vol. 6*, June pp. 5–75, 1767.

Quesnay, François: *François Quesnay. Œuvres Économiques Complètes et Autres Textes*. Théré, C.; Charles, L.; Perrot, J.-C. (eds.). Paris: Institut National d'Études Démographiques, 2005.

Reichwein, Adolph: *China and Europe: Intellectual and Artistic Contacts in the Eighteenth Century*. London: Kegan Paul, 1925.

Sabbagh, Gabriel: Quesnay's Thought and Influence Through Two Related Texts, *Droit Naturel* and *Despotisme de la Chine*, and their editions. *History of European Ideas*, 46(2), pp. 131–56, 2019.

Sabbagh, Gabriel: The First Appearances of Quesnay in German: About Sinophillia, Sweden and the Politics of Physiocracy *The European Journal for the History of Economic Thought*, 29, 2022 (forthcoming).

Schorer, Edgar: *L'influence de la Chine sur la genèse et le développement de la doctrine physiocratique*. Paris: Dormat, 1938.

Shrecker, J.E.: *The Chinese Revolution in Historical Perspective*. Westport, CT: Praeger, 2004.

Smith, Richard J.: *The I Ching: A Biography*. Princeton, NJ: Princeton University Press, 2012.

Steenge, Albert & van den Berg, Richard: Transcribing the *Tableau économique*. Input–Output Analysis à la Quesnay. *Journal of the History of Economic Thought*, 29(3), pp. 331–58, 2007.

Tan, Min: The Chinese Origin of Physiocratic Economics. In: Lin Cheng, Terry Peach & Fang Wang (eds): *The History of Ancient Chinese Economic Thought*, pp. 82–97. London: Routledge, 2014.

Van den Berg, Richard: Contemporary Responses to the *Tableau Économique*. In: S. Boehm, C. Gehrke, H.D. Kurz & R. Sturn (eds): *Is There Progress in Economics? Knowledge, Truth and the History of Economic Thought*. Cheltenham: Edward Elgar, pp. 295–316, 2002.

Volpilhac-Auger, Catherine: *Montesquieu*. Paris: Presses Paris Sorbonne, 2003.

Witzel, Morgen: *A History of Management Thought*. London: Routledge, 2012.

Ye, Tan: Etymological studies of "Chinese Economics". In: Lin Cheng, Terry Peach & Fang Wang (eds): *The History of Ancient Chinese Economic Thought*, pp. 166–80. London: Routledge, 2014.

# Section 2
# The traces of the past in the transition to modernity

# 17 Rethinking traditional attitudes towards consumption in the process of formation of Chinese economics (Late Qing and republican periods)

*Olga Borokh*

## Introduction

Social changes that took place in China in the late nineteenth century were accompanied by a rethinking of traditional ideas from the standpoint of their compatibility with the requirements of modernisation. Reformers Wei Yuan 魏源 1794–1857), Yan Fu 嚴復 (1853–1921), Liang Qichao 梁啟超 (1873–1929) and Tan Sitong 譚嗣同 (1865–98) proposed to change the view of consumption. They favoured the new ideology of "worship of luxury and elimination of thrift" ( *chong she chu jian* 崇奢黜儉).

The traditional attitude that for a long time defined consumer behaviour was the opposite: "to worship thrift and eliminate luxury" (*chong jian chu she* 崇儉黜奢 ). Justification of the legitimacy of wastefulness was aimed at stimulating consumption in order to expand the market and increase production. Chinese reformers considered the propensity to save and limited consumption as obstacles to the growth of national industry. If people are happy with what they have and do not seek to expand consumption, there are few opportunities for entrepreneurship. Wasteful consumption of the rich should not be condemned, as it can stimulate economic activity.

The tide of criticism against the normative "worship of thrift and elimination of luxury" peaked during the reform movement of 1898. However, the problem of savings as the source of economic development remained unresolved. If the rich spend all their money on luxury consumption, they will have no means to invest in new production, then industry will not develop and China will not be able to become rich and strong. It was necessary to explore deeply the sources of Chinese economic and ethical concepts in order to discover the positive meaning of the idea of thrift, to adapt it to the needs of the development of the market economy under conditions of backwardness, poverty and limited resources.

In the early twentieth century, the discussion of these problems became the task of Chinese economists. They assimilated the basic ideas of Western economics and from this standpoint sought to analyse the legacy of Chinese

DOI: 10.4324/9780367434496-26

economic thought. They investigated the diversity of ancient economic ideas in order to identify differences in the approaches of Chinese sages to human desires. The invariable component of these searches was attention to the relationship between consumption and production.

This study is based upon the analysis of the publications of four Chinese economists with American educational background from the early 1910s to the mid-1930s. Modern economic knowledge has become an integral part of their interpretations of traditional Chinese views on human desires and consumption.

## Chen Huanzhang and *The Economic Principles of Confucius and his School* (1911)

The views of Chen Huanzhang (Chen Huan-Chang 陳煥章, 1880–1933) were influenced by Chinese classical culture. In 1911 he received a doctorate from Columbia University for the thesis *The Economic Principles of Confucius and his School*. He was the only scholar who held both the highest Chinese degree of *jinshi* 進士 and an American doctorate in economics.

Chen Huanzhang embraced Western economics and sought to combine it with traditional Chinese economic thought. He presented the economic ideas of Confucius and his school while taking into account the division of economics into production, exchange, distribution and consumption accepted in Western economic science of that time. Chen Huanzhang reduced this scheme to two components: consumption and production. To substantiate this position, he referred both to classical Chinese texts and to the writings of Western economists who considered exchange and distribution as parts of production (Chen, Huazhang 2015, pp. 182–84).

He found arguments in favour of this division in the classic text of *The Great Learning* (*Da Xue* 大學) in the chapter "There is a Great Principle for the Increase of Wealth" (*shengcai you da dao* 生財有大道), which mentioned production and consumption and did not say anything about distribution: "There is a great principle for the increase of wealth: those who produce it should be many; and those who consume it, few. Those who create it should be rapid; and those who use it, slow. Then wealth will always be sufficient" (生財有大道，生之者眾，食之者寡，為之者疾，用之者舒，則財恆足矣).

Chen Huanzhang notes that the Great Principle makes production and consumption equal in rank, but production should exceed consumption:

> This is quite correct. If production were just equal to consumption, there could be not only no increase of production, but also no increase of consumption. The only means of extending consumption, is to produce wealth over and above the limit of consumption. This is the way to accumulate capital, and to make wealth always sufficient.
>
> (Chen, Huanzhang 2015, p. 182)

Chen Huanzhang referred to J.B. Clark's opinion that exchange is only a part of production because it produces either form utility, or place utility, or time utility. Distribution is closely related to production, since distribution is in accordance with the contribution of each individual to the product. "Indeed, production continues up to the time when consumption begins. Therefore, the "Great Learning" in dividing economics into two parts, instead of four, covers the whole ground" (Chen, Huanzhang 2015, p. 183).

The synthesis of the ideas of the Confucian Canon of *The Great Learning* with Western economics allowed Chen Huanzhang to divide the economic doctrine of Confucius not into four, but into two, parts by including exchange and distribution into the sphere of production. Although in the natural order production precedes consumption, for ease of presentation the scholar changed this sequence and began with consumption. He explained this by the fact that human wants were the basis of economic life and the object of production. In addition, the production section of the book needs to be much fuller than the consumption section, so "it seems best to discuss the more simple subject first and then the more complex one" (Chen, Huanzhang 2015, p. 184). This order of presentation was due not only to the aspiration to find the optimal structure. The starting point for Chen Huanzhang was that the purpose of production is consumption: if there are not those who consume, then why do we need those who produce?

Chen Huanzhang outlined the ideas of consumption of Confucius and his school in terms of the theory of desires, the theory of happiness, the theory of luxury and thrift, and the theory of special expenses such as on weddings, funerals and mourning, ancestor worship and social interaction.

He underlined that the true essence of the teaching of Confucius was not to eliminate desires, but to reduce their number and make indulgence to desires inadmissible. Chen Huanzhang noted that the teaching of T. Malthus was formulated on the same basis as that of Confucius. The doctrine of *An Essay on the Principle of Population* was based on the analysis of human desire of food and sexual relations. The "general system of philosophy" of Confucius was also built on desires that brings it closer to Western economic thought and makes it possible to see Confucius as an economist.

The problem of consumption was linked to the Confucian rules of ritual propriety, known as rites (*li* 禮). Chen Huanzhang divided the functions of these rules into two groups. The first is related to the satisfaction of wants and the second to the regulation of wants. Confucius believed that the satisfaction of desires was permissible within the constraints posed by rites. Confucius made "economics and ethics one system, and the satisfaction of human wants the first function of rites". According to Chen Huanzhang (2015, pp. 192–93), Daoism and Moism "are very unnatural and impracticable, because they do not satisfy human wants".

Confucius outlined four factors regulating human desires: moral control, social control, financial conditions and time element. Moral control represents the human capability of self-control, which is the most important regulator of desires (Chen, Huanzhang 2015, p. 197).

Social control is based on a hierarchical social order. In the moral sphere, it encourages people to struggle for virtue, not wealth. In the social sphere, it ensures that a person in a higher position will enjoy a better life. A similar idea of the importance of social differences to that of Chen Huanzhang is found in the *Political Economy* by N.W. Senior (1854), who pointed out that the duties of the higher members of society would not be performed properly if they did not cause respect from the bottom by demonstration of luxury (Chen, Huanzhang 2015, p. 201).

The third and most important reason relates to the economic sphere. The Confucians believed that wealth was limited and could not meet the needs of all people. If the standards of consumption are not set, no one will be satisfied because the desires are inexhaustible. Modern economic theory suggests that increased consumption leads to increased production. Confucius limited consumption because he saw no conditions to increase production. The combination of ethical and economic motivation suggested that if someone wanted to consume more, they would seek to provide more for society. Therefore, the regulation of consumption did not hinder the progress of society but contributed to it (Chen, Huanzhang 2015, p. 202).

The regulation of desires based on financial conditions means that consumption must correspond with the level of a person's income. A Confucian "noble man" with high moral qualities is aware of what corresponds to his position and wants nothing more than that.

According to Chen Huanzhang (2015, p. 206), when regulating desires it is also necessary to take into account the time element, referring to the period of time when wealth is spent. For example, in severe economic periods, it is necessary to reduce expenses to the minimum, to lower consumption and to launch no public construction works.

From the Confucian theory of desires, Chen Huanzhang moved on to the theory of happiness for the rich and poor. He noted that limiting the human desire for wealth could make people unhappy. To prevent this, Confucius allows everyone (rich or poor) to enjoy life and find pleasure in what they consume (Chen, Huanzhang 2015, pp. 209–10).

Confucius's craving for the "Golden Mean" was fully manifested in the sphere of consumption. Confucius objected to excessive luxury and excessive austerity (Chen, Huanzhang 2015, p. 244). This is evidenced by his statement that, "Extravagance leads to insubordination, and parsimony to meanness. It's better to be mean than insubordinate" (奢則不孫，儉則固，與其不孫也，寧固) (Analects VII, 36). Confucius preferred parsimony to extravagance, and the idea of the "Golden mean" was closer to economical consumption. Confucius was guided by the criteria of wasteful and economical consumption set out in the *Book of Rites* (*Li Ji* 禮記). The rites, including the rules of sacrifice, set standards for each social class.

Chen Huanzhang believed that the ideas of consumption differentiated by social ranks were rational and consistent with the principle of efficiency. Social standards, in addition to denoting differences in social status, have a significant impact on economic life:

> They make everyone satisfy his wants according to the standard of his class. They help to make the wealth that is produced suffice for the needs of consumers. They stimulate everyone to do his best in production for the sake of raising himself to a higher class. Therefore, Confucius prescribes the different standards for the different classes.
> 
> (Chen, Huanzhang 2015, p. 262)

Confucians saw the difference between individual and social spending. When money is spent for individual interest, one must be thrifty, but when it is for the public interest, one must be "liberal".

Chen Huanzhang described the idea of differentiated standards of consumption for different classes of society prescribed by Confucius as the Chinese equivalent of Western sumptuary laws. There is no doubt that such policies have slowed China's economic development. However, Confucius' views were not so much social as economic. He feared that the wealth produced would not be sufficient if the growth of human desires were boundless. Confucius accepted the law of diminishing returns, and this approach was justified by the fact that in ancient times the scale of production was limited.

Since Confucius allowed everyone to ascend to higher classes, anyone could increase their personal consumption as their social status became higher. Regulation of consumption cannot slow down economic development if the individual has the opportunity to take a higher place in society (Chen, Huanzhang 2015, p. 717).

In his book review John Maynard Keynes (1912, p. 584) praised Chen's work for its rich content and variety of economic topics. "His chapters are headed 'Factors of Production', 'Distribution', 'Public Finance', and so forth; but into this artificial scheme he has fitted a great deal that is charming and instructive." What Keynes called the "artificial scheme" was the most significant aspect of Chen Huanzhang's innovative approach. Before him, there were no attempts to structure Chinese economic ideas in accordance with Western concepts. Chen looked at Chinese thought from the point of view of the "scheme" created in another civilisation and analysed the teaching of Confucius from the perspective of consumption.

## Yuan Xianneng and *The Influence of Taoism and Related Philosophies on Chinese Economic Thought* (1930)

In 1929, Yuan Xianneng (Yuen Wen Peh 袁賢能, 1898–1983) received a doctorate from New York University. His dissertation, *The Influence of Taoism and*

*Related Philosophies on Chinese Economic Thought*, was focused on the economic ideas of Confucians and Daoists.

According to Yuan Xianneng (2013), p. 22), Confucians are "constructors" and interventionists. They see rituals and laws as a prerequisite for progress, and their weakening as immediately leading to economic disasters. Confucians emphasise the role of morality and of "noble men", not the role of institutions. They pay relatively little attention to production, and see the only way to well-being as lying in increasing the number of producers and reducing the number of consumers.

"Noble men" were encouraged to make every effort to regulate distribution and consumption for the sake of public welfare. Their ultimate goal in production and consumption is not to distribute according to the contribution of the factors of production, but rather to achieve the ideals of more equal distribution based on the needs of the individual and more equal consumption in accordance with moral and social responsibility (Yuan, Xianneng 2013, pp. 26–27). Here we can see a similarity between Confucian ideas and the views of socialists.

Yuan Xianneng believed that the theory of consumption, which was so "neglected in the West", could cause interest or at least curiosity among the students of modern economic science. Confucians see luxury consumption not only as a social and economic evil, but also as immoral behaviour. Useless waste is considered a sin. However, in cases of entertainment of friends and family, weddings and funerals, construction of public buildings, bridges and pagodas, open-handedness becomes a virtue and saving is considered stinginess. "This is the outline of the Confucian teachings on production, distribution and consumption, which have led the people to misery and poverty with which we are taught to be content" (Yuan, Xianneng 2013, p. 28).

The comparison of the Confucian moral doctrine with Western economic theories led Yuan Xianneng (2013, p. 30) to the conclusion that the West solves problems in accordance with the science of wealth by increasing production, and China is doing that in accordance with the science of poverty by reducing consumption.

In the East, priority is given to consumption, less to distribution and even less to production. In the West, the sequence is exactly the opposite: the desires should be satisfied, so production should be aligned with consumption. In the East, it is considered impossible to resist the natural order of production, so it was proposed to suppress desires and thus to adjust consumption to production (Yuan, Xianneng 2013, p. 43).

Since the Confucians looked for ways to solve economic problems in the sphere of consumption, not of production, and sought to establish control over consumption, the practical consequence was a need to have a large number of consumer items to be stored to get ready for possible economic difficulties. From the Confucian point of view, it was "the duty of the government as well as of the people to save food, rain-coats, rubber-shoes, and umbrellas for the rainy day". If in China the government and the rich people build numerous

Rethinking traditional attitudes    239

grain warehouses to prepare for unforeseen events, "in the West such a foolish step is more to be avoided than to be taken, for it will be more beneficial and logical to invest what one saves for further production instead of laying idle in the storehouse" (Yuan, Xianneng 2013, pp. 116–17).

Compared with Confucians, Daoists appear as liberals who advocate naturalness and call for non-action – they are "destroyers" (Yuan, Xianneng 2013, p. 32). In the sphere of consumption, they promote the abandonment of desires. They are satisfied with the most primitive housing, rough clothing and food; their main goal is to eventually completely get rid of all this, though it is unattainable in practice (Yuan, Xianneng 2013, p. 41).

Yuan Xianneng noted that the teaching of the Daoists was fundamentally related to the science of modern economics. In both cases, it is a question of finding ways and instruments to achieve the complete satisfaction of desires with the minimum effort. "[D]aoism starts where economics starts and ends where it ends. They both start from our desires and end in the satisfaction of our desire – welfare. Their purpose and aim are the same. Only the methods of approach are different" (Yuan, Xianneng 2013, p. 52). If economics calls to gratify desires, Daoism calls to suppress them.

Daoists are in favour of reducing consumption not because they oppose luxury and consider it immoral, and not because they seek to encourage the rich to take care of the poor. Instead, Daoists propose to reduce consumption and minimise it even when there is no difference in consumption between the rich and the poor, and each person receives a decent reward. The goal of reducing consumption is not to set aside funds for unforeseen needs, nor to accumulate capital for the expansion of production and the development of science.

Full satisfaction of desires is identical to complete absence of desires and the achievement of supreme happiness and immortality. Recalling that some practitioners of Daoism reduced their diets, Yuan Xianneng (2013, pp. 61–62) stressed that Daoist control over consumption cannot be equated with insufficient consumption, which can lead to physical suffering. The ultimate goal of Daoists was to achieve physical wellbeing and spiritual satisfaction.

Yuan Xianneng noticed that many people under-estimated Daoist methods of control over consumption. However, an effective control over food consumption helps to solve the problems that were studied by Malthus and Ricardo. Daoist control is added to the preventive and positive control of population growth. If food supply increases in arithmetic progression, the population grows in geometric progression. If we assume that the land resources are limited, but the demand for land decreases, and people gradually abandon the less fertile lands, then the return from the land will increase, not decrease.

Although this Daoist method of achieving the highest degree of wellbeing is not applicable in practice, according to Yuan Xianneng (2013, p. 64), "in theory, it is very logical". The desires are boundless: they cannot be satisfied even under the ideal system of production and distribution. However, human desires can be suppressed. If it becomes possible to control consumption painlessly, Daoist control will be carried out, then all desires will be satisfied. The difference between the two paths (Western and Daoist) is that unbounded desires cannot be satisfied, while limited desires can be satisfied.

Suppression of economic motivation of self-interest can lead to inefficiency of production, but the Daoists were ready to accept this. The problems arising from inefficient production can be solved by control over consumption. Serious efforts have been made to reduce consumption to zero. This opened the way to a spiritual state of satisfaction without consumption. Reducing consumption will reduce the demand for economic goods to such an extent that will make them free goods, and their utility will be free utility (Yuan, Xianneng 2013, p. 66).

Yuan Xianneng noted that China paid more attention to consumption than the West; this emphasis is present in both Daoist and Confucian teachings. Daoists wanted to reduce the level of consumption, believing that it harms the human mind: "All the attacks on luxury, all the eulogies for economy, and all the state interventions and supervisions of consumption must, according to Confucianism, be based on the central principle of virtue" (Yuan, Xianneng 2013, p. 109).

The book of Chen Huanzhang influenced Yuan Xianneng's thesis. However, Yuan Xianneng made greater use of modern Western economics to analyse and criticise Chinese economic ideas.

## Li Quanshi and *The Short History of Chinese Economic Thought* (1927)

In 1922, Li Quanshi (Li Chuan-Shih 李權時, 1895–1982) received a doctorate in finance from Columbia University for the thesis *Central and Local Finance in China: A Study of the Fiscal Relations between the Central, the Provincial, and the Local Governments*. Among his numerous books was the first outline of the history of Chinese economic thought written by a Chinese author, *The Short History of Chinese Economic Thought* (Li, Quanshi 1927). The book consists mainly of quotations from ancient texts and lacks theoretical generalisations. However, the publication is of interest as an example of the application of Western concepts and approaches to the presentation of traditional Chinese material.

Li Quanshi relied on the scheme of division into production, distribution, exchange and consumption adopted in Western economics. In accordance with these key topics, the ideas of ancient Chinese texts were summarised and analysed. In the chapter "On Desires and Consumption in China's Economic Thought Throughout History", Li Quanshi notes that desires and consumption are closely related, therefore they can be discussed together. He singles out in the history of Chinese thought the "school of few desires" (*guayulun pai* 寡欲論派), represented by Confucians and Mohists, the Daoist "school of rejection of desires" (*jueyulun pai* 絕欲論派) and the "school of connivance to desires" (*renyulun pai* 任欲論派) of Guanzi 管子, Yang Zhu 楊朱 and Sima Qian 司馬遷 (Li, Quanshi 1927, p. 59).

Among the representative views of the "school of few desires", Li Quanshi chose the words of Mozi 墨子 from the chapter "Befriending the Learned" (*Qin shi* 親士): "It is not that my wealth is not sufficient but that my passion yearns for more (to improve others' conditions)" (非無足財也，我無足心也). To characterise the views of Confucius, he uses the quote: "Noble man does not think about the satisfaction in food, does not care about the comfortable housing" (Analects, I, 14).

Through this example, it is possible to trace the process of formation of a set of quotations that were broadly accepted for description of economic views of ancient Chinese thinkers. The same quotations were used later by Tang Qingzeng. In the book of Li Quanshi one can see also quotes from other early Confucians (Mencius, Xunzi) and Daoists (Laozi).

The specifics in the interpretation by Li Quanshi of the Chinese ideas of consumption are most noticeable in attribution of Guanzi to the "school of connivance to desires". This analysis was supported by the quotation from the chapter "On Extravagance in Spending" (*Chi mi* 侈靡):

> those on high will indulge in extravagant spending while their subordinates will be given to luxurious living, and both the prince and his ministers will benefit accordingly. When both those on high and those below feel close to one another, the wealth of the prince and his ministers need not be hidden away. This being so, the poor will have work to do and food to eat.
> (Rickett 1998, p. 330)

Li Quanshi notes that the supporters of connivance to desires in the sphere of consumption did not advocate the worship of thrift (*chong jian* 崇儉), as can be seen from the chapter of *Guanzi* on luxury consumption. Those advocating "few desires" worship thrift; we can know that from the ancient ideas of "preference for thrift" (*ning jian* 寧儉) and "reduced expenses" (*jie yong* 節用). Ancient thinkers who advocated the renunciation of desires in the sphere of consumption advocated thrift (Li, Quanshi 1927, pp. 64–65).

Li Quanshi addressed the topic of consumption in many of his books and supplemented modern economic theories with Chinese ideas. In the *Theory of Consumption*, the final chapter was named accordingly to the traditional Chinese notions of "extravagance" and "thrift" (Li, Quanshi 1928b).

In 1930, *Jingjixue jikan* 經濟學季刊 (*Quarterly Journal of Economics*) published the review by Zhu Tonjiu of Li Quanshi's book *The Principles of Economics* (Li, Quanshi 1928a). The reviewer noted that the theory of consumption accounted for 138 pages or about one-fifth of the book. For comparison in Marshall's *Principles of Economics*, this share is one-tenth – that is Li Quanshi made this proportion twice as large. He placed the consumption at the beginning of the book, thus highlighting the importance of this problem. Li Quanshi wrote:

> Consumption is the goal of human life, production is the method of human life, if we talk about reality, sometimes the method is more important than

the goal, but from the point of view of theory, the goal is always more important than the method.

(Zhu, Tongjiu 1930, p. 232)

Li Quanshi's book *The Modern Chinese Economic Thought* also begins with the chapter "Modern Chinese Economic Thought About Consumption" (Li, Quanshi 1934, pp. 4–18). It consists of two parts: theory of desires; and theory of rationalisation of consumption. It can be concluded that Li Quanshi consistently emphasised the importance of consumption. He not only looked for its origins in ancient Chinese thought, but also underlined its connection with the modern development of China.

## Tang Qingzeng and *The History of Chinese Economic Thought* (1936)

In the 1920s, Tang Qingzeng (Tang Ching-tseng 唐慶增, 1902–72) studied economics at the University of Michigan and Harvard University. His book *The History of Chinese Economic Thought* (Tang, Qingzeng 2010) presented a systematic analysis of the economic ideas of Chinese thinkers of the pre-Qing period. In the Republican era, it represented the most advanced level of the study of the history of Chinese economic thought based on the methods and concepts of Western economics.

Tang Qingzeng underlined the importance of the problem of desires in Chinese tradition. He noted that there were few "correct judgments" on this question. Some thinkers who called for the suppression of desires, were in fact not for thrift but for stinginess. In the teaching of Laozi, the neglect of desires and their suppression reached the extreme. Other ancient thinkers, on the contrary, favoured following desires. They believed that the purpose of an individual life was the unbridled satisfaction of desires. The presence in Chinese economic thought of two opposite approaches to human desires has become an obstacle to its development (Tang, Qingzeng 2010, pp. 20–21).

The book is structured around the schools of ancient Chinese thought. Tang Qingzeng notes that many scholars called the teaching of Confucius about desires "quietism" (*jingjizhuyi* 靜寂主義). He concludes that Confucius did not advocate the abandonment of desires and that his views were not quietism. In peaceful and prosperous times, the pursuit of wealth and nobility is not reprehensible. Tang Qingzeng (2010, p. 82) stresses that seeking great profit should be encouraged and small profit should be condemned.

The teaching of Confucius about desires was not asceticism (*jinyuzhuyi* 禁欲主義). Confucius opposed the profit that was destroying individual virtue and morality, but he was not against the proper profit that supports human life. Tang Qingzeng concluded that the concept of interest (*li* 利) was not under interdiction in the teachings of Confucius and Mencius. Later Confucians misrepresented their views; the result was a taboo on the discussion of the problems of wealth. The original meaning of the economic ideas of Confucius and Mencius was lost, and this reduced people's interest in economic affairs.

Tang Qingzeng (2010, pp. 248–49) noted that economic views of Guanzi and his approaches to consumption were based on the idea of thrift. However, unlike Confucians, he was able to justify the benefits of thrift from an economic standpoint. He praised Guanzi's economic ideas (Tang, Qingzeng 2010, p. 239) and called him "a revolutionary in the history of Chinese economic thought". He maintained that Guanzi "really was a pure economist", "an outstanding person" among the representatives of various schools of Zhou and Qin dynasties, so his ideas deserved careful study.

Guanzi was opposed to the connivance to desires, emphasising that a "lazy and wasteful person is poor, persevering and thrifty is rich" (人惰而侈則貧，力而儉則富) in his chapter "On Conditions and Circumstances" (*Xingshi jie* 形勢解). A similar argument was applied to the state: waste leads to the exhaustion of resources and poverty of the population, so it is important for the authorities to set limits and be economical. Guanzi did not call the people to live in total simplicity. He argued that "thrift damages business, wastefulness damages the goods" (儉則傷事，侈則傷貨) in the chapter "Cheng Ma" (乘馬). In opposition to Li Quanshi, Tang Qingzeng claimed that the chapter "On Extravagance in Spending" "cannot represent the theory of consumption of Guanzi" (Tang, Qingzeng 2010, p. 251).

At the end of the book Tang Qingzeng added the table that classified the economic views of the ancient Chinese sages on desires and consumption:

- *Confucius.* The theory of limiting desires (*jieyulun* 節欲論) that can be named the doctrine of few desires (*guayulun* 寡欲論). Luxury and thrift are not perfect standards of consumption: the proper criterion is following the Mean (*zhongyong* 中庸). When comparing luxury and thrift, the latter is preferable.
- *Mencius.* The theory of limiting desires. He was able to understand the importance of desires that should be satisfied without stepping on the path of greed (*tan* 貪). Private interest (*si li* 私利) should not be pursued; it is necessary to promote public interest (*gong li* 公利).
- *Xunzi.* The theory of limiting desires. He developed a detailed theory of consumption, surpassing other sages of the Zhou and Qin dynasties. In his theory, desires are extremely important; they cannot be equated to human bad qualities (*e de* 惡德) and it is necessary to think up ways of their satisfaction. Desires are boundless and things are scarce, therefore conflicts among humans arise easily. The ritual is an instrument of regulation that limits inappropriate desires and encourages appropriate desires, thus preventing the emergence of conflicts.
- *Laozi.* The theory of renunciation of desires (*jueyulun* 絕欲論). He believed that all desires cause physical and spiritual harm, so they should be completely rejected to enable mankind to return to nature. Although he accented thrift, in fact it was stinginess (*se* 嗇).

- *Liezi* 列子. The theory of renunciation of desires. He forbade greed and ordered people to lead a life predetermined by fate.
- *Yang Zhu*. The theory of connivance to desires (*zongyulun* 縱欲論). He taught indulging desires without restraining their boundless growth. This is the complete opposite of the teaching of Laozi.
- *Zhuangzi* 莊子. The theory of renunciation of desires. He opposed material civilisation and taught that "without desires the world prospers" (*wuyu er tianxia zu* 無欲而天下足). Zhuangzi disapproved of growing desires that generate a strong craving for luxury and waste, resulting in severe free competition.
- *Mozi*. The theory of limiting desires. The theory of reduced expenses is an important part of his economic thought. Decisions about spending must be taken on the basis of appropriateness and utility (*xiaoyong* 效用). His ideas of "denunciation of music", "simplicity in funerals" and "condemnation of military attacks" came out of a utilitarian theory of limiting desires.
- *Guanzi*. The theory of limiting desires. Luxury is detrimental to capital (*mucai* 母財) and stinginess does not encourage private entrepreneurship. Both thrift and luxury are harmful. The teaching of Guanzi avoids extremes. He advocated savings to support consumption that should be suitable for human life, thus combining the ideas of Confucius and Mozi (Tang, Qingzeng 2010, pp. 448–50).

Tang Qingzeng structured the book according to ancient schools. His approach to traditional Chinese economic ideas was different from the methods of his predecessors.

## Conclusion

Studies in the problem of desires and consumption in ancient Chinese economic thought deepened the understanding of national specifics through comparison with Western economics. Chen Huanzhang (2015) and Yuan Xianneng (2013) presented Chinese ideas in accordance with American academic standards in their dissertations in the English language. Their study for Western doctorates contributed to the introduction of Chinese economic thought to foreign intellectuals.

The books of Li Quanshi and Tang Qingzeng were addressed to the Chinese audience. Both authors sought to systematise Chinese ideas in the framework of Western economics. Their pioneering works demonstrated that Chinese economic thought can be analysed as a part of the history of economic ideas of humankind. The scholars opened the path to comparative studies and synthesis of Chinese and Western economic concepts.

Radical critics of the early twentieth century blamed the tradition for China's economic backwardness and called for it to be completely abandoned. The Chinese economists demonstrated the variety of ancient views of consumption ranging from renunciation of desires to connivance to them. Confucian ideas of regulated consumption were elevated to the position of the "Golden Mean", combining the pursuit of desires with reasonable control over them. This interpretation of the past has opened the possibility to adapt the economic ideas of the early Confucianism to the needs of development and modernisation of China.

## References

Chen, Huanzhang: *The Economic Principles of Confucius and his School*. Beijing: Shangwu yinshuguan, 2015 [1911].
Keynes, John Maynard: The Economic Principles of Confucius and his School. *The Economic Journal*, 22(88), pp. 584–88, 1912.
Li, Quanshi 李權時: *Zhongguo jingji sixiang xiaoshi* 中國經濟思想小史 *(The Short History of Chinese Economic Thought)*. Shanghai: Shijie shuju, 1927.
Li, Quanshi 李權時: *Jingjixue yuanli* 經濟學原理 *(The Principles of Economics)*. Shanghai: Dongnan shudian, 1928a.
Li, Quanshi 李權時: *Xiaofeilun* 消費論 *(The Theory of Consumption)*. Shanghai: Dongnan shudian, 1928b.
Li, Quanshi 李權時: *Xiandai Zhongguo jingji sixiang* 現代中國經濟思想 *(The Modern Chinese Economic Thought)*. Shanghai: Zhonghua shujiu, 1934.
Rickett, W. Allyn: *Guanzi. Political, Economic, and Philosophical Essays From Early China, Vol. 2*. Princeton, NJ: Princeton University Press, 1998.
Senior, Nassau William. *The Political Economy*. London: Richard Griffin & Co. 1854.
Tang, Qingzeng 唐慶增: *Zhongguo jingji sixiang shi* 中國經濟思想史 *(The History of Chinese Economic Thought)*. Beijing: Shangwu yinshuguan, 2010 [1936].
Yuan, Xianneng (Yuen, Wen Peh): The Influence of Taoism and Related Philosophies on Chinese Economic Thought. In: *Yuan Xianneng zhushu wenji Shang juan* 袁賢能著述文集上卷 *(Collected works of Yuan Xianneng, Vol. 1)*. Beijing: Zhongguo shangwu chubanshe, pp. 1–168, 2013 [1930].
Zhu, Tongjiu 朱通九: Ping Li Quanshi zhu jingjixue yuanli 評李權時著經濟學原理 (Principles of Economics by Li Quanshi, book review). *Jingjixue jikan*, 1(1), pp. 231–45, 1930.

# 18 China's ancient principles of price regulation through market participation: The *Guanzi* from a comparative perspective

*Isabella M. Weber*

## Introduction

"One generally accepted assumption of Western economists is that, so far as ancient economic theories are concerned, only the Greeks and Romans developed anything worthy of study" (Hu, Jichuang 2009, p. i). In the spirit of such a dismissive view of China's ancient history of economic ideas, it is common practice to simply ignore the contributions of Chinese thinkers to the evolution of political economy.[1] Most standard textbooks in the field of the history of economic thought do not make any mention of Chinese texts. The common historiography still is the one reflected in Schumpeter's (1954) *History of Economic Analysis*. Schumpeter asserted that there was nothing worth studying between the ancient Romans and Greeks, and the Italian Scholastics. In his words, "So far as our subject is concerned we may safely leap over 500 years" (Schumpeter 1954, p. 70). One may add, inferring from Schumpeter's treatment of the ancient world, that in his view one may not only skip the Islamic contributions of thinkers of the stature of Ibn Khaldun who fall into Schumpeter's gap, but also safely ignore the ancient Chinese.

As a result of the attitude illustrated by Schumpeter's classic, historians of economic thought are rarely concerned with ancient Chinese contributions. A central inquiry in economic theorising since ancient times is the question of price determination. On this, as on many other core economic issues, China has a long history of theorising in the statecraft tradition. One text stands out in particular: the *Guanzi*. It is a core text in ancient Chinese economic thought on price stabilisation. As I develop in this chapter, the *Guanzi*'s approach to price regulation is encapsulated in the so-called "light–heavy" (轻重, *qingzhong*) principles, where *heavy* represents "important", "essential" or "expensive" and *light* connotes "unimportant", "inessential" or "cheap". In contrast to the lineage from the ancient Greeks and Romans to the Scholastics foregrounded by Schumpeter, the *Guanzi* is not concerned with the morally "just price" and the ideal order of things. Instead, as I derive here, it analyses the constantly changing forces that determine prices in the emerging market economy of its time. The

DOI: 10.4324/9780367434496-27

*The* Guanzi *from a comparative perspective* 247

Guanzi recommends that the ruler of the state study these empirical dynamics in order to manipulate them with the aim of enriching the state, creating wealth for the people and stabilising prices.

In its pragmatic outlook and focus on statecraft, the *Guanzi* is very different from its Greek counterparts, from Plato's quest for a utopian state and Aristotle's insistence on the distinction between natural and artificial social forms.[2] The *Guanzi* is not concerned with an ideal state, but with a feasible form of governance. A distinction between natural and artificial remains of little relevance to the *Guanzi*, since its aim is not to preserve a natural order but to channel the prevailing – or natural – forces so as to create wealth for the state. The questions pursued by Plato and Aristotle in their analysis of prices are normative: What price should be charged? What constitutes fraud? Why should greed and profit be condemned? They are concerned with the right price from the perspective of moral rules. In Roman legal thought, this moral inquiry later develops into laws that prescribe severe punishments against overcharging in response to inflation – as, for example, in the Diocletian's Edict of Maximum Prices (301 CE).[3] In contrast, we can think of the *Guanzi* as a very early form of positive economics that is less about how things ought to be and more about how they tend to be. The *Guanzi* proposes principles of price determination in the market that take greed, pursuit of profit and fraud as given. These principles of price determination are meant to serve the state in stabilising prices through commerce instead of through policing.

In the remainder of this chapter, I develop the *Guanzi*'s principles of price determination and regulation in the context of the economic challenges at the time. In the conclusion, I return to the comparative reflections just outlined. To be sure, I am not arguing that the *Guanzi* is representative of all of China's ancient tradition of economic thought – in fact, the basic logic of state market participation articulated in the *Guanzi* has been repeatedly and severely challenged from a moral and idealist viewpoint in major, reoccurring debates in China (Weber 2020; see also Chapter 15 in this volume on the Salt and Iron Debate). What I propose here is that the *Guanzi* merits comparative study. This chapter can only be a beginning of a much larger task.

## The *Guanzi*'s conception of price regulation through the market[4]

### *The historical context*

The Spring and Autumn (772–476 BCE)[5] and Warring States (475–221 BCE) periods, widely considered "China's golden age of culture" (Hu, Jichuang 2009, p. 19), were an "unusual age … when old orthodoxies had collapsed but new ones had not yet emerged" (Pines 2009, p. 220). It was "the age of the 'Hundred Schools'" (Pines 2018). During the Warring States period, economic considerations became increasingly important for government theory, and economic growth emerged as a major concern in light of constant warfare (Milburn 2007, p. 19). In many ways, this period laid the foundation for Chinese philosophy and long-standing social, economic and political practices. This is not to suggest that the period was followed by any form of stagnation or continuity, but it was a ground-breaking age for China's intellectual and institutional trajectory. Regarding economic questions, the writings collected in the so-called *Guanzi* (管子)[6] are the most important of these ancient contributions. The *Guanzi*, one of the largest of the ancient Chinese texts (Rickett 1993, p. 244), is considered by some to be the "most representative … of the emerging political economy of the Warring States era" (von Glahn 2016, p. 77).

Historical scholarship shows that the *Guanzi* was written by several anonymous authors, probably state planners and economic advisors (Chin 2014, p. 32; Hu, Jichuang 2009, p. 100). Irrespective of the precise date of its creation, which is subject to scholarly debate,[7] it is important that the *Guanzi* was composed in the context of turbulent times after the collapse of the Western Zhou and before the Qin dynasty unified China into a single empire for the first time. Most parts of the *Guanzi* were written in the form of dialogues between Duke Huan (桓公，685–643 BCE) of the state Qi and his adviser Guan Zhong （管仲， c. 710–645 BCE), with the latter providing answers to the questions of the duke (Chin 2014, p. 33; von Glahn 2016, p. 77). Guan Zhong is recognized as "one of the most renowned and influential statesmen in ancient China" (Hu, Jichuang 2009, p. 100). He was not an author of the *Guanzi*; The authors of the *Guanzi* referred to Guan Zhong to express their vision of what they imagined to be his economic policies during the rise of the state Qi to a temporary hegemon in the Spring and Autumn Period (Hu, Jichuang 2009, p. 100; Rickett 1998, p. 341; von Glahn 2016, p. 44).

The dialogues in the *Guanzi* are set in the context of deep social and economic change. A ritual order gave way to a time of war and chaos (Graham 1964, p. 29; von Glahn 2016, p. 82). New military and economic forces were unleashed as part of a process of "big fish eating small fish" (Li, Feng 2013, p. 182). Several hundred agrarian city states were merged into seven territorial, bureaucratic states (von Glahn 2016, p. 44; 82; Li, Feng 2013, p. 182). Institutions gradually developed that laid the foundation for a unified Chinese empire and shaped its future statecraft (Li, Feng 2013, p. 182; von Glahn 2016, p. 46). A deep transformation of production occurred in parallel with the emergence of a new political order. Family farms became the basic agricultural production unit (Li, Feng 2013, p. 189; von Glahn 2016, pp. 46, 82) and the iron revolution introduced new production techniques (Wagner & Needham 2008). Together, these changes brought about a drastic improvement in agricultural productivity, which in turn gave rise to increasing handicraft activities in households and, ultimately, to an enhanced functional and regional division of labour (Hu, Jichuang 2009, p. 19; von Glahn 2016, pp. 65, 82).

This transformation in production propagated a fundamental change in the organisation of commerce and created the need for a new form of state–market relations. Markets in the Western Zhou Period were under strict, direct government control, including price-setting (Hu, Jichuang 2009, pp. 7–8). Following the breakdown of the Western Zhou, a new urge for free trading of commodities emerged (Hu, Jichuang 2009, p. 19). The invention of coinage and the proliferation of currency by the state facilitated long-distance trade. Commerce flourished, and a new class of private merchants became prevalent (von Glahn 2016, pp. 46, 64). The rulers of the Warring States turned to this merchant class to assist them in establishing a new form of control over the economy (von Glahn 2016, p. 46). It is in this historical context that some writers of the *Guanzi* derived their remarkable recommendations on harnessing the newly unleashed market forces by the state. At the core of their program were price regulations based on the light–heavy (*qing zhong* 輕重) principles.

The next section introduces the basic theoretical outlook in the *Guanzi*. Following that introduction, we will turn our attention to the application in concrete policies.

*The light–heavy principles*

In the context of the fierce interstate competition of the Spring and Autumn Period, "all ducal states had been hankering for the art of 'making the state rich and the army powerful'" (Hu, Jichuang 2009, p. 120). The light–heavy principles were developed to meet these aims of strengthening state and army. They find their most systematic expression in the *Guanzi* (Chin 2014, p. 31; Hu, Jichuang 2009, p. 120). Enriching the country is the starting point: "a ruler who is good at ruling the state must first of all enrich his people, then govern them" (*Guanzi* as cited in Hu, Jichuang 2009, p. 102). As Rickett (1998, p. 338) explains in his introduction to the *Guanzi*:

> Qing 輕 means "light" and by extension "unimportant," "inconsequential," or "cheap." As a verb, it means to accord little or no value to something. Zhong 重 means "heavy," and by extension "important," "serious," or "expensive." As a verb, it means to value something. As a compound the two characters usually mean "weight."

Based on this literary meaning, Ye's (2014, p. 98) translation as "Weighing and Balancing Economic Forces" is apt. From the perspective of *qingzhong*, all economic phenomena can only be understood relationally; things can be heavy or light only in relation to other things. Heavy commodities are considered essential to production or human wellbeing, and light commodities are seen as inessential. But precisely what commodity is defined as heavy or light is subject to constant change and reflects the season of the year, production practices and market dynamics, among other factors. The task of economic policy is to weigh and balance, to use what is found to be heavy in order to offset what is light. Or, in the words of the *Guanzi*:

> To use the thing that is "heavy' to shoot at that which is "light", to use the cheap to level down the dear, these are the great advantages that can be drawn from the application of the "light–heavy" doctrine.
> (*Guanzi* as cited in Hu, Jichuang 2009, p. 127)

Hence the state should not work against the spontaneous forces inherent in the economy, society and natural environment; it should instead use these forces to first enrich and then govern the people while generating revenue for the state. State regulation must be based on detailed knowledge of the real conditions and their changes. To this end, the *Guanzi* recommended extensive empirical surveys and the use of statistics and calculations (Chin 2014, p. 42; *Guanzi* as in Rickett 1998, pp. 389–95; Hu, Jichuang 2009, pp. 155–7; von Glahn 2016, pp. 7–8). The state was to observe the movements in the market manifested in price changes as well as prevailing fundamental conditions such as population, natural resources, skills, seasonal changes and regional peculiarities. As far as the prices of specific commodities were concerned, the ruler had to understand the following principles, determining what was "heavy" or dear, and what was "light" or cheap: "When things are plentiful, they will be cheap; when they are scarce, they will be expensive" (*Guanzi* as cited in Rickett 1998, p. 384).

In modern language, this principle says that the price of a commodity is determined by its scarcity. But prices were also affected by a second principle: "Goods if concentrated will become 'heavy', but will turn 'light' once they are scattered about" (*Guanzi* as cited in Hu, Jichuang 2009, p. 124).

This pointed to the institutional structure of suppliers as one of the determinants of prices. If the goods are in the hands of few (i.e. they are monopolised), they will be expensive. If many suppliers offer identical goods, the goods will be cheap. In other words, scarcity is not simply about the absolute quantity of goods in the market, but also about the distribution of these goods across producers. If goods are concentrated in few hands, those in control of supply can generate artificial scarcity to charge higher prices. The *Guanzi* anticipated the idea of monopoly price markups.

Furthermore, the demand for goods influenced their price: "Goods worth being hoarded will become 'heavy', and conversely [if not worth hoarding] will become 'light'. Goods cornered will be 'heavy', or otherwise will be 'light'" (*Guanzi* as cited in Hu, Jichuang 2009, p. 124).

This principle suggests that goods that are demanded as a store of value of some sort, rather than to satisfy some immediate need or want, will increase in price when people try to hold onto their wealth in some physical, non-monetary form. When there is a rush on such goods and they are withdrawn from the market, they become scarce and hence expensive.

Finally, the government's taxation affected the price, according to the *Guanzi*: "An urgent decree to collect tax in the form of certain goods will make the goods in question 'heavy', but a go-slow decree will make them 'light'" (*Guanzi* as cited in Hu, Jichuang 2009, p. 124).

With regard to taxation, the writers of the *Guanzi* saw time as the crucial factor. If people have to pay a certain commodity as tax to the government in a rush, the price will shoot up, but when they have time to collect the required commodities, this will not be the case. In modern language, we call the underlying phenomenon a "demand shock".

All these principles build on the idea that relative value depends on supply and demand. But rather than focusing on the equilibrium between supply and demand, as economists are accustomed to do in modern neoclassical economics, the *Guanzi* explores reasons for change. The crucial point is that all these price-determining conditions were thought to vary depending on concrete circumstances. Things are not universally "heavy" or "light"; they change their designation depending on the context, which is analysed in ways more dynamic than a simple assessment of some given constellation of supply and demand. Therefore, the *Guanzi* suggests: "There is no rigid art of the 'light' and 'heavy', but to respond to anything that is showing signs of coming and to take advantage of any tidings heard" (*Guanzi* as cited in Hu, Jichuang 2009, pp. 127–28). As a result, the art of governing depended on being flexible: "The true king takes advantage of the situation, and the sage takes advantage of the principles of change" (*Guanzi* as cited in Hu, Jichuang 2009, p. 41).

However, it would be a mistake to conclude that the *qingzhong* principles only knew the movements in the market. *Qingzhong* economic policies aimed to use the individual pursuit of profit and self-interest to enrich the state while balancing and integrating the economy. When people valued something, it would become "heavy" or in the opposite case "light". Yet social wealth was defined not in terms of the subjective value, but rather in terms of the fundamentals of material wellbeing. In a vastly agricultural society, this was essentially the ability to cultivate the land to its fullest. Labour and land were the ultimate sources of wealth, and because the subsistence of people depended on grain, it was considered the most fundamental commodity in the *Guanzi*: "A man can't eat without grain, grain can't grow without land, land can't do without man, and man can't get rich without labour" (*Guanzi* as cited in Hu, Jichuang 2009, p. 104). Grain, being the centrepiece of wealth, takes the most crucial position in relation to all other commodities, and is hence of utmost importance in the *qingzhong* economic policy. Grain, it is suggested, determines the price of all other commodities, including money:

> The price of commodities will rise or fall along with the value of money, and it is grain alone that will determine whether they are expensive or cheap … When grain is expensive, all other things are cheap, when grain is cheap, all other things are expensive.
> 
> (*Guanzi* as cited in Rickett 1998, p. 367)

This means that the value of money moves in opposite directions. The price of grain affects all people in determining the general price level. At the same time, it affects the rural and urban populations in different ways. Even before the writing of the *Guanzi,* Li Kui 李悝 (455–395 BCE), the economic adviser to Duke Wen 文 of the Wen (Wei 魏) State, noticed that:[8]

> If grain … was very expensive it would injure the people (other than the farmers); while if it was very cheap it would injure the farmers … Consequently whether [the price was] very high or very low, the injury was one and the same.
> (*Han shu* quoted in Swann 1950, pp. 139–40, insertions in original)[9]

In the *Guanzi,* this notion is developed further. The balancing of the grain price becomes the core of the "art of planned fiscal management" (*Guanzi* as cited in Rickett 1998, p. 361), an art of government that aims to achieve stability and prosperity for the state using the principles of *qingzhong*. This policy of balancing the grain price is the subject of the next section.

### Balancing the grain price

Besides recognising grain as the "people's Master of Destiny" (*Guanzi* as cited in Rickett 1998, pp. 77, 384), the progression of the seasons is another condition that *qingzhong* economic policies take as a starting point. We read in the *Guanzi* that "the climatic changes of the four seasons and the rotation of day and night were objective laws. They could not be decreased if they were over-supplied and could not be increased if undersupplied" (Hu, Jichuang 2009, p. 105). From this, the following problem arises. *Qingzhong* suggests that the price depends on whether something is over-supplied or under-supplied. Depending on the season, grain is over-supplied (harvest) or under-supplied (spring). As a result, the price fluctuates – which is bad for both peasants and urban consumers. Thus, the ruler faced the question of how to balance the price of grain throughout the year. According to the *Guanzi*, "states that adhere to the way of a true king act in accordance with the seasons" (*Guanzi* as cited in Rickett 1998, p. 365). This suggests that, in general, the state must "make use of what is valued to acquire what is not valued and what has been acquired cheaply to ease the price of what has become too expensive" (*Guanzi* as cited in Rickett 1998, pp. 381–82). Furthermore, "when the prince mints coins to establish a money supply, the people all accept them as a medium of exchange" (*Guanzi* as cited in Rickett 1998, p. 380). Hence, the prince can issue money. "Therefore those who are skilled in government manage mediums of exchange in order to control the Masters of Destiny" (*Guanzi* as cited in Rickett 1998, p. 378). The government has a responsibility to stabilise the price of grain in order to stabilise the overall price level and the value of money.

This manifested as government purchase of surplus grain from the peasants in autumn, at harvest time, when it was over-supplied and its price was low – in other words, grain was "light" and money was "heavy". By demanding relatively large amounts, the government drove up the price of grain. It thereby balanced the relative quantities of money and grain in the market, prevented the downward movement of the grain price and protected the peasants from selling their grain at overly low prices to private merchants. In each locality, the government established public granaries to store the grain. In spring, when the farmers were ploughing and sowing, and in summer, when they were weeding, their grain reserves would run low. The supply of grain on the market was short, and the grain price was high. At that time, the government used parts of the grain stored away to increase the supply in the market. The government balanced the upshot in the price of grain and protected the peasants from having to buy grain at very high prices from private merchants.[10]

The scheme stabilised both the price of grain and the general price level. First, we have seen that in the *Guanzi*, the prices of all things depended on that of grain. Second, by participating in the market for grain, the state adjusted the money supply. Since the value of money, like that of all other commodities, was found to depend on its quantity, a change in the money supply would affect its value in relation to all other goods. In other words, it would change the overall price level.[11] According to the *Guanzi*, "When grain is cheap, he [the prince] exchanges money for food" (*Guanzi* as cited in Rickett 1998, pp. 377–78). In such a situation, money would be "heavy" and would buy a relatively great amount of grain, hence the price level was low. As the state bought a considerable amount of grain, the price of grain rose, but the value of money also fell, and hence a deflationary tendency was balanced. The opposite occurred in spring and summer, when grain was expensive. The state balanced the price of grain in money and the price of money in grain by balancing the quantities of money and grain in circulation. This is how the *Guanzi* envisioned the government to "manage mediums of exchange in order to control the Masters of Destiny" (*Guanzi* as cited in Rickett 1998, pp. 377–78). This was the basic scheme of grain price balancing. Beyond the immediate effects on prices, it had important implications for state revenues, inequality and famine prevention through counter-cyclical policies.

First, although the state balanced the price movements, it did not aim for complete stability – "When water is perfectly level, it will not flow" (*Guanzi* as cited in Rickett 1998, p. 308). The price of grain in autumn would still be higher than in spring and summer, but the price difference would be smaller than it had been without the state's participation in the market. As a result of the price difference, the state participation in the grain market generated government revenues. The state did not have to impose any direct taxes: "By taking advantage of government orders to move goods and money back and forth, there is no need to make any demands on the people in the form of special taxes and levies" (*Guanzi* as cited in Rickett 1998, p. 392). The rulers of the Western Zhou had fixed prices by decree and extracted surpluses from the people by direct taxation. In contrast, the new art of government was to use price fluctuations to enrich the country without undermining the enthusiasm of the peasants. Mastering this new "art of planned fiscal management" was "not something to create resentment among the people or ruin their aspirations" (*Guanzi* as cited in Rickett 1998, p. 362). Instead of taking away from the people by command, the state sold grain to the people when they needed it, thereby lowering the price, and bought grain from the people when they had it to sell, thereby raising the price. Instead of being subjected to direct taxation, the people would experience the state as a benevolent government. In sum, this approach would create "stability similar to placing a square object on the ground" (*Guanzi* as cited in Rickett 1998, p. 367).

Furthermore, the policy of balancing grain prices prevented great inequalities without making all people equal.[12] At the time, a class of private merchants was rising. In fact, the government learned the techniques of market participation from the merchants. As prices were no longer directly controlled by the state, it became apparent that, "As the harvest is bad or good, grain will be expensive or cheap" (*Guanzi* cited in Rickett 1998, p. 379). If the government did not utilise these price movements to generate public profit, private merchants would do so: "if the prince is not able to control the situation, it will lead to large-scale traders roaming the markets and taking advantage of the people's lack of things to increase their capital a hundredfold" (*Guanzi* cited in Rickett 1998, p. 379).[13]

The profit motive was not condemned morally in the *Guanzi* but instead faced as a reality: "it is the nature of men that whenever they see profit, they cannot help chasing after it" (*Guanzi* cited in Rickett 1998, p. 219). The task of the ruler was hence not to appeal to the morality of the people, but to use the prevailing interests and "regulate the people's profits" (*Guanzi* cited in Rickett 1998, p. 379). In order to do this, the state had to "maintain control over policies affecting prices" (*Guanzi* cited in Rickett 1998, p. 366). Land reform was not enough to prevent inequalities: "Even though the land may have been divided equally, the strong will be able to gain control of it; even though wealth has been distributed equally, the clever will be able to accumulate it" (*Guanzi* cited in Rickett 1998, p. 379). If the government failed to balance the grain price, "it will only result in the people below enslaving each other". When such "great inequality exists between rich and poor," the "multitude is not well governed" (*Guanzi* cited in Rickett 1998, p. 380). Hence, "Should the prince fail to maintain control over policies affecting prices … the economic policy of the state becomes meaningless" (*Guanzi* cited in Rickett 1998, p. 366).

Finally, and most essentially, the participation in the grain market allowed the state to accumulate grain in each locality and protect people from the consequences of natural disasters. An elaborate system of famine prevention worked hand in hand with a counter-cyclical fiscal policy. The government's task was to protect the people from the changes of the seasons, the climate and the market, and to ensure their access to daily necessities at all times. The state employed the people when the seasons did not require them to work in the field. In this way, the state prevented the source of wealth from drying up. The ruler was to practise frugality in normal times so as not to divert too much of the people's time from the fundamental occupation of agriculture. However, "prodigality should be adopted in a special situation" (Hu, Jichuang 2009, p. 116). If the people lost the foundation of their livelihood and could not work their land because of natural disasters, the state should offer them employment. At such times, the state should also encourage the rich to create work – for example, by encouraging them to have lavish funerals (*Guanzi* cited in Rickett 1998, p. 319). In sum, the *Guanzi* holds that those "who are good at ruling a state simply depend upon the situation to relax or intensify their demands" (*Guanzi* cited in Rickett 1998, p. 415).[14]

## Conclusion

We have seen that the *Guanzi* articulated distinct principles of government balancing of prices, market creation, famine prevention and monopoly control, which were developed in a period when "a new order emerged from great chaos" (*bo luan fan zheng* 拔亂反正). These policies aimed to protect the peasant majority from violent fluctuations, cycles and speculation in the context of the recently unleashed market powers and to increase commercialisation of society while enriching the state. Rather than working against powerful economic trends, this approach to economic policy suggested that the state should unleash and harness market forces in order to promote its wealth.

In the *Guanzi*'s conception, the state is both a market creator and a stabiliser. There is no clear separation of the bureaucracy and the private market; rather, the market economy is created and regulated through the state's direct commercial participation. The market without the state is conceptualised as inherently unstable, which becomes apparent in the violent price fluctuations and the threat of famine absent state participation. This means that from the perspective of the *Guanzi*, the nature of the market without the state is to not be in a position of rest or equilibrium. As such, there is no natural, uniform price to which sellers could adhere. The stable price only emerges as a result of the balancing by the state. But the *Guanzi* also insists that the act of balancing is never perfect and always involves imbalance. This stable price is an empirically determined price that emerges through the act of balancing the market. It cannot be theoretically derived or fixed by state order.

Conceptualising turbulence as an inherent feature of the market when left to its own devices is a fundamentally different starting point from that of ancient Greek philosophers such as Plato and Aristotle. Coming to the question of price determination from the angle of moral philosophy, they foreground the right behaviour on the part of the individual, not the structural features of the market. This leads to an emphasis on a moral obligation to charge a fair price that evolves in Roman law into the state's right to police and punish those who over-charge their customers. This is in sharp contrast to the *Guanzi*'s insistence on fluctuations of prices as ingrained in the dynamics of the market and the structures of the economy. Movements in prices in the *Guanzi* do not emerge from the individuals' wrong-doings, but from the normal and legitimate pursuit of self-interest. Therefore, prices can also not be stabilised by punishing individuals or by appealing to their moral obligations. Instead, price stabilisation from the *Guanzi*'s perspective requires the state to balance the structural

256  *Isabella M. Weber*

forces at play. We might want to think of the *Guanzi* as a precursor to monetary macroeconomics. In contrast, Plato and Aristotle paved the way for the Italian Scholastics' inquiry into the right price that prefigures the value theory of the classical economists.

Here, this comparative exploration of the *Guanzi* must remain preliminary. To comprehensively appreciate the differences and commonalities between ancient Greek, Roman and Chinese thought, a much larger research project is required. I hope this piece inspires some readers to move from Schumpeter's dismissal of Chinese contributions to curiosity for this tradition of thought.

## Notes

1. Hu's (2009) book *A Concise History of Chinese Economic Thought*, written in the 1960s and 1980s, remains by far the most comprehensive overview in English. Spengler (1964, p. 223) and Chang (1987, p. 481) observe that works on the history of Chinese economic thought outside China remain extremely scarce. Two recent volumes aimed at introducing key contributions of major Chinese historians of economic thought to an English-speaking readership suggest that this has not changed significantly in the past few decades (Lin, Peach & Wang 2014, 2019). Chen Huan-Chang's (1911a, 1911b) PhD thesis has for a long time been "the only major attempt to describe Confucian principles in economic terms to have appeared in English" (Witzel, 2002, p. xiv), and even though it was positively reviewed by Keynes(1912) in *The Economic Journal*, it was not followed up by work of similar depth. None of the major textbooks in the *Concise History of Economic Thought* contains a discussion of Chinese contributions.
2. My interpretation of Aristotle and Plato in this chapter is based on Schefold (2008).
3. See Baldwin (1959, p. 16) for a discussion of the place of the Diocletian's Edict in the lineage from Roman legal to Scholastic theories of the just price.
4. The following is an excerpt from my book How China Escaped Shock Therapy: The Market Reform Debate (Weber 2021, pp. 17–27, 37–41).
5. This period was chronicled in the *Spring and Autumn Annals*, sometimes attributed to Confucius, which gives it its name. Although the authenticity of Confucius's authorship is subject to debate, his life coincides with the time of writing (Li, Feng 2013, p. 161).
6. This chapter relies on the translation of the *Guanzi* by Rickett (1998) as well as on relevant secondary sources.
7. Rickett (1998), in the comments of his translation of the *Guanzi*, discusses the dating of each section in detail. See also Chin (2014, pp. 32–33) and von Glahn (2016, pp. 77–78).
8. Hu Jichuang (2009, p. 180) suggests that "Li Kui was not only a well-known statesman but also the earliest thinker to emphasize agriculture".
9. See Rickett (1998, p. 340) for elaborations on this passage.
10. The basic principles of this policy of grain price stabilisation are repeated in almost all the *qingzhong* dialogues in the *Guanzi*. This is a summary of the basic principles by the present authors. Variations on this scheme include (1) the use of loans to the peasants paid out in spring in grain and pegged to the high money price to be paid back when the price of grain is low in the fall (*Guanzi* cited in Rickett 1998, pp. 377–80, 343–44), and (2) the state purchase of clothes when they are cheap because grain is expensive; they are then sold by the state when clothes become expensive

in the fall at a time when grain is cheap (*Guanzi* cited in Rickett 1998, pp. 362, 367, 384, 391). Similar, yet less encompassing, policy proposals had previously been put forward by Fan Li (Chen, Huan-Chang 1911b, p. 568; Hu, Jichuang 2009, pp. 35–41; von Glahn 2016, p. 64) and Li Kui (Chen, Huan-Chang 1911b, p. 568; Hu, Jichuang 2009, pp. 179–84; Li, Feng 2013, p. 190; Spengler 1964, p. 228; von Glahn 2016, p. 55).

11  In the light of this insight, the *Guanzi* is found to be one of the earliest articulations of the quantity theory of money (Hu, Jichuang 2009, p. 131; Nolan 2004, p. 129; Rickett 1998, p. 4). If we consider the suggestions for counter-cyclical government spending, discussed later in this section, and the elaborations on hoarding, together with the grouping of different types of money according to their liquidity, a question for further research emerges: might we find not only the earliest articulation of the quantity theory of money in the *Guanzi* but also, thanks to its focus on transitional effects, a precursor to the breaking of a pure quantity theory as in Keynes' (1936) General Theory?

12  Or, as Hu (2009, p. 111) puts it, "The writer of *Guanzi* asserted that this inequality between rich and poor was an objective social reality, but his solution to the problem was merely to mitigate the antagonism, not to wipe it out entirely."

13  Such great inequalities are, for example, reported in the *Han Shu* to have occurred in the period 246–207 BCE. After the selling and buying of land was allowed, some individuals became very rich and brought both land and natural resources under their control. The poor had to cultivate the land of the rich and "had to give five-tenths [of the crop] for rent (*shui*)" (*Han Shu* cited in Swann, 1950, p. 182, insertion in original). "In profligacy and dissipation they [the rich] overrode government institutions; and they overstepped extravagance in order to outdo one another" (*Han Shu* cited in Swann 1950, p. 181). "Consequently the poor people wore at all times [garments in quality fit only] to be covering for cattle and horses. They ate, moreover food [of a standard suitable only] for feeding dogs and swine. ... The people, brought to grief, had no means of livelihood; and they became thieves and robbers" (Han Shu as in Swann 1950, p. 182, insertion in original).

14  This proposal for a counter-cyclical policy of government spending clearly anticipates, by 2000 years, Mandeville's (1970) *Fable of the Bees,* Malthus's letters to Ricardo (as in Keynes 1936, pp. 362–63), and Keynes' theory of effective demand. In light of Keynes' 1912 review of Chen Huan-Chang (1911b), which contains a treatment of grain price policies (pp. 568–85), the question emerges of whether Keynes might in fact have been inspired by ancient Chinese economic thinking.

## References

Baldwin, John W.: The Medieval Theories of the Just Price: Romanists, Canonists, and Theologians in the Twelfth and Thirteenth Centuries. *Transactions of the American Philosophical Society,* 49(4), pp. 1–92, 1959.

Chang, James L.Y.: History of Chinese Economic Thought: Overview and Recent Works. *History of Political Economy,* 19(3), 481–99, 1987.

Chen, Huan-Chang: *The Economic Principles of Confucius and His School, Vol. I.* New York: Columbia University Press, 1911a.

Chen, Huan-Chang: *The Economic Principles of Confucius and His School, Volume II.* New York: Columbia University Press, 1911b.

Chin, Tamara: *Savage Exchange: Han Imperialism, Chinese Literary Style, and the Economic Imagination.* Cambridge, MA: Harvard University Asia Center, 2014.

Graham, A.: The Place of Reason in the Chinese Philosophical Tradition. In: R. Dawson (ed.): *The Legacy of China.* Oxford: Oxford University Press, pp. 28–56, 1964.

Hu, Jichuang: *A Concise History of Chinese Economic Thought.* Beijing: Foreign Language Press, 2009.

Keynes, John Maynard: Review: The Economic Principles of Confucius and his School by Chen Huan-Chang. *The Economic Journal,* 22(88), pp. 584–88, 1912.

Keynes, John Maynard: *The General Theory of Employment, Interest and Money.* New York: Harcourt, Brace and World, 1936.

Li, Feng: *Early China: A Social and Cultural History.* Cambridge: Cambridge University Press, 2013.

Lin, Cheng; Peach, Terry; Fang, Wang (eds.): *The History of Ancient Chinese Economic Thought.* London: Routledge, 2014.

Lin, Cheng, Peach, Terry & Fang, Wang (eds): *The Political Economy of the Han Dynasty and Its Legacy.* London: Routledge, 2019.

Mandeville, Bernard: *The Fable of the Bees.* Harmondsworth: Penguin, 1970.

Milburn, Olivia: The Book of the Young Master of Accountancy: An Ancient Chinese Economics Text. *Journal of the Economic and Social History of the Orient,* 50(1), pp. 19–40, 2007.

Nolan, Peter: *China at the Crossroads.* Cambridge: Polity Press, 2004.

Pines, Yuri: *Envisioning Eternal Empire: Chinese Political Thought of the Warring States Era.* Honolulu: University of Hawai'i Press, 2009.

Pines, Yuri: Legalism in Chinese Philosophy. In: *Stanford Encyclopedia of Philosophy,* https://plato.stanford.edu/entries/chinese-legalism, 2018.

Rickett, W. Allyn: Kuan tzu 管子. In: M. Loewe (ed.): *Early Chinese Texts: A Bibliographical Guide.* New Haven, CT: Birdtrack Press, pp. 244–51, 1993.

Rickett, W. Allyn: *Guanzi: Political, Economic and Philosophical Essays from Early China. Vol. II.* Princeton, NJ: Princeton University Press, 1998.

Schefold, Bertram: Plato und Aristoteles (418/427–348/347; 384–322). In: J. Starbatty (ed.): *Klassiker des Ökonomischen Denkens: Erster Band von Platon bis John Stuart Mill.* München: C.H. Beck, pp. 19–55, 2008.

Schumpeter, Joseph A. *History of Economic Analysis.* New York: Routledge, 1954.

Spengler, Joseph: Ssu-Ma Ch'ien, Unsuccessful Exponent of Laissez Faire. *Southern Economic Journal,* 30(3), pp. 223–43, 1964.

Swann, Nancy Lee: *Food and Money in Ancient China: The Earliest Economic History of China to AD 25 (Han Shu 24).* Princeton, NJ: Princeton University Press, 1950.

von Glahn, Richard: *The Economic History of China: From Antiquity to the Nineteenth Century.* Cambridge: Cambridge University Press, 2016.

Wagner, D.B. & Needham, J.: *Science and Civilisation in China. Vol. 5. Chemistry and Chemical Technology. Party 11. Ferrous Metallurgy.* Cambridge: Cambridge University Press, 2008.

Weber, Isabella M.: *How China Escaped Shock Therapy: The Market Reform Debate.* Abingdon: Routledge, 2021.

Witzel, Morgen: Introduction. In: *The Economic Principles of Confucius and His School, Vol. I.* Bristol: Thoemmes Press, pp. v–xv, 2002.

Ye, Shichang: On Guanzi Qing Zhong. In: Lin Cheng, Terry Peach & Fang Wang (eds): *The History of Ancient Chinese Economic Thought,* pp. 98–106. London: Routledge, 2014.

# 19 Confucian entrepreneurship and moral guidelines for business in China

*Matthias Niedenführ*

Since the "Reform and Opening", widespread environmental degradation and loss of social cohesion in China, caused largely by unbridled economic growth, has contributed to a growing domestic discourse about business ethics, drawing on traditional Chinese philosophies as inspiration for indigenous forms of responsible business behaviour. Both scholars and business people have begun to explore ways of implementing Confucian values in a modern business environment, an approach known as "Confucian entrepreneurship" (*rushang* 儒商). This chapter traces the *rushang* phenomenon to historical bias against merchants in traditional society, examining some of the precursors of contemporary developments and the rehabilitation of both Confucianism and private entrepreneurship in the post-Mao era. It concludes with a short discussion of two case studies of contemporary "management with Chinese characteristics" (*Zhongguo tese guanli sixiang* 中國特色管理思想).

## Tensions between Confucianism and entrepreneurship

The term *rushang* contains two concepts: *ru*, the school of Confucianism, and *shang*, merchants as a social group. This term is in many ways contradictory, since there is a long history of Confucian bias against merchants. Confucian thinking as "one of the longest-continuing spiritual traditions in human history" (Tu, Wei-ming 2010, p. 37) deeply influenced and shaped the Chinese mind. Thoughts on commerce found in Confucian classical writing had an enormous impact on how merchant activity and motivations were seen in traditional Chinese society, as well as on the social status of people engaged in profit-oriented activities.

Confucianism emerged between the sixth and fourth centuries BCE during the Zhou-period (1046–256 BCE). The territory that today constitutes the Eastern part of China was then a plethora of smaller states, connected loosely by the ceremonial function of the Zhou rulers as arbiters of the "will of heaven" (*tianming* 天命). Their central power was declining, which led to numerous conflicts between rival states. It was also an age of invention, with diverse schools of thought – known as the "Hundred Schools" – competing for the

DOI: 10.4324/9780367434496-28

attention of state leaders. Among them, Confucianism ultimately prevailed in the Chinese cultural sphere.

Confucianism has little to say about transcendence; instead, it focuses on this world, being chiefly concerned with human beings and their interactions. Moral development – striving to become persons of "all-round virtues" (Liu, Hong 2018, p. 87) – is considered the ultimate goal (Fung, You-lan 1958, p. 69). The individual is conceived as a moral subject inseparable from the community to which they are connected via a web of hierarchical relationships (Lai 1995, p. 259). "Personhood [therefore] is not and cannot be compartmentalized: the self is at once social, moral, political, and intellectual" (Liu, Hong 2018, p. 17).

## Confucius's critical view of profit-making

Since merchant activity is intricately connected to human interactions, Confucian philosophers offer numerous statements about the morality of profit.

Confucius (*Kongzi*, 551–479 BCE), who lived during the "Spring and Autumn" period,[1] shaped what would later become known as "scholarly tradition" (*rujia* 儒家), or "Confucianism", and is considered its leading figure. His concern was the perceived moral decline of the troubled times in which he lived. He referred to much older writings, the "five classics", which describe a "golden age" of virtuous leaders (Yao, Xinxhong 2000, pp. 57–62), and surrounded himself with an entourage of disciples who compiled his sayings in the *Analects* (*Lunyu* 論語). This work offers repeated warnings against improper means of "personal gain" (*li* 利), and "exemplary persons" (*junzi* 君子) who strive for moral excellence are juxtaposed with "petty persons" (*xiaoren* 小人) who fail to bring their potential for virtue to fruition. Since virtue demands adequate treatment of people, virtue can be inhibited by concentrating on personal benefit: "Exemplary persons understand what is appropriate; petty persons understand what is of personal advantage (*li*)" (trans. Ames & Rosemunt 2010, p. 92).

*Junzi* are people who ignore personal advantage and "in sight of gain … think about appropriate conduct" (trans. Ames & Rosemunt 2010, p. 199). People motivated by profit, on the other hand, reap negative social reactions: "He who acts with a constant view to his own advantage will be much murmured against" (trans. by Legge 1893, p. 25). While profits were allowed in principle, they had to be gained in a morally acceptable manner.

Contemporary *rushang* still refers to a disciple of Confucius as the model for achieving this: Zigong 子貢 (520–456 BCE), who as the *Shiji* 史記 (Records of the Historian) mentions was a philosopher and diplomat, but also "made money by changing goods". The Song (960–1279) philosopher Zhu Xi 朱熹 (1130–1200) notes Confucius's praise for Zigong: "[Although] his goods are increased … his judgments are often correct" (Wang, Jianbao & Neidenführ 2019, p. 3).

## Mencius's rejection of profit

Mencius (*Mengzi*, 385–304 BCE) is considered the second-most influential thinker in Confucianism. Like his predecessor, he also advised rulers of different states. During the Warring States period, central power further eroded, leading to increased conflict. Many sovereigns followed an expansionist strategy, relying on advisers in statecraft, strategy and social order, but Mencius offered a vision of "benevolent and humane government" (*renzheng* 仁政) aimed at ensuring the loyalty of the people (Chan, Wing-Tsit 1969, p. 61).

Like Confucius, Mencius made it clear that "when self-interest comes into conflict with morality, it is self-interest that should give way" (Lau 1970, pp. xxi–xxii). Other statements, however, reveal that he was more critical of "profit" than his teacher in the *Analects*. The book *Mengzi* starts with the following passage: "The king said, '… may I presume that you are provided with counsels to profit my kingdom?' Mencius replied, 'Why must your Majesty use that word "profit"?'" (trans. by Legge 1895, pp. 1–2).

Mencius promoted "benevolence" (*ren* 仁) and "righteousness" (*yi* 義), arguing that a profit-oriented ruler sets a bad example, prompting a perilous wrestling for profit among his subjects, and that gain and virtue were mutually exclusive: "If you wish to understand the difference between Shun and Chih,[2] you need look no further than the gap separating the good and the profitable" (trans. by Lau 1970, p. 151).

The pursuit of profit is a source of social shame: "In the view of a superior man, as to the ways by which men seek for riches, honours, gain, and advancement, there are few of their wives and concubines who would not be ashamed and weep together on account of them" (trans. by Legge 1895, pp. 201–02).

This strain of Confucianism thus sees profit orientation as unbefitting of a man of virtue, especially for someone in a leadership position.

## Anti-merchant bias and social stratification

Merchants as a social group were gradually affected by this Confucian bias against profit orientation. During the Han dynasty (206 BCE–220 CE), Sima Qian 司馬遷 (c. 145–86 BCE) in the *Shiji* dedicated a chapter to "Biographies of Wealthy Merchants" (*huozhi liezhuan* 貨殖列傳). This chapter has been described as a "first, but pitifully abortive attempt to appreciate the role of mercantile activity and techniques" (L'Haridon 2015, p. 172). Although Han rulers had adopted Confucianism as the state philosophy, merchants were still quite accepted as a social group. But official histories of later dynasties did not mention merchants at all (ibid), showing an increasing state bias against merchants.

## Social stratification: The "four occupations"

In ancient times, Chinese society was classified into the "four peoples" (*simin* 四民), which entailed a clear ranking: educated officials (*shimin* 士民) at the top, followed by peasants (*nongmin* 農民) and craftspeople (*gongmin* 工民), with merchants (*shangmin* 商民) coming last.

The *Guliang* 穀梁傳 commentary dated to the Warring States period had still assigned merchants the second rank of the *simin*: "The people of old had four groups of people: there were officials, merchants, farmers and craftsmen" (trans. by CTP 2006).

But Xunzi 荀子 (c. 300–239 BCE), the third most influential thinker in Confucianism, shares Mencius's critical view of profit: "Even Yao and Shun could not get rid of the common people's desire for profit" (trans. by Hutton 2016, p. 304).

As a consequence, Xunzi relegated merchants to the lowest rank: "To treat farmer as farmer, the officer as officer, the craftsman as craftsman, and the merchant as merchant" (trans. by Hutton 2016, p. 75).

The thin strata of officials were appreciated for leadership and moral guidance based on classical education. Peasants benefited society by providing agricultural products, while craftspeople produced all kinds of goods. By contrast, merchants did not produce anything, but simply transported and exchanged items.

Almost 1800 years later, the Ming-era scholar Wang Yangming 王陽明 (1472–1529) was still referring to the order of "officials, farmers, craftsmen and merchants" (*shi nong gong shang*):

> In ancient times, the four groups of people worked hard in their industries but followed the same path … Scholars governed by cultivating, farmers nurtured growth by the use of tools, craftsmen employed the very best utensils, and merchants provided goods through exchange.
> (*Yangming Quanshu*, juan 25, in Ming, Xu 2016, p. 185, trans. by the author)

This order was cemented in a fixed expression in China, and was also adopted in other East Asian cultures – for instance, as *shi nō kō shō* in Japan.

## Hybrid scholar-merchants

The highest rank of the *simin*, the bureaucratic elite, was recruited through the meritocratic civil service examination system (*keju* 科舉). The *keju* limited hereditary positions and reinforced Confucian orthodoxy, turning the state into a "stable patrimonial order" (Ertman 2017, pp. 10–12). The system allowed even peasants to rise to high office, but the gentry class eventually succeeded in excluding merchants from this competition.

Scholars who also showed a concern for commercial success were few and far between, such as the Song era official Lu Xiangshan 陸象山 (1139–92). His family owned a trading warehouse, and according to Zhu Xi he advocated for "sons and grandsons to run a business". The diligence and sense of responsibility emphasised in his "family precept" (*jiaxun* 家訓) is recognised by Confucian family entrepreneurs even today (Wang, Jianbao & Niedenführ 2019, p. 4).

However, in Ming (1368–1644) and Qing (1644–1911) times, two new social trends of a downward mobility of scholars and an upward mobility of merchants emerged, which blurred the class boundaries, blending Confucianism and merchant activity. After a period of population growth, in which the number of official posts remained fixed, competition intensified. Disappointed examination candidates, unable to rely on their clans for continued support in pursuing a bureaucratic career, turned to business, "abandoning Confucianism and becoming merchants" (*qi ru jiu gu* 棄儒就賈) (Ming, Xu 2016, p. 1). This required harmonising clashes between group-specific values: the profit-averse values of the gentry and those of the merchants who relied on profit.

At the same time, affluent merchants aimed for social recognition by amalgamating practical business wisdom with scholarly ideals. They engaged in Confucian education and philanthropic activities, described as "being a merchant and appreciating Confucianism" (*gu er hao ru* 賈而好儒) (Ming, Xu 2016, pp. 21–23). These two trends converged in the evolvement of a new hybrid class of "scholar merchants" (Ming, Xu 2016, p. 1). For this phenomenon, two distinct terms appeared during these dynasties: during the Ming it was known as "*rugu* 儒賈", during the Qing as "*rushang*" (Ming, Xu 2015), both sharing the same meaning.[3]

Merchant groups with distinct qualities and codes of conduct, the *shangbang* 商幫, were formed in different regions, such as Anhui (*huishang* 徽商), Shaanxi (*jinshang* 晉商) and Zhejiang (*zheshang* 浙商). The *shangbang* are remembered for maintaining humanistic values alongside profit-seeking (RCCCE 2008). They supported their communities by filling gaps left by central authorities in the regional economy, supplying low-interest loans, grain sales at low prices during famines, infrastructural building and repair works, as well as organising militia defences (Ming, Xu 2015). Their stated values were often formulated as mnemonic mottos and disseminated through calligraphy and publications stressing virtue, as well as concrete business advice: "When dealing with people put trustworthiness and righteousness in high esteem … Even when the business landscape is changing and one hoards goods, one still does not use two different prices on the market" (Wang, Yan & Wang, Ruihui 2012, p. 347).

Lufrano describes them as "honourable merchants" who internalized Confucian values through the practice of "self-cultivation" (*xiuji* 修己), reaching a finely tuned disposition "which informed every act and decision" (Lufrano 1997, p. 60). Classical education permeated business practice, and instructive handbooks connecting practical knowledge with values considered beneficial to business were disseminated. The "honourable merchants" were able to "connect self-cultivation to the marketplace", fitting the family-run businesses into a "chain of causality linking the individual, the family, the state, and the world." (Lufrano 1997, p. 61)

# Rise, disruption and re-emergence of entrepreneur culture in China

## Reappraisal of entrepreneurialism with the arrival of Western influence

In late imperial China, an influx of Western technology and ideas challenged the established Confucian order and led to a surge in entrepreneurial activity.

While senior officials, such as Li Hongzhang 李鴻章 (1823–1901), in the "Self-strengthening Movement", established state-owned production facilities using Western technology, others, such as Zhang Jian 張謇 (1853–1926), ventured into private business. He was an "official-entrepreneur" who combined Confucian attitude with business acumen, founding numerous companies and schools. (Wang, Jianbao & Niedenführ 2019, p. 5).

Meiji Japan faced a similar challenge from the West and reacted with a modernisation programme of its own. Shibuzawa Ei'ichi 渋沢栄一 (1840–1931), the "father of Japanese capitalism", combined Confucian virtue ethics with modern business practices. Like Zhang Jian, he also founded hundreds of businesses and schools. In "The Analects and the Abacus", Shibuzawa clarified his concept of "scholarly soul and business talent" (Wang, Jianbao & Niedenführ 2019, p. 5).

> If you are biased towards the soul of the scholar and there is no business talent, the economy will come to self-destruction. Therefore, where there is a soul of a scholar, there must be the talent of a business person as well.
> (Shibuzawa 1998, pp. 18–19, trans. by the author)

Business practices informed by Confucian thinking and adapted by Japanese entrepreneurs such as Shibuzawa later became a resource for contemporary Chinese business people who aimed to integrate conscience with business decisions.

### Disruption of Confucian culture and entrepreneurism in China

After this brief surge, the tradition of Confucian entrepreneurship came to a standstill in twentieth-century China, with both Confucian culture and private entrepreneurship coming under attack. The pervasive influence of Confucianism on all aspects of society started to erode with late Qing intellectual debates critical of tradition. The demise of the imperial system in 1911 and subsequent iconoclastic modernisation movements in the Republican era further weakened traditional beliefs and social norms. Yet the term "*rushang*" did not completely vanish, still sporadically appearing in newspaper articles (Ming, Xu 2015).

Confucian entrepreneurship reached its lowest point when, following the founding of the People's Republic in 1949, Communist nationalisation policies targeted private entrepreneurs, leading to their mass exodus to Hong Kong and Taiwan. Mao Zedong's 毛澤東 (1893–1976) anti-traditional campaigns, most notably the Cultural Revolution (1966–76), eradicated the institutions of traditional culture and persecuted its proponents. As Levenson argued, Confucianism was rooted out and relegated to the museum (Billioud 2018, p. 2). The two elements of "Confucian entrepreneurship" – Confucian thinking and private entrepreneurship – thereby lost their foothold in mainland China.

## The return of the market and a Confucian revival

Opportunities to build businesses flourished again after 1978, when markets and private property were gradually reintroduced with the "Reform and Opening". The reforms raised living-standards, but also created social friction due to the dismantling of state enterprises, with many people joining the market economy.

Although liberalisation was limited to the economic sphere, with the political realm kept under tight control, there was a tentative relaxation of Communist anti-traditionalism as well, first in academia and then across society. Confucianism was again promoted within academic circles – for instance, through the establishment of dedicated research institutions, such as the Research Centre for Traditional Chinese Culture at Peking University (PKU) in 1992, and academic journals such as *Kongzi Yanjiu* 孔子研究 (Confucius Research) (Makeham 2011, p. 15).

The long-time rejection of tradition left a void in society. When the government restrictions were reduced, people from all walks of life became involved in a revival of Confucianism, triggering a "Confucian fever" (*ruxue re* 儒學熱) in the 1980s (Makeham 2011, p. 1). Further easing of social restrictions in the 1990s and 2000s allowed temples and shrines to resume operations (Billioud 2010, p. 220), enabling a dialogue between Confucianism and Buddhism, which helped to revive traditional practices, such as calligraphy, tea culture, medicine and martial arts (Ji 2018, p. 61). Scholars, business networks, and religious institutions from Taiwan, Hong Kong, and the diaspora, joined mainland actors to promote the revival of traditional culture. They share a belief that new generations need to know about their heritage in order to reassert a Chinese identity (Feng 2009).

While many were eager to learn from the developed West, interest in the neglected roots of Chinese culture had also grown. In the late 1990s, the "National Studies" (*guoxue* 國學) movement proposed classical teaching, as part of an "ardent pursuit of revitalizing traditional Chinese culture" (Tang 2015, p. 4). Unofficial learning institutions (*sishu* 私塾) emerged preaching "reading of the classics" (*dujing* 讀經) as an alternative form of education (Ji, Zhe 2018, p. 63). The *Analects* and its advice on social relations became particularly popular, as well as the *Dizigui* 弟子規 (Student's Rules), a primer written in Qing times, which was widely used until the early twentieth century to teach children Confucian virtues such as respect for the elderly (Ji, Zhe 2018, pp. 64–65).

This bottom-up phenomenon led to a top-down cooptation of traditional thinking, when the state increasingly advocated nationalism as an antidote against Western liberal values and identified tradition as useful for reinforcing patriotism. Hu Jintao's "society of humble prosperity" (*xiaokang shehui* 小康社會) employs a Confucian notion and fostered a re-traditionalisation of China. The 2004 establishment of Confucius Institutes was evidence of this about-face of the party concerning China's heritage. Xi Jinping's "Chinese Dream" (*Zhongguo meng* 中國夢) frequently references the values of village community life, such as harmony and filial piety. Xi called the "excellent traditional

*Figure 19.1* 2016 campaign poster in Beijing with an *Analects* quote
Source: photo by the author.

Chinese culture" (*Zhonghua youxiu chuantong wenhua* 中華優秀傳統文化) an "outstanding advantage of the Chinese nation" (*Guangming Ribao* 2019). The party-state started to promote conservative moral norms as "Chinese values", presented as equal or superior to individualistic Western values, which were portrayed as responsible for the moral decline of the West (Figure 19.1).

## Discourse and practice of contemporary Confucian entrepreneurship

### Re-emergence of Confucian entrepreneurship on the mainland

Half a century after the Cultural Revolution, there has thus been a "multifaceted revival" of Confucianism (Billioud 2018, p. 2), which serves as backdrop for a return of "Confucian entrepreneurship". The following different strands, both inside and outside China, shaped this process:

> Entrepreneurial culture infused with Confucian values had survived outside the mainland in the practices of entrepreneurs in "Cultural China" (Tu, Wei-ming 1991), i.e. Greater China and the diaspora, as well as in Korea and Japan. Ethnic Chinese (*huaren* 華人) in the South East Asian diaspora, who adhere to a Chinese heritage of language, festivities and education (e.g. Confucius schools), often had been restricted to commercial careers

due to policies denying them land ownership, for instance in Indonesia. *Huaren* were among the first to invest back in the mainland, and brought not only capital and skills, but also reimported Confucian entrepreneurial spirit. Business icons of the economic rise of East Asia, such as Inamori Kazuo (Japan) and Li Ka-Shing (Hong Kong), whose management styles underscore Confucian values, informs followers in China.

At the same time, a strong local identity re-emerged among a new generation of entrepreneurs in China, who looked for role models in their predecessors. Areas of entrepreneurial culture in the past again became home to contemporary *shangbang*, such as in Zhejiang, Jiangsu and Guangdong (RCCCE 2008). In the early 2000s, this increased interest led to a flurry of books and TV dramas (*lishiju* 歷史劇) about the *shangbang* – for instance, depicting the rise and fall of the Qiao 喬 family business in the Qing period. The community concern of the *shangbang* became a model for philanthropic action of modern-day entrepreneurs.

These first-generation local entrepreneurs built their companies as management autodidacts, lacking formal training. To assist them, they hired educated professionals, which in turn created a need to catch up in terms of education. While EMBA degrees from business schools offering Western management training proliferated, prestigious universities were attracted to the growing market for executive education to offer tailor-made courses in philosophy and *guoxue* 國學, such as the "Outstanding Leadership Class" at Tsinghua University.

While for some entrepreneurs, participation was merely "Confucian chic", a superficial interest in tradition to gain social recognition and networking opportunities (Yao, Xinzhong 2000); for others, it was part of an intrinsically motivated attempt to become "Confucian businesspeople" (*rushangren* 儒商人) (Billioud 2010, p. 204). They aimed to implement cultural knowledge in developing a corporate culture, which combines modern management and "China studies" (Yao, Xinzhong 2000) in a "Chinese-Western hybrid" (*zhongxi hebi* 中西合璧).

The term "*rushang*" re-emerged as well: in 1992 it was a byword for academics who had become business people, following the 1988 call of the "China Torch Program", which encouraged intellectuals to enter business. Efforts by academics to connect with diaspora entrepreneurs, such as the "Confucian Entrepreneur Conference" at Jinan University in 1994, also exhibited usage of the term (Ming, Xu 2015). In 1993, the TV drama *Rushang* portrayed an entrepreneur founding a joint venture in a special economic zone (Baike.com 2020).

### Discourse between business people and scholars

The emergence of regional associations of "Confucian business people", dedicated research institutes at universities, specialised conferences and study programs at business schools all over China attest to the significance of the *rushang* phenomenon.

While there have been *rushang* in China for over 20 years, research has not yet delivered a definition of what exactly constitutes a "Confucian entrepreneur". Some notions repeatedly occur: (1) success in business and recognition of both peers and the community; (2) rejection of exclusive use of Western management practices that fail to consider local conditions; (3) promotion of traditional values and commitment to their revival (*fuxing* 復興); (4) emphasis on business ethics; and (5) a patriotic claim for Chinese leadership in the world.

It is only since around 2010 that academic research and forums for discussion between business people and scholars have gathered pace in an effort to close the gap between normative prescriptions provided by scholars and the implementation of traditional values in real-life business settings. Some key philosophy scholars in the West with Chinese roots, who were custodians of Confucian culture during the iconoclastic phase of Communist rule, play a leading role here.

Among the most important figures is Tu Wei-ming 杜維明 (b. 1941), Chinese philosophy expert at Harvard and Berkeley, who has been a driving force of fostering humanities in China. He was involved in the 2006 creation of the "Center for Confucian Entrepreneurship and East Asian Civilization" at Zhejiang University headed by Zhou Shengchun 周生春, a former student. In 2013, as dean of the Institute of Advanced Humanistic Studies at PKU, he established the "Discourse on Confucian Entrepreneurs".

Another key player has been Cheng Chung-ying 成中英 (b. 1938), Chinese philosophy professor at University of Hawai'i, who triggered a discussion on Chinese values in management with his "C-theory" (Cheng 1992). He supports the "Bo'ao Confucian Entrepreneur Forum" (BCEF), established in 2016 by his former student Li Honglei 黎紅雷, who teaches "Corporate Confucianism" (*qiye ruxue* 企業儒學) at Sun Yat-sen University (Li, Honglei 2017).

Among a growing pool of people who employ the label "*rushang*" are business tycoons, who receive praise for their "Confucian business practices" (Yao, Xinzhong 2000). At the BCEF, a sub-forum of the Bo'ao Forum, thousands of entrepreneurs attended to see "Confucian Entrepreneur awards" being given to leaders such as Liu Chuanzhi 柳傳志 (Lenovo), Zhang Ruimin 張瑞敏 (Hai'er) and Yan Jiehe 嚴介和 (Pacific Construction Group), who all claim their business success is rooted in traditional culture.

Although the *rushang* is a niche phenomenon in private small and medium enterprises (SME), not in state-owned enterprises (SOE) under government control, it enjoys tacit government support. The participation of veteran high-level officials, such as diplomats Long Yongtu 龍永圖 and Sha Zukang 沙祖康, in the abovementioned forums, would be unthinkable without a green light from the authorities.

### Contemporary Confucian entrepreneur practice

To conclude this chapter, I present two cases that are part of an empirical study I conducted between 2017 and 2019, through qualitative interviews with entrepreneurs and their employees. Both belong to an exclusive group of companies who – after a specialised audit – received the label "Model Unit of Chinese Confucian Companies" from the China Confucius Foundation (CCF) and BCEF as part of their benchmark system (CCF 2018).[4]

## Mao Zhongqun 茅忠群 and the "Confucian way of FOTILE"

FOTILE Co. is a privately owned kitchen appliance-maker in Ningbo, Zhejiang. In 1996, Mao, a scientist by training, took the helm of his father's company and refocused production on European-style range hoods. An EMBA degree equipped him with modern management know-how, but his personal interest in Chinese culture made him enlist in *guoxue* courses at Tsinghua University. From 2008 onwards, he gradually reoriented FOTILE's corporate culture towards the inclusion of traditional knowledge, since he saw a mismatch between a purely Western approach to management and conditions in China, for instance an over-emphasis on the individual (CCF 2018).

This "implementation of culture" (*wenhua luodi* 文化落地) is an ongoing experimentation process of disseminating traditional values and practices to managers and employees, including daily readings of classics and reading requirements for new employees, especially the *Analects*. This "humanistic education" is supposed to support the "moral development" of employees and to create a "harmonious work atmosphere", which in turn is meant to positively reinforce diligence in providing excellent products and services.

Mao is convinced that leaders influenced by traditional culture will attract capable people:

> Through reading [the *Analects*] I discovered the need to particularly emphasize the moral character of leaders. That is to say, if as a leader you possess a very high moral character, you don't need to retain talented people through [socialising with them].
>
> (Interview, 20 September 2017)

This attention to "moral leadership" is reflected in recruitment and performance appraisals, which do not focus on professional skills alone but aim to "appreciate both virtue and ability" (*decai jianbei* 德才兼備). Managers are required to participate in the so-called "Five Ones" program: reading classics, doing good deeds, performing filial piety acts, correcting character flaws and setting ambitions.

FOTILE's company's stakeholder considerations include employee incentives in the form of "identity shares" (*shen'gu* 身股), a benefit-sharing scheme inspired by similar schemes of *shangbang* in the region. The company's mission is "cultural dissemination" (*wenhua chuanbo* 文化傳播) by way of free dissemination of *Analects*-copies, based on the notion that traditional culture can improve people's lives (CCF 2018).

## Wu Nianbo 吳念博 and the "happy enterprise" of GOOD-ARK

Suzhou Good-Ark Co., a diode manufacturer in Suzhou, was created in the early 1990s by Wu, a former teacher (Wu, Nianbo 2014). He obtained a philosophy degree from Nottingham University and frequently invites experts in Chinese tradition to assist in the development of the "Happy Enterprise" (*xingfu qiye* 幸福企業). This approach – in line with the local *shangbang* tradition rooted in family precepts – applies traditional family virtues to the company, notably *xiao* 孝 (filial piety). The company is regarded as a "big family", assigning a patriarchal role to the entrepreneur, whose care for employees is reciprocated by their loyalty.

Wu believes that the objective of a company is to sustain itself for the sake of social harmony and "employee happiness". This primary goal leads to profits as an "inevitable outcome" (Yu, Feng & Shen 2014). He has convinced several other companies to join the "Happy Enterprise Alliance".

GOOD-ARK's "Eight Module" system is centred on measures of "humanistic care," appreciation of employees and their families, and responsibility for the community and the environment. As with FOTILE, a core implementation tool for corporate culture is "humanistic education", including daily readings of the classics, such as the *Dizigui* and the *Sanzijing* 三字經 (Three Character Classic), with their emphasis on respect for elders (Wu, Nianbo 2014).

Numerous measures are designed to promote family values, such as a generous maternity leave, subsidies for employees' parents and children, and paid vacations for parents to visit their "left-behind children" in the countryside. To underscore *xiao*, Wu personally visits sick parents of employees in the hospital. Opportunities to volunteer for environmental and charity projects are intended to generate group cohesion and identification with the company (Wu, Nianbo 2014).

In both cases – FOTILE and GOOD-ARK – the traditional principle of "inner sage and outer king" (*neisheng waiwang* 內聖外王) is applied, which refers to the self-cultivation of an enlightened person and the application of knowledge in the community. In the context of the company, it aims at a transformative effect on managers and employees, but also on customers, suppliers and society (Figure 19.2).

## Conclusion

The management approach of "Confucian entrepreneurship" refers to traditional notions of family and community, and heavily emphasises "Chineseness". Some Western scholars have criticised the commodification of tradition in China as "a sign of its final demise" (Dirlik 1995, p. 273), arguing that Confucianism is manipulated to support any given agenda, a "chameleon" to underscore "Chinese uniqueness" (Kam 2011, pp. 77–78). Although this criticism can be directed at the nationalistic undercurrent of the *rushang* discourse, the described endeavours by entrepreneurs to implement humanistic management are not

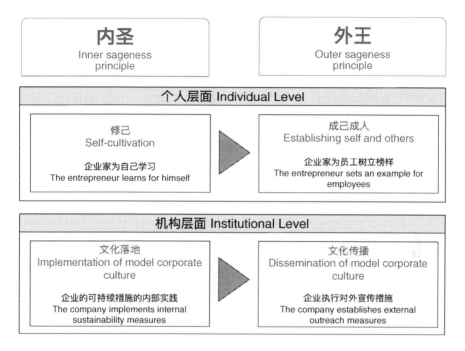

*Figure 19.2* The Neisheng-Waiwang principle in Confucian entrepreneurship
Source: illustration by the author.

without merit. Their management innovations solve a number of social stability issues on a meso-level in modern-day Chinese society.

The current attention on the *rushang* is rooted in the fact that the eradication of both entrepreneurship and Confucian influence on society during the twentieth century was so severe on the mainland that business people today are eager to consciously reconnect with the marginalised heritage in order to implement Confucian precepts in their daily business operations. This is a unique example of how the economic thinking of China's distant past can inform business decisions today.

"Management thinking with Chinese characteristics" regards traditional Chinese values as an important contribution to both China and global society. The international discussions about management – which are dominated by Western approaches – might benefit from considering the input of the contemporary *rushang*.

## Notes

1 The latter half of the Zhou period is divided into the "Spring and Autumn" (770–476 BCE) and the "Warring States" (475–221 BCE) periods.

2  Shun is considered a cultural hero, while Chih is an archetypical bandit.
3  In antiquity, a distinction was made between "*gu*" for settled merchants and "*shang*" for travelling traders (Durant, Lee & Schaberg 2016, p. 642), but this distinction was later lost.
4  For more details, see Niedenführ (2018, 2020).

## References

Ames, Roger & Rosemont Jr, Henry: *The Analects of Confucius: A Philosophical Translation*. New York: Ballantine Books, 2010.

Baike.com: Rushang 儒商 (Confucian Entrepreneur), www.baike.com/wiki 儒商 (retrieved 9 August 2020), 2020.

Billioud, Sébastien: Carrying the Confucian Torch to the Masses: The Challenge of Structuring the Confucian Revival in the People's Republic of China. *Oriens Extremus*, 49, pp. 201–21, 2010.

Billioud, Sébastien (ed.): *The Varieties of Confucian Experience: Documenting a Grassroots Revival of Tradition*. Leiden: Brill, 2018.

Chan, Wing-Tsit: *A Source Book in Chinese Philosophy*. Princeton, NJ: Princeton University Press, 1969.

Cheng, Chung-Ying: The "C"-Theory: A Chinese Philosophical Approach to Management and Decision-making. *Journal of Chinese Philosophy*, 19(2), pp. 125–53, 1992.

China Confucius Foundation (CCF): Zhongguo Kongzi Jijinhui 中国孔子基金会: „Zhonghua rushang qize shifan jidi" zai Ningbo Fangtai Jituan shoupai "中华儒商企业示范基地"在宁波方太集团授牌 (FOTILE Group of Ningbo receives the plaque "Model Unit of a Chinese Confucian Company), www.chinakongzi.org/rw/xszj/lihonglei/201804/t20180417_175717.htm, 2018

Chinese Text Project (CTP): *Guliang zhuan*, ctext.org/guliang-zhuan, 2006.

Dirlik, Arif: Confucius in the Borderlands: Global Capitalism and the Reinvention of Confucianism. *Boundary 2*, 22(3), pp. 229–73, 1995.

Durant, Stephen, Li Wai-yee & Schaberg, David: *Zuo Tradition: Commentary on the Spring and Autumn Annals*. Seattle, WA: University of Washington Press, 2016.

Ertman, T.C. (ed.): *Max Weber's Economic Ethic of the World Religions: An Analysis*. Cambridge: Cambridge University Press, 2017.

Feng, Xin-ming: Di Zi Gui: The Chinese Intellectual Heritage, http://tsoidug.org/dizigui.php, 2009.

Fung, You-Lan: *A Short History of Chinese Philosophy*. New York: Macmillan, 1958.

Hutton, Eric L.: *Xunzi – The Complete Text*. Princeton, NJ: Princeton University Press, 2016.

Kam, Louie: Confucius the Chameleon: Dubious Envoy for "Brand China". *Boundary 2*, 38(1), pp. 77–100, 2011.

L'Haridon, Béatrice: The Merchants in Shiji: An Interpretation in the Light of Later Debates. In: Hans Van Ess, Olga, Lomová & Dorothee Schaab-Hanke (eds): *Views from Within, Views from Beyond: Approaches to the Shiji as an Early Work of Historiography*. Wiesbaden: Harrasowitz, pp. 171–92, 2015.

Lai, Karyn L.: Confucian Moral Thinking. *Philosophy East and West*, 45(2), pp. 249–72, 1995.

Lau, D.C.: *Mencius*. Harmondsworth: Penguin, 2004 [1970].

Legge, James: *Confucius: The Confucian Analects, the Great Learning & the Doctrine of the Mean*. New York: Cosimo, 2009 [1893].

Legge, James: *The Chinese Classics, Vol. 2, The Works of Mencius*. Oxford: Clarendon Press, 1895.

Li, Honglei 黎红雷: *Rujia Shangdai Zhihui* 儒家商代智慧 (Confucian Business Wisdom). Beijing: Renmin, 2017.

Liu, Hong: *Chinese Business: Landscapes and Strategies*, 2nd edn. London: Routledge, 2018.

Lufrano, Richard J.: *Honorable Merchants: Commerce and Self-Cultivation in Late Imperial China*. Honolulu: University of Hawai'i Press, 1997.

Ji, Zhe: Making a Virtue of Piety: Dizigui and the Discursive Practice of Jinkong's Network. In: Sébastien Billioud (ed.), *The Varieties of Confucian Experience: Documenting a Grassroots Revival of Tradition*, pp. 60–89. Leiden: Brill, 2018.

Makeham, John: The Revival of Guoxue. *China Perspectives*, 1, pp. 14–21, 2011.

Mao, Zhongqun 茅忠群: Fangtai rudao zhi jiangxin shen'geng 方太儒道之匠心深耕 (Ingenuity in the Confucian Way of FOTILE). In: Li, Honglei 黎红雷: *Rujia Shangdai Zhihui* 儒家商代智慧 (Confucian Business Wisdom), pp. 378–92. Beijing: Renmin, 2017.

Ming, Xu 明旭: Cong caogen dao rushang de biange lilun 从草根到儒商的变革理论 (The Theory of the Change from the Roots to Confucian Entrepreneurship). *China Philanthropist*, 6, www.shanda960.com/shandaguan/article/4069 (retrieved 17 September 2016), 2015.

Ming, Xu 明旭: *Qi yu Zhi – Mingdai "Rugu" yixiang de xingqi* 气与志：明代"儒贾"意向的兴起 (Attitude and Will: The Emergence of the Concept of "Confucian Merchants" During the Ming Dynasty). Taibei: Hua Mulan Wenhua, 2016.

Niedenführ, Matthias: Management Innovation from China? The Emerging Trend of the "Confucian Entrepreneur". In *DCW Year Book* 2018. Cologne: DCW, pp. 67–76, 2018.

Niedenführ, Matthias: Humanistic Management with a Confucian Twist: The Case of FOTILE. In: Ernst, Von Kimakowitz, Claus Dierksmeier, Carlos Largacha-Martinéz & Hanna Schirovsky (eds): *Humanistic Management in Practice, Volume II*. London: Palgrave Macmillan, 2020 pp. 217–238.

Research Centre for the Culture of Confucian Entrepreneurs (RCCCE): *Rushang Wenhua Yanjiu Zhongxin* 儒商文化研究中: *Rushang renwu pian* 儒商人物篇 (Overview of Confucian Entrepreneurs), www.pku-rswh.com/personae.asp, 2018.

Shibuzawa, Ei'ichi 渋沢栄一: *Rongo to Soroban* 論語と算盤 (The *Analects* and the Abacus). Tokyo: Kadokawa Bunkō, 1998.

Tang, Yijie: *Confucianism, Buddhism, Daoism, Christianity and Chinese Culture*. New York: Springer, 2015.

Tu, Wei-ming: *Humanity and Self-Cultivation: Essays in Confucian Thought*. Berkeley, CA: Asian Humanities Press, 1979.

Tu, Wei-ming: Cultural China: The Periphery as the Center. *Daedalus*, 120(2), pp. 1–32, 1991.

Tu, Wei-ming: *The Global Significance of Concrete Humanity: Essays on the Confucian Discourse in Cultural China*. New Delhi: Centre for Studies in Civilizations, 2010.

Wang, Jianbao & Niedenführ, Matthias (trans.): The Confucian Entrepreneur: Model of a New Business Civilization. In: *Academy Association of Confucianism Germany 2019 Conference Proceedings*, 25 June 2019.

Wang, Yan 王艳 & Wang, Ruihui 王瑞辉: Dangdai shichang jingji chaoliu zhong rushang jingshen de queshi yu rushang wenhua de xiandai yiyi ji qijian xing 当代市场经济潮流中儒商精神的缺失与儒商文化的现代意义及其践行 (Lack of Confucian Merchants Spirit under Contemporary Market Economic Tide and Confucian Merchants Culture Modern Meaning and Practice). *Nongye Xiandaihua Yanjiu,* 33(3), pp. 346–49, 2012.

Wu, Nianbo: *From the Teachings of Sages to the Making of a Happy Enterprise: The "Family Culture" of Suzhou Good-Ark.* Suzhou: Suzhou Good-Ark, 2014.

Yao, Xinzhong: *An Introduction to Confucianism.* Cambridge: Cambridge University Press, 2000.

Yu, Howard, Feng, Xue & Shen, Hunter: Three Ways Ordinary Chinese Companies are Driving Innovation. *Forbes,* www.forbesindia.com/article/imd/three-ways-ordinary-chinese-companies-are-driving-innovation/38130/1 (retrieved 31 May 2018), 2014.

# Part IV
# Conclusions and perspectives

# 20 Towards a systematic comparison of different forms of economic thought

*Iwo Amelung and Bertram Schefold*

## Comparing economic thought in East and West: Initial conditions

Comparing the histories of Chinese and European ways of thinking about the economy can be useful when one wishes to understand differences in the governance of economic affairs between China and Western countries. It is fraught with difficulties and challenges, however, since it – like many comparisons – entails the danger of geographic and cultural essentialism. Moreover, economics was not a separate subject in premodern times, and what we regard as economic, how we isolate specific economic considerations in reflections on past economic action or as aspects of philosophical, political, even religious thought, depends on modern interpretations (Schefold 2018). Despite these reservations, which we discuss further below, it is possible to claim that Chinese economic thought from early on was almost always reflected upon in the context of the achievements and the failures of the state, while early observations of economic matters in the West are traditionally associated with the idea that there are economic forces that are autonomous and not easily controlled. The liberal tradition would emphasise the harmony that could result. Fronsperger, in the sixteenth century, thought the pursuit of individual utility could coordinate the manifold activities in town and country. He compared the result to the harmonious music produced by an organ with pipes of different length, and he referred back to antiquity and stoic philosophy (Schefold 2016a, 109–12). The stoics thought the world had been arranged by the Creator so that the Good resulted if everyone pursued their own proper interest, for evil forces could be turned to advantage if one knew what to make of them. The fight with my adversary will strengthen me. It is well-known that Adam Smith was greatly influenced by stoic ideas (Vivenza 1999). The pursuit of self-interest in the *Wealth of Nations* (Smith 1776) as the application of the stoic philosophical idea to the economic universe, leads to material gain. In *The Theory of Moral Sentiments*, Smith (1759) considered self-interest also in social intercourse, where it is more complex because I have to reckon with the sympathy of others who judge me according to whether I follow moral principles, and where there is not only exchange for mutual gain, but also benevolence and the generous

DOI: 10.4324/9780367434496-30

gift. That it is advantageous to buy cheap and to sell dear if one can is obvious, and we find this expressed as a trite principle by Xenophon in the fourth century BCE, but how far it is advisable to be led by it in order to accumulate wealth was controversial among the Greek philosophers. Aristotle argued that material objects – even slaves – were means to achieve a good life based on philosophical reflection, and this would show that having too much would lead away from the good life, as would having too little: the poor must struggle and sell their labour power, while the rich will endlessly worry about their wealth – and both were, each in their own way, concerned only with the instruments of the good life and not with the good life itself. The good life could be based, for instance, on an agrarian household of sufficient size to pursue philosophical, political and cultural activities.

The idea that the advantage in trading consists of buying cheap and selling dear, and that the pursuit of this principle leads to commodities flowing from where they are abundant and cheap to where they are scarce and demanded, was not absent from Chinese economic thought. It is expressed succinctly in a famous passage of the "Grand Historian" Sima Qian 司馬遷 (c. 145–90 BCE):

> What need is there for government directives, mobilisations of labour, or periodic assemblies? Each man has only to be left to utilise his own abilities and exert his strength to obtain what he wishes. Thus, when a commodity is very cheap, it invites a rise in price; when it is very expensive, it invites a reduction. When each person works away at his own occupation and delights in his own business then, like water flowing downward, goods will naturally flow forth ceaselessly day and night without having been summoned, and the people will produce commodities without having been asked … Is it not a natural result?
>
> (Sima 1993, p. 434)

Terry Peach (2019) has shown convincingly that this passage should not be misunderstood as an affirmative anticipation of Smithian ideas. He argues that the Grand Historian, in accordance with tradition, held that the excessive pursuit of material interests was a sign of decadence of the state rather than proof of its vigour. The rulers in the well-ordered monarchical state would order the social relations and keep the social classes apart; and the status of the trader – even if he grew rich – should not rival that of the elite. According to Peach, Sima Qian's "Biographies of the Money Makers" ("Huozhi liezhuan 貨殖列傳"), where the passage quoted can be found, is ironical and part of a surreptitious criticism of the policies of Emperor Wu of Han (156–87 BCE), into whose disfavour he had fallen and who even had him mutilated.

Early economic thought, both in Chinese and in Graeco-Roman antiquity, had in common that virtue should dominate over economic interests. We may imagine the roaming government advisers during the time after the marginalisation of Zhou rule and prior to the unification of the Qin dynasty, of which Confucius (551–479 BCE) was but one, and compare them with the roughly contemporaneous Ionian philosophers and then the philosophers of the Greek communities in the Mediterranean between the war with Persia and the beginnings of Hellenism. The rivalry of the city states also allowed migration, as in China, and favoured independent thinking, as exemplified by Aristotle, who came from Stageira, taught at Athens and had been the teacher of Alexander the Great in Macedonia. Economic thought had to be integrated with political circumstances in both the East and West, but these were vastly different. There was a rivalry of comparatively rich (that is, the elites were rich) territorial states on the territory of China, and a multitude of small and comparatively modest city states in the West, in which a middle class dominated and lived through periods of different political constitutions. The classical sequence was monarchy, aristocracy, tyranny and democracy, but tides could turn and the linear evolution could become cyclical. Each political change altered the political chances of the different strata. The thinkers in ancient China advised monarchical governments in a process of concentration that led to the formation of the empire. The city states of Graeco-Roman antiquity sat around first the Aegean Sea, and then the entire Mediterranean and the Black Sea like "frogs around the pond". The city states would fund colonies along the coasts, such as Athens in the Crimea, and there, new political constitutions could be tried. In China, the question always was how the duke, king or emperor should govern, where and how he would tax the people, and for whom and where he would spend the revenue, seeking to enhance his power but constrained by the need to keep the people content. By contrast, although the economic structure remained the same, the political forms changed in the Graeco-Roman world. The same Plato would see monarchy as the ideal from the abstract philosophical point of view and discuss this perspective in *The Republic*, as explained by Terry Peach in Chapter 14 of this volume. Then he would concede that the ideal state could not be realised in practice so he changed the order of preference of ideal states (monarchy better than aristocracy, aristocracy better than democracy) into the opposite when he looked at what could be realised in the dialogue *Politikos*. There the sequence became: democracy was more tolerable than the oligarchic state, and this was less bad than the tyranny, the worst of all. He discussed further variations in the *Nomoi* (*Laws*) in his later life. So the political forms were variable but, although they offered different chances to different sections of the populace, the fundamental economic organisation remained the same. As in China, the agricultural estates were the basis. A middle class of independent farmers dominated in the classical period, a modest number of slaves had to assist the relatively rich, and artisans in the city often were foreigners and of lesser influence. The main economic writings thus concerned the principles of householding of the individual estate or the city. The Greek perspective was bottom up, the Chinese viewpoint was top down.

The difference in the political perspective seems to correspond to different schools of thought that can be connected through different scientific traditions, indeed two different cosmological principles. As Joseph Needham has argued:

> There are two ways of advancing from primitive truth. One was the way taken by some of the Greeks: to refine the idea of causation in such a way that one ended up with a mechanical explanation of the universe, just as Democritus did with his atoms. The other way is to systematise the universe of things and events into a structural pattern which conditioned all the mutual influences of its different parts … the Greek Democritean approach may have been a necessary prelude to modern science … But … it is a mistake to think of this Chinese outlook on Nature as essentially primitive. It was a precisely ordered universe, not governed either by the fiat of a supreme creator-lawgiver, nor by the inexorable clashes of atoms, but by a harmony of wills, spontaneous but ordered in patterns, rather like the dancers in a country-dance, none of whom are bound by law or pushed by the others, but who cooperate voluntarily.
>
> (Ronan 1978, pp. 165–66)

Needham thus suggests a world view dominated by organicist considerations, which to a Western reader of text on historical, political and economic matters is striking, since at least economic theory started in the West time and again from mechanical analogies, and is still dominated by mechanistic thought. There was the Cartesian approach of the Physiocrats, the metaphor of gravitation in the Smithian foundation of the classical theory of value and the equilibrium concept of the neoclassicals, to mention only a few. Needham was fond to speculate that Western organicist tendencies were reinforced by Leibniz, who was influenced by what he learnt about Neo-Confucianism (Zhu Xi 朱熹) from the missionaries (Ronan 1978, p. 168). There are other attempts to find continuities and to characterise dominant ideas, such as Hermann-Pillath's attempt to characterise "ritual" as the unifying idea of the Chinese economic style (Hermann-Pillath 2017, p. 528). Examples are the re-emergence of lineages or of the belief that a cultural elite has the task of transforming Chinese society, whereas at least the liberal tradition in the West emphasises a spontaneous order. We thus observe a number of initial differences, which may help to explain the different trajectories of China and Europe shaping economic development and the evolution of economic and political thought. The "economic" is not easily perceptible in early written records, but the influence of the history of economic ideas became more important in the long run and is today a key to the understanding of ongoing transformations.

## Trajectories of economic thought

It was, of course, impossible to trace the entire trajectories of the two histories of economic thought in this book, let alone to deal in detail with their ramifications in different schools. We aimed instead at relevant and representative examples. That early beginnings were considered as being of special importance can be seen, as illustrated by Olga Borokh in Chapter 17, from Chen Huanzhang's 陳煥章 (1880–1933) work *The Economic Principles of Confucius and*

*His School.* And indeed, as late as the Qing dynasty, thinking about consumption and luxury laws was dominated by a maxim "to worship thrift and eliminate luxury" (Rosner 1974). Chen's normative approach stands in contrast to the contemporaneous work by Werner Sombart and Max Weber on the idea of a value-free science. The separation of norms and factual descriptions is often difficult, but the principle is easy to grasp in cases such as the analysis of consumption behaviour. Shifts in norms for consumption, such as whether smoking is a tolerable habit, could be analysed according to their origins and their direction, but the norms were, for the economists or social scientists, neither to be defended nor attacked. The formal theory of consumption behaviour had been developed by the neoclassical economists since the 1870s and earlier. The theory of indifference curves developed by Edgeworth and Pareto seems to be worlds apart from Chen's dedication to Confucianist ideas, yet the transition to a value-free and even positivistic approach to economics had many opponents in the West; we mentioned the German historical school in particular. Chen thus succeeded in showing that there had been economic thought in China. Confucianism as the dominant system of thought had largely shaped it, but it was closer to the Western historicist and organicist tradition than to the dominant neoclassical theory. The German historical school valued Smith's *Theory of Moral Sentiments* as a moral treatise. Economics was about development, and this meant not only growth and technical change as spontaneous processes, but also the development of the productive forces, supported by the government through the creation of schools of higher learning, and it meant the involvement of the state to support the unemployed and healthcare. Finally, promoted by all this, it meant the moral betterment of the nation and the world at large. Since they saw economic development as a qualitative transformation, they were interested in stages and societies different from those that had come about through the Industrial Revolution, so they would look for their comparisons to what the German professors – who had never been to the colonies – knew best: European antiquity.

Referring to antiquity of course was a common practice. The Romans looked back to classical Greek antiquity as an ideal; the Middle Ages did much to transfer that knowledge to later generations; the Renaissance tried to rediscover antiquity as a model. This was then contested in the *Querelle des anciens et des modernes* but, as far as the understanding of the *economic* differences between antiquity and modernity are concerned, the historical school was the great pioneer in the research into the matter. There resulted the famous debate between the primitivists and the modernists, which is of some relevance even today in ancient economic history, with questions that can also be asked in the Chinese case. The primitivists, in discussing the economy of Athens in particular, would take the texts about household economics literally. The number of slaves was thought to be small, the slaves were part of the family and the agricultural estate was largely self-sufficient, hence market relationships played a subordinate role. Production in the city was based on handicrafts with little standardisation, and citizens regarded their political and cultural pursuits as sufficiently important to subordinate business activities to these higher goals. The freedom of the citizen would be realised, as Aristotle had said, through gift-giving, which would enhance his prestige. Gift-giving would also largely determine the attitude of the citizen with regard to the state, for the state would avoid the build-up of bureaucratic structures by delegation and decentralisation. Individual citizens would assume specific responsibilities at their own expense – so-called liturgies, such as manning a ship for warfare – and would receive honours in return. The modernists, by contrast, would emphasise the similarity with the then modern institutions. They pointed to the fact that the rural estates produced commodities for the market, they spoke of factories when there was serial production in the city – for instance, of armaments – and they saw the city as a rational planner in the endeavour to collect different kinds of revenues, which were used for regular state activities. Both sides of the debate tried to understand economic history, but they were reading texts. Only the existence of the texts is historically certain; their contents may reflect biased views. The debate was therefore in its origin more about history of economic thought than about economic history; this has changed since because of archaeological finds, the discovery of inscriptions and more interdisciplinary research, which all help to establish the historical facts.

One can see a similar divide in the interpretation of Chinese antiquity, and it provides a dichotomy that is orthogonal to the distinction between different schools of thought, which in a heuristic rather than analytical fashion were framed as "legalism" and "Confucianism" (Pines 2018). Consider the Debate on Salt and Iron (*Yantie lun* 鹽鐵論), as discussed Qunyi Liu in Chapter 15. She argues that we simplify the complexity of the debate, using a schematic distinction, but it is not without foundation. A modernist might interpret the conception of Sang Hongyang 桑弘羊 to equalise prices by means of state trade in different parts of the country as the expression of rational planning, while a primitivist would see the endeavour of the ruler to reap the surplus by means of an improvised new institution in order to strengthen his power. The primitivist would see the meaning of the Confucian rituals as a practice of education and integration of the individual into their social role in the family and the state. As the debate was taken up again in the twentieth century, Confucian ideals and rituals were tools of oppression to many liberal intellectuals as well as to Maoist propagandists and modernist historians of economic thought who, rather than understanding the texts on their own terms, preferred to translate them into modern language and judge them according to modern values. This can be a virtue from the perspective of the history of economic analysis. For instance, the Confucian literati in the Debate on Salt and Iron complain that the iron tools sold by the state monopolies are expensive and of poor quality, so that some peasants have returned to wooden spades. Is this not an anticipation of the modern theory of monopoly pricing and a (liberal) critique of state interference? The primitivist would accept that agricultural life was to be dominated by the local gentry, who were to strengthen the social bonds between themselves, the farmers and tenants, and would accept that it was the role of the monarch and of the officials to benefit the people by keeping the weight of taxation low and using the proceeds for peaceful purposes. The ruler had to keep good order in the management of public affairs, and would subordinate his personal interest to the common good. Modernists of diverse persuasions might question most of these statements as ideological, and see the actors as pursuing their own material interests. More generally, primitivism meant that the sociological took precedence over the economic – and in this sense, by way of example, Richard Wilhelm (1873–1930) could be characterised as a sinologist, who was primitivist, with more understanding of Confucianism (Wilhelm 1930), while the Maoist critique was decidedly modernist and tended more towards legalism.

We think that these distinctions will help to interpret the contributions to this volume as elements for a comparison between Chinese and Western traditions of economic thought. Modernism and primitivism are approaches that only a few will want to pursue in their pure forms as extremes. Recent ancient economic history had learned to combine them and to seek the appropriate compromise in focusing on individual phenomena, with perhaps the prevailing trend being more modernist, while there has been a reaction in China to the extreme form of Maoist modernism; the resurgence of Confucianism is, to some degree, a primitivist response.

That it is indeed possible to identify economic thought, which can be framed as "legalist", is demonstrated in this book by Isabella Weber's study of the *Guanzi* 管子, with its ingenious proposals for controlling the price level through the timely increase or reduction of the money supply, and it is shown that such ideas form a pattern that recurs after more than 2000 years in pricing policies used in China's transition from Soviet-style planning to a market economy.

Qunyi Liu studies the continuities of the interactions between legalist and Confucian thought according to their later reconstructions from the Debate on Salt and Iron down to recent controversies. The same work is also fitting for a juxtaposition with Western thought: an essay by Schefold (2019) compares the economic arguments in the Debate on Salt and Iron with the pseudo-Aristotelian *Oeconomica* of the late fourth century BC and provides an example of how these were taken up in Germany in the seventeenth century

By and large, all these studies confirm that private economic activity in China is seen primarily in its interaction with the state, while most considerations of economic matters in the West begin with households as centres of production and consumption within a changeable political framework.

The social values and their ordering must correspond to the economic order. Ruling political elites often look down on merchants; at least two reasons are obvious. If the merchants are small traders, they have little significance; however, if they are rich, they may challenge the prerogatives of the elite. The reasoning may vary. Aristotle thought that trading was not a natural pursuit: traders were not productive in the same sense as farmers. In Chinese traditional thought, farming is one of the fundamental pursuits, and governments time and again would return to this theme. Legalists would remind the rulers that secondary occupations also were important, as did Sang Hongyang in the Debate on Salt and Iron. Nonetheless, the disdain for merchants would persist in traditional China, with ups and downs, regional variations and divergent social practices until recent times (Hua, Tengda 2020). The primacy of agriculture was re-emphasised in the eighteenth century by the physiocrats in Europe, in part with new reasonings. Richard van den Berg shows in this volume how it came to pass that the physiocrats portrayed the Chinese state as an ideal representation of physiocratic ideas: since production rested on agriculture, the emperor would collect the surplus and spend it again for the benefit of the people in a circular flow. Trade was unproductive and, for the physiocrats, this even applied to handicrafts, because the artisan only changed the form of natural products like wheat or leather by baking or upholstering, without being able to create them.

There is an asymmetry in this unity of basic doctrines in that, in the West, interest-taking was singled out as an activity to be banned or at least to be constrained on the basis of religious, philosophical and legal arguments. No such principled objection was raised in the East, although high interest could be seen as a calamity and the fate of poor people, unable to pay up, could be deplored. The book tries to explain this discrepancy in a series of accounts from both sides. Each focuses on one side, on particular periods, on specific phases of the evolution of economic thought; however, taken together, they furnish much material for comparison.

The history of the usury debate begins with the prohibition in the Old Testament against Jews lending with interest among one another, but they were allowed to lend to foreigners. Similar traditions existed in the Graeco-Roman world. Aristotle tried to justify the existing prejudice against interest-taking by buttressing it with a logical argument: that money was there to facilitate exchange, so to lend money and to ask for it to be returned with an increment was against its nature. Then came the Christian command to lend in order to assist others, without hoping for a return. During the first millennium, Christians thought that interest-taking was sinful because it reflected avarice but, when in the high Middle Ages commerce grew and interest-taking became more frequent and voluminous, the church began to intervene and to defend the prohibition of usury by means of more complex arguments. This also meant that exceptions had to be granted. From making a difference between conditions under which interest was licit and other conditions under which it was not, there arose a need to analyse the causes of the existence of interest. Hence the impetus was created to analyse this economic phenomenon causally and not to be content with the received moral rules. Chapter 7 by André Lapidus and Irina Chaplygina explained the theological reasonings of the church and their limitations. Much has been written about the subsequent Reformation and its impact on the economy, with Luther being conservative in regard to the critique of usury, while the Calvinists were clearly more open for money dealers and, eventually, industrial enterprise. In Chapter 8, Monika Poettinger focused on the beginnings of the Reformation and Luther's Catholic opponent Eck, who appears somewhat paradoxically as more liberal than the reformer. There then was economic progress in Europe, when new trading possibilities arose and monetary institutions developed. We learnt from Lilia Costabile in Chapter 12 that the institution of paper money in Europe began to take shape in Naples, and that it was also connected with the religious institutions.

This book presents these contrasting histories to enable us to compare the monetary evolution and the accompanying creation of a credit system with what happened in China. In Chapter 6, Yaguang Zhang, Yue Bi and Zyler Wang position Chinese monetary thinking by collecting evidence of how the Chinese judged foreign monies, comparing them with their own, and how monetary systems and ideas about them changed from early coinage to the first forms of paper money. Eventually, foreign silver became the main medium of exchange before modern monetary systems were adopted. In Chapter 5, Qiugen Liu discusses interest-taking in China with a multitude of facts, which require some interpretation. We are here confronted again with the text by Sima Qian, the Grand Historian, whom we cited in the first part of this chapter. What was interest? What was profit? Was profit really different from the salary of the manager? These are difficult questions since the texts do not use the modern concepts. It is clear, however, that interest rates tended to be high, and the agricultural surplus must on the whole have sufficed to pay those interest rates. As Pan Ming-te (1996, p. 112) observes regarding high interest rates, "Using rural credit to sustain their production was obviously a better alternative to peasants in Ming-Qing Jiangnan than not using it." No criticism of interest as such is voiced, but there are restrictions. There are also interest rate ceilings and a remarkable rule that appears in the Tang-dynasty and even earlier, which remains down to the Qing dynasty in the nineteenth century: the total of the outstanding debt shall not be more than the principal. The rule expresses the concern that interest debts should not accumulate to levels that are too high; the lender thus was forced to collect the outstanding interest regularly. Probably for the same reason, there are prohibitions on compound interest; the solution for the lender is to fix new contracts with the borrower for an increased principal as soon as outstanding interest payments have not been made. (See Chapter 9 by Bertram Schefold for a parallel development in the West.) What is perhaps most striking is that the state appears as a lender, not – as in the West most of the time – as a borrower, and this institutional fact gives rise to speculate about how people thought responsibilities should be divided. It is a paternal duty of the state to lend, and lending is possible if the state maintains granaries and is therefore able to provide loans in kind or even to donate in emergencies.

The usury debate in the West results in discussions about capital and profit; the conflicts about licit and illicit interest force it to shift from normative statements to causal explanations. Schefold starts with a discussion of the problem of usury as seen in Germany after the Thirty Years War by a Protestant lawyer, Kaspar Klock, who knew the scholastic discussions well. He is amazed at the multiplicity of contractual forms involving landed property, and believes that this variety is the result of concealing usury. He is especially interested in a construction, which he calls the "antichretic contract": a landowner arranges with an entrepreneur to leave to him his land for a certain number of years; the entrepreneur can use the proceeds of the land as he pleases, having paid a certain sum of money to the landowner. Leaving aside possible complicated additional arrangements, this appears to be a credit relationship. The proceeds from the land are interpreted as the amortisation of the loan. If the entrepreneur obtains a regular annual income from the land, each annuity can be seen as the sum of the repayment of the loan plus interest on the outstanding debt. Our lawyer, who is unable to calculate the interest implicit in this arrangement, cannot decide on rational grounds whether it is usurious or not; by the seventeenth century, this now means that the rate of interest exceeds the legal rate. We can compare this with Long Denggao's (2020) "Of the Analysis of Institutions for Land Transactions in Traditional China". Long and Xiang Chi, in Chapter 4, are also confronted with a multiplicity of institutions and contractual forms, but here they have nothing to do with the struggle to avoid usury, for interest is regarded as acceptable – even if the rates are high by European standards. The same arrangement as in the antichretic contract is here possible under the name of *dian* 典, but the interpretation is quite different. It is not considered a credit relationship, but as the selling of the surface of the land for a specific time period, and Long makes clear that "selling" is here possible because the Chinese distinguish between the surface of the land, the "skin", and the subsoil, the "bone", which are two different objects of property. The surface is for use and can be sold for a number of years. The specificity of the different interpretations, which are mathematically equivalent, can be defended only contextually. Different kinds of property-rights have evolved over the centuries. There is the critique of usury in the West that sharpens the eye for possibly usurious relationships, while Chapter 5 impresses the reader with the history of the institutions for purchases, which can in this case be analysed by going back to the Song-dynasty.

And now the great divide! Long, differing from interpretations of Sino-Marxism in Mao's time, asserts with self-confidence that the property rights of traditional China formed a well-functioning system, which permitted peaceful economic development on the basis of market relationships. Tenants, for him, are not like workers who are exploited by the landlord, as they were seen by the defenders of the communist revolution in the countryside, but entrepreneurs who combined the factors of production successfully, even if they did not own all of them, and their lot was not necessarily inferior to that of the farmer who worked with his family on their own land. This suggests that the revolutionary land reforms were not inevitable and needed to be put into practice because of exploitation by rich peasants and greedy landlords; however, other factors – such as the impact of inflation due to the constant internal and external wars with which China had to deal – have been more important.

Intellectual progress makes it possible to analyse the credit relationships mathematically from the late seventeenth century onwards. Leibniz, who was a pioneer of calculus, was inspired to use his mathematical techniques to analyse credit relationships. He was also a lawyer and as such, he was critical of usury in the sense of excessive interest charges. His mathematical analysis allowed him to draw a line between reasonable and licit credit arrangements and usurious relationships that the state was supposed to prohibit. Chapter 10 by Volker Caspari presents this entire evolution in the West in the perspective of modern economic theory. Modern intertemporal general equilibrium uses concepts that were first formed in the scholastic debates, when it was understood that to lend wheat at the time of the harvest and to demand the repayment at seed time could be usurious, even if exactly the same amount had to be given back as had been lent, for wheat is cheap at the time of the harvest and expensive at seed time so that, if one reckons in terms of money, the contract may involve high interest. This phenomenon is also described in Chapter 5 by Qiugen Liu. It should not come as a surprise to the modern economist who knows that, if relative prices change, the so-called own rates of interest of commodities are generally different.

## Economy and society, and the role of the state

The trajectory of economic thought that we have traced for the West is indicative of that transformation, which together with a great multitude of associated changes – partly well known, partly invisible – leads to modern capitalism, in which state and society trust in the power of the economy to develop autonomously with growing productivity. Social forms are not without influence on the economy – for instance, via demand – but social forms also have to adapt. It is an essential and recognised function of the state to correct the deficiencies that arise in the process but, according to the liberal conception, the state is not supposed to provide direction for the economy or to shape the social evolution that results from the free intercourse of the citizens.

It was believed in China after the Communist Revolution that the preceding modes of production had been exploitative, not only because capitalist forms of production had emerged under foreign influence, but also because the traditional form of society was interpreted as feudal – which meant other forms of exploitation. After the very successful economic reforms in China, this picture must be revised. Is the market economy of present-day China to be analysed in terms of the Marxian concepts of exploitation? Another aspect concerns the reinterpretation of traditional China. Here, a number of chapters provide evidence. First of all, Bin Wong argues in Chapter 1 that the monarchic form of government was not tyrannical in the sense of Plato, in that it was subject to law, it was supported by a well-educated bureaucracy and it followed the principle of benefiting the people. Chapter 2 by Elisabeth Kaske illustrates this. The system of the granaries was mentioned in several chapters, and there were also unconventional ways to raise money for the benefit of the people and, in particular, to overcome calamities. Office-selling, which to the modern mind is an expression of corruption, could be used in subtle ways to raise funds when there was hunger. For selling the honour of a decoration such as the right to wear a peacock feather does not necessarily imply that offices associated with relevant responsibilities were given to the wrong people. The Chinese state, which avoided going into debt, had to resort to other means in order to raise temporary finance.

It is difficult, but not quite impossible, to draw a line between generously benefiting the people and doing only what is most necessary in order to avoid uprisings, while the rulers reap what they can in order to pursue their own goals of a lavish life or power and conquest. Detailed empirical studies provide a differentiated picture. This is what Iwo Amelung attempts to do in his analysis of the expenditure on river works during the Qing dynasty in Chapter 3. River works were – and still are – a major block of expenditure, and their successful execution affected the lives of many people. The will – or rather the obligation – of the state to protect the population from inundations led into a contradiction, for the impositions on the same population should not be too high. In Chapter 19, Matthias Niedenführ shows what the revival of Confucian ideas may mean in business practice in modern China. Again, the borderline between serious commitment and false pretences can only be seen by going into detail.

The complement to these investigations is provided in Chapter 11 by Cosimo Perrotta and Chapter 13 by Hans-Michael Trautwein on the changing status of labour and social policies in the West. Perrotta focuses on the changing status of the labourer. The free citizen of antiquity leaves work to others (to the slaves) if possible, while the church turns work into a dedication. Whether the poor should be supported by charity or systematically be put to work, and whether an advantage should be sought by mobilising a national workforce to create commodities for export as a basis for national power were highly controversial questions discussed in religious contexts between the advent of Christianity and the turn to mercantilism, which England took successfully while Spain tumbled into a re-feudalisation. Trautwein confronts the macroeconomic perspective in discussing the modern welfare state in two variants, Germany and Sweden, between the 1950s and 1980s. Ordoliberalism was the dominant ideology in Germany. It stressed individual responsibility and subsidiarity: the delegation of social tasks to the smallest unit that could fulfil it. Social expenditure by the state could then be kept low, but at the same time the goal of international competitiveness was given a high priority, implying the need for the state to foster education and to raise general productivity. The Swedish model appealed more to solidarity, tried to achieve a fairer income distribution by highly progressive taxation, and attempted to ensure full employment by active labour market policies and a solidaristic wage policy, complemented by a comprehensive social assistance and a strong work ethic. Taken together, the chapters illustrate how the sociological aspects of economic governance evolve in reaction to the particular problems posed by the transformations of the economy. This means that democratic governments exhibit less pretension to be able to shape societal developments.

## The emergence of the history of Chinese economic thought

Comparing the histories of Chinese and European economic thought is a complex task; it depends on the vantage point taken. We have endeavoured to compare like with like, ancient thought with ancient and modern with modern. We now reflect once more on how economic thought as a subject was constituted, focusing on China, and then turn to the concluding question, which is at present discussed rather intensively by Chinese economists, namely to what extent perceived "Western economic theory" possesses validity for China and whether it would not be necessary to develop something like "Chinese economic theory", based on traditional Chinese approaches and congenial to the often quoted "special Chinese circumstances". This discourse is not new; it first appeared during the Republican period of China, when a considerable number of scholars claimed that "traditional Chinese economic thought" not only had the potential, but actually had made major contributions to the economic wisdom of the world (see also Chapter 17 by Olga Borokh).

The question of economic thought has never been completely neglected since, but it has drawn less attention than macro-economic history analysis or, for that matter, expeditions into other realms of thought such as philosophy, literature, logic or science. There certainly were scholars who were of the opinion that there was not much history of economic thought to be done. This neglect, however, has been corrected by publications by Ying Ma and Hans-Michael Trautwein (2013), Cheng Lin, Terry Peach and Wang Fang (2014, 2019) and others. There also has been a marked increase on research on the question of the ideas guiding Chinese officials who had to handle economic issues in their respective jurisdictions. Different from earlier assumptions, which were quite widespread for a long time, Chinese scholar-officials were well aware of the extent to which the wellbeing of the people was related to economic development, and thus needed to have an interest in the workings of the "hardware" of the empire (Dunstan 1996; Rowe 2018; Zanasi 2020).

Every attempt to assess Chinese economic thought is fraught with some serious methodological problems. Most important here is that, as we have stressed several times, "economics" as a field of knowledge did not exist in traditional China. This was also true of Europe up to the sixteenth century; this does not, of course, mean that there were no persons thinking about economic problems – there certainly were; however, they did not do so within a framework even vaguely resembling "economics", as it emerged as a field of knowledge only in Antonio Serra in 1613 (Patalano & Reinert 2016) and in Antoyne de Montchrétien (1615), if we leave aside the ancient use of the Greek term "οἰκονομία πολιτική" ("Political economy") for the householding of the state (Schefold 2016b). Economics as an academic discipline arose in nineteenth-century Europe. The modern Chinese term for economics, *jingjixue* 經濟學, came to China from Japan at the beginning of the nineteenth century. There is not the slightest doubt, however, that economics as a modern academic discipline was appropriated from the West, and the main aim, when appropriating economic knowledge and economic theories in late nineteenth- and early twentieth-century China, was to attain the same level of wealth and power, which the Western countries – and increasingly Japan – had acquired at the beginning of the twentieth century.

Reconstructing the history of economic thought for periods in which the concept did not exist is a task not confined to China, but the history of its solution is special because Western economic thought and theory were seen as a remedy for the Chinese woes, and first Chinese translations of Western economic thought, such as Fawcett's *Manual of Political Economy* in 1883, make this very clear. This can be seen from the title – the Chinese title *Fuguoce* 富國策 retranslated literally as "Strategies to enrich the country", a term that actually for some time was used as a translation for the whole subject of "economics". In 1886, Jevons' *Primer on Political Economy* (originally 1878) was published in translation as *Fuguo yangmin ce* 富國養民策 (literally "Strategies to Enrich the Country and Nourish the People"). Other assorted publications soon followed. It can be said that they greatly suffered from a lack of consistent terminology, and even more from a lack of interest accorded to the new subject by scholars and officials. Without going into details, we should note briefly that early translations – especially Yan Fu's 嚴復 (1853–1921) translation of Adam Smith, which was finished in 1900, put a very strong emphasis on the tangible effects of economic doctrines and economic thought. For Yan Fu, Adam Smith appears like a sage, whose ideas more or less single-handedly brought about the wealth and power that England enjoyed at the end of the nineteenth century (Schwartz 1964, p. 114). It needs to be stressed, however, that for Yan Fu and other early translators of Western economic thought, it was not the wealth of the individual that was important, but rather the wealth of the country or the nation, which in turn could transform into power. While most early translations are not really related to the Chinese situation, it is possible to find instances, which may help to demonstrate that translators such as Yan Fu were quite perceptive in discovering basic differences between Western and Chinese economic thought. In the preface to the translation, Yan notes that,

> unless we make every effort to change our mental habit of shunning all talk of interest (*li* 利), unless we resolutely break our attitude of emphasizing agriculture and suppressing commerce, our wealth will remain undeveloped … if interest is taboo there can be no science of economics.
> (Schwartz 1964, p. 123)

A little later an increasing number of works on Western economics began to be translated into Chinese from the Japanese. And it was only then that the word *Jingjixue*, which was used in Japan to translate economics but actually was based on the traditional Chinese concept of *jingshi jimin* 經世濟民 ("govern the world and relieving the people"), became popular in China as well (Masini 1993, pp. 183–84). That these terminological issues were considered as of greatest importance can be seen from the fact that Yan Fu himself still chose to employ a phonological transcription for economics when dealing with the Western science of economics, since he thought that *jingjixue* was too charged with traditional notions, and thus would confuse readers rather than providing the conceptual clarity that was so urgently needed (Lippert 2004). It is still unclear, however, when the term *jingji sixiang* 經濟思想 – which today is used for "economic thought" –showed up in the sinophone world for the first time. One early reference is an article from 1903, which quite typically did not refer to the Chinese tradition, but rather linked the development of "economic thought" to civilisational development as represented by the advanced countries of the West and their strict time-regimes (Gongfazi 1903).

While of course the late imperial government had an economic policy and late Qing bureaucrats and thinkers were busy to shape the Chinese economic system along the lines of Western and Japanese models, understandably there was only limited interest in the Chinese economic tradition. Why should one deal with something that apparently was one of the main causes for the desperate situation into which China had been led since the middle of the nineteenth century?

During the next stage of the introduction and reception of Western economic knowledge, an expansion and stabilisation can be observed. This went hand in hand with a rapid expansion of technical terms, soon covering all aspects of Western economics as well as first attempts at lexicalisation. This expansion of the translated body of knowledge in many cases implied a negative evaluation of knowledge resources, which partially reflected Western views of the Chinese tradition, but was mainly brought about by the fact that the new knowledge tended to stress the supposed deficits of indigenous knowledge in a clearly visible way. Since in this stage the conceptional and institutional basis of the new field of knowledge began to play an even greater role, indigenous forms of knowledge continued to become further delegitimised.

It only was during a third stage of translation, dissemination and appropriation, which was highly indebted to the increased importance of translations from the Japanese, that a more systematic dealing with aspects began, which can be considered as belonging to the realm of economic thought.

Indeed, until the 1920s, looking into traditional Chinese economic thought in China itself was rather rare. The nearest we have is the so-called "Theory of the Chinese origins of Western thought" (*Xixue zhongyuan* 西學中源), which was quite ubiquitous in late nineteenth and early twentieth-century China and extended to almost all subjects. It basically postulated that different aspects of Western thought – especially the natural sciences – had their origins in China. While this idea was later discarded in many respects, the *Xixue zhongyuan* theory was of great importance for "rediscovering" – and at times "inventing" – the Chinese tradition. Important and less important works of Chinese antiquity now were read along the lines of Western academic traditions (Quan, Hansheng 1935). In respect to economic thought, probably the most significant contribution was Liang Qichao's 梁啟超 (1873–1929) *Biography of Guanzi* (*Guanzi chuan* 管子傳), published in 1909. This, on the basis of Western works – namely

Adolf Wagner's *Finanzwissenschaft*, which had been translated into Japanese in 1905 – discovered *Guanzi*'s economic thought, which at time was interpreted as being near to the so-called Younger German Historical School, in contrast to Adam Smith's economics, based on individualism and the free market. Liang also found other aspects of Western economic and fiscal practices such as cameralism in Guanzi (Liang, Qichao 1909). The discovery of such similarities was a remarkable achievement (see also Chapter 18 by Isabella M. Weber), even if Liang often overstated his case: similarity is not the same as full anticipation, let alone proof of direct influence. There were others arguing along similar lines. Especially interesting is an article that was published in the *Eastern Miscellany* (*Dongfang zazhi* 東方雜誌) in 1905; it blamed later Confucians for the non-development of China:

> This all is the economic science of the late Zhou-period, how could anybody claim that China in antiquity did not have economic science? But once we arrive at the time after the Qin and Han, the scholar officials begin to highly praise life and taboo the character li for profit and even arrive at the idea that "Righteousness does not regard profit". This was practised for several thousand years and became common. And it is the reason why the economic science of antiquity perished and why the art of enriching the country was not transmitted, so that the country suffers from being poor.
> ("Lun Zhongguo gudai jingjixue" 1905)

It is, of course, extremely hard if not impossible to validate the correctness of such far-reaching claims. We quote them here since they demonstrate how the reception of Western economic thought and different doctrines resulted in a rereading and rearranging of the Chinese tradition, and thus was a major factor for the reconstruction (or outward construction) of Chinese "schools" of economic thought, or maybe even the "invention" of traditions in the sense of Hobsbawm (1983).

Liang Qichao's articles and book greatly contributed to the emergence of something like a canon from which to quote when speaking about economics in ancient China (Liang, Qichao 1999). Research into the history of Chinese economic thought did not develop much further during the 1910s and 1920s, since this was a period in which China's situation was perceived as being so desperate that for many Chinese scholars and intellectuals completely doing away with the Chinese tradition seemed to be the only reasonable approach for solving China's problems. We have, however, one major exception, which interestingly was not directed towards China, but rather towards a foreign audience, namely Chen Huanzhang's (1881–1933) abovementioned massive *The Economic Principles of Confucius and his School*. Chen here basically tried to defend Confucianism, highlighting the supposed contributions of Confucius to a market economy. The book met with a rather enthusiastic response in the West – Keynes (1912), for example, wrote a review – but it was completely ignored in China, since it was written in English. It was translated into Chinese only about ten years ago. The situation began to change in the mid-1920s only when an increasing number of Chinese scholars – many of them trained economists – delved deeply into the Chinese tradition and began to publish a considerable number of works related to traditional Chinese economic thought.

For reasons of space, we will not go into detail here, but instead focus on a representative and arguably one of the most important works of the period, which was published by Tang Qingzeng 唐慶增 (1902–1972) in 1936 as *A History of Chinese Economic Thought* (Borokh 2013). Tang Qingzeng was an economist trained at Harvard University. He was well versed in research on historical thought, and had published a book on the main schools of Western economic thought. Tang had taught the history of economic thought for some years, and this had included the history of Chinese economic thought. His original plan had been to cover the whole period of Chinese history – in the end, only the first volume was published, which only covered the pre-Qin period, which Tang considered – as he explicitly writes – to be the most important period for the formation of Chinese economic thought. Tang explains that the basic reason for his interest in Chinese economic thought was that the economic systems were locally different and that early economists, such as William Petty and others, had always worked on economics with a view to their own country. According to Tang, such an approach was completely missing with regard to China. Tang's book was quite innovative in many aspects, but why did he write it in the first place? Most important, probably, was a feeling – which was quite widespread at that time – that the Chinese tradition in worldwide academic thinking was not taken as seriously as it should have been. Tang says:

> The net of [publications on] the economic thought of all countries is tightly knit, only China has been left out. The American Haney, moreover, has ridiculed Chinese economic thought as being childish [child economics]. This is a humiliation for the Chinese scholarly world, I am really heartbroken about it. In order to further the point of the scholarly endeavours, which our country originally had, it is urgently necessary to research the economic history of our country.
>
> (Tang 1936, p. 5)

This idea came together with another point: that the West did not even realise the extent to which it was indebted to China for its development. Tang Qingzeng insisted that French physiocratic thought was greatly influenced by Chinese ideas (on this, see Chapter 16 by Richard van den Berg):

> Ancient Chinese economic thought actually exercised a significant influence on the countries of the West.; the most noticeable was the [influence] on French physiocrats. This influence was deep but not comprehensive, it was limited only to one period and one school. Nevertheless, the influence [of ancient Chinese economic thought] on the history of Western economic thought was much more important than of doctrines of Rome, of ideas of

Christianity, of the Bible etc. While Chinese and Western researchers of the history of economic thought of the West know and value the doctrines of Rome, they bypass in silence the ancient Chinese economic ideas. It means that, while enumerating historical events, they forget the ancestors.

(Tang 1936, p. 366)

Tang Qingzeng even went one step further and claimed that traditional Chinese economic ideas, through the physiocrats, influenced the founder of English classical economics, Adam Smith. This hypothesis permitted the identification of a Chinese contribution to the tradition of liberalism, which is usually considered to epitomise Western economic thought. The Chinese ideas that were most important here were Confucian in nature.

The second reason pointed out by Tang for his endeavour was that, in his view, economic theory always had been related to the peculiarities of certain countries. This had been true for William Petty, for example, whose ideas were based on the English example and applied to England, and it was true for other countries as well, so this idea also needed to be taken into account for China.

According to Tang Qingzeng's third reason, economic development was based on a certain system (*zhidu* 制度), which was closely tied to the special situation of the country, and this in turn was related to economic thought. Modern Chinese reviewers of Tang Qingzeng here interestingly relate Tang's ideas to later ideas of path-dependency, likening him to economists such as North. The influence of the German historical school is visible. Tang himself, however, had something different in mind, which deserves a longer quotation:

Contemporary China's economic problems are extremely complex, including the financial and monetary system, agriculture etc. Common to all of them is the urgent need of reform. In order to find an appropriate solution, it is necessary to have sound economic thought. But the economic problems of our country are special in nature, it is necessary that our compatriots devise a good method. We cannot only indiscriminately copy new Western explanations and phrases. It is possible that this is successful, but if we want to produce economic thought, which is appropriate for our special situation of the country, this is not possible without doing research in the history of Chinese economic thought. Scholars need to take into account the contents of China's contemporary economic system, but they at the same time need to carefully do research into the merits and failures of past Chinese economic thought. It is necessary to adopt the successful ideas and produce new thought, in order to solve current economic problems.

(Tang 1936, p. 4)

This, of course, is a rather normative statement. Tang Qingzeng nonetheless makes a concentrated and systematic effort to live up to it. He systematically looks into the economic ideas of all Chinese intellectual schools of pre-Qin times. To what extent he really fulfils his own claim to present a real and substantial Chinese alternative of economic thought, however, is rather difficult to say. Tang basically investigates the different trains of thought, and relates and classifies them according to Western economic doctrines such as "liberalism", "mercantilism", "socialism" and so on. He makes no secret of his favourite, namely liberal economic thought, which he finds in Confucius, as mentioned above. In order to be successful in this respect, he needs to make some re-evaluations. He claims, for example, that the common idea that Confucius was "anti-merchant" and "pro-agriculture" is too simplified. He does this by stressing certain ideas from the *Lunyu*, such as "benevolence without great expenditure" (*hui er bufei* 惠而不費), which he sees as proof of Confucius's opposition to "intervention" and his propagation of *laissez-faire* (Tang, Qingzeng 1936, pp. 75–76). Tang not only stressed the "active" and "positive" aspects of Chinese economic thought, but tried to look into the causes of its backwardness as well. These include Chinese family structures, geographical constraints and supposed deficits of the Chinese "national character", such as conservatism; believing in luck rather than doing business; and too much stress on secrecy. It is interesting here how Tang stresses that China lacked a clear-cut concept of economics – which, of course, is an entirely justified observation. As we have pointed out already, Tang Qingzeng's approach was not singular. His book, however, probably was the most ambitious and most systematic one published.

In 1943, Chiang Kai-shek 蔣介石 (1887–1975), then president of war-torn China, published a book entitled *China's Economic Theory*, in which he deplored that, since being exposed to Western economic thought, "nobody is speaking about China's own economic principles" (Chiang Kai-shek 1943, p. 252). Yet he arrived at conclusions that were completely different from those of Tang and rather stressed those scholars and officials commonly seen as state interventionists – such as Guanzi, Wang Anshi 王安石 and others. According to Chiang Kai-shek, neither liberal economic thought nor Marxism was appropriate for "China's social situation" and "people's livelihood necessarily must be based on 'planned economy'" (Chiang, Kai-shek 1947, p. 277).

After 1949, under the circumstances of accelerated economic construction, which clearly was based on the Soviet model, explorations of traditional Chinese economic thought played no important role. The great exception was the work by Hu Jichuang 胡寄窗 (1902–93), which set modern research into the history of Chinese economic thought on a new course and to which several contributions in this volume are indebted. Hu's work, published in Chinese in three volumes (1962–81; English version 1988) (Hu, Jichuang 1988), was comprehensive, and he strove for objectivity. However, when in the last phase of the Cultural Revolution the "Discourse on Salt and Iron" *Yantie lun* was used in order to justify Maoist approaches to the Chinese economy, the aims were ideological on all sides (see Chapter 15 by Qunyi Liu).

## Conclusion: The significance of the history of Chinese economic thought today

It only is in recent years that dealing with traditional Chinese economic thought has clearly gained importance and is taught in many universities. Tang Qingzeng, for one, who was a rather marginal figure in China after 1949, has been rediscovered abroad as well as in China itself. Olga Borokh has claimed that this may be due to his clearly pronounced position in economic liberalism. We would stress that his *History of Economic Thought* fits quite well into a more general line of scholarship, which tries to centre on traditional Chinese thought.

There is a clear relationship here with the Chinese renaissance of "National learning" (*guoxue* 國學), which has become increasingly visible since the mid-1990s. "National learning" actually is a term borrowed from the Japanese. It hints at research on traditional Chinese literature (the "canon") by using traditional philological and academic ideas. This approach became popular for the first time in the 1920s, but was more or less completely discarded later. Its recent renaissance has witnessed attempts to expand the scope of "national studies", which is now considered by some as extending to the natural sciences as well. While it is of interest to note that Tang Qingzeng had stressed the importance of "national learning" for his own approach, for us it is more important to point out that the re-emergence of "national learning" has a close relationship to the application of postcolonial thought in China. Its character was thus transformed from conservative to anti-hegemonical, directed against supposed efforts of the former colonial powers to resurrect their dominance by means of "discursive hegemony", as has been stressed times and again.

Whatever the reason may be, there is no doubt that "national learning" has enjoyed a very high degree of visibility and importance during the last few years. Many Chinese universities now boast institutes dedicated to the cause. We would like to suggest that this is the main background for the growing importance accorded to traditional Chinese economic thought. In this way, it becomes part of an approach that stresses Chinese exceptionalism since, according to this view, "universal science" does not manage to shed its "colonial" baggage. This approach is particularly visible in the realm of economic reasoning, and has become even more pronounced since Xi Jinping 習近平 took power. One of the reasons for this development is the Chinese economic miracle, which has greatly boosted Chinese self-confidence. As a representative, we quote Zhou Wen 周文, a professor of economics at Fudan University, one of the best universities of China:

> China's rise has two layers of implications: 1. It means that the period of more than 300 years, in which Westcentrism guided economic science, has come to an end, and it also means that the period, in which China was the "docker" of Western economic concepts and the horse-racing course for Western economic technical terminology has come to an end. Modern Western economics is the summarization of Western experiences. During

the last hundred years not only economics but the complete system of philosophy and social sciences has been enveloped into a Western-centred hegemonic discourse system. But it was China's rise that deconstructed the Western discourse system. 2. The transformations of the world and its new structure reveal that the explanatory force of Western economics is getting smaller daily and demonstrate the inherent contradictions of the system. If Chinese economy is able to form an efficient theoretical system for these two questions, it will be able to independently form its own school and by means of this will be able to occupy a leading position within the forest of economics.

(Zhou, Wen 2017a)

In another context, Zhou Wen (2016) demands that China needs to stop as soon as possible merely "danc[ing] in the Western cage" of economic education and instead should summarise the Chinese experience scientifically.

Recently, after the 19th party congress, Zhou even demanded that the Nobel Prize committee should look eastwards, because according to this logic – which entirely mirrors the logic employed by Tang Qingzeng – the Chinese economic miracle must have been based on a considerable amount of economic expertise – which, of course, was Chinese rather than Western (cf. Chapter 18 by Isabella M. Weber). Chinese economists have thus made great contributions to the world and, even more importantly, in this way Chinese economic wisdom would push forward the economic development of the world. For this, he even could refer to a statement from Milton Friedman – who, ironically, quite often is credited with having had a substantial impact on the Chinese economic reform – that whoever could solve China's economic problems deserved a Nobel Prize. Zhou Wen refrains from suggesting any specific person, although he most likely would have thought of Justin Yi-fu Lin 林毅夫, professor of economics at Peking University and former chief economist of the World Bank (Zhou, Wen 2017b).

The Western observer who notes the defiant undertone of such statements may decide to wait and see. It would be wrong, however, to denounce Chinese economic thought as a mere fabrication. The point that needs to be taken into account is rather the question of commensurability – or, to put it differently, what is the *tertium comparationis* when relating Chinese and Western "economic thought"? Dealing with this question alone is a dauntingly difficult task. The question becomes even more complicated because there is no escape from employing concepts and terms, which are ultimately derived from Western economic sciences – that is, based on the translation efforts of the early twentieth century (which include, as just noted, even the designations for the discipline itself). This can easily result in a discursive imbalance, since it quite often leads to the discovery (or construction) of deficits on the Chinese side – or, to put it differently, it is only a short distance from incommensurability to a supposed "lack" of something, which in turn can be employed to explain China's historical "lagging behind" or "non-development". Unfortunately, it is almost impossible to escape from this predicament. Up until now, there has been no framework based on Chinese indigenous categories and concepts, which could be used to understand and analyse not only Chinese traditional "economic thought", but also the European experience past and present. One good example of the difficulties that this approach inevitably entails is Schurman's (1956) take on the question of property, in which he claims that, "Traditional property concepts in China were far from the concept of Freies Eigentum which is at the basis of modern capitalist society." Schurman's example might be overly simple, but it is still quite instructive to imagine a Chinese scholar who has read a number of lexicon entries on "property" in the West and then is shocked about what is supposedly missing in China. Quite typically, the reverse approach is nowhere adopted, let alone the beholders undergoing the effort, as done by Long Denggao and Xiang Chi in Chapter 4, to highlight the flexibility and positive contributions of Chinese systems of property to consolidate and develop the Chinese rural economy.

Max Weber is perhaps most prominent among the scholars who stress the lack of Western concepts in the Chinese tradition. Pointing out the "deficits" of non-Western civilisations and societies served as the methodological device to highlight the peculiarities of Western (or, better, Protestant) modernity. Even though Weber's black-and-white comparisons were carried out in a quite sophisticated way, and yielded some valuable insights for understanding developments on both sides, they more often than not tend to exaggerate or even make absolute differences, which in turn are used to analyse differing development trajectories of which only one – the European/Western one – will lead to "modernity". Sociologists such as Eisenstadt and others have tried to balance such cultural-deterministic approaches by intensively questioning the prerequisites of modernity and coming up with concepts such as "alternative" or "multiple" modernities (Dirlik 2013; Eisenstadt 2000). However, sociology is of limited use where we are concerned with a broader problem in the history of knowledge. Weber, carried away by audacious historical visions and restrained by a sharp sceptical intellect, was prone to limiting himself to negative characterisations when he dealt with Western history: the political capitalism of Roman antiquity lacked the ascetic spirit that helped to introduce modern capitalism; modern capitalism in its iron cage lacked the humanity and the aesthetic genius of the renaissance, and so on. If one really wants to apprehend a distant past and hopes to get inspiration for the present, one must overcome self-imposed limitations and recognise, and up to a point identify with, different values and different ways to seek truth. The humanities have confronted this task – remember Herder, Goethe and Dilthey. Research into the history of European economic thought has also lived with the tension between modern values, which are not fixed but often ambiguous, and values of the past. The usury problem, as discussed in this volume, is an example. We have stressed the progressive conceptual evolution leading to modern theories of interest, but we also mentioned the thread leading to Marx and the critique of capitalism.

We are convinced that the potential of the history of Chinese economic thought has not been exhausted. The reader of this book will have encountered a number of attempts at positive characterisations of the Chinese tradition in this field. They are inevitably reconstructions insofar as the subject "economics" did not exist, and also because we are looking for modern understanding, inspiration – perhaps even relevance and applicability. From the point of view of rational modern Western democracy or Sino-Marxism, the past is mainly peopled with monarchists who tended to believe in ghosts, but left behind stupendous artefacts and challenging ideas. How to make sense of these distant worlds? Needham interpreted Chinese science in general as organicist. Herrmann-Pillath (2017) proposes a Chinese economic style, a concept taken from the so-called Youngest Historical School in Germany, also used by one of us (Schefold 1994) and based on the idea of an economic spirit or mentality, which has the advantage of linking economic history with economic thought. Herrmann-Pillath proposes to look at the rituals as an expression and stabiliser of this spirit in the Chinese case. Bin Wong, in Chapter 1, starts from the political ideas of benefiting the people. Confucianism is mentioned in several places as a principle that ties economics to ethics. There is no lack of different approaches. They are similar and hang together or form pairs of opposed doctrines that show their dynamic potential in their interaction, such as "Harmony of Diversity" and "Great Uniformity" (Zhong 2013).

On the one hand, it is true that mechanistic economic theorising seems not to be endogenous in China and arrived there only in the late nineteenth century, transforming, with liberalism and Marxism, the autochthonous teaching. On the other hand, given the nature of Chinese scholars as potential advisers to the competing states in antiquity and their role as potential officials, especially from the installation of the examination system onwards, the past and present fixation of Chinese economics on the state is no surprise and is clearly reflected in many of the contributions of this volume. It represents an alternative approach to economics that –– albeit only in parts – overlaps with heterodox currents in the West. In the long run, a synthesis will have to emerge. The discursive imbalance, deplored by authors such as Zhou Wen, will be reduced. Autochthonous characterisations of Chinese economic schools such as "Legalism" will often, but not generally, be preferable to imported terms such as "mercantilism" – which, by the way, is also a reconstruction, while "physiocracy" and "Confucianism" were programmatic terms that were introduced and used by the schools themselves. And why not reverse the game and write a comparative paper on whether Sir William Petty was a Legalist?

Given these considerations, arriving at a comprehensive understanding of present-day Chinese economic thought is likely to remain an elusive goal for some time to come, for the contrasts are many, even while some fundamental traits can be reliably identified. Engaging in a dialogue on the question of the history of economic thought, as provided by this volume, is not only a fruitful intellectual challenge, but will help us to better understand the next steps.

Independently of utilitarian considerations, the history of premodern and early modern Chinese economic thought is a treasure trove rich in insights about state, economy and society. The visual character of this literature, the pointed formulations, the intimate relationships with Chinese ethical thought with its maxim for the government "benefiting the people" – the central theme of this book – are reasons why this tradition is a key to the understanding of one of the greatest cultures of the world and an inspiration for others.

## References

Borokh, Olga: Chinese Tradition Meets Western Economics. Tang Qingzeng and His Legacy. In: Ying Ma and Hans Michael Trautwein (eds): *Thoughts on Economic Development in China*. London: Routledge, pp. 136–74, 2013.

Chiang Kai-shek: *China's Destiny and Chinese Economic Theory – with Notes and Commentary by Philip Jaffe*. London: Dobson, 1947.

de Montchrestien, Antoine: *Traicté de l'oeconomie politique*. F. Billacois, ed. Paris: n.p., 1999 [1615].

Dirlik, Arif: Thinking Modernity Historically: Is "Alternative Modernity" the Answer? *Asian Review of World Histories*, 1(1), pp. 5–44, 2013.

Dunstan, Helen: *Conflicting Counsels to Confuse the Age: A Documentary study of Political Economy in Qing China, 1644–1840*. Ann Arbor, MI: Center of Chinese Studies, 1996.

Eisenstadt, Shmuel N.: Multiple Modernities. *Daedalus*, 129(1), pp. 1–29, 2000.

Gongfazi 功法子, "Guomin zhi jingji sixiang yu shijian" 國民之經濟思想與時間 (The Economic Thought of the Citizens and Time). *Yishu huibian*, 2(11), pp. 106–07, 1903.

Herrmann-Pillath, Carsten: *China's Economic Culture. The Ritual Order of State and Markets*. London: Routledge 2017.

Hobsbawm, Eric: Introduction: Inventing Traditions. In: Eric Hobsbawm & Terence Ranger (eds): *The Invention of Tradition*. Cambridge: Cambridge University Press, pp. 1–14, 1983.

Hu, Jichuang: *A Concise History of Chinese Economic Thought*. Beijing: Foreign Languages Press, 1988.

Hua, Tengda: *The Development of Commerce and the Status of Merchants in Ming China: Economic Thought and Economic History*, Ph D thesis, Frankfurt am Main, 2020.

Keynes, John Maynard: Review of The Economic Principles of Confucius and his School by Chen Huan-Chang. *The Economic Journal*, 22(88), pp. 584–88, 1912.

Liang, Qichao 梁啟超: Guanzi zhuan" 管子傳 (Biography of Guanzi). In: Liang Qichao, *Liang Qichao quanji*, Beijing: Beijing chubanshe, pp. 1858–1906, 1999 [1909].

Lin, Cheng, Peach, Terry & Fang, Wang: *The History of Ancient Chinese Economic Thought*. London: Routledge, 2014.

Lin, Cheng; Peach, Terry & Fang, Wang: *The Political Economy of the Han Dynasty and Its Legacy*. London: Routledge, 2019.

Lippert, Wolfgang: The Formation and Development of the Term "Political Economy" in Japanese and Chinese. In: Michael Lackner & Natascha Vittinghoff (eds): *Mapping Meanings: The Field of New Learning in Late Qing China*. Leiden: Brill, pp. 119–28, 2004.

Lun Zhongguo gudai jingjixue 論中國古代經濟學 (On Economics in Ancient China), *Dongfang zazhi* 2(1), 1905.

Ma, Ying & Hans-Michael Trautwein, *Thoughts on Economic Development in China*. London: Routledge, 2013.

Masini, Federico: *The Formation of Modern Chinese Lexicon and its Evolution Toward a National Language: The Period from 1840–1898*. Berkeley, CA: University of California Press, 1993.

Pan, Ming-te: Rural Credit in Ming-Qing Jiangnan and the Concept of Peasant Petty Commodity Production. *The Journal of Asian Studies*, 55(1), pp. 94–117, 1996.

Patalano, Sophus & Reinert, Rosario (eds): *Antonio Serra and the Economics of Good Government*. Basingstoke: Palgrave Macmillan, pp. 166–90, 2016.

Peach, Terry: Sima Qian and *laissez-faire*: Satire on a "Discordant and Degenerate Age". In: Lin, Cheng, Terry Peach,& Fang, Wang (eds): *The Political Economy of the Han Dynasty and Its Legacy*, pp. 175–94. London: Routledge, 2019.

Pines, Yuri: Legalism in Chinese Philosophy. In: Edward N. Zalta (ed.): *Stanford Encyclopedia of Philosophy*, Stanford, CA: Stanford University Press, 2018.

Quan, Hansheng 全漢昇: Qingmo de Xixue yuanchu Zhongguo shuo 清末的西學源出中國說 (The late Qing Theory that Western Learning Has Its Origin in China). *Lingnan xuebao*, 4(2), pp. 57–102, 1935.

Ronan, Colin A.: *The Shorter Science and Civilization in China: An Abridgement of Joseph Needham's Original Text, Vol. I*. Cambridge: Cambridge University Press, 1978.

Rosner, Erhard, Luxusgesetze in China unter der Manchudynastie (1644–1911). *Saeculum*, 25, pp. 325–37, 1974.

Rowe, William T.: *Speaking of Profit. Bao Shichen and Reform in Nineteenth Century China*. Cambridge, MA: Harvard University Asia Center, 2018.

Schefold, Bertram: *Wirtschaftsstile Bd. 1: Studien zum Verhältnis von Ökonomie und Kultur*, Frankfurt a.M.: Fischer Taschenbuch Verlag, 1994.

Schefold, Bertram: *Great Economic Thinkers from the Classicals to the Moderns. Translations from the Series Klassiker der Nationalökonomie*. London: Routledge, 2016a.

Schefold, Bertram: Political Economy in the Pseudo-Aristotelian Oeconomica II and the German Cameralist Klock. *History of Economic Thought and Policy*, 2, pp. 59–72, 2016b.

Schefold, Bertram: Die Bedeutung des ökonomischen Wissens für Wohlfahrt und wirtschaftliches Wachstum in der Geschichte. In *Sitzungsberichte der Wissen schaftlichen Gesellschaft an der Johann Wolfgang Goethe-Universität, Frankfurt am Main*, Stuttgart: Steiner, 2018.

Schefold, Bertram: A Western perspective on the Yantie lun. In: Lin, Cheng, Terry Peach,& Fang, Wang (eds): *The Political Economy of the Han Dynasty and Its Legacy*, pp. 153–74. London: Routledge.

Schurman, H.F.: Traditional Property Concepts in China. *The Far Eastern Quarterly*, 15(4), pp. 507–16, 1956.

Schwartz, Benjamin: *In Search of Wealth and Power: Yen Fu and the West*. Cambridge, MA: Harvard University Press, 1964.

Sima, Qian: *Records of the Grand Historian, Han Dynasty II*, translated by Burton Watson, rev. ed. New York: Columbia University Press, 1993.

Smith, A.: *The Theory of Moral Sentiments*. London: Andrew Millar, 1759.

Smith, A.: *The Wealth of Nations*. London: W. Strahan & T. Cadell, 1776.

Tang, Qingzeng 唐慶增: *Zhongguo jingji sixiang shi* 中國經濟思想史 (A History of Chinese Economic Thought). Shanghai: Commercial Press, 1936.

Vivenza, Gloria: Ancora sullo stoicismo di Adam Smith. In: *Studi Storici Luigi Simeoni*, 99, pp. 97–126, 1999.

Wilhelm, Richard: *Chinesische Wirtschaftspsychologie*. Leipzig: Deutsche Wissenschaftliche Buchhandlung, 1930.

Zanasi, Margherita: *Economic Thought in Modern China. Market and Consumption, c. 1500–1937*, Cambridge: Cambridge University Press, 2020.

Zhong, Xiangcai: Harmony of Diversity and Great Uniformity. Two Trains of Thought in the Economics of Ancient China. In: Ma, Ying & Hans-Michael Trautwein (eds.): *Thoughts on Economic Development in China*, pp. 194–209. London: Routledge, 2013.

Zhou, Wen 周文: Jingjixue xu zhengtuo Xifang guannian qiulong 經濟學須掙脫西方概念囚籠 (Economics Needs to Escape from the Cage of Western Concepts). *Huanqiu shibao*, 2 February 2016.

Zhou, Wen 周文: Jingjixue de Zhongguo jingjie 經濟學的中國境界 (The Chinese Boundaries of Economics). *Guangming ribao*, 11 October 2017a.

Zhou, Wen 周文: Jingjixue nuojiang pingwei ying xiang dong kan 經濟學諾獎評委應向東看 (The Price Committee for the Nobel Prize in Economics Should Look East). *Huanqiu shibao*, 10 October 2017b.

# Index

*Achsenzeit* xiii
Ailly, Pierre de 150
Alberti, Leon Battista 150
Alexander the Great 279
Althusius, Johannes 172, 182n1
*Analects* of Confucius 202, 236, 241, 260–1, 264–6, 269
Antichretic contract 121–2, 126, 129, 286; *see also* Florencourt, Carl Chassot de; Klock, Kaspar
Aquinas, Thomas: commenting on Aristotle 97; on money loans 93–5; on poverty 148–9, 155n11; and his theory on usury 95–6, 98–101, 108, 120, 133–4
Aristotle: biographical note on 279; compared to ancient Chinese philosophers xiii; on fair prices 255–6, 256n2; on frugality 145, 150, 155n1, 155n3; on gift-giving 282; on the good life 278; on money 108, 284; on natural and artificial social forms 247, 283; on usury 120; *see also* Aquinas, Thomas, *Yantie Lun*
Augustine 147, 155n5
Auxerre, William of 95, 101

Baily, Francis 127
Ban, Gu 78
Bao, Shichen 41
Baudeau, Nicolas 219–21, 227n6, 227n8, 227n9
Böhm-Bawerk, Eugen von 138, 141
Bonaventura 133
Bortkiewicz, Ladislaus von 123, 125
Bracciolini, Poggio 150
Brixiensis, Stephanus Federicus 113

Calvin, Johannes 114
Calvinism xv, 120, 172, 284

Cameralism 119–20, 128; *see also Guanzi*
Cantillon, Richard 218, 226n1
*Carentia pecuniae see* Usury
Carli, Gian Rinaldo 160, 167n2
Cartalism 158–9
Cassel, Gustav 176
Cato 121
Chao, Cuo 20, 30n1, 208
Charles V (Holy Roman Emperor) 153, 161
Charles VIII (of France) 160
Chen, Hongmou 8
Chen, Huanzhang: combining Western and Chinese economic thought 234–5; on Confucius 234–7; influencing Yuan, Xianneng 240; on production and consumption 234–7; *see also* Keynes, John Maynard
Chen, Longzheng 68
Cheng, Chung-ying 268
Chiang, Kai-shek 295
Chrysostom, John 94, 96
Church Fathers: and canonical law 107; and the prohibition of interest 94–5, 108, 125; on poverty 145, 148–9
Clark, John Bates 141, 235
Clement V 108
Cochlaeus, Johannes 112, 114
Confucianism: anti- 202, 206–7, 209–10; and the criticism of profit-making 260–2; and consumption 240; and development 245; and food security 19, 24; in the Han-dynasty 204, 211; and *laissez-faire* economics 205; and merchants 259, 262–3; Neo- 20, 280; and paternalism 43; as a programmatic term 299; revival of 265–6; and Richard Wilhelm 283; *see also Analects*

## 304  Index

of Confucius; Confucius; Leibniz, Gottfried Wilhelm; *runshang*
Confucius xiii–xiv, 189, 200n8, 209–10, 241–4, 256n5, 260–1, 265–6, 269, 278, 280, 292, 295; *see also Analects* of Confucius; Chen, Huanzhang; Confucianism; Quesnay, François
*Contractus trinus see* Eck, Johann
Copronimo, Constantino 160
Corvée labour: and land tenure 54, 68; privilege of exemption from . . . by making contributions 20; in Qing times 35; restriction of 200n12; and river control 33, 35–6; *see also* Yongzheng
Courçon, Robert of 94–5, 98, 100–1
COVID-19 pandemic 15
Cultural Revolution xvi, 202, 205, 207, 209, 266, 295; *see also* Mao, Zedong

Dai, Junyuan 39, 43
*Damnum emergens see* Usury
D'Andrea, Giovanni 108
Daoguang Emperor 40–1, 43, 83–4
Daoism 221, 223, 235, 238–41
Daszyńska-Golińska, Zofia 215–6
Davanzati, Bernardo 158, 160–2, 167n4
Davis, John Francis 129
Deng, Xiaoping 5, 208–9
*Dian* (典) land right: definition of 50–1, 61n2, 61n3; compared to other forms of land transactions 52, 61n2, 286; and its contribution to economic stability 53; in the Qing dynasty 53–4; in the Song dynasty 51, 53; in the Tang dynasty 51, 53
Dilthey, Wilhelm 298
Diocletian 247, 256n3
Dominic of Guzmán 148
Du Halde, Jean Baptiste 218
Du, Yannian 189
Duns Scotus 133

Eck, Johann: biographical note on 110, 115n9; his contemporary reception 115n11; on the *contractus trinus* 111–4, 116n16, 116n17, 116n18, 116n19; and his theory on usury 112–4
Edgeworth, Francis Ysidro 281
El Amine, Loubna 7
Elizabeth I (of England) 152
Erhard, Ludwig 174–5
Eucken, Walter 174

European Union 11, 171, 173, 176, 181
Eyb, Gabriel of 113

Famine Relief: 19–20, 26–8, 29, 43–4, 65, 68; *see also* Jiaqing, Qianlong
Fan, Daren 208
Fang, Xiaoru 204
Fawcett, Henry 290
*Fede di credito* 162–4, 166
*Fede di deposito* 163
Feudalism 146–7, 207, 210
Ficino, Marsilio 150, 155n13
Fisher, Irving 136
Florencourt, Carl Chassot de: as a "calucalting jurists" 120, 125, 128; on the antichretic contract 121–2, 129; the calculation of loan payments 126–7; on Leibniz' s calculation of the *interusurium* 125
Foreign Currencies in Ancient China: exchange ratios and influences of 79–82, 86; shape and structure of 78–9; *see also* Ming Dynasty; Qing Dynasty
Francesco da Empoli 109–10
Francis of Assisi 148
Frederick II (Holy Roman Emperor) 160–1, 166n1
Friedman, Milton 297
Fronsperger, Leonhard 277
Fugger, Jacob 110, 112–13, 115n8, 116n15
Funi, Yang'e 84

Gaetanus 113
Galiani, Ferdinando 159, 162, 167n8
Gauss, Friedrich 127
Gerard of Siena 108
Glahn, Richard von 43, 83, 256n7, 257n10
Goethe, Johann Wolfgang von 298
Gong, Zizhen 85
Good Governance xv, xvi, 7–8, 10–1, 15, 23
Graeco-Roman antiquity: city states in 279; compared to Chinese economic thought 189–90, 200n5, 246–7, 256, 278–9; labour in 145–6; usury in xv, 119, 284; *see also* Han Dynasty
Granaries: and their expansion to support people's livelihoods 9; as food security 19–20; local 21; providing loans 8, 63, 65, 68, 285; public 253; in the Song dynasty 65

Gratian (canon lawyer) 93, 96
Great North China Famine (1877–1879) 24, 27
Gregory VII 147
Gregory IX 100, 120
Gregory of Nazianzus 94
Gu, Yanwu 85
Guan, Zhong 248
Guangxu Emperor 42–3
*Guanzi*: cameralism in the 292; compared to ancient Greek philosophy 246–7, 256; on consumption 241, 243; and the grain price 252–5, 257n10; historical context of the 247–9; and interest rates 70; and light-heavy principles 249–52; on money 257n11, 283
Guo, Congju 28
Guo, Moruo 203, 206–7
Gustafsson, Björn 5

Hammurabi 135
Han, Fei 189
Han, Seunghyun 25
Han Wudi (Emperor) 207
Hayek, Friedrich August von 137
He, Changqun 207
He, Liangjun 85
He, Shen 69
He, Weifang 12
Henry VII (of England) 152
Henry VIII (of England) 152, 155n14
Henry of Susa 108
Herder, Johann Gottfried 298
Hermann-Pillath, Carsten 280
Hong, Zun 78
Hu, Angang 10–1
Hu, Jintao 14, 265
Hu, Weixin 206
Hua, Guofeng 209
Huan of Qi, Duke 248
Huan, Kuan 202–4, 206
Huan, Tan 64
Huang, Zhongmo 84
Huang, Zongxi 85
Hudson, Geoffrey Francis 215, 221
Humanism 106, 112, 116n14
Huo, Guang 202, 206, 208

Ibn Khaldun 246
Industrial Revolution 54, 59, 153, 281
Innocent III (Pope) 148
interest rates: commodity 133, 135, 137; compound 66, 70–1, 73, 119, 123–9, 130n1, 285; money 133, 136–7, 139; natural 135, 138; prohibition of xv, 70–1, 94, 96, 108, 110, 119–20, 123–5, 129–30, 130n1, 165, 284–5; *see also* Church Fathers; *Guanzi*; Keynes, John Maynard; Leibniz, Gottfried, Wilhelm; Loans; Ming dynasty; Qing Dynasty; Wicksell, Knut; Yuan Dynasty
*Interusurium see* Florencourt, Carl Chassot de; Leibniz, Gottfried Wilhelm

Jacobsen, Stefan Gaarsmand 221, 223, 227n8
Jamieson, George 129
Jaspers, Karl xiii
Jevons, William Stanley 290
Jia, Sixie 204
Jiang, Shoupeng 22
Jiang, Qing 207
Jiang, Xiaocheng 70
Jiaqing: and expenditure control 43; and famine relief 25; and office selling 21, 23, 25; pawnshops under the reign of 69; and river control 39, 43
Jin, Fu 34–5
John of Austria 162
Juan de Medina 154
Justinian 106, 108, 125

Kästner, Abraham Gotthelf 127
Kangxi Emperor 34–6, 39, 43–4, 80, 84
Keynes, John Maynard: and the *General Theory* 137, 257n11; and the liquidity premium 138; on macroeconomic stabilisation 174, 176, 179; and own rates of interest 137–8; reviewing Chen, Huanzhang's book 237, 256n1, 257n14; and the saving-investment relation 135, 139
Klock, Kaspar: on the antichretic contract 121–2; and the School of Salamanca 120, 128; on usury 120–1, 285
Knobloch, Eberhard 124
Kroll, Jurij 211–12

*laissez-faire* economics 205, 227n10, 295; *see also* Quesnay, François
land tenure: concentration of 58–9; equalisation of 58; forms of 49–50; in modern times 60; of wealthy landowners 57; *see also* Ming Dynasty; Qing Dynasty; Yuan Dynasty
Laozi 210, 216, 241–3

306  Index

legalism 189, 204–5, 207, 211, 282–3, 299; see also Mao, Zedong
Le Goff, Jacques 95
Leibniz, Gottfried Wilhelm: as a "Calculating Jurist" 120; and the mathematical analysis of the *interusurium* 122–4, 286; and Neo-Confucianism 280; on compound interest 123–5, 130n1; on usury 120, 122–3, 125, 286
Lempp, Johann Jakob 110
Leo X 112
Lessius, Leonard 120
Li, Hongbin 85
Li, Honglei 268
Li, Hongzhang 26–7, 29, 264
Li, Keqiang 13
Li, Kui 206, 252, 256n8, 257n10
Li, Lillian 27
Li, Liuru 205
Li, Mingwei 81
Li, Quanshi 240–4
Li, Si 189, 200n3
Liang, Qichao 204, 208, 233, 291–2
Lin, Biao 209–10
Lin, Justin Yi-Fu 297
Lin, Zexu 86
Linguet, Simon Nicolas Henri 220–1, 227n6
Liu, Chuanzhi 268
Liu, Shaoqi 208
loans: cash- 65; consumptive 67, 68, 94–5, 102; contracts 69–70; government 24; high-interest 66, 68, 72; non-profit 63; private 64–5, 71; with a collateral 51, 67, 69; see also Aquinas, Thomas; Florencourt, Carl Chassot de; Granaries; Ming dynasty; Qing dynasty; Tang dynasty; Yuan dynasty
Lombard, Alexander 93
Long, Yongtu 268
Lu, Xiangshan 262
*Lucrum cessans* see Usury
Lufrano, Richard J. 263
*Lunyu* see *Analects* of Confucius
Luo, Feng 82
Luther, Martin xv, 114, 284

Maffei, Aldo 218, 226n3
Magnus, Albertus 133
Malthus, Thomas Robert 235, 239, 257
Mandeville, Bernard 150, 257n14
Mann, Michael 211

Mao, Zedong: and the Cultural Revolution 264; and entrepreneurship 269; and the industrialisation 10; and legalism 210; post-era 259; and the *Yantie Lun* 205, 207
Mao, Zhongqun 269
Marshall, Alfred 241
Marx, Karl: and the translation of the *Capital* 74; on exploitation 140–1, 287; see also Sino-Marxism
Maverick, Lewis A. 215–6, 218, 226n4
Medici, Cosimo de' 109–11
Meidner, Rudolf 176–8
Melanchthon, Philip 114
Melon, Jean-François 218
Mencius xiii, 189, 210, 223, 241–3, 260–2
Mercantilism: British 128; in contrast to early Chinese policies of ensuring people's livelihoods 7; and labour xvi, 288; Neo- 171, 176; and poverty 151; usury discussions in 119–20, 125
Metallism 158–62, 166, 167n3, 167n4, 167n6; see also Ricardo, David
Meun, Jean de 150, 155n12
Mevius, David 122
Michiel (Domenico Michiel, Doge of Venice) 160–1
middle class: in antiquity 279; China's . . . compared to other countries 6; creation of an urban 5, 11; in the Middle Ages 147; of peasants in the agricultural era 59, 279
Ming Dynasty: economic pragmatism during the 204, 209; foreign currencies during the 82–4, 86; land transactions during the 51, 53, 55; loans and interest rates 67–8, 72–3; and merchants 262–3; office selling during the 20; see also paper money
modernism 281–3
modernity 111, 281, 298
Montanari, Geminiano 158, 161–2, 167n6
Montchrétien, Antoyne de 289
Montesquieu, Charles-Louis de Secondat Baron de 224
moral hazard 101, 134, 170–1
Morgan, Augustus de 127
Morse, Hosea Ballou 82
Müller-Armack, Alfred 174–5, 182n6
Murthy, Viren 6
Mu, Tianyan 84
*Mutuum* 95–100, 121

Myrdal, Alva 176
Myrdal, Gunnar 176

Needham, Joseph 279–80, 299
New Catholic View on the Economy 107, 110, 114
Ni, Mo 80
Nuccio, Oscar 107, 115n4, 115n5

Ockham, William of 115n12, 133, 150
office selling: in Qing times 19–22, 30; history of 19–21; and provincial governors 20, 25; *see also* Jiaqing; Qianlong
Olivi, Peter John (Pèire de Joan-Oliu) 110, 133, 148, 155n9
Opium War 21, 225
Ordoliberalism 171, 174, 176, 182n7, 288
Oresme, Nicole 150

Pan, Ming-te 285
paper money: in the Ming dynasty 158; in the Song Dynasty 77, 158; in the Yuan Dynasty 77, 158; in Naples xvi, 158, 162, 164, 166, 285; issued during the siege of Leyden 160; Pareto, Vilfredo 281
Passow, Richard 127
pawnbroker 69, 125, 129, 162–3; *see also* Jiaqing; Qianlong
Pedro de Toledo (Viceroy of Naples) 165
Peng, Xinwei 77
people's livelihood and wellbeing (*minsheng* 民生) xv, 5, 6, 10, 12–15, 43, 295
*Periculum sortis see* Usury
Petty, William 293–4, 299
Pfautz, Christoph 125
physiocracy: cartesian thought in 280; critics of 221; influenced by Chinese economic thought 215–7, 221, 293; modern reception of 203–4; and its portrayal of the Chinese state xvi, 284; as a programmatic term 299; *see also* Tang, Qingzeng
Pierozzi, Antoninus 108
Piketty, Thomas 6
Pinot, Virgile 218
Pirckheimer, Willibald 112–14, 115n13, 116n20
Plato: and forms of government 247, 287; and *Nomoi* 200n18, 279; and *Politikos* 279; on poverty 198; on prices 247, 255–6, 256n2; and *The Republic* xvi, 190. 197, 279; *see also* Xunzi
Plutarch 113
*Poena conventionalis see* Usury
poverty: absolute 5, 6, 11; in antiquity 145; and land tenure 59; in the Middle Ages 146–8; in the 14th and 15th century 149–50; in 16th and 17th century England 151; relief 170, 173; Yuan, Xiannang on 238; *see also* Aquinas, Thomas; Church Fathers; Mercantilism; Plato; Xunzi
Priddat, Birger P. 221
primitivism 281–3
property rights: corporate 49–50, 56, 58; development of different 51, 53–5, 59–60, 286; independent 57; and the physiocrats 222–6; private 49–50, 59, 140, 222–6; in relation to the rate of profits 140–1

Qianlong Emperor: and famine relief 21, 23; and office selling 21, 23, 29–30; and river control 38–40, 43–4; and pawnshops 69
Qin Shihuang (First Emperor of Qin) 207
Qing Dynasty: and foreign currencies 82–5; and the promotion of agricultural production 7; collapse of the 208; encouraging private investments 14; land tenure in the 52–4, 57; loans and interest rates in the 67–9, 71, 74; river control in the 34–8, 42–3; *see also* Corvée Labour, *Dian* Land right; Office selling
Qiu, Jun 204
Quesnay, François: on Confucius 222, 227n8; and *laissez-faire* economics 221, 223; and "legal despotism" 219, 221, 224, 226; and the "natural law" 219, 221–2; sources of his writings xvi, 215–9, 226n1, 226n2, 226n3, 226n5; and the *Tableau Économique* 219–21, 225, 227n6, 227n7

Rehn, Gösta 176–8
Reichwein, Adolph 215–6
Reinhard, Wolfgang 21, 24
Renaissance xiii, 110, 114–15, 281, 298
Ricardo, David: on consumption 239; on metallism 159; on the rate of profits 140–1; on spending 257n14

river control 33, 35, 40–3; *see also* Corvée labour; Jiaqing; Qianlong; Qing dynasty; Yellow River; Yongzheng
Robertson, Dennis Holme 159
Röpke, Wilhelm 174
Rosano, Genesio 113
Roscher, Wilhelm 122
Rousselot de Surgy, Jacques Philibert 218–19, 221, 224, 226n3, 226n5, 227n8
Rowe, William 8
*Rushang* ("Confucian Entrepreneurship"): contemporary 260, 271; definition of 259, 268; in Ming times 263; in Qing times 263–4; re-emergence of 267

Sai, Lu 66
Salutati, Coluccio 150, 155n13
San Bernardino of Siena 109, 134
Sang, Hongyang 202–6, 282, 284
Sassanid Empire 77, 82
Scheurl, Christoph von 112
Schmoller, Gustav von 115n11, 120
Schneider, Dieter 127–8
School of Salamanca 119–21; *see also* Klock, Kaspar
Schorer, Edgar 215
Schumpeter, Joseph 115n6, 246, 256
Serra, Antonio 289
Sha, Zukang 268
Shang, Yang 20, 204, 206
Shibuzawa Ei´ichi 264
Sicular, Terry 5
Sima, Qian 63–4, 77, 200n3, 240, 261, 278, 285
Sino–Japanese War (1894/95) 20, 22
Sino–Marxism xv, 33, 67, 208, 286, 299
Smith, Adam: and China 290, 294; and the German historical school 292; on indirect taxes 121; influenced by Stoic ideas 277; and the market economy 190; *see also* Tang, Qingzeng
Socrates xiii, 145
solidarity 170–2, 174–7, 179, 181, 182, 182n1, 182n2, 288
Sombart, Werner 281
Song Dynasty: coinage in the 78–81, 83; and office-selling 20; Southern 66, 189, 204; *see also Dian* land right; Granaries
Soto, Domingo de 154
Sraffa, Piero 127, 137, 141
Starkey, Thomas 151–2
subsidiarity xvi, 170–2, 174–6, 181–2, 182n1, 182n2

Summenhart, Konrad 110, 114
Sun, Yat-sen 9, 24, 58, 205, 268

*Tableau Économique see* Quesnay, François
Taiping Rebellion 21, 42
Tan, Min 221, 226n4
Tan, Sitong 233
Tang Dynasty: coinage in the 77–9; loans in the 63–5, 69; *see also Dian* land right
Tang, Qingzeng: on Adam Smith 294; on ancient Chinese economic thought 215, 227n10, 241–4, 293, 295; emancipation from Western economic theories 216; on physiocracy 215, 293; reception of 296–7
Tian, Qianqiu 203, 206
Tocqueville, Alexis de 225
Tolomei, Claudio 150
Tolstoy, Leo 216

Usury: negotiating power and 93–5, 98–9, 102–3; *carentia pecuniae* and 99; *damnum emergens* and 98–9, 121, 133–4; *lucrum cessans* and 98–9, 108–9, 120–1, 133–4; *periculum sortis* and 120; *poena conventionalis* and 98; *see also* Aquinas, Thomas; Aristotle; Eck, Johann; Graeco-Roman antiquity; Klock, Kaspar; Leibniz, Gottfried Wilhelm; Mercantilism

Valla, Lorenzo 150, 155n13
Verbiest, Ferdinand 80
Vives, Luis 154

Wagner, Adolf 182n8, 292
Waldes, Peter 148
Wang, Anshi 65–6, 204, 206, 295
Wang, Liqi 206–7
Wang, Yangming 262
Warring States-period (475–221 BCE) xiii, 6, 53, 63, 247–9, 261, 271n1
Weber, Max: on "deficits" of non-Western societies 298; and "ideal types" 173; and the protestant ethic 150; and "rational" capitalism 128; and value-free science 281
Wei, Yuan 33, 38, 41, 233
welfare state: in Britain 182n5; in Germany 171, 175, 179, 181, 288; in Sweden 171, 176, 179–81, 288; providing social security 152, 170; *see also* Wicksell, Knut
Weng, Shupei 79

Wicksell, Knut: on savings and investment 135, 138–9; and the "natural" rate of interest 135, 138–9; inspiring the Swedish welfare model 176
Wilhelm, Richard 283; *see also* Confucianism
Wittfogel, Karl August 33, 42–3, 44n1
Wu, Jing 39, 40
Wu, Nianbo 270
Wu, Qi 206

Xi, Jinping xvii, 13, 265, 296
Xia, Mingfang 42
Xiang, Jing 20
Xenophon 155n3, 278
Xunzi: on activities of the state 195–6; biography of 189; compared to Plato xvi, 189–91, 197–9; on poverty 192; on profits 262; on society 193

Yan, Congjian 81
Yan, Fu 233, 290
Yan, Jiehe 268
Yang, Shuda 204–6
Yang, Zhu 240, 244
*Yantie Lun* (debate on salt and iron): compared to the pseudo-aristotelian *Oeconomica* 211, 283; historical context of 82, 202–3; literary classification of the 204; modern reception of the xvi, 204–9, 282, 295; and Sang Hongyang 284; *see also* Mao, Zedong
Yellow River: floods of the 21; maintenance of the 9, 23; and river control 33–8, 41–3, 44n2

Yinghe 23
Yongzheng: and contribution campaigns 22; and the expansion of agricultural production 7; and the expenditure for river control 33, 36, 38–9, 43
Yuan, Cai 65
Yuan Dynasty: coinage in the 81; interest rates and loans in the 65–7; land tenure in the 53; and office selling 20; *see also* paper money
Yuan, Xianneng 237–40, 244; *see also* poverty

Zeng, Guoquan 27–28
Zigong 260
Zhang, Jian 264
Zhang, Peilun 29
Zhang, Ruimin 268
Zhang, Zhixiang 204
Zhao, Dingxin 210–11
Zhao, Yi 70
Zheng, He 80
Zhenzong 83
Zhou, Enlai 208–9
Zhou, Haiwen 211
Zhou, Hui 79
Zhou, Shengchun 268
Zhou, Wen 296–7, 299
Zhou, Xueguang 211
Zhu, Cai 24
Zhu, Tonjiu 241
Zhu, Xi 20, 260, 262, 280
Zhu, Zhengcheng 83
Zucman, Gabriel 6